Cuba, the United States, and the Post–Cold War World

Contemporary Cuba

Florida A&M University, Tallahassee
Florida Atlantic University, Boca Raton
Florida Gulf Coast University, Ft. Myers
Florida International University, Miami
Florida State University, Tallahassee
University of Central Florida, Orlando
University of Florida, Gainesville
University of North Florida, Jacksonville
University of South Florida, Tampa
University of West Florida, Pensacola

Contemporary Cuba
Edited by John M. Kirk

Afro-Cuban Voices: On Race and Identity in Contemporary Cuba, by Pedro Pérez-Sarduy
and Jean Stubbs (2000)

Cuba, the United States, and the Helms-Burton Doctrine: International Reactions,
by Joaquín Roy (2000)

Cuba Today and Tomorrow: Reinventing Socialism, by Max Azicri (2000);
first paperback edition, 2001

Cuba's Foreign Relations in a Post-Soviet World, by H. Michael Erisman (2000);
first paperback edition, 2002

Cuba's Sugar Industry, by José Alvarez and Lázaro Peña Castellanos (2001)

Culture and the Cuban Revolution: Conversations in Havana, by John M. Kirk
and Leonardo Padura Fuentes (2001)

Looking at Cuba: Essays on Culture and Civil Society, by Rafael Hernández,
translated by Dick Cluster (2003)

Santería Healing: A Journey into the Afro-Cuban World of Divinities, Spirits, and Sorcery,
by Johan Wedel (2004)

Cuba's Agricultural Sector, by José Alvarez (2004)

Cuban Socialism in a New Century: Adversity, Survival and Renewal,
edited by Max Azicri and Elsie Deal (2004)

*Cuba, the United States, and the Post–Cold War World: The International Dimensions of
the Washington-Havana Relationship*, edited by Morris Morley and Chris McGillion
(2005)

Cuba, the United States, and the Post–Cold War World

The International Dimensions of
the Washington-Havana Relationship

Edited by Morris Morley
and Chris McGillion

University Press of Florida
Gainesville/Tallahassee/Tampa/Boca Raton
Pensacola/Orlando/Miami/Jacksonville/Ft. Myers

Library of Congress Cataloging-in-Publication Data
Cuba, the United States, and the post–Cold War world: the international dimensions
of the Washington-Havana relationship / edited by Morris Morley and Chris McGillion.
p. cm.—(Contemporary Cuba)
Includes index.
ISBN 0-8130-2827-2 (alk. paper)
1. United States—Foreign relations—Cuba. 2. Cuba—Foreign relations—United States.
3. United States—Foreign relations—1989– . I. Morley, Morris H. II. McGillion, Chris, 1954– .
III. Series.
E183.8.C9C8295   2005
327.7307291'09'049—dc22   2005042231

The University Press of Florida is the scholarly publishing agency for the State University
System of Florida, comprising Florida A&M University, Florida Atlantic University, Florida
Gulf Coast University, Florida International University, Florida State University, University
of Central Florida, University of Florida, University of North Florida, University of South
Florida, and University of West Florida.

University Press of Florida
15 Northwest 15th Street
Gainesville, FL 32611-2079
http://www.upf.com

If ever there was in the history of humanity an enemy who was truly universal, an enemy whose acts and moves trouble the entire world, threaten the entire world, attack the entire world in any way or another, that real and really universal enemy is precisely Yankee imperialism.

Fidel Castro, January 1968

I'm amazed that there's such misunderstanding of what our country is about that people would hate us. I am—like most Americans, I just can't believe it because I know how good we are.

George W. Bush, October 2001

Contents

Foreword

This book will undoubtedly prove controversial. Its thesis—that the role of the United States as a "lone cowboy" is misguided and counterproductive—is illustrated, and illustrated well, in its relationship with revolutionary Cuba. It is particularly relevant, perhaps, in the wake of the overthrow of Saddam Hussein and the U.S. role in Iraq (increasingly seen as an occupation rather than a liberation). Once again single-minded determination (and shortsighted ideological considerations) have held sway over common sense and solid analysis. "Regime change" and "weapons of mass destruction" have been thrust into Washington's international agenda, as the presidency of George W. Bush has sought to imprint its hegemony upon several areas of the developing world.

Unilateralism has undoubtedly become the major approach of U.S. foreign policy during this administration, which has refused among other things to accept the Kyoto accord on global warming, an international treaty banning land mines, or even membership in the International Criminal Court. In Iraq, notwithstanding support from Great Britain and members of the rather threadbare "coalition of the willing," it is eminently clear that the Bush administration's obsession with overthrowing the Hussein dictatorship took precedence over virtually all other considerations. The thesis of the "lone cowboy" again seems pertinent.

Nowhere is this unilateral approach to foreign policy seen more clearly—or for a longer period—than in the troubled U.S. relationship with Cuba. Some forty-five years after the revolutionary government of Fidel Castro overthrew Fulgencio Batista, the rhetoric emanating from the Bush White House remains as harsh as ever. Meanwhile, the international community has moved on, often critical of the Cuban revolution's approach to civil and political rights, but keen to normalize relations with Havana. Indeed, as a traditionally stalwart supporter of Washington such as the Dominican prime minister has noted, "If [the United States] haven't realized the Cold War is over, we have."

There is no doubt that the government headed by Fidel Castro is polemical and that the revolutionary government skillfully plays on nationalist rhetoric and crises (real and imagined), presenting the island as a victim of imperialist aggression. It is also true that the Cuban president has an uncanny ability to infuriate friend and foe alike with his iconoclastic approach on a whole host of matters, including a foreign policy that is totally sui generis. Indeed, in recent years the Cuban president has roundly condemned several Latin American and

European countries for their criticism of the Cuban human rights situation. At the same time, with one major exception, at present Cuba has normal diplomatic relations with virtually the entire world.

This collection of essays reveals just how isolated Washington is in its approach to dealing with revolutionary Cuba. In November 2003, some 179 countries voted against the U.S. embargo at the U.N. General Assembly. (Only three—the United States, Israel, and the Marshall Islands—voted in support of it.) Moreover, the European Union took Washington to the World Trade Organization to protest the 1996 Helms-Burton legislation, noting angrily that "this extraterritorial extension of U.S. jurisdiction has no basis in international law." The foreign minister of Canada, the major trading partner of the United States, also weighed into the debate: "This is bullying," noted Lloyd Axworthy with irony. "But in America you call it global leadership." While many nations are upset with the human rights situation in Cuba, they have sought to maintain a more balanced overview of the Cuban situation—and to resist the pressures emanating from Washington for some forty-five years.

The response to the "Cuban question" from the United States—with some notable exceptions—has been consistent during this time. In fact, some ten presidents have maintained the same approach—seeking the overthrow of the Castro government and the installation of a friendly regime. Unfortunately for Washington the strategy has repeatedly failed, causing one to wonder why the game plan has not been changed.

The irony of this situation is that Cuba represents no plausible threat to the United States. Indeed, Havana has sought to cooperate with the United States on a number of matters, ranging from drug interdiction to immigration matters. In addition, it was one of the first countries to offer its airports for U.S. planes to land after the September 11, 2001 terrorist attacks. And, despite the existence of an "embargo," the United States is currently the seventh largest supplier of goods to Cuba—some $250 million of agricultural goods were bought in 2003 alone and $718 million since December 2001. Strange, but true . . .

Despite this reality, however, ideology (and the political clout of conservative Cuban American exiles in South Florida) continue to influence U.S. policy towards this small island of 11.2 million. President George W. Bush has illustrated this unilateral approach well, in typical blunt style: "At some point we may be the only ones left. That's ok with me. We are America."

This anthology seeks to counterpose diverse international reactions to this policy, revealing both the isolated position of Washington and its attempts to exercise its substantial influence. While U.S. hegemony remains strong in the wake of the end of the Cold War, the resulting unipolar world order has not witnessed the peace dividend, much less the stability, that had been hoped for following the demise of the Soviet Union. Instead, we see the apparent application of the "Might is Right" axiom by the surviving superpower and a determination on the part of Washington to play the role of the "lone cowboy" in international politics. This book questions the legitimacy (and the efficacy) of such an approach—and offers some useful lessons in evaluating this strategy.

John M. Kirk, Series Editor

Introduction

The post–Cold War international environment has had a contradictory effect on Havana and Washington: whereas the former systematically reversed what U.S. policymakers previously described as "obstacles" to improved bilateral ties, the latter deepened its adversarial posture. Beginning in the late 1980s, Havana withdrew its troops from Africa, halted its export of revolution to Latin America, drastically reduced its military-security ties with the former Soviet Union, began a measured integration into the capitalist world economy, and accelerated efforts to restore ties with governments irrespective of their political outlooks. None of these shifts, however, produced a softening in the U.S. policy of hostility toward the Cuban Revolution. On the contrary, under both Republican and Democratic administrations Washington has tightened the economic noose, heightened ideological warfare, and sought to further "run down" the Cuban economy to eliminate even the vaguest possibility of a competitive regional alternative to the highly polarized free market model championed by the U.S. in the Third World.

If Havana's post–Cold War behavior is largely explained by necessity, Washington's is largely explained by opportunity. Ever since the first strains began to appear in the Soviet Union's grip on superpower status during the Gorbachev era, the United States seemed intent on recreating a world of uncontested American supremacy. In the aftermath of victory in the first Gulf War, George H. W. Bush declared that American leadership and power were prerequisites for a stable international order; that "American leadership [means] economic, political and, yes, military"; and that, in all three areas, it embodied "a hard nosed sense of American self-interest."[1] Bill Clinton and his senior foreign policy advisers also stressed the importance of continued U.S. global leadership, or what National Security Council Adviser Anthony Lake termed "enlargement." In a major September 1993 policy speech, Lake spelled out the administration's global strategy: "Only one overriding factor can determine whether the U.S. should act multilaterally or unilaterally, and that is America's interests. We should act unilaterally when that will serve our purpose."[2]

The presidency of George W. Bush began with reassuring words about the U.S. commitment to multilateralism. But, following the September 11, 2001, terrorist attacks on New York and Washington, the Bush administration was in no mood to allow U.S. interests to be compromised by the need to work cooperatively with other nations. The president expanded even further on this disposition to "go-it-alone" in his 2002 *National Security Strategy of the United States*. On matters of security, the message was particularly blunt: "we will not hesitate to act alone, if necessary, to exercise our right of self-defense *by acting preemptively*" (our emphasis).[3] The era of containment and deterrence was over, replaced by a new, proactive imperial doctrine.[4]

The George W. Bush White House has been far more consistently head-strong and unilateral in its pursuit of U.S. interests across a broad range of issues: withdrawing from both the Kyoto Protocol on climate change and the 1972 Anti-Ballistic Missile Treaty (in order to begin development on a missile defense shield, dismissing the concerns of European allies); rejecting membership in the International Criminal Court and refusing to join efforts to strengthen measures against biological weapons; opposing a worldwide ban on antipersonnel land mines; criticizing the limitations imposed by the Comprehensive Test Ban Treaty; giving a cold shoulder to the 2002 Johannesburg Earth Summit on sustainable development; and, in 2004, consenting to Israel's annexation of Palestinian territories in the West Bank despite this being contrary to United Nations resolutions, a violation of international law on military expansion and population transfers, and an affront to the overwhelming weight of world opinion.

Most divisive of all, however, was the Bush decision to go to war in Iraq without specific authorization from the United Nations Security Council and against the opposition of important continental allies, notably France and Germany. Responding to Bush's designation of Iraq as a sponsor and supporter of international terrorism, and thus a legitimate target in America's open-ended global "war on terror," Germany's foreign minister Joschka Fischer commented that the "international coalition against terror does not provide a basis for doing just anything against anybody—and certainly not by going it alone."[5] The European Union's external affairs commissioner Chris Patten was equally blunt; the U.S., he said, seemed to be heading into "unilateralist over-drive."[6] Both remarks echoed the earlier words of Canada's foreign minister Lloyd Axworthy when protesting the extraterritorial provisions of the 1996 Helms-Burton legislation ratcheting up U.S. economic sanctions against Cuba: "This is bullying. But in America you call it global leadership."[7]

Washington's increasingly unilateralist approach to international politics in the new millennium mirrors its historic attitude toward the Cuban Revolution: from its barely concealed hostility toward the Castro leadership in 1959 through its multitrack efforts (military, covert, economic, political) to topple the regime from power over the following half century.[8] Crucial to the revolution's survival was the Soviet Union's protection and economic support. But the collapse of the Soviet Union and its Eastern European empire revived U.S. hopes that the right mix of economic coercion and ideological warfare could now bring Cuba to its knees. Predictions of the rapid disintegration of an economy heavily dependent on Moscow's largesse encouraged first George Bush, and then Bill Clinton, to adopt a policy approach based on increased diplomatic hostility and a tightening of the economic screws in the hope of finally translating into reality the long-held strategic objective of consigning the Cuban Revolution to history. This, in large part, accounted for the manifest absence of reciprocal responses to the changes that had taken place in the island's foreign and domestic policies.[9]

The George W. Bush administration was even less disposed to couch the goal of "regime change" in diplomatic language. In his May 2001 Cuba Independence Day address, the new president declared that goal a "moral statement" made by the United States on behalf of the people of Cuba.[10] This stance was in sharp contrast to that adopted by most of America's allies who, even before the official end of the Cold War, were demonstrating a willingness to "engage" the Castro regime in order to promote political and economic reforms, rather than pursuing confrontation and subversion to topple it from power. Undeterred, Washington has gone to great lengths to enlist or cajole other countries to fall in line with its Cuban agenda. But the gap between this ambition and other countries' responses demonstrates the extent to which the new global environment has proved more complicated than American policymakers had envisaged. The disintegration of the Soviet Union may have shifted the balance of power on a world scale in favor of the U.S., but it simultaneously diminished the reliance of America's allies on its security umbrella. This lessened need has translated into a greater assertion of independence from Washington, in particular a reluctance by other countries to subordinate their foreign economic policies to White House diktats. As a result, intercapitalist economic competition in the post–Cold War era has intensified, not diminished, and any automatic expectations of broad international support for U.S.-led political, diplomatic, economic, or military campaigns have been well and truly dashed.

This development has particularly weakened Washington's efforts to contest Cuba's expanding economic links with the rest of the world. *First*, U.S. allies have become much more assertive about their preferred approach for encouraging change on the island and correspondingly less disposed to genuflect to American prescriptions. There is no clearer evidence of this cleavage than the rapidity with which Latin American nations have restored diplomatic relations with Cuba and Europe's insistence that dealing with Fidel Castro's government is not incompatible with urging internal reforms. *Second*, Washington's alliance partners are reluctant to forgo trade and investment opportunities in a relatively small but nonetheless lucrative market simply to pay homage to the will and whims of American policy. Europe, Canada, Latin America,

Japan, and China have all shown a keen interest in exploiting an economy off limits to American traders and investors and in using Cuba as a springboard for even more ambitious commercial ventures in the Caribbean and beyond.

Third, America's allies are determined to resist pressures to stay out of the Cuban economy because of the precedent it could set in other global markets. Hence the vociferous denunciations of both the elder Bush's decision to expand trade sanctions—principally through the 1992 Cuban Democracy Act, which targeted overseas subsidiaries of U.S. corporations—and Clinton's decision to sign onto the even harsher extraterritorial 1996 Cuban Liberty and Democratic Solidarity (Helms-Burton) Act. Western capitals from Ottawa to Mexico City to London denounced these unilateral projections of domestic laws beyond America's national boundaries, formed diplomatic alliances to fight such legislation, passed retaliatory measures to protect their Cuba-based investors and traders, and protested the threat that these U.S. actions posed to the letter and the spirit of global free trade agreements.

Fourth, the heavy-handed—or what French president Francois Mitterrand once termed "primitive"—White House approach on Cuba has inadvertently forced America's allies to tune an array of economic, diplomatic, and juridical initiatives to the defense of their commercial relations with Havana.[11] In the process, they articulated, developed, refined, and defended a rationale for doing business with the Caribbean island broadly described as "constructive engagement"—an approach based on reintegrating Cuba back into the regional and international communities as the best way to encourage genuine internal economic and political reform. To the advocates of constructive engagement, the U.S. strategy of confrontation leading to regime change is seen as anachronistic and/or counterproductive. Since September 2001, this dispute over whether to engage or confront Cuba has been writ large in the broader struggle over whether international problems should be addressed through diplomacy and negotiation or through a ham-fisted approach determined and directed by Washington.

This collection details the evolving relationship between Cuba and the international community since the end of the Cold War. It examines the U.S. response to these developments including: (a) the extent to which the U.S. has sought to obstruct Cuban efforts to "reach out" to the rest of the world; (b) the obstacles employed and instruments used by U.S. policymakers to contain these efforts; (c) why American policy has targeted some aspects of Cuba's efforts at global and regional reintegration more than others; and (d) the extent to which U.S. policymakers have been forced to operate within certain constraints that, on occasion, required the White House to modify the style if not the substance of its preferred approach. Underlying each of these issues are the tensions that U.S. policy toward the government in Havana have generated in Washington's relations with other countries—over matters ranging from trade and investment, to security concerns, to multilateral cooperation, to respect for the rule of international law. These tensions have not resulted in the kind of disharmony between the U.S. and its major allies that characterized the 2003–04 Iraq conflict. On the other hand, they have a longer, more diverse and comprehensive history, and thus provide better insight into the development of these contrasting approaches. In this way, the essays that follow make a unique contribution to our understanding of the direction of contemporary American foreign policy.

In a wide-ranging account of U.S.-Cuban relations since the end of the Cold War, *William LeoGrande* details the unremittingly hostile White House policy toward Fidel Castro's government, which shows no signs of abating. On the contrary, the administration of George W. Bush has further widened the gulf between Washington and the international community over Cuba by more aggressively and publicly advocating regime change, intensifying efforts to foment an internal challenge to the revolutionary leadership, and engaging in failed attempts to implicate the island in the "axis of evil" of so-called rogue states—thus making it a potential target in the U.S. "war on terror." This chapter provides the necessary context for examining the nature of Cuba's relations with the rest of the world, the global response to this "reaching out" and the extent to which it diverges from American policy, the problems the latter have generated in Washington's relations with its allies, and the current state of Cuba's relations with Russia, Europe, Canada, Latin America, and the rest of the Third World.

During the Cold War no relationship was more critical to the survival of the Cuban Revolution—or more annoying from Washington's perspective—than Havana's economic and security links to the Soviet Union. Mired in a deepening political and economic crisis at the end of the 1980s, however, and with its Eastern European empire unraveling, Moscow was increasingly exposed to U.S. demands that it sever its ties with Fidel Castro's government in return for desperately needed economic assistance. George Bush Sr. took advantage of the weaknesses and vulnerabilities of Mikhail Gorbachev to demand that he cut Cuba adrift as the quid pro quo for Western aid and loans.[12] Bill Clinton applied similar pressure on the fledgling Russian Federation—albeit largely at the behest of anti-Castro legislators. George W. Bush finally managed to persuade Moscow to abandon its last significant investment in the island—the Lourdes intelligence gathering facility—as a gesture of Russian commitment to bury the past and negotiate a new relationship with the United States for the 21st century.

The irony is that despite this insatiable U.S. demand for concessions, Washington did not deliver substantial assistance to an accommodating Gorbachev and his successors. *Nicola Miller's* incisive analysis of the shifts and changes in Soviet/Russian-Cuban relations since 1989 concludes that this perceived lack of reciprocity has had a powerful impact on Moscow's current thinking about Cuba. There is now growing support for the argument that too much has been sacrificed in Cuba to curry favor with the Cold War "victor." Any consequent review of long-term economic and military interests in Cuba could pose problems for future relations between Russia and the United States, particularly given the triggers mandating U.S. retaliation for certain forms of Russian-Cuban cooperation specified in the Helms-Burton legislation.

The relationship between America and Europe is more pivotal to the success of the global free trade regime than any other and, hence, the division over Cuba has always contained within it a potential for creating bigger and more significant conflicts between historic allies. *Chris McGillion* provides a thorough assessment of the impact of America's Cuba policy on the broader transatlantic economic debate, centered on the passage and consequences of the 1992 Cuban Democracy Act and the 1996 Helms-Burton legislation. This extraterritorial application of U.S. domestic laws generated major inter-Alliance frictions, reaching a peak after Bill Clinton signed Helms-Burton into law. Individually, European governments condemned this encroachment on their sovereignty and threatened reprisals; collectively, the European Union, outraged by what it viewed as a direct challenge to international law, took its complaint to the World Trade Organization (WTO) and raised the prospect of a transatlantic trade war if it got no satisfaction. Such a dire outcome has failed to eventuate, but the reason that gave rise to it has still not been comprehensively addressed.

While George W. Bush has been no less inclined than his predecessor to lobby Congress to remove the more contentious "global reach" provisions of Helms-Burton, a potential new source of conflict has emerged between the U.S. and its European allies. The latter have developed a significant commercial stake in Cuba, which they show no signs of surrendering to American competitors in the post-Castro era. As well, the Europeans have cultivated extensive ties with those government officials and other political "influentials" in Cuba who are more likely to inherit the reins of political power than Washington's allies among the Miami exile leadership and the island's dissident community. For these reasons, another transatlantic contest over Cuba cannot be ruled out in the future.

If the United States and much of the rest of the world have diverged when it comes to dealing with Cuba—the former advocating confrontation, the latter favoring engagement—nowhere has this been more evident than in the case of Canada. Bilateral ties between Havana and Ottawa waxed and waned during the first three decades of the revolutionary regime amid the ups and downs of the Cold War and the personal outlooks of individual prime ministers. Still, Canada's basic policy position stayed remarkably consistent over this period. The Canadian approach to Cuba has been dictated by national interest tempered by a concern not to take measures that might rupture Canada's far more important relationship with its powerful southern neighbor. Since the end of the Cold War, both sides have displayed a pragmatism that ensures their differences over Cuba do not get out of hand. Ottawa has been careful to defer to Washington on discrete issues of critical importance to the White House. For its part, the U.S. has not allowed its repeated displeasure over Canada's more friendly approach toward Cuba to trigger any precipitate action that might endanger the larger bilateral relationship. Still, as *Peter McKenna* and *John Kirk* show in their nuanced critique, this arrangement has not been without its problems. Moreover, it remains one that requires an inordinate degree of careful management over an issue that should be peripheral to the mutual interests of both countries. The most recent echo of these divergent approaches toward Cuba has emerged in negotiations for a hemisphere-wide free trade agreement—with the U.S. insisting on unbridled market access, while Canada advocates a treaty sensitive to Latin America's social development and incorporating a degree of protection for local entrepreneurs until they are able to compete on a more equal footing.

Latin America's post–Cold War relationship with Cuba is not altogether dissimilar to that of Canada's. *Morris Morley's* exploration of the Cuba–Latin America–United States triangle contrasts the region's sophisticated post–Cold War approach toward Cuba—based on the notion that a business-like relationship is not incompatible with disagreement and criticism—with the unyielding, hardline stance adopted by Washington. By the end of the 1990s, the imperial state's decades-long isolation policy had effectively collapsed. Cuba had reestablished full diplomatic relations with virtually every country in the region, economic ties with a substantial number, and had been readmitted into numerous hemispheric organizations. A visibly frustrated White House has been forced to adapt to this new reality. Its opposition has been reduced to largely empty gestures such as imploring governments to demand a quickened pace of domestic reform on the island in return for normalization of bilateral ties or symbolic gestures like directing U.S. embassies to make perfunctory diplomatic démarches to host country foreign offices favoring any thaw in official relations.

Nonetheless, hemispheric support for Cuba's reintegration into the inter-American system coexists with sensitivity to specific U.S. concerns on the part of most countries, not least due to their vulnerability to White House economic pressures. This has been most evident in the region's reluctance to vigorously support Cuba's readmission to the Organization of American States (OAS), where the U.S. has waged a determined campaign to keep Havana out of the peak hemispheric body, including letting it be known that trade and aid agreements were at stake for any Latin country not prepared to play by America's rules. Ironically, U.S. policymakers can take some of the credit for the significant improvement in relations between Cuba and Latin America since the end of the Cold War: it was they who encouraged the process of redemocratization in countries that have emerged as some of Havana's staunchest political and economic allies and who, in more recent years, have tested Washington's commitment to democracy in the region by more forcefully articulating their policy differences with the northern giant.

The manner in which the U.S. has sought to constrain Cuba's global "outreach" similarly has created major new imperatives for Havana to redevelop ties of solidarity with Third World countries and to play a leadership role in their collective challenge to imperial state interests on issues ranging from debt and development, to security, to environmental protection and social advancement. As *H. Michael Erisman* demonstrates, Washington's politics of hostility have not only forced Havana to look for political allies and trade partners wherever it can find them in Africa, Asia, and the Middle East, but also allowed the Cubans to portray their treatment at American hands as emblematic of the fate of Third World countries in an era of uncontested U.S. global power. Paradoxically, Havana has pursued this objective in the very international organizations the U.S. was instrumental in setting up and increasingly seeks to politicize—above all the United Nations and its various agencies and commissions. But Cuba has also attempted to breath new life into parallel institutions such as the Non-Aligned Movement (NAM) and the Group of 77 developing nations. Indeed, given the largely hostile Third World response to the Bush administration's wars in Afghanistan and Iraq and the potential threat to other countries inherent in the open-ended "war on terror," Cuba's election to chair the NAM in 2006 raises the possibility of new conflicts erupting between the organization and Washington.

Collectively, these regional and country studies reveal a number of contradictions in U.S. policy toward Cuba. The *first* is that between the narrow political considerations that drive the policy and American national interest. Domestic factors, not least the continuing efforts to secure the Florida–New Jersey "Cuba vote" and to mollify congressional hardliners, have skewered Washington's approach to Cuba. Explaining the White House refusal to normalize ties with Havana, one senior Clinton foreign policy adviser put it in these terms: "There are no votes riding on how we deal with Indonesia, and not many on how we deal with China. [But] Castro is still political dynamite."[13] Neither the Clinton nor the George W. Bush White House has budged from this assessment even though a rival constituency comprising the U.S. business community, the agricultural sector, and human rights groups began mobilizing in the late 1990s to garner support for easing, if not lifting, the embargo. For both, the notion of a Cuba policy based on national interest remains subordinate to electoral calculations about placating parochial groups of right-wing Cuban-Americans.

Second is the contradiction between America's professed commitment to free trade and its Cuba policy. Since the 1990s, the nation's multinational business community has depended on foreign markets for a growing proportion of its profits. This trend has reinforced Washington's determination to break down barriers to U.S. capital and commerce and to champion this approach in the interests of global economic health and development. The prime ideological instrument in this drive has been the free trade doctrine. For more than a decade, U.S. officials have argued in every regional and global forum that free trade is the cornerstone of American foreign economic policy—and synonymous with American "global leadership" in the post–Cold War era.

Yet this doctrine conflicts with the restrictive trade practices supported by the White House and Congress to obstruct and limit Cuba's economic ties with the rest of the world—a policy inconsistency that has encouraged rivals around the world to view America's embrace of free trade as a self-serving policy to be used only when it serves U.S. political interests. In an era of heightened competition for global market share, economic competitors are not prepared to sacrifice investment or commercial opportunities to satisfy the requirements of American foreign policy. Nor are they willing to be bullied into severing normal economic ties with an internationally recognized and legitimate government in order to accommodate White House domestic imperatives. Consequently, U.S. actions have created tensions and disputes with a number of key allies, even threatening the viability of instruments of global dispute resolution such as the WTO and raising the possibility of a cross-Atlantic trade war.

Third is the contradiction between Cuba's efforts to become a member of the international community in good standing and the refusal of Washington to halt its unrelenting ideological war against Fidel Castro's government. The U.S. approach to Cuba remains embedded in Cold War rhetoric far more than it does in the realities of Cuba's international behavior in the post–Cold War era. Today, the more Cuba opens up to the world, the more intense the U.S. rhetorical onslaught seems to become. This dynamic could be observed in the aftermath of the September 11 attacks on New York and Washington: Bush officials responded to Cuba's expressed sympathy over the victims, its offer of support, its denunciation of terrorism, and its cooperation in housing suspected Al Qaeda prisoners at Guantánamo Bay by attempting to paint the Castro government as a supporter of terrorism and to implicate it in efforts to develop weapons of mass destruction with which to threaten the "Free World."

By contrast, European, Asian, Latin American, and Canadian governments have not only recognized and responded to positive developments inside Cuba and to its foreign policy shifts but also encouraged political, economic, cultural, and scientific contacts with the island. Thus the U.S. pursues a phantom ideological war that fails to evoke sustained international support. There can be no more graphic evidence of this than the annual United Nations General Assembly vote calling for an end to the American embargo. Every year since 1992, the White House has been humiliated: on no occasion have more than three other countries lined up with U.S. in opposing the lifting of the blockade. The only conclusion that can be drawn is that Washington's approach lacks all credibility and is self-defeating: it isolates the U.S. and allows Cuba's revolutionary leadership to limit the scope and pace of political reform on the island in the interests of "defense" and to cast human rights and pro-democracy advocates as puppets of a foreign, hostile power.

The U.S. refusal to consider serious negotiations with Cuba in the absence of regime change has been the hallmark of post–Cold War American policy worldwide. Yet Cuba has not only survived the collapse of the Soviet Union and a resurgent American imperialism, but has also repositioned itself internationally, normalizing ties with key U.S. allies in Europe, Latin America, and Asia and beginning the process of assuming its place in regional and international forums from which it had long been ostracized or excluded.

Today, Washington's uncompromising hostility toward Cuba almost totally isolates it from the rest of the international community, contradicts its professed commitment to free trade principles, undermines international laws, weakens its claim to global leadership, and creates problems for America's overseas investors and traders. The vast majority of countries fail to comprehend the logic of a policy approach still based on the proposition that of all former Cold War socialist bloc nations, only Cuba is immune from engagement as a step toward normalizing bilateral relations. This approach is seen as anachronistic, irrational, and presumptuous. America's allies place a much higher value on encouraging economic ties and political dialogue, on multilateralism and consensus building. This is the approach that they calculate will more likely produce desired changes in Cuba's political economy and limit friction between Havana and other nations over the issue of differing internal policies. The international dimensions of Washington's Cuba policy since the end of the Cold War and across a range of issues, more starkly than any other foreign policy issue, reveal the degree to which U.S. policymakers have exhibited a striking lack of realism about America's capacity to impose its political and economic will in a global environment unsympathetic to its imperial ambitions.

Notes

1. "America Must Remain Engaged," U.S. Department of State, *Dispatch*, December 21, 1992, 893–95.

2. "From Containment to Enlargement," U.S. Department of State, *Dispatch*, September 27, 1993, 658–64.

3. "Full Text: Bush's National Security Strategy," *New York Times*, September 20, 2002.

4. For an analysis, see Walter LaFeber, "The Bush Doctrine," *Diplomatic History* 26, no. 4 (Fall 2002): 543–58.

5. Quoted in "Germany Warns U.S. Against Unilateralism," *BBC News Online*, February 12, 2002.

6. Quoted in Jonathan Freedland, "Breaking the Silence," *The Guardian* (U.K.), February 9, 2002.

7. Quoted in David E. Sanger, "Talk Multilaterally, Hit Allies With Stick," *New York Times*, July 21, 1996, E3.

8. See Morris H. Morley, *Imperial State and Revolution: The United States and Cuba, 1952–1986* (New York: Cambridge University Press, 1987).

9. For an extended discussion, see Morris Morley and Chris McGillion, *Unfinished Business: America and Cuba After the Cold War, 1989–2001* (New York: Cambridge University Press, 2002).

10. "Remarks by the President in Recognition of Cuba Independence Day," White House, Office of the Press Secretary online, May 18, 2001, transcript/audio file. Three years later Bush was no less committed to at least ensuring that the Cuban Revolution would not survive the Castro era. See Colin Powell, *Report to the President: Commission for Assistance to a Free Cuba*, U.S. Department of State online, May 6, 2004. Also see "U.S. Seeks to Subvert Succession in Cuba," *New York Times*, May 6, 2004 and Christopher Marquis, "Bush Proposes a Plan to Aid Opponents in Cuba," *New York Times*, May 7, 2004.

11. Quoted in Charles Trueheart, "U.S. Hard-Line Stance on Cuba Draws Icy Reviews from Trading Partners," *Washington Post*, September 10, 1994, A18.

12. See Michael R. Beschloss and Strobe Talbott, *At the Highest Levels* (London: Warner Books, 1993), passim; Morley and McGillion, *Unfinished Business*, 22–24.

13. Quoted in D. E. Singer, "Real Politics: Why Suharto is In and Castro is Out," *New York Times*, October, 31, 1995, 3.

I

The United States and Cuba

Strained Engagement

William M. LeoGrande

The sanctions our Government enforces against the Castro regime are not just a policy tool; they're a moral statement.

George W. Bush, May 18, 2001

At each other's throats for the past forty-five years, Cuba and the United States remain, in the words of a former head of the American Interests Section in Havana, "the closest of enemies."[1] Since 1898, no relationship has been more important for Cuba than its relationship with the United States. From the Bay of Pigs to the fall of the Berlin Wall, Moscow took Washington's place as Cuba's hegemon, but the looming U.S. threat meant that relations with Washington remained critically important. When the Cold War ended, so too did the geographically implausible triangular relationship between Cuba and the two superpowers, leaving Cuba alone once again to confront what José Martí called the "turbulent and brutal North."[2]

Since George W. Bush became president, the Cuban and U.S. governments have not had much direct interaction other than trading invective. Like hostile next-door neighbors who have built a tall fence between their properties, they rarely see one another, but delight in hurling insults back and forth. This is hardly a new development. Although Presidents Gerald Ford and Jimmy Carter sought to normalize relations with Cuba in the 1970s, their efforts faltered over Cuba's support for liberation struggles in Africa. No U.S. president since has made a serious effort to negotiate normalization. With U.S. foreign policy adopting a more aggressive posture toward adversaries under the mantle of the war on terrorism, U.S.-Cuban relations appear destined to get worse before they get better. Yet despite the persistent hostility between the two countries, the relationship is by no means static. The end of the Cold War set off a cascade of significant changes in U.S. interests, Cuban interests, and the domestic political dynamics that shape policy on both sides of the Florida Straits.

Before 1991, Cuba's partnership with the Soviet Union and ideological antagonism toward the United States made it a security issue for Washington. Aiding revolutionaries in Latin America, sending troops to Africa, denouncing global capitalism in the Non-Aligned Movement—at every juncture, Cuba stood opposed to U.S. foreign policy. With the collapse of the Soviet Union, however, any plausible Cuban threat evaporated. The troops came home from Africa; Cuba stopped promoting revolution in Latin America; military ties to Moscow were severed; and even the Russian intelligence facility at Lourdes was closed. Castro continued to denounce global capitalism, especially as manifested in U.S. proposals for a Free Trade Area of the Americas (FTAA), but Cuba was no longer seen as a model by the underdeveloped world. By the mid-1990s, virtually all U.S. security concerns about Cuba were gone, yet Washington's antagonism remained undiminished.

As the security issue faded from the U.S. agenda, the promotion of democracy rose to replace it. The idea that U.S. foreign policy should promote democracy has a long pedigree, but it was eclipsed during most of the Cold War by the realist argument that security and the balance of power were preeminent concerns. When the end of the Cold War made containment irrelevant as an organizing principle for foreign policy, "democracy promotion" emerged as a consensus alternative. George H. W. Bush, Bill Clinton, and George W. Bush all embraced this new aim, though not (as China policy demonstrated) to the exclusion of more traditional economic and security interests. In Cuba, however, where security concerns were nil and potential economic interests modest, the promotion of democracy became a key element in the revised agenda of U.S. demands. This shift in the U.S. rationale made normalization even more difficult, because Washington was now demanding not just an end to objectionable Cuban behavior abroad but to the very character of the socialist state.

There were countervailing forces, however. As the Cuban economy integrated into global markets and opened up to foreign direct investment, the potential economic benefit for the U.S. business community came into clearer focus. By the late 1990s, a growing lobby of farm interests, travel and entertainment companies, and pharmaceutical manufacturers were working for a relaxation of U.S. policy. In addition, the Cuban-American community was changing with the regular flow of new immigrants whose reasons for departure were more economic than political. That, plus the aging of the original exile generation, produced a more heterogeneous community with more heterodox politics.

Commerce Trumps Anticommunism: The Eroding Power of the Cuba Lobby

The explanation for the persistence of the Cold War in the Caribbean lay in U.S. domestic politics, in particular, the considerable political clout of the conservative Cuban-American lobby. In the early 1970s, Secretary of State Henry Kissinger and Assistant Secretary for Latin America William D. Rogers could contemplate normalizing relations with Cuba, confident they would face no domestic opposition of any consequence except perhaps some demonstrative acts by Cuban exile terrorists.[3] No president since has enjoyed that luxury.

The political and financial power of conservative Cuban-Americans, organized most effectively in the 1980s by Jorge Más Canosa in the Cuban American National Foundation (CANF), gave the community virtual veto power over U.S. policy. Wealthy, well-organized, single-minded, and strategically concentrated in the key electoral states of Florida and New Jersey, Cuban-Americans dominated the issue field. CANF directors and their political action committee, the Free Cuba PAC, contributed hundreds of thousands of dollars to dozens of sympathetic congressional and presidential candidates in each election cycle—a total of several million dollars since 1979.[4] Any public official who even hinted at a policy of engagement with Cuba came under attack. When Senator Lowell Weicker (R-Conn.) traveled to Cuba in October 1980, met with Castro, and returned to advocate normalizing relations, CANF made an example of him by working diligently, and successfully, to defeat him for reelection.[5] Jorge Más Canosa's ready access to Congress and even to the White House was testimony to CANF's success at positioning itself as the voice of Cuban-Americans.[6]

Although polls showed that a majority of the U.S. public in the 1980s and 1990s continued to favor normalization of relations with Cuba, the issue was not highly salient.[7] No domestic group stood to reap any significant gain from a relaxation of relations, at least in the short term, so there was no countervailing constituency to the Cuba lobby. Successive presidents have followed the path of least political resistance by leaving the policy of hostility in place.

The first crack in the Cuban-American right's policy dominance was the embargo's loss of legitimacy after the Cold War. Without a national security rationale, the embargo looked less and less justified. In light of Cuba's economic hardship, it looked downright cruel. When it included food and medicine, the embargo against Cuba constituted the most severe sanctions Washington maintained against any country in the world, including countries with notably worse human rights records (such as Indonesia under Suharto and Afghanistan under the Taliban) and reputed terrorist states (such as Iran and Saddam Hussein's Iraq). Every year since 1992, the United Nations General

Assembly has voted overwhelmingly in favor of a resolution calling on Washington to end the embargo, in 2002 by the largest margin ever: 173 to 3 with four abstentions.

The suffering endured by ordinary Cubans during this crisis prompted a significant humanitarian response in the United States. A number of new and existing nongovernmental organizations (NGOs) launched relief projects, including Pastors for Peace (which refused on principle to seek the required licenses from the U.S. Treasury Department), U.S.+Cuba Medical Project, Madre, and Catholic Relief Services (CRS). From 1992 to 2001, the Treasury Department granted licenses for $334 million in humanitarian medical assistance.[8] Except for CRS, these NGOs combined their direct aid campaigns with popular education projects aimed at mobilizing public opinion against the embargo on humanitarian grounds. In Congress, Democrats introduced legislation to exempt sales of food and medicine from the embargo, arguing that U.S. policy aggravated the shortages in Cuba, especially of medicine.

Despite their undiminished hatred of Fidel Castro, Cuban-Americans were also moved by the plight of their brethren and responded by increasing the flow of in-kind assistance and cash remittances. Cuban-Americans had been sending such aid ever since 1978, when family visits were first authorized by the U.S. and Cuban governments. The growth of in-kind assistance was slow during the 1980s, however, because the Cuban government sharply curtailed the number of Cuban-American visitors after the 1980 Mariel boatlift crisis, and mail service was unreliable. Getting cash to Cuba faced similar obstacles, and until 1993, it was illegal for Cubans to hold U.S. currency, so dollars could only be used on the black market. Nevertheless, by 1990, rough estimates of the cash remittances being sent to Cuba totaled about $150 to $200 million annually.[9] Desperate to acquire hard currency, the government legalized the holding of dollars in 1993 so that it could capture part of the remittances stream. By 1994, the estimated value of private cash transfers to Cuba had risen to $500 million a year.[10]

Conservatives in the Cuban-American community, led by the CANF, initially opposed sending remittances on the grounds that they helped Castro stabilize the economy and therefore prolonged his rule. During the 1994 rafters crisis President Clinton bowed to CANF's lobbying by cutting off cash remittances and ending most charter flights, making family visits more difficult. But such measures were not universally supported among Cuban-Americans, many of whom were more immediately concerned with the well-being of their families than with punishing Fidel Castro.[11] Many in the community simply ignored the new rules. Bolstered by improved mail and telephone service, the family ties between Cubans in the United States and Cubans on the island had become too well established and too important to be so easily severed. The prohibition on remittances had no noticeable effect on the availability of dollars in Cuba. Cuban-Americans simply sent funds through third countries or carried them by hand, traveling through Mexico, Jamaica, or the Bahamas.[12] In 1998, after Pope John Paul II's visit to Cuba, Clinton lifted the restrictions on remittances, and by the end of the decade, they reached between $800 million and a billion dollars annually.[13]

Divisions in the Cuban-American community over family contacts were the first indication that the political power of the Cuban-American right was eroding. CANF's unrelenting opposition to family visits, as well as humanitarian assistance and remittances, even in the face of Cuba's economic crisis, now put it at odds with many of its own constituents. In October 2000, a majority of Cuban-Americans favored a national dialogue between Cubans abroad and Castro's government over family issues, unrestricted travel to Cuba, and the sales of medical supplies and food, numbers that had all increased since 1997.[14]

Cleavages within the community were sharp; older Cuban-Americans who left Cuba in the 1960s and 1970s tended to take a much harder position than younger ones who left in the 1980s and 1990s or who were born in the United States. The later immigrants, from the boatlift onwards, were primarily economic rather than political refugees. Unlike the exiles of the 1960s, they did not harbor the same depth of ideological animosity toward the Cuba they left behind. These later arrivals were overwhelmingly in favor of family travel and humanitarian trade, whereas the older Cuban-Americans were opposed.[15] "There's a split in the Cuban American community . . . between those who still have relatives there and those who don't," explained the director of the Cuban Research Institute at Florida International University, Lisandro Pérez. "Most of the Cuban-American leadership are people who came here in the 1960s and 1970s. They are not likely to have family in Cuba anymore. Among recent emigres, however, the concern is to help their families."[16]

These cleavages opened more political space in Miami for moderate Cuban-Americans. The Committee for Cuban Democracy (CCD), headed initially by Bay of Pigs veteran Alfredo Duran, became a significant alternative voice in the late 1990s, as did Cambio Cubano, led by former political prisoner Eloy Gutiérrez-Menoyo.[17] The pope's visit and his call for Cuba "[to] open itself to the world and . . . the world [to] open itself up to Cuba" gave further legitimacy to Cuban-Americans who favored a U.S. policy of greater engagement.[18]

In November 1997, Jorge Más Canosa died of cancer, depriving the Cuban-American right of its most dynamic, charismatic, and politically astute leader. His dominance of Miami's political scene was so great that there were no obvious successors to fill his shoes. In Más Canosa's shadow, other leaders did not flourish. His son, Jorge Más Santos, took over as CANF's chairman, but his strengths were more as a businessman than a politician.[19] Without Más Canosa's hand at the helm, CANF seemed adrift, lacking a clear strategy. At the moment of transition, it had to face its greatest challenge: the arrival of Elián González in late November 1999.

Rescued at sea floating in an inner tube after the boat carrying his mother and several other would-be "refugees" sank in the Florida Straits, six-year-old Elián became an immediate icon to the Cuban-American community—the miracle boy saved by divine intervention, the symbol of Cuba's youth, of Cuba's future. To most members of the community, Elián's future belonged in the United States as vindication of the choice they had made in leaving Cuba. That this small boy should be returned to Castro, to the Cuba of socialism-or-death, was unthinkable.[20] A *Miami Herald* poll found that ninety-one percent of Cuban-Americans in South Florida believed Elián should stay in the United States.[21]

The dilemma for Cuban-American leaders, including CANF, was that most U.S. citizens saw Elián's case as a matter of parental rights rather than a symbolic confrontation with Cuban communism. Support for sending the boy back to Cuba with his father grew from fifty-six percent in January 2000 to sixty-seven percent in April.[22] Sixty percent supported the federal government's decision to forcibly seize Elián from his Miami relatives. Republicans were almost as likely as Democrats to favor returning Elián to his father, a fact which no doubt muted Republican criticism of the Justice Department's decisions.[23]

For many Cuban-Americans, however, the forcible removal of Elián from his Miami relatives and his return to Cuba produced a sense of betrayal unmatched since President John F. Kennedy refused to use U.S. military forces to save the doomed Bay of Pigs invasion in 1961. Demonstrators trampled the American flag and denounced their adopted homeland in front of the television cameras. Cuban-American local officials implied they would not obey federal authority or even control civil disorder. Anglo counterdemonstrators threw bananas at Miami's city hall to symbolize their anger at living in a "banana republic."[24]

This paroxysm of rage proved disastrous for Cuban-American political influence beyond Miami. At a moment when most U.S. citizens were paying attention to Cuba—moments that are rare—Cuban-Americans appeared lawless, fanatical, and contemptuous of America.[25] "The picture that is being painted is an unstable Miami," lamented Governor Jeb Bush, "a Miami that cannot control itself."[26] Lawmakers who had been content to leave Cuba policy to the Cuban-American community began to have second thoughts.

CANF in particular lost influence. Its inability to persuade the White House to keep Elián in the United States represented the foundation's first major defeat after a string of victories stretching from the establishment of Radio Martí to the passage of the Cuban Liberty and Democratic Solidarity Act (Helms-Burton). In Miami, rivals on the right openly challenged the efficacy of

CANF's Washington-focused strategy of lobbying the political establishment, prompting CANF to announce a new program of direct aid to Cuban dissidents.[27] In Washington, not only was the wisdom of CANF's hard line called into question, so was its political muscle. Legislators who opposed CANF's demands to keep Elián in the United States suffered no negative political consequences, proving that the foundation was not invincible after all. Like the China lobby that held U.S.-China relations hostage for nearly a generation, CANF proved to be a paper tiger.

In an effort to refurbish CANF's image and influence, Jorge Más Santos shifted toward the political center. He supported holding the Latin Grammy Awards in Miami, despite the participation of Cuban artists. When Cuba sought to buy food and medicine from the United States in the aftermath of Hurricane Michelle, CANF did not oppose the sales, nor did it oppose former president Jimmy Carter's trip to Cuba in 2002.[28] When George W. Bush considered banning remittances and direct flights to Cuba in 2003, CANF opposed the sanctions because of the impact they would have on Cuban families—a 180-degree reversal of its position during the 1994 rafters crisis.[29] So stark was CANF's shift to the center that a recalcitrant minority of hardliners on its board felt that the younger Bush had betrayed the legacy of his father, and they resigned in protest.[30]

The declining political power of the Cuban-American right coincided with the mobilization, for the first time, of an organized constituency with an interest in improving relations with Cuba—the business community. For years, business had been notoriously absent from the debate over Cuba. Even after the end of the Cold War, when business played a key role in pressing for normal trade relations with China and Vietnam, interest in Cuba was negligible. Cuba's potential market was much smaller than Vietnam's, not to mention China's, but the main reason for the lack of corporate interest was Cuba's uninviting business environment.

When Castro first opened the island to joint ventures in the 1980s, the laws governing foreign investment were strict and inflexible, reflecting the government's residual ideological hostility. After the Soviet Union collapsed, however, Cuba began to actively court foreign investment. In 1995, the investment law was amended to allow 100 percent foreign ownership in certain industries, and bureaucratic reforms made Cuba more attractive. By 2001, there were 392 joint ventures with partners around the globe.[31]

As European trade and investment grew, U.S. corporations began to worry about losing a potentially lucrative market to foreign competitors. "We're saying on behalf of the American business community that it's time to look at this another way," said Thomas J. Donohue, president of the U.S. Chamber of Commerce after a three-day visit to Cuba in 1999. "Who does well there? It's the Canadians, the Germans, the French, the Italians. All of our friends. . . . Ask

Bill Marriott or the guys at the Hilton, do they want to let everybody else in the world buy up those beaches? We need a new approach."[32]

Cuba also became a focal point for the business community's discontent with Washington's use of unilateral economic sanctions in general. Ironically, the 1996 Helms-Burton law crystallized this discontent because its extraterritorial pretensions threatened to disrupt trade relations with Europe, Canada, and Latin America. Business associations were drawn into lobbying on Cuba to pressure the White House to waive implementation of Title III of the law (which enables Cuban-Americans to sue foreign corporations in U.S. courts if they "traffick" in expropriated property).[33] Shortly thereafter, the Chamber of Commerce, the National Association of Manufacturers, and the National Trade Council (representing some five hundred multinational corporations) began to develop a coordinated lobbying strategy against unilateral sanctions.[34]

In early 1998, coinciding with the pope's trip to Cuba and his call for an end to the U.S. embargo, Americans for Humanitarian Trade with Cuba was inaugurated. Organized by the Chamber of Commerce, this coalition was an unusual alliance of some 600 business organizations and 140 religious and human rights groups dedicated to repealing the embargo on food and medicine. The effort was endorsed by a pantheon of prominent former officials including former treasury secretary Lloyd Bentsen, former Federal Reserve chairman Paul Volcker, former World Bank president A. W. Clausen, former U.S. trade representative Carla Hills, and former National Security Council (NSC) adviser and secretary of defense (in the Reagan administration) Frank Carlucci.[35] By focusing specifically on food and medicine, this coalition was able to harness both the humanitarian impulses that arose in response to Cuba's economic hardship and the pecuniary interests of the business community—a combination that proved surprisingly powerful.

The growing chorus of voices in favor of reexamining policy toward Cuba included some high profile conservatives. In 1998, a constellation of Republican luminaries called upon President Clinton to appoint a bipartisan national commission to reassess U.S. policy. The initiative was endorsed by former secretaries of state Henry Kissinger, George Shultz, and Lawrence Eagleburger, former secretary of defense Frank Carlucci, former secretaries of agriculture John Block and Clayton Yeutter, former Senate majority leader and White House chief of staff Howard Baker Jr., along with several dozen U.S. senators and congressmen.[36] Although Clinton rejected the idea, prominent Republicans went on to create the Cuba Policy Foundation, headed by Ambassador Sally Grooms Cowal, to lobby for a new policy. In 1999, the supremely establishmentarian Council on Foreign Relations launched a task force on U.S.-Cuban relations that concluded with a call for new initiatives from Washington.[37]

At first, conservative Cuban-Americans and their allies on Capitol Hill were confident that with the Congress under Republican control, they could turn back any legislative effort to ease the embargo. "It's the same people, with the same proposals, with the same votes, and they will lose graciously, as they always have," said Senator Robert Torricelli (D-N.J.).[38] Representative Ileana Ros-Lehtinen (R-Fla.), one of the three Cuban-American members of Congress, reacted contemptuously to the formation of Americans for Humanitarian Trade with Cuba. "This is really an unholy alliance between the usual suspects who are always anti-embargo, the church groups and now, Wall Street," she said. "The greedy businessmen, the Chamber of Commerce, won't do away with the embargo."[39]

In August 1999, however, to the surprise of almost everyone, the Senate overwhelmingly approved a proposal by conservative John Ashcroft (R-Mo.) to end all U.S. embargoes on food and medicine, including the one against Cuba. Republican leaders in the House prevented the proposal from being considered there, but it reappeared in 2000, sponsored by another farm state Republican in a tight race for reelection, Representative George Nethercutt (R-Wash.). In the midst of the election campaign, a moment when American politicians are notorious for avoiding controversy, large majorities in both chambers of the Republican-controlled legislature voted to lift the ban on selling food and medicine to Cuba and the ban on travel. In the conference committee, however, Republican congressional leaders used their control of the rules to impose a compromise that lifted the embargo on sales of food and medicine, but denied Cuba any U.S.-government or private-sector financing to make purchases. This financial straitjacket meant that the practical effect of lifting the food and medicine embargo was minimized, and the Cuban government initially denounced the measure as a fraud.[40] As part of the compromise, the travel ban was retained as well. Nevertheless, the bipartisan support that the measure received in both the House of Representatives and Senate demonstrated that the strength of the political forces defending the status quo was on the wane.

Congress Gets Bush-Whacked

With congressional momentum moving against the embargo, the election of George W. Bush came in the nick of time for the hardliners on Cuba. Having gained the presidency by virtue of a few hundred votes in Florida, Bush was especially attentive to the Cuban-American constituency, eighty percent of which voted for him. Conservative Cuban-Americans, long a key element of Florida governor Jeb Bush's coalition, had ready-made access to the Bush White House. Bush appointed more Cuban-Americans to senior positions than any president before him. Mel Martinez, a political ally of Jeb, was appointed secretary of Housing and Urban Development, becoming the first Cuban-American member of the cabinet. Otto Reich, Bush's choice to be assistant secretary of state for the Western Hemisphere, was notorious for demonizing opponents when he ran Ronald Reagan's public diplomacy operation—so notorious, in fact, that he could not win Senate confirmation and took office through a recess appointment. Reich's deputy, Lino Gutiérrez, was also a former Reagan official. Colonel Emilio González was named to the NSC staff as director for the Caribbean and Central America, covering Cuba. Mauricio Tamargo, Ileana Ros-Lehtinen's former chief of staff, was appointed chairman of the Foreign Claims Settlement Commission (with jurisdiction over Cuban-American claims against Cuba under Title III of Helms-Burton and existing U.S. compensation claims for property nationalized in the 1960s). Adolfo Franco, a Republican congressional staffer, became Latin America administrator for the U.S. Agency for International Development (AID). From the State Department to the NSC to AID, conservative Cuban-Americans were on the front lines of Bush's foreign policy apparatus dealing with Latin America. This president would be a bulwark against efforts to dilute the embargo. "We have an insurance policy in George W. Bush," said Cuban-American House member Lincoln Díaz-Balart (R-Fla.). "You're not going to see George W. Bush betray the Cuban-American community."[41]

Bush gave his first speech on Cuba in May 2001, celebrating the anniversary of Cuba's independence from Spain. Declaring sanctions to be a "moral statement" as well as a policy instrument, he promised to fight any effort to relax them "until this regime frees its political prisoners, holds democratic, free elections, and allows for free speech." Further, Bush promised a more proactive approach. "The policy of our Government is not merely to isolate Castro but to actively support those working to bring about democratic change in Cuba," he said, including providing them with material support.[42] Two months later, Bush outlined a series of new measures, including tougher enforcement of the travel ban (which tens of thousands of Americans were ignoring), limits on remittances, and the new regulations governing humanitarian assistance. He also reiterated his determination to actively support Cuban opponents of the Castro government. "I will expand support for human rights activists, and the democratic opposition," he declared, "and we will provide additional funding for non-governmental organizations to work on pro-democracy programs in Cuba."[43] He would not, however, provoke a confrontation with European allies by allowing Cuban-Americans to sue European firms for lost property under the Helms-Burton law. A few days after his tough public speech, Bush quietly extended Clinton's policy of waiving implementation of Title III.[44]

By most estimates, the total number of Americans visiting Cuba annually was 150,000 to 200,000, most of them Cuban-Americans visiting family. Some thirty thousand others traveled legally under approved licenses, and the rest (somewhere between twenty and fifty thousand) traveled illegally.[45] Increased travel to Cuba was not just a foreign policy problem for Bush; it was a domestic problem as well. Besides depositing hard currency in Castro's coffers, travelers demystified Cuba and made it more difficult to maintain a demonized public image of Fidel Castro. The travel section of every major newspaper ran stories about Cuba as an attractive tourist destination, and every bookstore featured travel guides to Cuba from all the major publishers. As more and more people went and recounted their experiences to family and friends, Cuba seemed more and more like just another tropical island, albeit a little threadbare, not the archenemy of the Bush administration's rhetoric. The Cubans themselves were well aware of this dynamic and sought to encourage it by welcoming American tourists. "Each one who comes, goes back to the United States and tells the truth about Cuba," said Foreign Minister Felipe Pérez Roque. "They say they have been to hell, but hell is not as hot as it had been depicted."[46]

During the Clinton presidency, efforts by the Treasury's Office of Foreign Assets Control (OFAC) to enforce the travel ban were not very intense. The number of enforcement actions varied annually from a low of 46 to a high of 188 in 2000. In 2001, however, under the new regimen of tougher travel rules, the Bush administration undertook 766 enforcement actions.[47] Additionally, it made the application process for new licenses more complicated, slowed down the processing of applications, and turned down applications more frequently. In early 2003, the administration adopted new regulations ending "people-to-people" exchanges that were not part of regular academic programs of study, a category that included most legal travelers who were not Cuban-Americans.[48] The decision to tighten travel restrictions was not a popular one. In 2001, a poll undertaken for the Cuba Policy Foundation found that Americans favored unrestricted travel to Cuba by a wide margin, sixty-seven percent to twenty-four percent. In early 2003, a poll of Cuban-Americans in South Florida found them evenly split: forty-six percent in favor of unrestricted travel, forty-seven percent against.[49]

For Cubans seeking to visit the United States, the process became even more onerous. Some eighteen thousand visas were granted to Cuban visitors in 2001, only seven thousand in 2002.[50] Cuban officials seeking to meet with U.S. businessmen to buy food and medicine were denied visas, including the head of Cuba's food import enterprise. Visas for Cuban musicians were held up so long that twenty-two of them missed the 2002 Grammy Awards ceremony, which had been moved to Los Angeles from Miami for fear of violence by anti-Castro extremists. Of the 106 Cuban scholars who sought visas to participate in the

2003 Latin American Studies Association (LASA) professional meeting, only about half received them.[51]

The new Congress was undeterred by the new president's hard line on Cuba and picked up where the old Congress had left off. In July, the House of Representatives voted 240 to 186 in favor of an amendment to the Treasury appropriation offered by Jeff Flake (R-Ariz.) to end the travel ban, eight votes more than the same proposal had gotten in 2000. An amendment by Charles Rangel (D-N.Y.) to end the embargo entirely made a surprisingly strong showing, losing 201 to 227.[52] In the Senate, Byron Dorgan (D-N.D.) promised he would offer Flake's amendment when the Senate version of the bill came to the floor. He also planned to propose an amendment to the agricultural appropriation that would lift the ban on private financing of food and medicine sales. His plans were derailed, however, by the September 11, 2001 terrorist attacks on New York and Washington, after which national unity was a high priority for Congress, especially in the field of foreign policy. "The terrorist attacks and the change in climate at the moment made it an inappropriate time to address this issue," said Dorgan, explaining why he decided not to offer his amendments on either travel or food sales. In conference committee on the Treasury bill, the House language lifting the travel ban was dropped, in part because the Republican leaders in the House opposed it and in part because Bush threatened to veto it if the language was retained.[53]

The View From Havana: Economics in Command

For Cuba, the end of the Cold War changed everything. The economic shock that accompanied the collapse of Europe's socialist bloc compelled Cuba to reintegrate its economy with global markets. That, it turn, made rapprochement with the United States advantageous in a way that it had not been in the 1970s and 1980s. Not only was the U.S. market a natural one for Cuba, it was also the main point of origin of tourists bound for the Caribbean and the main source of direct foreign investment in the region.

Cuba's economic restructuring in the 1990s also made the socialist state more vulnerable. The contraction of the state sector of the economy, the proliferation of private entrepreneurs and private markets, the de facto privatization of agriculture, the growing social inequalities based on access to dollars—all these developments undermined the core values of Cuban socialism and hence regime legitimacy. Ending the U.S. embargo was therefore important for economic recovery, but also fraught with political risks: would the benefits of enhanced economic growth outweigh the socially disruptive effects of marketization?

The loss of Soviet economic assistance, which totaled at least three billion dollars annually, sent the Cuban economy into a tailspin that lasted until 1994. The gross domestic product shrank by more than a third, imports fell by more than half, and unemployment swelled as factories closed for lack of critical inputs. Cuba's leaders were forced to implement a series of economic reforms aimed at making the island competitive in the world market and at stimulating domestic production through the introduction of market incentives. For the first time since the early 1960s, U.S. economic sanctions became a significant obstacle to Cuban prosperity.[54]

Conservatives in the United States, hopeful that the collapse of the Cuban regime was imminent, tried to accelerate the process by tightening the embargo in areas where it had become lax. The 1992 Cuban Democracy Act (CDA) sponsored by Congressman Robert Torricelli reinstated the ban on trade with Cuba by the subsidiaries of U.S. corporations in third countries (a measure lifted by Gerald Ford in 1975), thus halting some $768 million in annual trade, ninety percent of which involved Cuban imports of food and medicine.[55] In 1996, Senator Jesse Helms (R-N.C.) and Congressman Dan Burton (R-Ind.) cosponsored the Cuban Liberty and Democratic Solidarity Act to deter foreign corporations from investing in Cuba by making them subject to law suits in U.S. courts if they "trafficked" in property confiscated from U.S. citizens, including naturalized Cuban-Americans. The Helms-Burton legislation also inscribed the embargo into law, preventing the president from simply revoking the executive orders that originally imposed it and normalizing relations.[56]

The U.S. embargo hampered Cuba's economic recovery in a variety of ways. Because it had to conduct most of its trade with Europe rather than the nearby United States, Cuba's shipping costs, especially for bulk commodities like exported sugar and imported grain, were far higher.[57] This expense was exacerbated by a provision of the embargo prohibiting ships that call in Cuban ports from entering U.S. ports for six months. Goods produced under patent only by U.S. corporations (including many pharmaceuticals) were unavailable to Cuba. The 1992 CDA purportedly legalized the sale of medical supplies, and the 2000 Agricultural Appropriations Act did the same for food, but restrictions in the laws limited the practical feasibility of such sales.[58] A number of independent studies have documented the deleterious impact of U.S. sanctions on the Cuban health care system.[59]

The embargo complicated Cuba's effort to diversify away from sugar production and into tourism. The United States is the country of origin for most of the Caribbean tourist trade and the main source of foreign direct investment in Latin America. Although Cuba enjoyed considerable success in developing tourism, the future expansion of this sector was limited so long as the United States prohibited tourist travel to the island. A U.S. government study estimated that if sanctions were lifted, between 100,000 and 350,000 additional U.S. residents would travel to Cuba annually (approximately doubling the current number), and these visitors would provide Cuba with between $90 million and $350 million in revenue.[60]

Finally, Cuba's isolation from international financial institutions meant that the impact of adjusting to the shock of the Soviet collapse fell fully on the shoulders of Cuban consumers. Neither the International Monetary Fund (IMF) nor the World Bank was available for emergency infusions of cash and credit. Cuba withdrew from these institutions in the 1960s and has been prohibited from participating in the Inter-American Development Bank (IADB) since its membership in the Organization of American States (OAS) was suspended in early 1962. U.S. policy opposed allowing Cuba back into any of these institutions. Although Fidel Castro had nothing but scorn for the IMF, calling it a "sinister" tool of the United States that has perpetuated the subjugation of the underdeveloped nations, he was less critical of the World Bank and IADB.[61]

For all these reasons, Cuba has had a compelling economic interest in normalizing its commercials relations with the United States. With the embargo inscribed in law by Helms-Burton, however, the only hope for loosening it lay in cultivating political constituencies in the United States that could pressure Congress to rewrite the law. Havana has been solicitous of three such constituencies: moderate Cuban-Americans, grassroots NGOs that have taken advantage of people-to-people contacts, and the business community.

As described earlier, demographic changes in the Cuban-American community have made it less monolithic politically. The Cuban government tried to encourage and capitalize on that change by differentiating its traditional enemies from the Cuban-American community at large. In the early years of the revolution, all those who went into exile were denounced as *gusanos* (worms). In later years, as more and more emigrants left for economic reasons and sent remittances to family back home, the *gusanos* became the "Cuban community abroad." Only the community's unreconstructed hardliners were singled out for the government's venom, routinely referred to as the "Miami terrorist mafia."[62] Raúl Castro explained the distinction: "The émigré community cannot be considered as a monolithic bloc of traitors of the nation, supporters of the blockade and of the overthrow of the Revolution. Those who are part of the exile mafia with extreme right-wing views and terrorist behavior manipulate, to some extent, the Cuban émigré community in [the United States]. Another minority is growing, brave émigrés who defend Cuba. A large number simply want to have normal contact with their relatives and live in peace with their country of origin."[63]

In 1994, the Cuban government invited over two hundred exiles to a "Nation and Migration" conference in Havana to begin the process of "normalizing" relations between the island and the diaspora. It was the first significant meeting between the government and the exile community since the 1978

"Dialogue" at the height of President Jimmy Carter's efforts to improve U.S.-Cuban relations. The agenda was dominated by issues of travel and family contacts. The island government agreed to lift a number of restrictions on travel by exiles and even offered to allow them to invest in Cuba on the same terms as any foreign investor. The unspoken hope was that easier travel would produce more travel and more external support for family members in Cuba. Nor was the government unaware of the potential political impact in the United States. "If they want to invest here, they now have a better understanding of the importance of lifting the embargo," observed Cuban official spokesman Miguel Alfonso.[64] Conference participants were criticized vociferously by Miami conservatives but, as polls showed, most Cuban-Americans agreed with the sentiments of Dr. Bernardo Benes, who led the 1978 dialogue. "Right now, Cuba is a house on fire and it's not the time to ask who is to blame," he declared. "The priority is to put out the flames and save the children inside the house."[65]

Several months later, Cuba's foreign minister, Roberto Robaina, met secretly in Spain with the leaders of three moderate exile opposition groups, two of which maintained explicit ties to dissidents on the island.[66] A second Nation and Migration conference was held the following year, and unlike the first conference, invitations were not restricted to those who were generally supportive of the revolution. Over 350 participants came from thirty-four countries.[67] A third conference was scheduled for April 2003, with anticipated participation of over one thousand people, but was cancelled amidst the furor caused by Cuba's arrest of seventy-five dissidents.[68]

Easing travel restrictions for Cuban-Americans was by no means risk free for the Castro government. The first time it threw open the doors to returning emigrants, in 1978, nearly 150,000 flooded the island in just over a year. Their obvious wealth compared to that of ordinary Cubans exacerbated smoldering discontent due to an economic downturn Cuba experienced in the late 1970s. The result was the Mariel boatlift crisis. But like so many of the potentially destabilizing reforms Cuba had to make in the 1990s to survive the "Special Period," economic necessity trumped political sensitivity, and Cuba-U.S. travel was allowed to expand.

Faced with antagonism from official Washington, the Cuban government has long tried to build bridges to sympathetic Americans in the hope that their influence might mitigate U.S. hostility. This strategy was largely ineffective when travel to Cuba was illegal for everyone in the United States except journalists, academics, and Cuban-Americans. But when President Clinton allowed travel for religious, humanitarian, and people-to-people cultural exchanges, almost two hundred NGOs launched programs in Cuba, sending some thirty thousand people annually.[69] The humanitarian efforts, especially by churches, to aid Cuba in the depth of its economic crisis created permanent linkages, in much the same way that Cuban-Americans were forging (or reforging) family connections. A Sister Cities movement arose, for example, linking seventeen Cuban cities with U.S. cities. Robert Torricelli and Bill Clinton embraced people-to-people contacts, anticipating that such exchanges would help create in Cuba a constituency for changing the Cuban regime. An unanticipated result was that such contacts created a constituency in the United States for changing U.S. policy.

An even more important one was developing within the farming and business sectors. At first, the Cubans reacted badly to the limitations on financing that Republican congressional leaders imposed on the sale of food and medicine in 2000. The conditions were "humiliating" said Vice President Carlos Lage, and until they were changed, Cuba would not buy "a single grain of rice or a single aspirin."[70] The Cubans seemed to think that if there were no sales, the business lobby would return to Congress and force it to remove the onerous financing conditions. The actual effect of the Cuban boycott was just the opposite. After several years of tough congressional battles, the business community had nothing to show for it. They had won the right to sell food and medicine to Cuba, but the Cubans weren't buying. Some business lobbyists began to wonder if trying to do business with Cuba was more trouble than it was worth.[71]

In November 2001, Cuba was hit by Hurricane Michelle, a category four storm, the worst in half a century. Although there were few fatalities, Michelle caused an estimated $1.8 billion in damage, destroying large portions of the sugar, citrus, banana, and tobacco crops.[72] The United States offered emergency disaster relief, but Cuba took the opportunity to ask instead to purchase food and medicine on a "one time" basis to replenish depleted stocks.[73] The hurricane gave the Cubans an opportunity to step down from their intransigent position on sales without losing face. A few months later, the Cubans announced they would continue purchasing food under the terms of existing U.S. law.[74]

In the last few weeks of 2001, Cuba bought $35 million worth of food from U.S. firms and another $165 million in 2002.[75] "American business has been reintroduced to Cuba," said John Kavulich, president of the U.S.-Cuba Trade and Economic Council. "We're back, and this is irreversible."[76] The Cubans were careful to spread their contracts around for maximum political effect, even when it was not the most economical approach. Like savvy U.S. defense contractors, they made sure that as many congressional districts as possible had some stake in the sales. By late 2002, businesses in twenty-seven states had contracts with Cuba. "At the end of the day, it's all about politics," explained a Cuban official.[77]

The resumption of trade with Cuba, the first trade of any significance with U.S. firms since 1962, reenergized the business community's interest.[78] State and local officials from around the United States began traveling to Havana to seek out opportunities for their constituents, and almost all of them were received by Castro personally. U.S. diplomat Vicki Huddleston dubbed the performance Castro's "charm offensive."[79] Governor George Ryan of Illinois went to Cuba twice; Governor John Hoeven of North Dakota visited and returned with $2 million in sales contracts; and Governor Jesse Ventura of Minnesota went with a retinue of businessmen for a four-day food and agribusiness trade show. Even local officials from Tampa and the Florida Keys made the journey.[80]

These trips infuriated the Bush administration. It refused to grant a license to a Farm Foundation delegation that included several top agribusiness executives and two former Secretaries of Agriculture (both Democrats). But when elected officials made the trip, there was not much the White House could do to stop them.[81] It may have been no coincidence that when, in November 2002, the State Department expelled four Cuban diplomats as punishment for the Ana Belen Montes espionage case, one of the diplomats expelled from his post at the Cuban Interests Section in Washington was the liaison to the U.S. business community.[82]

Moreover, on the eve of the September 2002 Food and Agriculture Exhibition, the State Department's senior latin Americanist, Otto Reich, publicly excoriated U.S. businesses for rushing to Cuba for contracts. Comparing Castro to Hitler, he called participants in the trade show Castro's "props" and accused them of acting against the national interest, especially in light of Cuba's alleged bioweapons program. "It would be one of the greatest ironies in history if the wealth of the American private sector is what keeps that failed government from finally collapsing," Reich said. Then he urged Governor Ventura and his delegation to "refrain from sexual tourism" during their trip.[83]

When the trade show opened, with 288 exhibitors from thirty-three states, the newly appointed head of the U.S. Interests Section, James Cason, made a point of attending to warn participants that Cuba was an "international deadbeat," already behind in debt payments to various European governments and firms. Cuba had a "Jurassic Park economy," Cason quipped, and would not be a sound business partner.[84] Despite Cason's warnings, exhibitors signed $66 million in new contracts with Cuban trade representatives.[85]

Both the Bush administration and the Cuban government foresaw that the growing trade in food and medicine could have deleterious political implications for the rest of the embargo. Food and medicine were the proverbial crack in the dam. As Cuban foreign minister Pérez Roque put it, food sales were "an example of what the future could hold" for relations between the two countries.[86] Otto Reich's spin was different, but the point was the same: "What we believe [Castro] wants to do here is to entice the U.S. agricultural community

. . . with cash purchases so that we open up markets and have, quote, normal trade relationships."[87]

After 9/11: The "War on Terror" and Cuba Policy

During his first few months in office, George W. Bush pledged that Latin America would be the focus of his foreign policy, and his close relationship with Mexican president Vicente Fox seemed a bellwether. The September 11 attacks upended that agenda. All other issues took second place to the war on terrorism, centered on the Muslim world. Latin America was peripheral to this conflict and slid from the top of the White House agenda to the bottom. Relations with key Latin allies like Mexico and Chile blew hot and cold depending upon their willingness to back Washington's "antiterrorism" efforts in Afghanistan and Iraq.[88]

With the attention of senior Bush policymakers focused in the Eastern Hemisphere rather than the Western, mid-level officials sought to cultivate attention for their favorite policy initiatives by recasting them as ancillary to the war on terrorism. Thus, the war in Colombia, which before September 11 had been justified as a war on drug trafficking, was quickly reframed as a war on terrorism, with the guerrilla movements and paramilitaries both added to the State Department's list of terrorist organizations. Congressional restrictions that prevented U.S. military aid from being used to fight the guerrillas were lifted and aid to the Colombian military increased.[89]

Hardliners in the Cuban-American community and the Bush administration seized on the terrorism issue as rationale for a more confrontational policy toward Cuba and to fend off growing congressional pressures to relax the embargo. On September 20, 2001, speaking before Congress, Bush had drawn the line starkly: "Either you are with us or you are with the terrorists," he declared. "From this day forward, any nation that continues to harbor or support terrorism will be regarded by the United States as a hostile regime."[90] Cuba, the hardliners pointed out, had been on the State Department's list of state sponsors of international terrorism since the list's inception in 1982, and it maintained friendly relations with other states on the list, including Libya, Syria, Iran and Iraq.[91] The signs for Cuba were ominous.

Cuba's security concerns vis-à-vis the United States have always had two dimensions: fear that the United States might seek to redeem its defeat at the Bay of Pigs by launching a direct invasion, and fear that the United States would exploit internal discontent to subvert the socialist state. The end of the Cold War did not mean a reduction of Cuba security worries. If anything, it meant just the opposite. Although in the waning years of the Cold War, the Soviet military commitment to Cuba had been largely abandoned and economic aid had dwindled, the Cubans still depended on the Soviets for all their military equipment and most of their trade.[92] Not only did the disappearance of the Soviet Union leave the Cubans alone to face the harsh discipline of the international market, it also left them alone to face the unrivaled military power of the United States.

As the Cuban economy spiraled downward, the armed forces were not spared the budget axe. From 1989 to 1999, the size of the regular armed forces fell by eighty percent, from 297,000 troops to just 50,000. Expenditures fell sixty-four percent (in constant dollars) from $1.73 billion to $630 million, down from 2.9 percent of GNP to just 1.9 percent (ranking Cuba 87th of 167 countries, right below Laos and Fiji).[93] The severe shortage of petroleum Cuba experienced in the mid-1990s meant that the armed forces rarely trained, and seventy-five percent of its heavy equipment was mothballed. Required to produce all of its own food and much of its budget, the military shifted its activities from war readiness to business.[94] The Special Period transformed the Cuban armed forces, the U.S. Defense Department reported, "from one of the most active militaries in the Third World into a stay-at-home force that has minimal conventional fighting ability."[95] Gone were the halcyon days when the Cubans defeated the South Africans in Angola and the Somalis in the Ogaden desert.

With no Soviet patron and a decrepit military of its own, Cuba had no chance whatsoever of deterring or fending off a military attack by the United States. The best it could do was seek sanctuary in the bulwarks that small powers have longed used to shield themselves from great power pretensions— international law and the good offices of the international community. Never more than a slender reed, these safeguards looked especially precarious when George W. Bush declared the new doctrine of unilateral preventive war and invaded Iraq, despite majority opposition on the United Nations Security Council.

On September 11, 2001, Cuba was one of the first countries to express condolences to the United States and offer help.[96] As commercial flights were grounded and airports closed all across America, Cuba offered its airports to any U.S. plane that needed a place to land. The tone of the Cuban response shifted from sympathy to concern after Bush's September 20 speech to the Congress. While reiterating Cuba's opposition to terrorism in principle and its determination to prevent any terrorist attack against the United States being launched from Cuba, Castro also began to speak out vigorously against a unilateral U.S. military response. On September 22, Castro called terrorism "dangerous and ethically indefensible," and described the September 11 attacks as "a huge injustice and a great crime . . . atrocious and insane." Nevertheless, he argued, the attacks should not be used as an excuse to "recklessly start a war." Bush's speech to Congress, he warned, signaled a U.S. strategy to act "under the exclusive rule of force, irrespective of any international laws or institutions." The United Nations was being "simply ignored [and] would fail to have any authority or prerogative whatsoever" if the United States could go to war whenever and against whomever it pleased. Castro was clearly worried that Cuba could end up a target of such unilateralism, although he thought "it will not be easy to fabricate pretexts to do it."[97]

Over the next year, Cuba's strategy would be to do everything possible to demonstrate its opposition to international terrorism and its willingness to cooperate to eradicate it, while at the same time arguing strenuously that the United States did not have the right to wage war unilaterally. Cuba signed all twelve international protocols against terrorism, and did not object—even offering to cooperate with the provision of some services—when the United States decided to use Guantánamo naval base as a detention center for suspected Al Qaeda and Taliban prisoners. Cuba proposed three draft agreements to the United States on cooperation against terrorism, drug trafficking, and people smuggling, issues on which the two countries had mutual interests. Washington did not respond.[98]

Against this background, Otto Reich, assistant secretary for Western Hemisphere Affairs, launched a review of policy toward Cuba with the aim of seeking new ways to promote a "rapid and peaceful transition to democracy." Foremost among them was to increase support for opposition elements on the island.[99] But the outcome of the policy reviewed seemed more rhetorical than substantive. When Bush's "New Initiative for Cuba" was announced in May 2002, it sounded a lot like the old initiative from May 2001: hold firm against efforts to relax the embargo, strengthen TV and Radio Martí, intensify enforcement of the restrictions on travel, and increase support for Castro's opponents. The rhetoric ratcheted up considerably, however. To a Cuban-American audience in Miami, Bush described Castro as "a brutal dictator who cares everything for his own power and nada for the Cuban people . . . [who] clings to a bankrupt ideology that has brought Cuba's workers and farmers and families nothing-nothing-but isolation and misery." Any Cuban who dissented could only expect "jail, torture, and exile." Bush promised to veto any effort to relax the embargo, because trade with Cuba would do nothing more than "line the pockets of Fidel Castro and his cronies."[100]

Castro responded in kind, referring specifically to the Miami speech as "arrogance, demagogy and lies," and charging Bush with having promised the Cuban-American right before the election that he would destroy the Cuban Revolution. "These [plans] did not exclude assassinating me." Since September 11, Bush had resorted to "the rule of Nazi concepts and methods" in his dealings with the rest of the world, Castro charged, and his intimate relationship with Cuban-American terrorists in Miami "completely undermines his moral authority and disqualifies him as a world leader to fight against terrorism."[101] Castro pointed out that 3,478 Cubans had died in terrorist attacks launched from the United States, many with U.S. government complicity, and a number of those responsible still resided openly in Miami.[102]

Despite the escalating war of words between Washington and Havana, the September 11 attacks made the Cuban threat look puny by comparison. Critics argued that if Washington was to rally a broad international coalition for the fight against terrorism, it could not afford to risk its own credibility by continuing to brand Cuba a terrorist state for political reasons.[103] Richard Nuccio, who had been Clinton's special adviser on Cuban affairs, had tried in vain to get Cuba dropped from the terrorist list when he was in government, because there was no evidence that the Cubans were engaged in or supporting acts of international terrorism any longer. No one in the intelligence community disputed the facts, according to Nuccio, but no one in the Clinton White House was willing to weather the political firestorm sure to be unleashed if Cuba was dropped from the list.[104]

When the State Department's new list was released in May 2002, Cuba was still on it. The rationale was that Cuba had vacillated over the war on terrorism, because Castro had denounced U.S. military action in Afghanistan as excessive. The report also repeated prior charges that Cuba harbored fugitives from U.S. justice, terrorists from the Fatherland and Liberty (ETA), and Colombian guerrillas.[105] Critics noted that the Basques were in exile in Cuba at the request of the Spanish government; the Colombians were there because Cuba was serving as a neutral site for ongoing peace negotiations between the guerrillas and the Colombian government; and the U.S. fugitives were there because the United States and Cuba did not have a functioning extradition agreement.[106] Moreover, there was no evidence in the report that Cuba had actually *done* anything to provide "support for acts of international terrorism"—the statutory criterion for membership on the terrorist list.[107]

But the deficiencies of evidence in the State Department report on global terrorism were dwarfed by the furor that erupted when Under Secretary for Arms Control and International Security John R. Bolton accused Cuba of developing biological weapons. In a May 2002 speech to the conservative Heritage Foundation, entitled, "Beyond the Axis of Evil," Bolton elevated rogue states Libya, Syria, and Cuba to evil's second tier (below Iran, Iraq, and North Korea) because of their efforts to acquire weapons of mass destruction. "The United States believes that Cuba has at least a limited offensive biological warfare research and development effort," Bolton said. "Cuba has provided dual-use biotechnology to other rogue states."[108]

U.S. concerns about Cuba's biotechnology industry dated to the early 1990s. The advanced technology Cuba acquired to produce commercial pharmaceuticals had the potential for dual use; like similar technologies in a host of other countries, it was equally capable of producing biological weapons.[109] The charge that Cuba actually was producing such weapons gained currency in

Miami in the late 1990s, when defector Alvaro Prendez claimed that Cuba had Soviet medium range missiles armed with biological warheads aimed at South Florida. The State Department spokesman dismissed the charges, saying, "The U.S. government follows the matter of weapons of mass destruction very closely, and we can assure you that we know of no reason to be alarmed."[110]

The issue was revived in 1998, when Ken Alibek, former deputy director of the Soviet Union's biological weapons program, described how circumstantial evidence had convinced his boss, Yuri Kalinin, that Cuban biotechnology was being used for weapons development.[111] Once again, the State Department issued a denial, saying, "We have no evidence that Cuba is stockpiling or has mass-produced any BW [biological warfare] agents." On background, U.S. officials were even more definitive: "None of what we know adds up to Cuba having offensive biological warfare capabilities. We get lots of reports from defectors and others, but when we go to check them out it's always second and third hand, and the stuff doesn't check out."[112] In 1998, a Defense Department report to Congress reiterated concerns about the potential for biological weapons development provided by Cuba's biotechnology industry, but did not claim that any weapons program was underway.[113]

Bolton's speech, by contrast, seemed to announce that U.S. fears had been realized, that the Cubans had launched a weapons program. But senior officials began backing away from the claim almost immediately. The day after Bolton's speech, Secretary of Defense Donald H. Rumsfeld dodged the issue by claiming, "I haven't seen the intelligence." A few days later, Secretary of State Colin Powell, commented: "As Under Secretary Bolton said recently, we do believe that Cuba has a biological offensive research capability. We didn't say that it actually had such weapons, but it has the capacity and the capability to conduct such research."[114] That was not quite what Bolton said. He did not say the Cubans had the "capability" to do biological weapons research, something that had been known for years. He said they had a "research and development effort" underway.[115]

To confuse matters even more, it turned out that Bolton was repeating language that Carl Ford, assistant secretary of state for Intelligence and Research, had used in congressional testimony in March. However, Ford's two sentences on Cuba were buried in a longer report on the global threat from weapons of mass destruction and so they went largely unnoticed.[116] Ford subsequently testified, under oath, that the language about Cuba had been cleared by the intelligence community and reflected its collective judgment, one unchanged since a 1999 National Intelligence Estimate on the matter. But he hastened to draw a distinction between Cuba's limited developmental offensive biological warfare research effort and a weapons development program. "We've never tried to suggest that we have the evidence, the smoking gun, to prove proof positive that they had a program. A program suggests to us something far more substantial than what we see in the evidence. But we feel very confident about saying that they're working, working on an effort that would give them a BW, a limited BW offensive capability . . . . Clearly we're suggesting that Cuba is working on biological weapons."[117]

That seemed unequivocal, but Ford's account began to waver as he was questioned by the senators. What started out sounding like a research "effort" to develop weapons began to dissolve back into a mere capability. "Cuba has in our judgment the trained personnel, medical and scientific, the knowledge as supported by their research into various diseases, both human and animal. They have the research facilities, including biocontainment facilities. They have everything you need to build an offensive biological weapon. They don't need anything else. The difference between that and a program is an arbitrary intelligence community judgment, that to have a program, you need to be able to have a factory that tests the weapon, that puts the weapon in a bomb or a shell and/or does research and development on that sort of weapons program, and has a unit within the military specifically designated for a weapons capability. . . . We don't see that in Cuba."[118]

What evidence the government had remained classified, but Ford admitted that it had not come from anyone actually working on biological weapons in Cuba, even though a number of scientists had defected, including José de la Fuente, former director of research and development at the Center for Genetic Engineering and Biotechnology, Cuba's main biomedical research institute. De la Fuente denied that he had seen or heard any evidence of Cuban biological warfare research before leaving Cuba in 1999. "All our information is indirect," Ford acknowledged.[119] Congressman Tim Roemer (D-Ind.), a member of the House Intelligence Committee, said flatly that Bolton's charges were false.[120]

Whatever the truth of Cuba's alleged bioweapons "effort," it was hard not to think that the Bolton speech was intentionally timed to make a big media splash just before former president Jimmy Carter's trip to Cuba. Bolton, a conservative political appointee, had chosen a major public forum to announce three potential additions to the "axis of evil," though in the Cuban case, the intelligence assessment had not changed in three years, despite Bolton's insinuation to the contrary. Just a few months before, at a United Nations conference in Geneva, Bolton had accused five countries of secretly developing biological weapons, and Cuba was not among them.[121]

The impending Carter trip was embarrassing to President Bush, who had been promising a tougher policy on Cuba, and he tried to dissuade Carter from going. The trip was sure to give renewed impetus to congressional efforts to relax the embargo—which the White House opposed. Reinforcing the perception that politics lay behind the timing of the Bolton bombshell, it turned out that Assistant Secretary Reich—whose reputation for partisan manipulation of policy issues during the Reagan years was well earned—had been pressing the intelligence community to allow public dissemination of the bioweapons assessment.[122]

Carter was convinced the timing of the Bolton speech was designed to distract attention from his trip and diffuse its policy impact. While in Cuba, he responded by pointing out that in the intelligence briefings he received before departing for Havana, no one mentioned biological weapons development. "There were absolutely no such allegations made or questions raised," Carter said. "I asked them myself on more than one occasion if there was any evidence that Cuba has been involved in sharing any information with any country on earth that could be used for terrorist purposes. And the answer from our experts on intelligence was no."[123]

Fidel Castro denounced Bolton's claim in no uncertain terms, as a "diabolical fabrication" and an "infamous slander" designed to prevent Congress from easing the embargo. "In our country . . . no one has ever thought of producing such weapons," Castro insisted, and he offered any international agency the right to inspect Cuba biotechnology facilities.[124]

Sure enough, when Congress again took up proposals to lift the travel ban and the restrictions on food sales, opponents relied on the biological weapons charge as the centerpiece of their strategy to block the proposals. In July, Congressman Flake again offered his amendment prohibiting enforcement of the travel ban to the Treasury appropriation in the House. Unlike prior years, however, conservative Republicans mounted a vigorous opposition because the same language had already been inserted into the Senate bill, making it harder to strip out in the conference committee as the leadership had done two years in a row. The leadership structured the floor debate to Flake's disadvantage, forcing members to vote first on an amendment by Intelligence Committee Chairman, Porter J. Goss (R-Fla.). The Goss amendment made lifting the travel ban contingent on a presidential certification that Cuba was not aiding terrorists, developing biological weapons, or providing bioweapons technology to others.

The essential hollowness of the administration's bioweapons argument was underscored by its ineffectiveness as a legislative device. Even Goss, who was well versed in the evidence by dint of his position, did not repeat Bolton's claims. Nor would he go so far as to argue that Cuba was a state sponsor of international terrorism. "Whether it is a terrorist sponsor today remains a difficult, open question," he acknowledged, "and one which our executive agencies are working on."[125] The House rejected the Goss amendment handily, 182 to 247, and went on to pass the Flake amendment 262 to 167, even in the face of a presidential threat to veto the bill. In all, seventy-three Republicans deserted Bush and their House leadership to support Flake. The House then quickly passed amendments to lift the financial limit on remittances to Cuba and to allow private financing of agricultural sales. Only Rangel's perennial bid to lift the embargo completely was beaten back, 204 to 226.[126]

"Those votes reflected a nation that's got a different attitude on the subject than it had three, four, five years ago," observed Dick Armey (R-Tex.), Republican majority leader.[127] Armey himself was a good example of how attitudes were changing. Upon announcing his decision to retire, Armey admitted that his support for continuing the embargo against Cuba had been based on party and personal loyalty. "What you see in the House of Representatives and what you see by way of individual votes—my own is an example—is loyalties to your friends," he said. The embargo, he predicted, would be lucky to survive another year.[128]

Survive it did, however, once again by virtue of a legislative sleight of hand of the Republican congressional leadership. In the Senate, where Dorgan was expected to successfully amend the Agriculture appropriation to lift the ban on private financing for farm sales to Cuba, the leadership avoided the vote by simply preventing the bill from ever coming to the floor. They did the same with the Treasury bill. Both bills were among the eleven that had to be combined into an omnibus appropriation, but in the process of crafting the omnibus, all the provisions on Cuba were dropped because President Bush threatened to veto the entire bill and bring the government to a halt rather than relax sanctions against Cuba.[129] "People are wrong to underestimate what it means to have President Bush on our side," said Diaz-Balart, one of the most stalwart anti-Castro legislators.[130]

"Going Backward": New Provocations and New Anxieties

For Cuba, the U.S. invasion of Iraq was even more disconcerting than the war against the Taliban. At least in Afghanistan, the Taliban had, in fact, been sheltering and supporting Al Qaeda. But there was no verifiable link between Saddam Hussein and the September 11 attacks, and the claims that Iraq weapons of mass destruction (WMD) posed an imminent threat to its neighbors were, at the very least, debatable. More importantly, the United Nations inspection regime was addressing the issue of Iraq's WMD when the United States simply swept it aside and went to war. What was to stop Washington from declaring Cuba's notional bioweapons program an imminent threat at least as serious as Saddam Hussein's elusive WMD? Washington had already declared Cuba a terrorist state, and Bush had promised that any state supporting terrorism would be regarded as "hostile regime." He avowed the right of the United States to take "preemptive action" against its enemies, and Bolton, in his speech claiming that Cuba was developing biological weapons, warned that countries developing WMD "can expect to become our targets."[131]

While these developments suggested the Bush administration might be trying to create an excuse to attack Cuba directly, Castro was equally concerned with the threat to internal security. In 1992, the CDA added a new dimension to U.S. policy to complement the three decades-old economic sanctions regime. The idea of promoting people-to-people contacts, which President Bill Clinton embraced, sought to foster the development of Cuban civil society. This new facet of U.S. policy was dubbed "Track II" (Track I being the economic sanctions). People-to-people contacts, through academic and cultural exchanges and improved air and telecommunications links, served a clear humanitarian purpose by easing the lives of ordinary citizens on both sides of the Florida Straits. But Track II had a double edge. From the outset, Washington conceived of these contacts as a way to subvert the Cuban government. That was how the policy was promoted when first introduced by Congressman Robert Torricelli, author of CDA. Drawn from the experience of Eastern Europe, Track II was founded on the assumption that people-to-people contacts would promote the diffusion of ideas, strengthen independent nongovernmental organizations, and thereby erode the political control mechanisms of the authoritarian state. The Eastern European communist regimes "ultimately fell from the power of ideas," Torricelli argued.[132] By analogy, Castro would, too.

The Clinton administration was enamored of this approach, largely because Richard Nuccio, the president's special adviser on Cuban affairs, authored the original Track II provisions of the CDA when he worked for Torricelli. As described by Under Secretary of State Peter Tarnoff, Track II aimed to "empower those living under [the regime's] yoke to be able to continue their struggle for democratic reform and human rights. . . . These actions are intended to give hope to legitimate opponents of the regime to allow them to sustain the risks and pressures of maintaining their struggle for democracy."[133] Under the rubric of Track II, the Clinton White House improved telephone links with the island, allowed Cuban-Americans to send remittances to their relatives, allowed U.S. NGOs to provide humanitarian aid to NGOs in Cuba, and loosened travel restrictions for professional, religious, and humanitarian purposes.[134]

In addition to allowing the expansion of academic and cultural contacts, Torricelli's 1992 law also authorized Washington to take a more direct role, providing funding for "the support of individuals and organizations to promote nonviolent democratic change in Cuba."[135] President Clinton announced the first grant under this title of the law in October 1995, providing funding to Freedom House to disseminate information in Cuba and to aid former prisoners.[136] "We believe that reaching out today will nurture and strengthen the fledgling civil society that will be the backbone of tomorrow's democratic Cuba," explained Clinton. "We will continue to help Cuba's democratic opposition and the churches, human rights organizations, and others seeking to exercise the political and economic rights that should belong to all Cubans."[137] The 1996 Helms-Burton law expanded the "democracy-building" mandate of this overtly political program, authorizing assistance to democratic and human rights groups in Cuba, and humanitarian aid for former political prisoners and their families.[138]

George W. Bush's pledge to increase U.S. support for opposition elements on the island was immediately manifested through increased funding for "democracy programs" aimed at Cuba and a more aggressive posture by the U.S. Interests Section in Havana. During the Clinton presidency, AID spent about $10 million on the Cuba program. Bush raised the annual budget from $3.5 million in FY2000 to $5.0 million in FY2001 and $7.0 million in FY2004. The money was distributed to U.S. NGOs to finance programs designed to support Cuban human rights activists, independent journalists, independent trade unionists, former political prisoners, and nongovernmental organizations. At least until 2003, there was a prohibition on delivering any of the funds in cash to Cuban clients, both because of concerns about accounting standards and because of the risk entailed for recipients due to Cuba's stringent laws prohibiting such funding. Consequently, the support provided tended to be mostly in the form of material goods (computers, cameras, etc.) and published materials critical of the Cuban government. However, some participating U.S. organizations also delivered privately raised cash to Cuban clients along with the goods paid for by AID. An evaluation of the project conducted in 2001 noted that it was very difficult to deliver much actual material assistance to clients in Cuba because of Cuban government controls.[139]

It did not escape Fidel Castro's notice that Washington envisioned Track II as an instrument of subversion. "It seeks to destroy us from within," he declared in July 1995, "to infiltrate us, weaken us, to create all types of counter-revolutionary organizations, and to destabilize the country. . . . These people want to exert influence through broad exchanges with diverse sectors they consider vulnerable."[140] Predictably, the Cuban government reacted harshly to Washington's attempts to foster internal dissension, treating all dissidents as if they were foreign agents and looking with suspicion at all Cuban contacts with foreigners.

In early 1996, after the passage of Helms-Burton, Raúl Castro denounced Cuban intellectuals for having developed dangerously close ties with U.S. groups and foundations. Cuba's economic crisis had created "feelings of depression and political confusion," he acknowledged. The party needed to wage a "battle of ideas" to explain these events, lest people lose faith in socialist values and be seduced by capitalist consumerism. "We must convince the people, or the enemy will do it." He went on to describe Track II efforts to create an independent civil society as an attempt at "internal subversion. . . .

The enemy does not conceal its intention to use some of the so-called nongovernmental organizations (NGOs) established in Cuba in recent times, as a Trojan horse to foment division and subversion here." As an object, negative lesson, Raúl singled out the Central Committee's own research centers, especially the Center for the Study of the Americas (CEA), which had fallen prey to U.S. efforts at "internal subversion."[141]

Shortly thereafter, the Cuban National Assembly adopted the Law for the Reaffirmation of Cuban Dignity and Sovereignty as a response to the passage of Helms-Burton. The Cuban law criminalized "any form of cooperation, whether direct or indirect, with the application of the Helms-Burton Act," including providing to the U.S. government information relevant to the law, receiving resources from the U.S. government to promote the law, spreading information provided by the U.S. government promoting the law, or cooperating with the mass media to promote it. In short it criminalized a wide swath of common dissident activity, especially if it was supported by the United States.[142]

In January 1999, President Clinton announced a series of measures ostensibly aimed at easing relations with Cuba somewhat. At the time, Clinton was under pressure to appoint a bipartisan commission to review bilateral relations, which, with an eye on the Cuban-American vote, he was loath to do on the eve of Al Gore's 2000 election campaign. Although he rejected the idea of a commission, Clinton loosened restrictions on religious, humanitarian, and professional travel, expanded direct air flights to Cuba from cities other than Miami, and offered to restore direct mail service. But he added two additional measures that made the Cuban government apoplectic: he allowed anyone in the United States to send remittances to anyone in Cuba, whereas previously remittances had been restricted to family members. That meant individuals or foundations could send money directly to Cuban dissidents. And Clinton promised to allow sales of agricultural inputs to independent farmers "for the purpose of promoting economic activity that is independent of the Cuban Government."[143]

"What the hell is this?" stormed National Assembly president Ricardo Alarcón. "Now, in order to intensify their war against Cuba in the political and ideological areas, in the field of subversion . . . they have come across the idea of using other American institutions not only the government. . . . Foundations, non-governmental organizations, whatever, can finance people who are not their relatives." Such a regulation could only have "a clearly subversive, counterrevolutionary, interventionist purpose," he argued. "Every American buy a Cuban!" He didn't think much better of the farm provisions.[144]

The Cubans struck back with new legislation, the Law for the Protection of Cuban National Independence and the Economy (Law No. 88), making it illegal to disseminate subversive material from the United States, collaborate with foreign mass media for subversive purposes, hinder international economic relations, or receive material resources from the U.S. government.[145] That effectively meant that any Cuban involved with AID's democracy promotion program was breaking the law.

The need for unity in the face of the U.S. threat, the equating of dissent with treason, are themes that have suffused Cuban politics since 1959. When Oswaldo Payá's Varela Project successfully organized the fragmented dissident movement to collect eleven thousand signatures calling for a referendum on democratic change, the government's response was to mobilize millions to sign petitions calling for a constitutional amendment declaring socialism "untouchable." The government's action was framed not as a response to the Varela Project, however, but as a response to George W. Bush's May 20, 2002, "New Initiative for Cuba" speech, in which he promised a tougher U.S. policy lasting until Cuba abandoned its socialist system.[146]

In a spectacular show of its organizational muscle, the government's mass organizations mobilized over eight million people in just a few days to sign the petition. The drive was launched with patriotic speeches and rallies on the 101st anniversary of the Platt amendment. It was, said Fidel, "a convincing and fitting response to the uninvited liberator, W. Bush."[147] Although many Cubans had at least some notion of the Varela Project (Jimmy Carter praised it in his televised speech in Havana, which was reprinted in *Granma*), Cuban officials almost never mentioned it, except to demean it as nothing more than a U.S. government plot. The Varela organizers were "on the U.S. government payroll," claimed Foreign Minister Felipe Pérez Roque.[148]

During the months in which the dissident movement was gathering signatures on the Varela petition, the U.S. Interests Section began to promote opposition activity more aggressively. Shortly after Bush's inauguration, Vicki Huddleston, the chief U.S. diplomat in Havana, started handing out shortwave radios, especially to dissidents with whom she met periodically. She described her efforts as a new, "robust" outreach policy made possible by the new administration in Washington. "Now I'm really able to push the envelope," she explained. Cuban officials protested that her behavior was improper, but to no avail. "This is sheer intervention in our internal affairs," complained one official. "They did that in Eastern Europe, and they think they have a right to do it in Cuba. We won't allow it."[149]

When private protests brought no surcease, Castro himself publicly reproached the U.S. diplomats, warning: "The U.S. government is also making a mistake if it expects that people who work as hired hands of a foreign power will go unpunished. . . . Nor should he [Bush] think that those who visit Cuba under some disguise or other to bring in money and to conspire openly against the Revolution will find things easy; nor that officials of his Interests Section have any right to run all over the country as they please . . . to organize rings of conspirators." U.S. diplomats were acting in ways inconsistent with their diplomatic status, Castro charged. "We are not willing to allow our sovereignty to be violated or to allow the norms that govern diplomatic behavior to be flouted in a humiliating manner." He threatened to abrogate the migration agreement with the United States and close the Interests Section.[150]

In September 2002, James Cason replaced Vicki Huddleston as head of the Interests Section, and he took an even more outspoken public stance in support of the dissidents. He not only met with them frequently, but he offered them the use of the Interests Section and his residence for meetings. He attended meetings in their homes, including some to which the international press was invited. He traveled around the island meeting with dissident groups in far-flung towns. On March 6, in a speech to the National Assembly, Castro publicly condemned Cason's disparaging remarks about the Cuban government at a press conference held at the home of prominent dissident Marta Beatriz Roque, calling it a "shameless and defiant provocation." He repeated his threat, first made in June 2002, to close the Interests Section: "Cuba can easily do without this office, a breeding ground for counterrevolutionaries and a command post for the most offensive subversive actions against our country." But he also speculated that perhaps the Bush administration was intentionally trying to provoke him into severing what formal ties existed between Washington and Havana.[151]

Rather than strike at the Interests Section, Castro struck at the dissidents. On March 18, state security began rounding up dissidents across the island, charging them under both the 1996 Law for the Reaffirmation of Cuban Dignity and Sovereignty and the 1999 Law for the Protection of Cuban National Independence and the Economy. After summary trials closed to international observers, seventy-five of the accused were found guilty and sentenced to long terms in prison, ranging from six to twenty-eight years. At the trials, a number of prominent, longstanding members of the dissident movement revealed themselves to be state security agents who testified against the accused. The government insisted that the defendants were not being jailed for opposing the government, but for conspiring seditiously with the United States. Evidence introduced at the trials demonstrated that many of the accused had been in close contact with the U.S. Interests Section and may have received material assistance of various kinds either from the U.S. government or from U.S. organizations funded under AID's democracy promotion programs.[152]

At first glance, the timing of the arrests was difficult to decipher. There was no obvious reason to suddenly round up the dissident movement's leadership after having tolerated them (albeit not without ongoing harassment) for several years. Some observers suggested that the Cubans were using the war in Iraq as cover for the crackdown, but the timing was not really fortuitous. The European Union (EU) had just opened an office in Havana and resumed discus-

sions about admitting Cuba to the Cotonou Agreement providing trade preferences to former colonies—discussions broken off in 2002 because of Cuba's
unwillingness to accept EU human rights conditionality. In Geneva, the United
Nations Human Rights Commission (UNHRC) was on the eve of its annual
debate over Cuba's human rights record, a debate that was a perennial ideological battlefield between Washington and Havana. The Cubans took these
debates very seriously, even though the commission had no enforcement
power. To the Cubans, international opinion as expressed through the United
Nations represented an important bulwark against U.S. attack. Finally, the
arrest of the dissidents came just as the U.S. Congress was beginning to take up
a new round of legislative proposals to lift the travel ban and expand sales of
food.

Predictably, the arrests touched off a firestorm of international protest and
hurt Cuba's interests in all these venues. Surprisingly, however, the Bush
administration's reaction was relatively mild. Bush took the opportunity to
blast Castro rhetorically, but the two principal responses discussed inside the
administration—cutting off remittances and halting direct flights to Cuba—
were both opposed by the CANF. In the end, neither was adopted. Instead,
Washington expelled fourteen Cuban diplomats for improper conduct, but did
little else.[153] Proponents of free trade and travel admitted that Castro's actions
had dealt their cause a blow. "There is a parallel here between this administration and the Castro government," said Congressman Bill Delahunt (D-Mass.).
"They are both going backward."[154]

At root, the dissidents' arrest reflected internal Cuban politics as much as
foreign policy. A confluence of events made Cuban officials particularly worried that the United States was planning on using the dissidents to spearhead a
more aggressive U.S. policy and that this strategy might be poised for success.
After September 11, 2001, the Cuban economy dipped into recession for the
first time since 1994. The slump in international tourism reduced earnings
from Cuba's tourism industry, which had been the economy's engine of growth
in the 1990s. The recession in the United States also hurt Cuba because Cuban-
Americans in South Florida (also a major tourist destination) could not afford
to send as much money in remittances. Finally, the declining world market
price for sugar rendered much of Cuba's sugar industry uneconomical, and the
government finally took the difficult decision to close a large portion of it
down for good.[155]

In the past, economic hardship has been a bellwether of discontent and
increased pressures for migration. The 1980 Mariel boatlift was preceded by
recession, as was the 1994 rafters crisis. The latter was also accompanied by a
series of hijackings, one of which touched off the riot on the Malecon, the first
overtly antigovernment demonstration since 1961. Since the 1995 U.S.-Cuban
migration agreement, migration pressure in Cuba had been eased somewhat by

the orderly emigration of twenty thousand Cubans annually to the United States. In 2002–03, however, the processing of visas for Cuban emigrants slowed dramatically. Five months into the year, only 505 visas had been processed, compared to over 7,000 the year before. The State Department explained the delays as a result of more elaborate screening procedures adopted after September 11. The Cubans, however, were convinced that the Bush administration was delaying the visas to shut off the safety valve of migration, in the hope that discontent on the island would boil over.[156] There was precedent for that tactic. When Ronald Reagan came to office in 1981, several thousand former political prisoners were awaiting visas to enter the United States under an agreement negotiated by the Carter administration. Reagan halted the processing.[157]

At the same time that the approval of visas slowed, Bush officials warned the Cubans that a migration crisis like 1980 or 1994 was "unacceptable," and would be regarded as "an act of war."[158] Nevertheless, Cubans who stole or hijacked boats and planes to get to Florida were routinely paroled into the community and almost never prosecuted, thus creating no disincentive for hijackers. A wave of hijacking attempts in early 2003 indicated that discontent and migration pressures were rising in tandem with the economy's decline. To Fidel, it appeared that the Bush administration was intentionally creating the conditions for a migration crisis that could then be used as "a pretext for a military aggression against Cuba."[159] Anxious to halt the hijackings, the government took the drastic step of executing three young men who tried unsuccessfully to hijack a ferry to Miami.

One important difference between the 1980 and 1994 crises, and the problems Cuba faced in 2003, was the strength of the dissident movement. In 1980, there was none. In 1994, it was minuscule, and its leaders were more often in jail than they were free. By 2003, however, the government had lost its tight grip on civil society as a result of the economic and social changes forced on Castro after the Soviet collapse. The Varela Project disproved the conventional wisdom that Cuba's dissidents were too fragmented to cooperate effectively, too few to have any impact, and too isolated to reach out to anyone beyond their own immediate circle of family and friends. The project's ability to get over eleven thousand people to sign a petition that effectively declared themselves in opposition to Cuba's socialist system came as a shock to most observers, and it must have been an even greater shock to Cuba's leaders. The government's massive mobilization to preempt the Varela petition with one of its own was evidence of how seriously the political elite regarded the challenge. Varela's success implied that it might have the potential to take advantage of growing discontent and channel it into political action. Moreover, the Bush administration had openly declared its intention to strengthen the internal opposition, had doubled AID funding for that purpose, and had given the

Interests Section free rein to publicly and aggressively embrace the dissidents and encourage them.

Washington's embrace of the dissidents proved to be the kiss of death. It enabled prosecutors to portray the defendants as U.S. agents, thereby branding dissent as equivalent to treason. Not only did the government demolish the dissident movement, it also sent a clear warning to others who might be tempted to voice opposition to Castro's leadership. For Castro, the point of the arrests was to project an image of strength and implacable determination to resist U.S. pressure.

In September 2003, the House of Representatives voted, for the fourth year in a row, to halt enforcement of the travel ban. The margin (227 to 188) was smaller than in 2002, but in light of the nearly universal condemnation of the Cuban government's imprisonment of dissidents the previous spring, the resilience of the majority in favor of lifting the travel ban was surprising.[160]

A few weeks later, before the Senate took up the travel ban, President Bush publicly reiterated his commitment to keep the ban in place and tighten its enforcement. Tourism would only serve to "prop up the dictator and his cronies," Bush argued, while feeding an "illicit sex trade . . . encouraged by the Cuban government." At the same time, he announced the creation of a Commission for Assistance to a Free Cuba, in order to "plan for Cuba's transition from Stalinist rule to a free and open society, to identify ways to hasten the arrival of that day."[161]

On October 23, the Treasury appropriations bill came to the Senate floor and Byron L. Dorgan offered his amendment to halt enforcement of the travel ban, using exactly the same language approved by the House of Representatives. Despite the president's threat to veto any legislation easing travel to Cuba, the Senate overwhelmingly rejected the Republican leadership's effort to table Dorgan's amendment, 59 to 36, and then adopted it. It was the first time the Senate as a whole had voted on the issue since 1999, when the effort to end the travel ban was defeated, 43 to 55. Thirteen Republicans switched sides in the interim.[162]

The House's efforts to end the travel ban in 2001 and 2002 were blocked in conference committee. Because there was no similar provision in the Senate version of the appropriations bills, the Republican leadership had a ready-made excuse for dropping the Cuba provision because the two bodies were "in disagreement." In 2003, however, the House and Senate were not in disagreement over Cuba; both had adopted identical language. Under Congress' own rules, a provision not in disagreement should not be open to modification by the conference committee. Fidelity to the rules, however, was not the Republican leadership's strong suit. They simply dropped the Cuba language from the bill, and the Republicans they appointed to serve on the conference committee went along.[163]

By threatening to veto the Treasury and Transportation appropriation, President Bush won a victory over the congressional majority that favored ending the travel ban to Cuba, thereby solidifying his support among conservative Cuban-Americans in South Florida. His victory may well have been pyrrhic, however, because it generated considerable anger among the majority of members whose will the president thwarted.

In May 2004, just as the presidential campaign was heating up, the White House received the report of the Commission for Assistance to Free Cuba that President Bush had appointed in October. Having taken no public testimony and consulted no one outside the administration other than the most conservative Cuban-American legislators, the commission reported a menu of options, all of which Bush promptly accepted. The unabashed aim of the commission's recommendations was to subvert the Cuban government, "to bring about an expeditious end to the Castro dictatorship."[164] The core strategy was to further constrict the flow of hard currency (via new regulations on travel and remittances) to Cuba in order the cripple the economy, stoke popular discontent, and precipitate Castro's collapse—the same familiar formula on which the embargo was based and that had failed to succeed for forty-five years.

Conclusion

By 2003, a transition was already well underway in Cuba—from a centrally planned economy insulated from the world market by its membership in the socialist camp to an economy responsive, by necessity, to market forces, both internal and external. The long-term political implications of this economic transformation were as yet unclear. Cuba's leaders hoped to follow the path blazed by China and Vietnam, in which economic reform was combined with continuing political hegemony for the Communist Party. But they feared the fate of Eastern Europe and the Soviet Union where reform led to political disintegration.

This strategy of accommodating economic reality while trying to maintain political control had significant foreign policy implications. The economic imperative was to foster better relations with Cuba's principal trading partners and, of course, the largest potential partner, the United States. The political imperative was to isolate the polity somehow from the corrosive political effects of greater economic openness. More travel and tourism meant more potential for ideological "contamination" and anger over "tourist apartheid." More foreign direct investment meant reduced control over development priorities. In the case of the United States, this conundrum was further complicated by the long history of U.S. hegemony over the island, the revolutionary leadership's pride at having rescued Cuba from that hegemony, and Washington's ongoing determination to restore it by replacing the Cuban regime with a pro-U.S. democracy. As Castro himself said, the revolution was largely defenseless in the face of U.S. power, except for the "battle of ideas," the determination of Cubans to preserve their revolutionary achievements. In that sense, Fidel Castro's struggle to maintain Cuba's sovereignty and independence from the United States was at root a struggle for the hearts and minds of the Cuban people. And for that reason, dissidents, especially those who identified and associated with the United States, were seen as traitors.

On both sides of the Florida Straits, policymakers shared the same uncertainties about the interplay of political and economic forces. In Washington, they debated whether the economic changes underway on the island would catalyze political change or would simply strengthen the government by enhancing economic growth. With this dynamic in mind, U.S. policy was designed to limit contacts to those that would have the most destabilizing effects while providing the fewest economic resources for the government.[164] In Havana, policymakers debated the same issue in different terms: whether the economic transition would reinforce their legitimacy by boosting growth or would corrode party control. In the realm of foreign policy, this uncertainty translated into a deep ambivalence, especially regarding the United States. Improved relations held the promise of economic bounty, but also the potential poison pill of resurgent U.S. hegemony. Improved relations meant a reduced risk of attack, but also the loss of the revolution's symbolic enemy, around which Fidel had so often and so effectively rallied the Cuban people to his side. The future of U.S.-Cuban relations depended upon how long the economic forces pulling the two countries together could be resisted by the hardliners in each camp who feared the domestic political consequences of closer relations.

Cuba's broader diplomatic and economic relations were also deeply affected by the bilateral relationship with the United States. Although no major country in the world supported Washington's policy of hostility and pressure against Cuba, relations between Havana and Canada, Europe, and Latin America repeatedly proved vulnerable to flare-ups in relations with the dominant global power. At moments of heightened tension, Latin and Atlantic allies might disagree with U.S.-Cuba policy, but the issue was never important enough for them to put their own bilateral relations with Washington at risk. The Cubans were inclined to see this pragmatism on the part of Europe and Latin America as a lack of principle and to say so publicly, uncouched in diplomatic niceties.

Serious friction arose with Canada in 2001, when Castro denounced Prime Minister Jean Chrétien for giving in to U.S. pressure to exclude Cuba from the Third Summit of the Americas.[165] In 2002, Castro blasted Mexican president Vicente Fox and Foreign Minister Jorge Castañeda when he was asked to leave a 2002 United Nations development summit in Monterrey because President

George Bush refused to attend if Castro was present.[166] In 2003, when Cuba arrested and imprisoned scores of dissidents for receiving U.S. support, Castro responded to European criticism by accusing the EU of being Washington's pawn and then leading a million protestors to the Spanish and Italian embassies.[167] In short, Cuba's diplomatic relations with both Latin America and Europe tend to be held hostage by Havana's conflict with Washington. Despite the need for Cuba to cultivate good relations with these continents, Castro cannot quite forgive them for being the friends of his enemy and refusing to forsake their friendship with United States over the issue of Cuba.

As of 2004, U.S. policy toward Cuba was in flux. In office was a president as hostile to Fidel Castro as any since Ronald Reagan, in part because of the predominance of Reagan veterans in his foreign policy apparatus. Despite overwhelming evidence to the contrary, for example, Bush officials still continue to insist that Cuba "remains a terrorist and BW [biological weapons] threat to the United States."[168] But the political dynamics underlying American policy were changing, as evidenced by the sharp turnabout in Congress since the passage of Helms-Burton in 1996. Despite Bush's visceral dislike of the Cuban regime and his close political alliance with the most hardline elements of the Cuban-American community in Miami, he was constrained in his ability to intensify sanctions against Cuba by farm-state Republicans, by Republican businessmen, and by moderate Cuban-Americans. As Congressman Jeff Flake observed, "At some point, farm-state politics trumps Florida politics."[169]

Notes

1. Wayne S. Smith, *The Closest of Enemies* (New York: W. W. Norton, 1987).

2. Martí letter to Manuel Mercado, May 18, 1895, quoted in Piero Gleijeses, *Conflicting Missions: Havana, Washington, and Africa, 1959–1976* (Chapel Hill: University of North Carolina Press, 2001), 13.

3. For a discussion of William D. Rogers' May 17, 1975, report to Henry Kissinger, see Peter Kornbluh and James Blight, "Dialogue with Castro: A Hidden History," *New York Review of Books*, October 6, 1994, 45–49.

4. The Cuban-American lobby's influence is documented extensively in Morris Morley and Chris McGillion, *Unfinished Business: America and Cuba After the Cold War, 1989–2001* (New York: Cambridge University Press, 2002).

5. Mark Silva, "VP Pick Makes Foundation's Choice Less Clear," *Miami Herald*, August 9, 2000.

6. Peter H. Stone, "Cuban Clout," *National Journal*, February 20, 1993, 449–53; John Newhouse, "A Reporter at Large: Cuba," *New Yorker*, April 27, 1992; Paul J. Kiger, *Squeeze Play: The United States, Cuba, and the Helms-Burton Act* (Washington, D.C.: Center for Public Integrity, 1997), 28–44 and "The Cuban American National Foundation," *International Studies Quarterly* 43 (1999): 341–61.

7. William Watts, *The United States and Cuba: Changing Perceptions, New Policies?* (Washington, D.C.: Potomac Associates and Johns Hopkins University, 1989), 9; "Carter Trip to Cuba Reflects U.S. Sentiment: Engagement Supported by American People, Congress," press release, Washington, D.C., Cuba Policy Foundation, May 10, 2002.

8. U.S. Department of State, Bureau of Western Hemisphere Affairs, "Humanitarian Assistance to Cuba," fact sheet, September 7, 2001 and "Humanitarian Assistance," November 8, 1999.

9. "Cubans Complain Sanctions Are Hitting Them While Missing Mark of Castro," *Baltimore Sun*, September 2, 1994.

10. Sergio Díaz-Briquets and Jorge F. Pérez-López, "Refugee Remittances: Conceptual Issues and the Cuban and Nicaraguan Experiences," *International Migration Review* 31, no. 2 (Summer 1997): 411–37.

11. Morley and McGillion, *Unfinished Business*, 71–81; Jon Nordheimer, "Cuban Group Forges Link to Clinton," *New York Times*, August 26, 1994; William Booth, "Tighter Policy Exposes a Rip in Anti-Castro Fabric," *Washington Post*, August 24, 1994.

12. Jonathan Decker, "Smuggling Cash to Cuba Rises in Defiance of Embargo," *Christian Science Monitor*, May 24, 1995.

13. Juan O. Tamayo, "Cuban Economy Abominable in 1998," *Miami Herald*, July 9, 1999.

14. See *Preliminary Results, Florida International University (FIU) Cuba Poll 2000* (Miami: FIU Institute for Public Opinion Research, October 2000); Guillermo J. Grenier and Hugh Gladwin, *FIU 1997 Cuba Poll* (Miami: FIU Institute for Public Opinion Research, 1997).

15. See *Preliminary Results, FIU Cuba Poll 2000*.

16. Rebecca J. Fowler, "Cash Flow to Cuba Barred," *Washington Post*, August 21, 1994. For a detailed look at the links between Cubans abroad and family on the island, see Susan Eckstein and Lorena Barberia, "Grounding Immigrant Generations in History: Cuban Americans and Their Transnational Ties," *International Migration Review* 36, no.3 (2002): 799–38.

17. Max Castro, "Transition and the Ideology of Exile," in *Toward a New Cuba: Legacies of a Revolution*, ed. Miguel Angel Centeno and Mauricio Font (Boulder: Lynne Rienner, 1997), 91–108.

18. Richard Boudreaux and Mark Fineman, "Catholic Leaders See the Start of New Cuban Era," *Los Angeles Times*, January 26, 1998; Mike Clary, "Pope's Cuba Visit Fosters Attitude Shift," *Los Angeles Times*, February 28, 1998.

19. Guy Gugliotta, "Cuban American Foundation Is Determined Not to Founder After Loss of Its Leader," *Washington Post*, January 21, 1998.

20. See, for example, Eunice Ponce and Elaine De Valle, "Mania over Elián Rising," *Miami Herald*, January 10, 2000.

21. Oscar Corral, "Elián Custody Case Unites Miami's Cuban-Americans," *Milwaukee Journal Sentinel*, April 23, 2000.

22. David W. Moore, "Americans Approve of U.S. Government Decision to Return Boy to Cuba," *Gallup News Service Poll Releases*, January 12, 2000; Frank Newport,

"Majority Support for Elián Raid Continues, Even Though Public Disapproves of Method," *Gallup News Service Poll Releases*, May 2, 2000.

23. Mireidy Fernandez et al., "Polls Show Americans Split on Using Force: Most Backed Reunion of Father and Son," *Miami Herald*, April 25, 2000; "Most Say Elián Belongs with Dad," *Miami Herald*, April 4, 2000.

24. Karen Branch, "Penelas Put Himself into Prominent Spot with Tough Talk," *Miami Herald*, March 31, 2000.

25. Alfonso Chardy, "Cuban-American Leaders Aim to Separate Local Issues, Castro," *Miami Herald*, May 5, 2000.

26. Quoted in Don Finefrock, "Businessman Criticizes Fellow Cubans," *Miami Herald*, April 28, 2000.

27. Morley and McGillion, *Unfinished Business*, 158–63; Scott Wilson, "In Miami, Cuban Exile Group Shifts Focus," *Washington Post*, September 14, 2000.

28. Alan Sayre, "U.S. Ships Food to Cuba for Hurricane Relief," *Miami Herald*, December 17, 2001; Carol Rosenberg, "Pair Asked Bush to Block Carter's Trip," *Miami Herald*, May 7, 2002.

29. Christopher Marquis, "U.S. May Punish Cuba for Imprisoning Critics," *New York Times*, April 17, 2003.

30. Dana Canedy, "Cuban Exile Group Split as Hard-Liners Resign From Board," *New York Times*, August 8, 2001.

31. Jorge F. Pérez-López, "The Cuban Economic Crisis of the 1990s and the External Sector," *Cuba in Transition: Volume 8* (Miami: Association for the Study of the Cuban Economy, 1998), 386–413; Omar Everleny Pérez Villanueva, "Foreign Direct Investment in Cuba," in *Development Perspectives in Cuba*, ed. Pedro Monreal (University of London: Institute of Latin American Studies, 2002), 47–68.

32. Quoted in Karen DeYoung, "U.S. Businesses Encouraged to Explore Trade with Cuba," *Washington Post*, July 28, 1999.

33. Thomas W. Lippman, "Business Groups Urge Clinton to Disallow Suits Over Seized Property in Cuba," *Washington Post*, July 6, 1996.

34. Louis Uchitelle, "Who's Punishing Whom? Trade Bans Are Boomerangs, U.S. Companies Say," *New York Times*, September 11, 1996.

35. Thomas W. Lippman, "Business-Led Coalition Urges U.S. to Relax Embargo on Cuba," *Washington Post*, January 14, 1998; Tim Weiner, "Pope vs. Embargo," *New York Times*, January 21, 1998.

36. Tim Weiner, "Anti-Castro Exiles Won Limit on Changes," *New York Times*, January 6, 1999. The commission's Web site describes its intended agenda.

37. *U.S.-Cuban Relations in the 21st Century* (New York: Council on Foreign Relations, 1999). The Cuba Policy Foundation closed its door in 2003, partly for financial reasons and partly in reaction to Castro's arrest of seventy-five dissidents.

38. Quoted in Gugliotta, "Cuban American Foundation."

39. Quoted in Weiner, "Pope vs. Embargo."

40. Steven A. Holmes and Lizette Alvarez, "Senate Approves Easing Sanctions on Food to Cuba," *New York Times*, October 19, 2000; "Chaos Reigns in U.S. Politics," editorial, *Granma* (Havana), October 16, 2000 (English translation provided by the Cuban Interests Section, Washington, D.C.).

41. Quoted in Miles A. Pomper, "Sentiment Grows for Ending Cuba Embargo, But Opponents Say Bush Will Stand Firm," *Congressional Quarterly Weekly Report*, February 9, 2002, 408 (hereafter cited as *CQWR*).

42. U.S. Department of State, Office of International Information Programs, "Transcript: Bush Signals Support for Sending Aid to Dissidents in Cuba," May 18, 2001.

43. "Statement: Toward a Democratic Cuba," *Weekly Compilation of Presidential Documents: Administration of George W. Bush* (July 13, 2001): 1036–37.

44. Christopher Marquis, "Bush Forgoes Trying to Bar Cuba Deals By Foreigners," *New York Times*, July 17, 2001.

45. Mark P. Sullivan, *Cuba: U.S. Restrictions on Travel and Legislative Initiatives*, report for Congress, *Congressional Research Service*, April 22, 2003, 5.

46. Quoted in Ginger Thompson, "Cuba, Too, Felt the Sept. 11 Shock Waves, with a More Genial Castro Offering Help," *New York Times*, February 7, 2002.

47. "Americans Who Make Trips to Cuba Without Ok Could Be Prosecuted," *Houston Chronicle*, March 2, 2003; Mark Sullivan, *Restrictions on Travel*. As of December 2003, the Bush administration had undertaken over 1,400 enforcement actions. See Peter Slevin, "Crackdown on Cuba Travel Angers Some," *Washington Post*, December 9, 2003.

48. David D. Kirkpatrick, "U.S. Halts Cuba Access by Educational Groups," *New York Times*, May 4, 2003.

49. Andrea Elliott and Elaine De Valle, "Cuban Community Split on Policy," *Miami Herald*, February 13, 2003.

50. Tracey Eaton, "Travel Permits Harder to Come by Under Bush Administration," *Dallas Morning News*, March 23, 2003.

51. Nancy San Martin, "U.S. Food Sales to Cuba Far Exceed Planned Amount," *Miami Herald*, April 3, 2002; David Segal, "Visa Delays Cost Cuban Musicians—Law Keeps 22 From Latin Grammys," *Washington Post*, September 19, 2002; Burton Bollag, "Closing the Gates: A Cuban Scholar Shut Out," *Chronicle of Higher Education*, April 11, 2003. The Bush administration denied visas to *all* Cuban scholars scheduled to participate in the 2004 LASA International Congress.

52. Flake amendment, H.AMDT.241 to H.R.2590, *Congressional Record*, 107th Cong., 2nd sess., July 25, 2001, H4599–4604, H4607; Rangel amendment, H.AMDT.242 to H.R.2590, *Congressional Record*, 107th Cong., 2nd sess., July 25, 2001, H4604–08.

53. Quoted in Keith Perine, "Conferees Purge Controversial Items from Treasury-Postal Service Bill," *CQWR*, October 27, 2001, 2548.

54. The next few paragraphs are adapted from William M. LeoGrande and Julie M. Thomas, "Cuba's Quest for Economic Independence," *Journal of Latin American Studies* 34, no.2 (May 2002): 325–63.

55. Juan Triana Cordovi, "Cuba's Economic Transformation and Conflict with the United States," in *The United States and Latin America*, ed. Victor Bulmer-Thomas and James Dunkerley (Cambridge: Harvard University Press, 1999), 247–66; Richard Garfield and Sarah Santana, "The Impact of the Economic Crisis and the U.S. Embargo on Health in Cuba," *American Journal of Public Health*, January 1997, 15–20.

56. On the political maneuvers that led to Helms-Burton's passage, see Morley and McGillion, *Unfinished Business*, 98–130.

57. U.S. International Trade Commission, *The Economic Impact of U.S. Sanctions with Respect to Cuba* (Washington, D.C.: February 2001), chapter 5 passim. This report estimates that U.S. producers could capture as much as eighty to ninety percent of the Cuban market for imported wheat, rice, and feed grains because of the cost differential.

58. Under the 1992 law, licenses for medical supplies would only be granted if the U.S. government could verify that the supplies were being used appropriately, a stipulation the Cuban government rejected. Under the 2000 law, Cuba was denied any U.S. government or private sector financing to purchase food or medicine. This financial straitjacket meant that the practical effect of lifting the food and medicine embargo was nil, and the Cuban government denounced the measure as a fraud. See *Granma* editorial, "Chaos Reigns."

59. Garfield and Santana, "Impact," 15–21; Gustavo C. Roman, "Epidemic Neuropathy in Cuba: A Public Health Problem Related to the Cuban Democracy Act of the United States," *Neuroepidemiology* 17, no.3 (1998): 1111–16; American Association for World Health, *Denial of Food and Medicine: The Impact of the U.S. Embargo on Health and Nutrition in Cuba* (Washington, D.C.: March 1997); "The Politics of Suffering: The Impact of the U.S. Embargo on the Health of the Cuban People, Report to the American Public Health Association of a Fact-Finding Trip to Cuba, June 6–11, 1993," *Journal of Public Health Policy* 15, no.1 (Spring 1994): 86–107.

60. U.S. International Trade Commission, *Economic Impact of U.S. Sanctions*, 4–21. The American Association of Travel Agents has a much higher estimate: one million U.S. tourists going to Cuba the first year after sanctions are lifted, rising to as many as five million annually. See Appendix to the preceding report, D-31.

61. Address by Dr. Fidel Castro Ruz, opening session, Group of 77 South Summit Conference, Havana, April 12, 2000, *Granma Internacional Digital*.

62. See, for example, speech by Dr. Fidel Castro Ruz, opening ceremony of the First National Olympics of Cuban sport, Plaza de la Revolución, November 26, 2002, *Cuba.cu*/gobierno/discursos/2002.

63. Raúl Castro, "The Political and Social Situation in Cuba and the Corresponding Tasks of the Party," *Granma Internacional Digital*, March 27, 1996.

64. Deborah Ramirez, "Exiles End Conference by Meeting Castro Focus on Bid to Ease Travel, Investment," *Montreal Gazette*, April 25, 1994; Howard W. French, "Havana Woos Exiles, Easing Visits and Dangling Financial Carrot," *New York Times*, April 25, 1994.

65. Quoted in David Adams, "Exiles Meet Cuban Officials," *St. Petersburg Times*, September 11, 1994.

66. They were Alfredo Duran (Cuban Committee for Democracy), Ramon Cernuda (Coordination Committee of Human Rights Organizations), and Eloy Gutiérrez-Menoyo (*Cambio Cubano*/Cuban Change).

67. Larry Rohter, "In Move to Improve Relations With Exiles in U.S., Cuba Eases the Way for Investment," *New York Times*, November 7, 1995.

68. Anita Snow, "Cuba Postpones Immigration Conference," *Associated Press*, April 4, 2003.

69. Mark Sullivan, *Restrictions on Travel*, 5.

70. Quoted in Tim Johnson, "U.S. Farmers Elated Over Cuba Trade," *Miami Herald*, November 16, 2001; Holger Jensen, "Cuban Embargo: Close, but No Cigar," *Rocky Mountain News* (Denver), March 12, 2001.

71. Tim Johnson, "Cuba Declines U.S. Aid, Wants to Pay for Relief," *Miami Herald*, November 10, 2001; see also Johnson, "U.S. Farmers Elated."

72. Martin Merzer, "Isidore Eyes Mexico—800 Cuban Homes Hit," *Miami Herald*, September 21, 2002; Kevin Sullivan, "After the Storm, Cubans Survey Losses," *Washington Post*, November 7, 2001; Vivian Sequera, "Cuba, Hit Hard by Michelle, Turns to Task of Recovery," *Boston Globe*, November 7, 2001.

73. "Four U.S. Companies Sign the First Trade Deals With Cuba," *New York Times*, November 22, 2001.

74. "Food, Drug Industries Size up Cuba Market," *Miami Herald*, January 25, 2002.

75. Juan O. Tamayo, "Report Cites U.S. Benefits of Cuba Trade," *Miami Herald*, January 28, 2002; Tim Johnson, "U.S. Support of Embargo on Cuba Is Holding—but for How Long?," *Miami Herald*, December 22, 2002.

76. Quoted in Patrick Rucker, "Americans Prizing Open Cuban Trade Door," *Financial Times* (U.K.), October 1, 2002.

77. Quoted in James Flanigan, "U.S. Business Likes Cuba, but Obstacles Remain," *Los Angeles Times*, May 15, 2002. Also see David Gonzalez, "Cuba Receives U.S. Shipment, First Purchase Since Embargo," *New York Times*, December 17, 2001; Kevin Sullivan, "At Havana Trade Show, They're Talkin' Turkey," *Washington Post*, September 26, 2002.

78. Christopher Marquis, "U.S. Is Reportedly Prepared to Allow Food Sales to Cuba," *New York Times*, November 15, 2001; Tim Johnson, "Freighter Leaving for Cuba with U.S. Corn," *Miami Herald*, December 14, 2001.

79. Quoted in Elaine Del Valle, "Q&A—Veteran Leader Speaks about Dissidents, Castro and the U.S. Role," *Miami Herald*, March 3, 2002.

80. Kevin Diaz, "Ventura Puts Another Bite in Cuba Embargo," *Minneapolis Star Tribune*, September 24, 2002; "Castro Surprises Pensacola Group," *St. Petersburg Times*, September 11, 2002; Jennifer Babson, "Economic Links Aim of Cuba Visits," *Miami Herald*, August 11, 2002; Kevin Diaz, "Politics Will Ride with Governor on Trade Trip to Cuba," *Minneapolis Star Tribune*, September 22, 2002.

81. E. A. Torriero, "Farm Group's Trip to Cuba Hits Federal Roadblock," *Washington Post*, January 6, 2002.

82. Glenn Kessler and Karen DeYoung, "U.S. Moves to Expel 4 Cuban Diplomats," *Washington Post*, November 6, 2002. Ana Belen Montes was the senior analyst covering Cuba at the Defense Intelligence Agency. She was arrested in October 2001 and pled guilty to espionage on behalf of Cuba in March 2002.

83. Quoted in Rob Hotakainen, "Administration Advises Ventura: Don't Visit Cuba," *Minneapolis Star Tribune*, September 7, 2002; Mark Brunswick, "Ventura Seeks White House Apology," *Minneapolis Star Tribune*, September 10, 2002.

84. Quoted in Nancy San Martin, "U.S. Official Dampens Trade-Show Enthusiasm with Talk of Cuban Credit," *Miami Herald*, September 29, 2002; Sullivan, "Talkin' Turkey."

85. Rucker, "Trade Door."

86. Quoted in Karen DeYoung, "U.S. Food Sale Is Hailed by Cuban Minister 'Positive Gesture' Could Aid Relations, He Says," *Washington Post*, November 29, 2001.

87. Quoted in Craig Gilbert, "Cuba Woos Heart of U.S. with Trade," *Milwaukee Journal Sentinel*, August 18, 2002.

88. Ginger Thompson with Clifford Krauss, "Antiwar Fever Puts Mexico in Quandary on Iraq Vote," *New York Times*, February 28, 2003; Larry Rohter, "Chile Feels the Weight of Its Security Council Seat," *New York Times*, March 11, 2003.

89. Glenn Kessler, "Powell Pledges More Support for Colombia's Anti-Rebel War," *Washington Post*, December 5, 2002.

90. "Address Before a Joint Session of the Congress on the United States Response to the Terrorist Attacks of September 11," *Weekly Compilation of Presidential Documents: Administration of George W. Bush* (September 20, 2001): 1347–51.

91. See, for example, the questions asked of Secretary of State Powell by Ileana Ros-Lehtinen (R-Fla.) and Robert Menendez (D-N.J.), in "Recent Developments in the International Campaign Against Terrorism," *Hearing of the House International Relations Committee*, October 24, 2001, Federal News Service.

92. Soviet leaders told Raúl Castro in 1980 that Cuba would have to be prepared to defend itself in the event of a U.S. attack. "La URSS nos abandono en 1980: Raúl Castro Ruz," *El Sol de Mexico*, April 22, 1993.

93. U.S. Department of State, Bureau of Verification and Compliance, *World Military Expenditures and Arms Transfers 1999–2000* (Washington, D.C.: 2002).

94. Juan Carlos Espinosa, "Vanguard of the State: The Cuba Armed Forces in Transition," *Problems of Post-Communism* 48, no.6 (November-December 2001): 19–30; Richard L. Millet, "From Triumph to Survival: Cuba's Armed Forces in an Era of Transition," in *Beyond Praetorianism*, ed. Richard L. Millet and Michael Gold-Biss (Boulder: Lynne Rienner, 1996), 133–56.

95. U.S. Department of Defense, Defense Intelligence Agency, "The Cuban Threat to U.S. National Security," May 6, 1998.

96. Text of the Cuban message is quoted in a speech by Dr. Fidel Castro Ruz, "None of the Present World Problems Can Be Solved with the Use of Force," September 11, 2001.

97. Speech delivered by Cuban president Fidel Castro in San Antonio de los Baños, Havana, September 22, 2001.

98. Statement from the Ministry of Foreign Affairs, "The Cuban Government Submits to the United States a Set of Proposals for Bilateral Agreements on Migratory Issues, Cooperation in Drug Interdiction and a Program to Fight Terrorism," Havana, March 17, 2002, *Cuba.cu*/gobierno/discursos/2002.

99. Andres Oppenheimer and Tim Johnson, "U.S. Policy on Cuba to Receive Full Review," *Miami Herald*, March 8, 2002; Tim Johnson, "Reich Vows to Defend Cuba Embargo," *Miami Herald*, March 13, 2002.

100. Bush gave two speeches on May 20, 2002, "Remarks Announcing the Initiative for a New Cuba," and "Remarks on the 100th Anniversary of Cuban Independence, Miami, Florida," *Weekly Compilation of Presidential Documents: Administration of George W. Bush*, 852–58.

101. Speech by Dr. Fidel Castro Ruz, president of the Republic of Cuba, at the Extraordinary Session of the National Assembly of People's Power, Havana, June 26, 2002; remarks by Dr. Fidel Castro Ruz, president of the Republic of Cuba, at a rally held in General Antonio Maceo Square, Santiago De Cuba, June 8, 2002, *Granma Internacional Digital.*

102. Fidel Castro Ruz, "Extraordinary Session" speech and "rally" remarks above; also see key address by Dr. Fidel Castro Ruz, at a massive demonstration commemorating the 25th anniversary of the terrorist act against a Cubana jetliner off the coast of Barbados, Revolution Square, October 6, 2001, *Cuba.cu,* <www.cuba.cu/gobierno/discursos/2001/ing/f061001i.html>.

103. Kevin Sullivan, "U.S. Is Urged to Remove Cuba From List of Terror Sponsors," *Washington Post,* September 29, 2001; Anya K. Landau and Wayne S. Smith, "Keeping Things in Perspective: Cuba and the Question of International Terrorism," Washington, D.C., Center for International Policy, November 20, 2001; Phil Peters, *Cuba, the Terrorism List, and What the United States Should Do* (Arlington, Va.: Lexington Institute, November 20, 2001).

104. On-the-record presentation by Richard Nuccio at a panel, "Cuba's Presence on the State Department's List of Countries Supporting Terrorism," Georgetown University, Washington, D.C., October 11, 2001. Also see Maya Bell, "Experts Debate Taking Cuba off Terrorism List," *Orlando Sentinel,* April 7, 2002.

105. U.S. Department of State, Counterterrorism Office, *Patterns of Global Terrorism, 2001,* May 21, 2002.

106. For a detailed refutation of the State Department's accusations, see Wayne Smith, "CIP Challenges State Department's List of Terrorist States," Washington, D.C., Center for International Policy, May 24, 2002; Anya K. Landau and Wayne S. Smith, "Cuba on the Terrorist List: In Defense of the Nation or Domestic Political Calculation?," *International Policy Report,* Washington, D.C., Center for International Policy, November 2002, 1–10.

107. See Public Law 87–195, sec. 620A, "Prohibition on Assistance to Governments Supporting International Terrorism," *Foreign Assistance Act of 1961* in U.S. Congress, Senate Foreign Relations Committee and House International Relations Committee, *Legislation on Foreign Relations Through 2001,* 7–65, 293–95.

108. "Beyond the Axis of Evil: Additional Threats from Weapons of Mass Destruction," remarks to the Heritage Foundation, Washington, D.C., May 6, 2002.

109. U.S. Congress, Office of Technology Assessment, *Technologies Underlying Weapons of Mass Destruction* (Washington, D.C.: GPO, December 1993), 85, 237.

110. Quoted in Juan O. Tamayo, "U.S. Downplays Rumors of Cuban Germ Missiles," *Miami Herald,* February 4, 1997. Prendez also claimed that the Cuban Center for Genetic Engineering and Biotechnology was secretly a military installation producing biological weapons, a charge that was disproved when the center's research director, José de la Fuente, defected in 1999.

111. Ken Alibek, *Biohazard: The Chilling True Story of the Largest Covert Biological Weapons Program in the World* (New York: Random House, 2000), 273–77.

112. Quoted in Juan O. Tamayo, "U.S. Skeptical of Report on Cuban Biological Weapons," *Miami Herald,* June 23, 1999.

113. The unclassified report's section on biological weapons read: "Cuba's current scientific facilities and expertise could support an offensive BW program in at least the research and development stage. Cuba's biotechnology industry is one of the most advanced in emerging countries and would be capable of producing BW agents" (U.S. Defense Intelligence Agency, "The Cuban Threat to U.S. National Security," May 6, 1998). One press report quoted a classified annex to the DOD report that went a step further: "According to sources within Cuba, at least one research site is run and funded by the Cuban military to work on the development of offensive and defensive biological weapons" (quoted in Martin Arostegui, "Fidel Castro's Deadly Secret: Five BioChem Warfare Labs," *Washington Times Insight Magazine*, July 20, 1998). In his Heritage Foundation speech, Bolton belittled the DOD report for playing down the Cuban threat because the lead analyst in preparing it was Ana Belen Montes, who subsequently pled guilty to spying for Cuba. The report, however, was the product not just of DIA, but of the entire intelligence community.

114. Rumsfeld quoted in Senate Foreign Relations Committee, Subcommittee on Western Hemisphere, Peace Corps and Narcotics Affairs, *Cuba's Pursuit of Biological Weapons: Fact Or Fiction?*, 107th Cong., 2nd sess., June 5, 2002, 13; U.S. Department of State, Office of the Spokesman, "Powell Says Cuba Has Biological Weapons Research Capacity," May 13, 2002.

115. For a careful look at the evidence on Cuba's alleged bioweapons program, see Anya Landau and Wayne Smith, "CIP Challenges Bolton on Cuba Bio-Terror Charges," press release, Washington, D.C., Center for International Policy, May 8, 2002; Landau and Smith, "CIP Special Report on Cuba and Bioweapons: Groundless Allegations Squander U.S. Credibility on Terrorism," press release, Washington, D.C., Center for International Policy, July 12, 2002.

116. Prepared statement of Carl W. Ford Jr. before Senate Foreign Relations Committee, "Reducing the Threat of Chemical and Biological Weapons," March 19, 2002, Federal News Service. Ford said Cuba had "at least a limited, developmental offensive biological warfare research and development effort."

117. Senate Foreign Relations Committee, *Cuba's Pursuit*, 15, 32.

118. Ibid., 36. Bolton's other charge was that Cuba provided dual use biomedical technology to "rogue states." Cuba itself acknowledged exporting biomedical technology to fourteen countries, with contracts pending in ten others. Only one, Iran, was by U.S. terms a "rogue state" (see response by President Fidel Castro Ruz to the statements made by the United States government on biological weapons, May 10, 2002, *Granma Internacional Digital*). There was no evidence that Iran was using Cuban technology to produce biological weapons. The trade relationship by itself triggered U.S. concerns, as Carl Ford explained: "The connection with biological weapons with Iran and other places is based on simply the fact that they are involved in economic, commercial relations with Iran on biomedical devices, capabilities, and research" (*Cuba's Pursuit*, 41).

119. *Cuba's Pursuit*, 35. De la Fuente is quoted in Tim Johnson, "Talk of Cuba's Germ Warfare Potential Could Affect Embargo," *Miami Herald*, May 7, 2002.

120. Tim Johnson, "U.S. Rejects Carter's Plea to End Embargo on Cuba," *Miami Herald*, May 16, 2002.

121. The five were made up of the original "axis of evil" (Iran, Iraq, and North

Korea) plus the other two countries Bolton denounced in his Heritage Foundation speech (Syria and Libya). Judith Miller, "U.S. Publicly Accusing 5 Countries of Violating Germ-Weapons Treaty," *New York Times*, November 19, 2001.

122. Johnson, "Cuba's Germ Warfare."

123. Quoted in David Gonzalez, "Carter and Powell Cast Doubt on Bioarms in Cuba," *New York Times*, May 14, 2002.

124. Castro responded to Bolton in his key address at the open forum held in Sancti Spiritus Province, May 25, 2002, and in his May 10, 2002 response to the U.S. government on biological weapons.

125. *Congressional Record*, 107th Cong., 2nd sess., July 23, 2002, H5267.

126. *Congressional Record*, 107th Cong., 2nd sess., July 23, 2002, H5267–H5273, H5291–H5306. Also see Andrew Taylor, "Travel to Cuba, Contract Quotas Draw Veto Threat on Spending Bill," *CQWR*, July 20, 2002, 1952 and "Bush May Christen His Veto Pen on Treasury-Postal Spending Bill," *CQWR*, July 27, 2002, 2053.

127. Quoted in "Veto Pen."

128. Quoted in Edward Epstein, "Retiring Armey Holds Nothing Back; Candor Resonates Across House Aisle," *San Francisco Chronicle*, August 16, 2002.

129. Joseph J. Schatz, "Fiscal '03 Spending Omnibus Struggles Toward Finish Line Amid a Chorus of Warnings," *CQWR*, February 8, 2003, 340.

130. Quoted in Keith Perine, "Presidents, Lawmakers Alike Caught Up in Cuba Embargo's Power to Polarize," *CQWR*, May 18, 2002, 1270.

131. President's address, "Terrorist Attacks of September 11"; also see "Commencement Address at the United States Military Academy in West Point, New York," *Weekly Compilation of Presidential Documents: Administration of George W. Bush* (June 1, 2002), 944–48; Bolton, "Axis of Evil."

132. *Congressional Record*, 107th Cong., 2nd sess., September 22, 1992, H9086.

133. Testimony before Senate Foreign Relations Committee, Subcommittee on Western Hemisphere, Peace Corps and Narcotics Affairs, May 22, 1995 (transcript available from LexisNexis Congressional Universe).

134. Secretary of State Madeleine K. Albright, "Opening Remarks on Cuba at Press Briefing followed by Question and Answer Session by other Administration Officials," Office of the Spokesman, Washington, D.C., March 20, 1998; also see "Statement on United States Policy Toward Cuba, January 5, 1999," *Public Papers of the Presidents of the United States: William J. Clinton, 1999*, vol. 1 (Washington, D.C.: GPO, 1999), 7–8.

135. See section 5g, *Cuban Democracy Act of 1992*, Public Law 102–484, 102nd Cong., 2nd sess., October 23, 1992.

136. "Remarks at a Freedom House Breakfast, October 6, 1995," *Public Papers of the Presidents of the United States: William J. Clinton, 1995*, vol. 2 (Washington, D.C.: GPO, 1995), 1544–51.

137. "Remarks to the Cuban-American Community, June 27, 1995," *Public Papers of the Presidents of the United States: William J. Clinton, 1995*, vol. 1 (Washington, D.C.: GPO, 1996), 953–55.

138. See section 109a, *Cuban Liberty and Democratic Solidarity Act of 1996*, Public Law 104–114, 104th Cong., 2nd sess., March 12, 1996.

139. U.S. Agency for International Development, *Evaluation of the USAID Cuba Program*, <www.usaid.gov/locations/latin_america_caribbean/> (see especially the chapter, "Program Effectiveness and Compliance").

140. Fidel Castro speaks at Moncada ceremony, July 26, 1995, Latin American Network Information System (LANIC), Castro Speech Database, <www1.lanic.utexas.edu/project/castro/1995/>.

141. "The Political and Social Situation in Cuba and the Corresponding Tasks of the Party," *Granma International Digital*, March 27, 1996.

142. Quoted in Julio Garcia Luis, ed., *Cuban Revolution Reader: A Documentary History* (Melbourne: Ocean Press, 2001), 280–85.

143. Secretary of State Madeleine K. Albright, "Statement on Cuba," Office of the Spokesman, Washington, D.C., January 5, 1999.

144. Ricardo Alarcón Quesada, "What they have done is to inform the world that the blockade stays in place, that they will try to foster it, to convince others, to make more propaganda, while they continue on that road doomed to failure," *Granma International Digital*, January 8, 1999.

145. Andres Oppenheimer, "Cuba: Back to Darkness," *Miami Herald*, March 18, 1999.

146. See, for example, "Discursos pronunciados en el Acto Solemne, el 20 de junio del 2002, Intervención de Ricardo Alarcón de Quesada, Presidente de la Asamblea Nacional del Poder Popular," 20 de junio del 2002, *Cuba.cu*, <www.cuba.cu/gobierno/documentos/2002/esp/a200602e.html>.

147. Information offered to the people by Dr. Fidel Castro Ruz, president of the Republic of Cuba, in a television and radio appearance, June 13th 2002, *Cuba.cu*, <www.cuba.cu/gobierno/discursos/2002/ing/f130602i.html>.

148. Quoted in Kevin Sullivan, "Anti-Castro Forces Mount Petition Drive," *Washington Post*, April 28, 2002.

149. Quoted in Kevin Sullivan, "In Havana, U.S. Radios Strike Note of Discord," *Washington Post*, May 5, 2002; Fred Bernstein, "Lighting Matches in Cuba on the 4th," *New York Times*, July 4, 2002.

150. Dr. Fidel Castro Ruz, "Extraordinary Session" speech.

151. Speech made by Dr. Fidel Castro on the current world crisis, on the occasion of his inauguration as president of the Republic of Cuba, Havana, March 6, 2003, *Granma Internacional Digital*.

152. Press conference by Cuban foreign minister, Felipe Pérez Roque, "On the mercenaries at the service of the empire who stood trial on April 3, 4, 5 and 7, 2003," Havana, April 9, 2003, *Granma International Digital*; Tracey Eaton, "Cuban Spies Say They Used Pro-Democracy Funds," *Dallas Morning News*, May 18, 2003.

153. Karen DeYoung, "President Criticized Over Past Pledges About Cuba," *Washington Post*, May 21, 2003.

154. Quoted in David Gonzalez, "Cuban Crackdown on Critics Stalls a Drive to Ease U.S. Embargo," *New York Times*, April 13, 2003.

155. Daniel Schweimler, "Sugar and Tourism Force a Bitter Pill on Cubans," *Financial Times*, July 9, 2002; Mary Jordan, "Ending an Era, Cuba Closes Sugar Mills," *Washington Post*, July 29, 2002.

156. Cuban foreign minister Pérez Roque, "mercenaries" press conference.

157. Smith, *The Closest of Enemies*, 263–64.

158. Quoted in Karen DeYoung, "Cuba Denounces Diplomats' Expulsions," *Washington Post*, May 15, 2003.

159. Special presentation by Dr. Fidel Castro Ruz at the televised roundtable, "On recent events in the country and the increase of aggressive actions by the United States government against the Cuban people," April 25, 2003, *Cuba.cu*, <www.cuba.cu/gobierno/discursos/2003/ing/f250403i.html>.

160. Paul Richter, "House Votes to Ease Travel to Cuba," *Los Angeles Times*, September 10, 2003.

161. Quoted in Edwin Chen, "Bush Steps Up Effort to Destabilize Castro's Regime," *Los Angeles Times*, October 11, 2003.

162. Kathryn A. Wolfe, "Mindful of Florida's Clout, Conferees Drop Cuba Travel From Transportation Bill," *CQWR*, November 15, 2003.

163. Christopher Marquis, "Bush's Allies Plan to Block Effort to Ease Ban on Cuban Travel," *New York Times*, November 13, 2003.

164. For an especially good explanation of this logic, see Susan Kaufman Purcell, "Why the Cuban Embargo Makes Sense in a Post–Cold War World," in *Cuba: Contours of Change*, ed. Susan Kaufman Purcell and David Rothkopf (Boulder: Lynne Rienner, 2000), 81–104. A November 2003 report to Congress by the Treasury Department's Office of Foreign Assets Control revealed the extraordinary lengths to which the Bush administration is prepared to go in waging economic war against Cuba. The report acknowledged that while there were only four treasury officials assigned to investigate the Osama Bin Laden and Saddam Hussein money trails, nearly two dozen treasury officials were assigned to catch individuals or organizations violating the U.S. economic embargo of Cuba! See Nancy San Martin, "More Focus on Cuba Embargo than Terror Trail is Questioned," *Miami Herald*, April 30, 2004.

165. Response by President Fidel Castro Ruz to a question posed by the moderator of a round table discussion on a statement made by Canadian prime minister Jean Chrétien during the III Summit of the Americas, April 25, 2001, *Cuba.cu*, <www.cuba.cu/gobierno/discursos/2001/ing/r250401i.html>.

166. Political statement by Dr. Fidel Castro Ruz, president of the state council of the Republic of Cuba, Havana, April 22, 2002, *radioreloj.cu*, <www.radioreloj.cu/discursos/declaracion_fidel-ingles.htm>.

167. Statement from the Ministry of Foreign Affairs, Havana, June 11, 2003, *Cuba.cu*, <www.cuba.cu/gobierno/documentos/2003/ing/r110603i.html>; "Huge March in Havana Protests European Criticism of Castro," *New York Times*, June 13, 2003.

168. Under Secretary of State for Arms Control John Bolton in March 2004 testimony before the House International Relations Committee, quoted in "Cuba a Bioweapons 'Threat,' U.S. Says," *Miami Herald*, March 31, 2004.

169. Quoted in Perine, "Cuba Embargo's Power," 1270.

2

Trying to Stay Friends

Cuba's Relations with Russia and Eastern Europe in the Age of U.S. Supremacy

Nicola Miller

We have always abandoned Cuba. When we had to withdraw the missiles in 1962 we didn't ask Fidel. . . . When we withdrew the brigade that had been there for several decades, again we consigned the Cubans to the background. We never consulted with our allies, we never took them into account. It was the same when we broke off economic relations. And now history is repeating itself.

Nikolai Leonov, former Soviet intelligence officer, 2001

The conclusive moves in the endgame of Cuba's alliance with the USSR have been well-documented.[1] As Cuban officials lamented, thirty years of collaboration were cast aside in as many months. Indeed, the marriage of convenience was dissolved as rapidly as it had been contracted, and with the same heedlessness of the consequences—for either side—by the dominant partner.[2] The beginning of the end can be dated to April 1989, when Soviet president Mikhail Gorbachev went to Havana, signed a twenty-five-year Friendship and Cooperation Treaty, and made reassuring noises about each socialist country pursuing its own path to a more dynamic economy. That year, Cuba continued to receive uninterrupted Soviet deliveries of virtually all of its fuel supplies, a high proportion of its other mineral requirements, and most of its wheat imports. In turn, Cuba supplied the USSR with 3.5 million tonnes of sugar (the bulk of Soviet sugar imports, and more than a quarter of total consumption), over half of its imports of citrus fruit, and significant quantities of nickel and cobalt concentrate. But in Moscow the Friendship Treaty was seen more as a vehicle for extracting concessions from Castro than as one for granting favors to him.

As pro-market reformers began to seize the political initiative throughout the Eastern bloc countries, pressures were rapidly accumulating against any international relationship based on ideological solidarity. In January 1990, the members of Comecon (the Council for Mutual Economic Assistance), meeting in Sofia, Bulgaria, denounced the existing mechanisms of cooperation between them as Stalinist and obsolete and voted to trade henceforth on the basis of world market prices and hard currency. A year later, the budget for aid to Cuba was reduced by the Supreme Soviet from an estimated 3 billion rubles per annum to 55.7 million rubles.[3] In mid-1991 Comecon and the Warsaw Pact dissolved themselves in rapid succession; in August the Communist old guard's attempt to restore the Soviet Union to the status quo ante was defeated; in September Gorbachev suddenly announced, without consulting or even informing Castro, that Soviet troops would be withdrawn from Cuba; and by the end of the year Cuba's main ally, the USSR, no longer existed. The subsequent Russian Federation, headed by Boris Yeltsin, initially sought to distance itself as completely as possible from the Cuban Revolution: military aid ceased, and trade between the two states dwindled away—a contraction in economic activity estimated at forty to forty-five percent—leaving Cuba to survive, as best it might.[4]

If that had truly been the end of the affair, then Cuba's relations with Russia after the Cold War could have been conveniently summarized in a few paragraphs with accompanying tables of shrinking import-export data (as can be done for Havana's ties with most of its former Eastern bloc partners—see Appendix, Table 1). There are, however, two major reasons why this is not the case. One is that the United States—the ever-present third party to the Soviet-Cuban relationship—has proved notoriously unwilling to abandon a Cold War stance towards Fidel Castro (and it *is* that personal), despite having come to a rapprochement with Vietnam, leading to the exchange of ambassadors in 1996.[5] As a result, Cuba continued to provide Russian leaders with some residual bargaining power in their own relationship with Washington. One persistent thorn in the side of U.S.-Russian relations throughout the 1990s was Lourdes, the huge electronic surveillance station that the Russian government maintained near Cienfuegos until October 2001, when President Vladimir Putin announced—in the aftermath of September 11—that it would be closed, along with Russia's naval base at Cam Ranh Bay in Vietnam. Up to that moment, however, the United States repeatedly used Cuba as a probe of Russian intentions, so that the Washington-Moscow-Havana triangle remained just as worthy of analysis, if not as immediately significant, as it had been during the Cold War.

The other key reason for the continuing importance of the Moscow-Havana relationship is that Russian policymakers themselves soon began to have second thoughts about their hasty abandonment of Cuba. This was partly because of the U.S. attitude; partly because the Russian authorities came to see relations with Latin America as an increasingly important plank of their new multilateral foreign policy; and partly because they found that they missed the guaranteed supplies of Cuban sugar. By the mid-1990s, the "sacrifice" of good relations with Havana was openly being criticized as "imprudent and irrational," and initiatives were undertaken to revive ties.[6] What was presented by both Russia and Cuba as a sequel to their previous relationship, although it now appears to be little more than an epilogue, began in 1996, when new foreign minister Evgeny Primakov visited Cuba, and peaked in December 2000 when President Putin himself spent four days on the island. During the second half of the 1990s, Cuba became an important touchstone for debates about how foreign policy should develop in post-Soviet Russia. In light of these concerns, the analysis below traces Russian-Cuban relations and the impact of U.S. policy on these relations through three distinct periods: "breakdown" (1989–91); "distancing" (1992–94); and "rapprochement" (1995–2001). It then examines the current trade relationship between the two countries and concludes with an assessment of the state of the relationship and its prospects, particularly in the context of post-9/11 developments.

The Breakdown in Soviet-Cuban Relations (1989–1991)

It has been argued that Gorbachev was "more patient and understanding with Castro than with any other prime Third World client."[7] There is indeed much evidence that he was not unsympathetic to the Cuban Revolution and, in any case, was genuinely reluctant to force conformity on Soviet allies. During his 1989 visit to Havana, Gorbachev recalled, he reassured Castro: "What we are doing now is necessary for us. But that does not mean you have to do the same thing. You are in a completely different country and a different situation. Our attitude is one of confidence in what you do. . . . It is your choice, and no questions about it arise on our part."[8] Castro trusted Gorbachev personally, maintaining a distinction—even after the fall of the USSR—between Soviet leaders who had acted in the full knowledge that they were "murdering socialism" and others, like Gorbachev, who had sought only to reform it.[9] By 1989, however, there were three major sources of tension in the Soviet-Cuban relationship, none of them new, but all by that time reaching crisis point. In ascending order of importance from Moscow's point of view, they were: Castro's attitude towards perestroika; the question of Soviet aid to Cuba; and Cuba's role in regional conflicts, both in southern Africa and in Central America. The year 1989 was a crucial one, because the incoming U.S. administration of George Bush vigorously set about trying to resolve outstanding issues between Washington and Moscow and identified Soviet policy towards Cuba as a key indicator of how far Gorbachev was committed to a new approach to international relations.

Castro was critical of perestroika from the outset (1985): he always insisted that socialist ills could not be treated with capitalist medicines. At first, he voiced his doubts privately to Soviet officials; later, as the increasingly unregulated Soviet media began to publish critical accounts of economic conditions in Cuba, Castro retaliated with public defenses of Cuba's own rectification policy (introduced in 1986) and denunciations of Soviet reforms, which he saw as inimical to socialism.[10] Nor did Gorbachev's opening to the West meet with approval in Havana: Cuban leaders were particularly unconvinced by the Soviet claim that arms limitation and reduction agreements between the superpowers made for a more secure world. Castro maintained at the time—and he has not changed his view subsequently—that it was absurd and tragic that the USSR was dissolved, primarily because it had played an indispensable role in balancing the power of the United States.[11] In the Cuban leader's opinion—and it has largely been vindicated—Washington would prove to be ruthless in extracting maximum advantage from the collapse of the Soviet bloc, especially in relation to the developing world.[12]

Policymakers in Moscow initially hoped that Castro could be persuaded to become more flexible and to apply at least some of the principles of perestroika to the Cuban economy (like the Vietnamese leaders, whose initial wariness had been replaced by enthusiasm by late 1988). But Gorbachev's visit to Havana in April 1989 definitively put paid to any such hopes. That in itself might not have mattered had Cuba's economy been doing well. Soviet leaders would probably not have opposed rectification if it had worked (that is, their concerns were pragmatic rather than ideological). They became increasingly concerned, however, about the inability of the Cuban government to improve economic performance and thereby reduce its dependence on Soviet aid. As the issue of aid to client states became more and more contentious in both the Soviet Congress of Peoples' Deputies and the media, it became correspondingly harder for the Soviet government to justify high Cuba subsidies to its own immiserated population that, moreover, had ever greater access to the means to express resentment about such an outflow of resources. A notorious list published by *Izvestiya* in March 1990 brought to light the fact that Cuba was by far the USSR's largest debtor.[13]

Especially after the rejection of socialism by East European countries in 1989, the remaining socialist states attracted a lot of attention in the Soviet press, much of it highly critical. In a context where little was known about conditions in countries such as Cuba, it was easy to replace the previously romanticized picture with one that was all negative. There was a tendency to personalize regimes, and Castro's denunciations of the profit motive struck many people in the Soviet Union as all too reminiscent of Stalinism, which had become an all-purpose pejorative for anything about the past that anybody wanted to reject. Widespread coverage in 1989 of the trial and execution of

Cuban general Arnaldo Ochoa Sánchez and the imprisonment of Interior Minister José Abrantes Fernández, both convicted of corruption (a euphemism for drug smuggling), only served to confirm such impressions.

Official advocates of the "new political thinking" all emphasized that economic relations with Cuba would be "streamlined to ensure maximum mutual benefits for both parties."[14] But this was easier said than done, because aside from all the political difficulties entailed, no one could agree on how to calculate the balance of advantage between the two partners. It was claimed in hostile sections of the Soviet press that aid to Cuba was running at $5–$6 billion per annum in the late 1980s and constituted ten percent of the USSR's balance of payments deficit. But such figures were vigorously disputed by Cuba's supporters within the Moscow establishment.[15] They made a case that this alleged level of subsidy was "an invention of the CIA," because trade had been conducted on a barter basis, with accounts in transferable rubles.[16] CIA calculations were based, they pointed out, on an artificial exchange rate of 0.62 rubles to the dollar. When the Soviet government introduced a tourist ruble in 1990, the rate of exchange was officially set far lower at 6.2 rubles to the dollar (the open market rate being 27.5 rubles to the dollar). So if the Soviet Union paid, say, 0.26 rubles per pound for sugar, the CIA exchange rate resulted in a calculation that Moscow was paying forty-two cents per pound, when the world market price (WMP) was eight cents. But if the same transaction was calculated at the tourist rate of exchange, then it worked out at just over four cents per pound, that is, about half the WMP.[17] Defenders of Cuba argued that the Cubans had provided the Soviet Union with a reliable supply of sugar, nickel, and citrus fruits, for which Moscow would otherwise have had to pay precious hard currency, and that Cuba had also provided invaluable services, such as shipping facilities. They also emphasized that the Soviet Union had often sent inferior quality goods to Cuba in fulfillment of its side of the barter trade.

As will be seen below, the argument that Soviet-Cuban trade was by no means exclusively to Cuba's advantage was later shown to carry weight. Critics of the relationship countered, however, that the USSR could have earned far more than the $1.5–$2 billion needed to pay for Cuban products by selling oil on the world market instead of sending it to Cuba. Such disputes are ultimately irresolvable. But perhaps the nub of the situation was captured by Castro himself when, in late 1991, he observed that given the relative prices of oil and sugar by that time, in order to buy the thirteen million tonnes of oil Cuba consumed annually at world market prices, it would need to sell more than ten million tonnes of sugar, which it had never succeeded in producing.[18] The advantages for Cuba of a secure source of its strategic imports and a guaranteed outlet for its main exports far outweighed the losses made in those years when it paid over the odds for Soviet oil (notably 1986–90) or was paid less than the world market price for sugar.[19]

In any case, however the historic balance of advantage between the Soviet Union and Cuba is assessed, by 1990 the market reformers who argued that the Soviet government could no longer afford to subsidize economically unviable allies were manifestly in the ascendant. It was made clear to Cuba that their economic relationship with Moscow was to be restructured, slowly but surely, along market lines. Instead of the customary automatic renewal of trade agreements, no formal basis for trade between the two countries in 1990 was established until Leonid Abalkin, vice president of the Soviet Council of Ministers and head of the Intergovernmental Soviet-Cuban Commission on Economic and Scientific-Technical Collaboration, traveled to Havana in April of that year. After the negotiations, Abalkin publicly made positive statements about the prospects for economic collaboration, but ominously also mentioned the need to adapt to world market conditions.[20] A Soviet-Cuban trade agreement for 1991, signed only at the last minute in December 1990, and for just one year instead of the usual five, stipulated the gradual introduction of market prices and—the key point, which effectively eliminated subsidies—accounting in dollars. Castro had already been warned that Cuba would be expected to repay its debt to Moscow, and in dollars, starting in 1995.[21] By the end of 1990 Cuba had received twenty percent less Soviet oil than in previous years (at a time when the crisis in the Gulf had almost tripled oil prices), as a result of which a national emergency—the "Special Period in Peacetime"—was declared. Cuba's economic difficulties were compounded by the loss of its most important trading partner in Eastern Europe, the German Democratic Republic, which was subsumed into a reunified Germany on October 3, 1990.

The issue of aid was highly visible, but Soviet policy towards Cuba as the Cold War wound down was largely determined by the fact that Gorbachev needed Castro's cooperation to end the proxy wars the United States insisted should be part of negotiations between the two superpowers. In relation to Africa, Cuban collaboration was relatively easy to obtain, the bottom line being that they simply could not afford to support a military presence there that the Soviet Union was not prepared to finance. In any case, the Cuban military was overstretched by its African commitments, and the level of casualties was becoming uncomfortably high. Cuban troops were brought home from Ethiopia in September 1989. In southern Africa, Castro initially engaged in some brinkmanship, irritating the Soviet government by expanding Cuban forces in Angola by about thirty percent without prior consultation, stationing them provocatively close to the Namibian border, and seeking to establish conditions for their withdrawal, such as the ending of apartheid, which precluded any basis for negotiation with South Africa.[22] In response to such criticisms, the Cubans would probably say, and not without justification, that the

United States has always set them impossible conditions for negotiation on any issue. But Cuban influence in Moscow, which had traditionally bypassed the Soviet Foreign Ministry for the Communist Party Central Committee, was on the wane as Eduard Shevardnadze moved to assert his authority as foreign minister. Cuba was informed that the Soviet Union intended to support U.S. peace initiatives in southern Africa. The Cubans won a significant concession in insisting that they be party to multilateral talks on the independence of Namibia. From that point on, however, the newly collaborating superpowers set the agenda, although Castro played them off against each other with his customary panache and secured an agreement that enabled him to preserve political capital both at home and abroad.[23] The Cuban government signed up to the peace accords of December 1988 and had duly withdrawn its troops from Angola by the end of May 1991.

Central America was far more problematic, however, because the stakes were higher on all sides. In the United States, the desire to see the Sandinista revolution in Nicaragua overthrown had become the cause célèbre of the Republican Right, which bitterly resented the refusal of a Democrat-dominated Congress to grant military aid to the U.S.-backed counterrevolutionary forces (known as the contras). The acrimony was intensified by the scandal that broke in late 1986, when it was made public that some members of the Reagan administration had been secretly raising money to fund the contras by selling weapons to Iran in exchange for the release of American hostages held by terrorist groups backed by Tehran. By the end of Reagan's second term in office (1985–88), the issue of involvement in Central America had become symbolic of the profound disagreements within the U.S. policy-making establishment about the role that the United States should play in the world after Vietnam. The issue also became a test case of the respective strengths of Capitol Hill and the White House.

Thus when George Bush assumed the presidency in January 1989, having stated in his inaugural address that it was time to bury the legacy of Vietnam for good, the first major foreign policy issue he tackled was Central America. Bush had campaigned on a pledge to restore military aid to the contras, but it soon became clear that he would be unable to secure the necessary votes in Congress to do so. To the president and his secretary of state, James Baker III, resolving the Central American crisis was crucial to their plans for shaping the post–Cold-War world, because any major new initiatives—on drugs, terrorism or nuclear nonproliferation—would require congressional support, which in turn created the need to establish a bipartisan consensus. In his memoirs, Baker expressed the view that "every important achievement" in U.S. foreign policy since the Second World War had enjoyed bipartisan support. Although he was a supporter of military aid to the contras, he saw Central America as "the Vietnam of the 1980s" and maintained that Reagan's policies had left President

Bush with "a legacy of enormous suspicion and mistrust," which had to be overcome before the new administration could pursue its self-assigned role as architect of the new world order.[24] He started from the premise that a diplomatic solution might be possible, "but not without Moscow's help."[25]

In order to win Soviet cooperation, Baker had first to secure his home front. He began by appointing Bernard Aronson, a Democrat who supported aid to the contras but who was above all committed to consensus building, as assistant secretary of state for inter-American Affairs. Having thereby signaled a strong commitment to bipartisanship, and building on the personal trust that he himself enjoyed, Baker spent most of March 1989 bargaining with congressional leaders over what to do about the Sandinistas. The pressure to make a deal was acute because the last installment of the previous allocation of so-called "humanitarian" aid to the *contras* was due to expire on March 31. Baker championed the Esquipulas peace plan, signed in August 1987 by all five Central American nations but consistently rejected by the Reagan White House, as "an opportune vehicle around which to fashion a new policy."[26] On the basis of the president's new willingness to accept a nonmilitary resolution of the conflict, the secretary of state finally secured a bipartisan accord, signed in late March. The compromise was that the contras were granted a further $50 million in humanitarian aid, subject to congressional review after eight months; the administration agreed to accept the result of an election in Nicaragua, assuming that the Sandinistas could be induced and/or intimidated into complying with Esquipulas; and the White House was granted leeway to seek a diplomatic solution with Gorbachev.

The Bush administration then proceeded to turn Central America into a test case of Soviet willingness to apply "new thinking" in their foreign policy. In discussions with his Soviet counterpart, Eduard Shevardnadze, throughout the rest of 1989, Baker repeatedly made it clear that the United States saw Soviet "mischief in our hemisphere" as the key stumbling block to warmer relations between the two superpowers.[27] Most sources agree that the Soviet Union had suspended direct arms supplies to Nicaragua at the end of 1988. In May 1989, Gorbachev told Bush this, without consulting either Castro or the Nicaraguan president, Daniel Ortega.[28] His visit to Cuba had apparently confirmed his fear that the Cuban leader could not be shifted from the position that the Esquipulas peace accords were merely a political means of bringing about what the U.S.-backed contras had failed to achieve militarily, namely the overthrow of the Sandinistas. In response to the consternation that Gorbachev's announcement to Bush created in Havana and Managua, Shevardnadze sent Georgi Mamedov, deputy head of the U.S. and Canada Directorate, and Yuri Pavlov, head of the Latin American Directorate, to visit both capitals, proposing regular tripartite consultations to coordinate Central American policy. Pavlov reported that although Managua initially showed some enthusiasm for this idea, the Cubans were unresponsive and it was therefore dropped. From then on, Cuba was increasingly regarded in Moscow as an obstacle to a peaceful settlement.[29]

The Cubans continued to ship light weapons to Nicaragua, persisting with an earlier Soviet-Cuban arrangement whereby weapons for Nicaragua were sent first to Cuban ports, causing James Baker to complain during Soviet-American talks in Wyoming that the Sandinistas had received more weapons in 1989 than they did before the Soviet Union had supposedly stopped its supplies.[30] Soviet officials also strongly suspected Cuba of continuing to supply weapons to the Farabundo Martí National Liberation Front (FMLN) guerrillas in El Salvador, particularly when they launched a major offensive in November 1989 using Soviet surface-to-air missiles (SAMs) supplied via Nicaragua. Officials in Moscow were infuriated by Castro's subsequent protests that he knew nothing about plans for the November offensive and his denials of Cuban involvement in transportation of SAMs through Nicaragua to El Salvador. Soviet leaders had, of course, for many years taken refuge in the claim that they could not control Castro, so the skepticism of U.S. policymakers is understandable. But in this instance it seems that he was indeed acting against Soviet wishes. The Foreign Ministry, at least, saw the Castro government's active support for the FMLN as a deliberate "attempt to torpedo Soviet policy in Central America" and proclaimed "a curse on both their houses."[31] Increasingly, from that moment on, Shevardnadze ignored Castro. In February 1990, he accepted Baker's proposal to express joint U.S.-Soviet opposition to any external military aid to Central America and their shared commitment to respect the results of free and fair elections in Nicaragua. Cuban troops were withdrawn from Nicaragua in March 1990, after the Sandinistas had lost the elections. Havana's military aid to the FMLN was eventually curtailed in April 1991, and Castro accepted the United Nations–brokered peace settlement in El Salvador early in 1992.

There is little doubt that Soviet leaders found Castro unhelpful and intransigent on the issue of Central America. They were not prepared, however, to bend to U.S. pressure on how to conduct their relations with Cuba. The United States went much further than trying to force the Soviet Union to prevent the Cubans from supplying weapons to El Salvador. From the Malta Summit of December 1989 onwards, the Bush administration sought to persuade Moscow to cut its ties with Cuba altogether. In July 1990, Bush publicly stipulated three conditions for U.S. aid to the Soviet Union, one of which was the ending of relations with Cuba. (The others were pro-market reforms and cuts in defense spending.) Gorbachev's consistent response was that the best way for the United States to bring about a reduction in Soviet-Cuban cooperation would be for Washington to normalize its own relations with Castro.[32] Moreover, measures were taken to ensure that the Cubans could maintain a high level of deterrence against U.S. military action. In May 1991 a consignment of MiG-29 planes (albeit delayed since late 1989) was sent to Cuba. The Cubans had their supporters in the Soviet Ministry of Defense, many of whom were committed to the strategic benefits of the alliance. So long as Gorbachev still had significant power in the Soviet Union, U.S. demands "that Moscow join the efforts of Washington and Miami to strangle Cuba [were] really too much to ask."[33]

The situation was changed dramatically, however, by the attempted coup of August 1991, after which Gorbachev and Yeltsin, coexisting in uneasy partnership until Gorbachev's resignation in December, agreed on little else apart from the need to cooperate with the West in order to unlock economic aid and trade. During James Baker's visit to Moscow in September 1991, Gorbachev agreed not only to withdraw the Soviet brigade from Cuba, but also to make an announcement to that effect at the joint press conference, thereby infuriating the Cubans, who once again found that a decision crucially affecting their security had been taken over their heads. Baker, surprised by a policy that he thought "wouldn't go over all that well in Moscow" either, especially with the Soviet military, was convinced that the main motivation for the withdrawal from Cuba "was to clear the way for stronger U.S. support."[34] With hindsight it is clear that the United States did not deliver on their unspoken side of the deal. The only major Western initiative to help the Russian economy convert to capitalism was the 1992 Paris Club decision to defer the repayment of Soviet debt for ten years.

The Cubans, with their long and bitter experience of being a small and vulnerable nation, were more realistic than their Russian counterparts about what to expect from Washington. Bush and Baker heeded Gorbachev's injunctions to talk to the Cubans in one respect only. In November 1990, when the U.S. was trying to mobilize support on the United Nations Security Council (UNSC) for a resolution authorizing the use of force to bring about Saddam Hussein's withdrawal from Kuwait, Cuba occupied a seat as a nonpermanent member of the Security Council. Havana had supported the key Resolution 660 of August 2, 1990, which condemned the Iraqi invasion, and had also backed the majority of subsequent resolutions on the issue. The day before Resolution 678, giving Iraq a specific deadline for withdrawal, came up before the Security Council, Baker had a two-hour meeting with Shevardnadze and then conferred with Cuban foreign minister, Isidoro Malmierca. This was the first official high-level meeting between the United States and Cuba since the 1981 meeting between Secretary of State Alexander Haig and Cuban vice president Carlos Rafael Rodríguez. Technically, Baker says, it was in his role as president of the Security Council that he was meeting with Malmierca, not as U.S. secretary of state. In trying to shift Malmierca away from his declared position that a resolution involving a deadline made war all but inevitable, and that such a war would result in high oil prices and economic disaster for the world's poor, Baker suggested—not very subtly, as he himself admitted in his memoirs—that Cuba would find itself completely isolated if it failed to support the resolution. Unsurprisingly, Malmierca dug his heels in, and Baker ruefully acknowledged: "It had been a long shot; even in the face of pressure from their longtime Soviet benefactors, Cuba would stand fast."[35]

In the new context created by Soviet reform and the fall of the Berlin Wall, the Cuban government found that the tactics it had employed to manage its dependence on Moscow over three decades—namely, strategic loyalty mixed with a persistent and public refusal to accept the role of junior partner, laced with a degree of unpredictability and brinkmanship—no longer sufficed. Cuban leaders, long habituated to state-controlled media, did not adapt easily to the rapid emergence of public debate in the Soviet Union. They analyzed developments with acuity and prescience, such as the problems posed for them by the rise in power of the Soviet Parliament, but seemed far less able to respond flexibly to meet them. Castro knew how to play a live crowd well enough, but not, it seemed, the more diffuse and fickle audience of public opinion. For example, the Cuban government famously offered places for up to ten thousand children who had been victims of the Chernobyl disaster to go to Cuba for treatment. Injured veterans from the Soviet occupation of Afghanistan were also rehabilitated on the island. These initiatives backfired, however, because although the humanitarian impulse was widely acknowledged, Cuba's very capacity to offer such facilities served as a vivid reminder that the supposedly "poor" developing nation, subsidized by the "rich" Soviet Union, was in fact more advanced in sectors of intense popular concern such as health care.[36] Cuban official statements also had a less than tactful tendency to imply that their solidarity with the USSR in these instances was equivalent to Soviet support for the Cuban Revolution over the course of three decades.

Castro's vociferous public complaints about the difficulties caused by delays in Soviet shipments did little to help the situation. Even though he repeatedly acknowledged that many of these problems were beyond the control of the Soviet government,[37] his detailed indictments of them did not endear him either to Soviet officials, who felt that they were indeed doing their best to get supplies through to Cuba against difficult odds,[38] or to the Soviet public. Castro was motivated primarily, of course, by the need to ensure that the Cuban population did not blame his own government for the shortages. To some extent officials in Moscow were prepared to accommodate that political necessity, but petty acts of protest—such as refusing to refuel Aeroflot planes en route to Latin America—strained their patience.[39] Most of the problems experienced by the Cubans were an inevitable if unintended consequence of the decentralization of economic activity in the USSR, which meant that contracts were "no longer signed just with the Soviet state, but also with countless Soviet firms involved in production, transportation, and various other aspects of the process."[40] There seems to have been no official decision to exert economic pressure on Castro to implement policies more to Soviet liking, a fact that many Soviet officials felt was insufficiently appreciated in Havana.

Thus it transpired that Soviet-Cuban relations during 1990–91 played out the limitations of the Friendship and Cooperation Treaty that Gorbachev had signed in April 1989.[41] The treaty had no strategic value, making no reference to defense cooperation or even to consultation in the event of a threat from a third party. It was a pale shadow of documents that the USSR had signed under the same name with India, Egypt, and Iraq in the 1970s. To some extent it reflected Gorbachev's new thinking in foreign policy and was an attempt to keep Castro in line with that approach. In return, the Soviet leaders omitted any mention of the Nuclear Non-Proliferation Treaty, which Cuba had not signed, or of Latin America as a nuclear-free zone. Mostly, however, it displayed the traditional Soviet caution—at least since the 1962 Cuban Missile Crisis—about overreaching themselves in order to support Cuba. The treaty specifically stated (Article 12) that Soviet-Cuban friendship was not directed against any third country. In any case, it lasted barely more than twenty-five months, let alone twenty-five years, for it effectively became a dead letter after the demise of the USSR.

Distancing Havana: Courting Washington (1992–1994)

At first, Havana had some reason to hope that Boris Yeltsin would be favorable to the Cuban Revolution; he had visited Havana twice in November 1987, on his way to and from Nicaragua, and been given a warm welcome. Former ambassador to Cuba, Yuri Petrov, who had become head of Yeltsin's private staff, was seen as a promising channel of communication.[42] But Yeltsin's immediate priority was to put as much distance as possible between Soviet foreign policy and that of his own government. Given the emphasis on "de-ideologization," high-profile Cuba was bound to be a casualty. During this period, Castro's government even lost Russia's political support on issues of human rights. Although it had been a tenet of Gorbachev's new political thinking that human rights should no longer be subordinate to the principle of nonintervention in the affairs of other nations, in practice the USSR had continued to defend Cuba's record in international fora. This remained official policy despite the fact that unfavorable hearings on Cuban human rights cases in the Russian Parliament were an important element in turning Russian public opinion against Cuba. In late 1991, local organizations had been established in Moscow to campaign against alleged Cuban human rights violations, and the influential anti-Castro Cuban American National Foundation (CANF) was also permitted to establish an office there. In both 1990 and 1991, however, the

Soviet government refrained from voting with Bulgaria, Hungary, and Czechoslovakia in support of the annual U.S.-sponsored resolutions condemning Cuba's human rights record at the United Nations Human Rights Commission (UNHRC). From 1992 to 1995, however, the Russian Federation voted against Cuba. In February 1992, Sergei Kovalev, a former Soviet dissident who was appointed Russia's representative at the UNHRC, went so far as to apologize publicly on behalf of the Russian government for its past support of Cuba.[43] That bleak year for Cuba, the Russian Federation even abstained in the annual United Nations General Assembly (UNGA) resolution condemning the U.S. blockade.

In line with the political renunciation, one of the new Russian government's earliest acts was to stop cheap loans and subsidies to Cuba. Yeltsin courted Washington's favor by announcing to the U.S. Congress that Russia "has corrected the well-known imbalances in its relations with Cuba," and he pandered to public opinion at home by telling St. Petersburg dockers that fifty thousand tons of food intended for Cuba would be kept for the city's own residents.[44] When the 1991 trade agreement expired, attempts by the Cubans to renegotiate a preferential deal were ignored in Moscow, and the only agreement secured was an exchange of 1.8 million tonnes of oil for 1 million tonnes of sugar at prices just below the world market level. All trade in other goods ceased: Cuba could not even obtain from the Russians supplies of the fertilizer needed to cultivate the sugar cane that Russia still wanted to buy. Support for Cuba was portrayed by Russia's new generation of technocrats as one of the USSR's classic mistakes—a costly squandering of resources in the pursuit of inappropriate aims.

In East Europe, most of the new postcommunist governments also wanted to distance themselves from Cuba, making debt settlement a precondition of further economic ties. Czechoslovakia refused at the end of 1990 to continue hosting the Cuban Interests Section in Washington, which was transferred to the Swiss Embassy. Bulgaria and Romania continued to buy Cuban sugar—albeit at significantly reduced levels—to compensate for the slump in their own production of sugar (from beet) during the early to mid-1990s, but Cuba lost the German and Czech markets altogether. (Poland, a major sugar producer in its own right, had never been important.) It also became far more difficult for Cuba to import the spare parts needed for its Hungarian buses, Czech-made electric generators for sugar mills, and Romanian diesel engines for lorries.[45] East European countries had accounted for only about fifteen percent of Cuba's total trade, but the goods supplied were crucial to strategic sectors of the economy such as construction, transportation, and the sugar industry. Cuba's isolation was only marginally alleviated by the fact that most of the former USSR republics chose to maintain relations. Havana's policy was to recognize them all and to preserve trade where possible, but together (Ukraine, Byelorussia, Kazakhstan, Kyrgyzstan, Azerbaijan, Tajikistan, Latvia, and Lithuania) they accounted for only a small percentage of Cuba's sugar exports and an even tinier proportion of its sharply reduced import total (see Appendix, Table 1). As a measure of the overall closing down of Cuba's supply lines, the total trade turnover between Cuba and former Soviet bloc countries in 1993 was less than seven percent of its 1989 level.

Cuba found that there were hidden consequences, too, of the economic dislocation in Russia. Mineral products flooded onto the world market, lowering the price of nickel (Cuba's second most important export), among others. World food prices rose, because of the sharp reduction in Russian cereal production. Oil became more expensive, partly because of a downturn in Russian production and partly because of the 1991 Gulf War. Within Cuba itself, the government estimated that there were some six hundred uncompleted projects dependent upon Soviet aid and technical assistance.[46]

The most important of these projects—the unfinished nuclear plant at Juragua—became a focus for all the tensions inherent in the new relationship between Russia and Cuba. The Soviet Union had initially agreed to build Cuba a nuclear reactor in 1976 as one element in a broad strategy to reduce Cuban dependence upon Soviet oil supplies. Work did not begin until 1983, however, and it was later interrupted because of the accident at Chernobyl in 1986. The reactors at Juragua are almost completely different from those at Chernobyl, but the disaster made the Soviet government more hesitant about supplying technology—and finance—to Cuba.[47] Hence, Juragua was still some way short of completion when the Soviet Union collapsed at the end of 1991. It was designed to supply about ten percent of Cuba's electricity needs, saving about 1.2 million tonnes of oil per annum. The new government of the Russian Federation initially agreed in principle to finish building the two reactors, but insisted that Cuba pay in hard currency for future supplies of equipment and technical assistance. The Russians also stipulated that Cuba would have to obtain part of the automated system from a third country. Cuban protests that such conditions were completely impossible for them to meet given that they had no access to international credit facilities were ignored.

The Cuban government, estimating that they would have to find at least $400 million in hard currency, unilaterally announced the suspension of work on the plant in September 1992, saying that they were unable to meet Russia's financial demands.[48] At this stage, work on the Juragua-1 reactor itself was nearly complete, although only just over a third of the equipment for it had been assembled; work on the second reactor (Juragua-2) was only about one-quarter completed.[49] Yuri Pavlov explains that the problem for the Russians "was that the maintenance of the equipment already installed required almost as much expense in hard currency as the completion of the construction. If the project collapsed, then Russia would lose its right to ask for repayment of Soviet investment in [it]."[50] In July 1993, Russia agreed to provide a $30 million credit to implement the measures necessary to make the plant safe in its incomplete state. Attempts in 1993–94 to interest European and Latin American companies in the contract to complete the work were all unsuccessful, and the project appeared to be at an impasse.

Russia's complete cold-shouldering of Cuba did not last long, however. Several of Yeltsin's advisers, including Yuri Petrov, were arguing that Russia's own economic situation was too precarious to rely wholly on trade in hard currency. Above all, the Russians found it highly inconvenient to do without guaranteed supplies of Cuban sugar, which had mainly been consumed in Russia itself (Cuba's 3.5 million tonnes accounting for nearly half of Russia's annual 8–9 million tonnes). Russian sugar consumption fell during the 1990s to about 4.5–5 million tonnes per annum, the level at which experts expect it to stabilize.[51] The need for imports was not reduced correspondingly, however, because Russia's own sugar production, from beet, also fell, due to the withdrawal of state subsidies and a host of other factors that resulted in low yields. Production also declined sharply in the newly independent Ukraine, which had accounted for half of Soviet beet sugar.[52] In any case, the reduction in consumption was largely in industry: Russian households continued to consume relatively large quantities of sugar, because they relied on their own preserves, pickling, and alcohol production. Sugar was a highly sensitive commodity, therefore, and the incoming Russian government did move to sign an oil-for-sugar deal with Cuba early in 1992, which resulted in about one million tonnes being imported via this route.[53] This was not enough, however, and sugar shortages, which were widely attributed to reduced imports from Cuba, did not help to reconcile an often-recalcitrant population to market reforms. Such shortages were a telling reminder that, as I have argued elsewhere, the original Soviet-Cuban trading relationship was based on a perfectly rational exchange of oil for sugar.[54]

The key explanation for continued Russian interest in Cuban sugar lies in timing: the Cuban harvest runs from December to April when there is a gap both in domestic beet production and in supplies from Southern Hemisphere producers such as Brazil or Australia. Contrary to what is often claimed, a lot of Cuban sugar found its way to Russia in 1992 (2.9 million tonnes according to the International Sugar Organization), but more than half of it was sold at inflated prices via third parties as Yeltsin's government sought to make up for its early mistake in not buying enough sugar from Cuba during the first half of the year.[55] A senior government official later admitted that in 1992 Russia "lost a lot of money by repurchasing Cuban sugar from third countries," mostly former Soviet republics.[56] It seemed to make far more sense for the Russian government to deal directly with Cuba.

Many Russian experts on Cuba soon began to argue for the continuation of ties in all spheres, largely on the grounds that the United States was using the issue of relations with Cuba as a means of applying pressure to Russia. This was the interpretation placed on the 1992 Cuban Democracy Act (CDA)—reestablishing U.S. sanctions against foreign cargo ships calling at the island—by Alexei Yermakov, the newly appointed Foreign Ministry spokesman on Cuba.[57] In summit talks, American officials continued to insist on raising the question of Russia's ties with Cuba, yet there was little sign that further concessions would obtain the aid that Yeltsin sought to restructure the Russian economy, all of which strengthened the position of those in Russia who had never been convinced by the reformers' pro-Western policies. The Russian military were particularly unhappy about the abrupt abandonment of Cuba, a key strategic asset and their most useful ally during the Cold War (after all, Cuban troops had fought and helped to win two wars in Angola and one in Ethiopia). Warm personal ties between senior Soviet-era military leaders and the Castro brothers were not an insignificant factor.[58] More mundanely, Cuba was also seen as a good market for secondhand military equipment that could no longer be offloaded elsewhere. It also helped that Castro became more accommodating: in September 1992, he withdrew his insistence that the departure of the Soviet combat brigade be linked to United States' withdrawal from Guantánamo Bay. Moreover, against all the odds, he was still in power, a fact that provoked astonishment and admiration in roughly equal proportions in Moscow. As a result of these accumulated pressures, after over a year of estrangement, a senior Cuban delegation was received in Moscow in November 1992, when trade and shipping agreements were signed that made provision for another oil-for-sugar barter deal. By the end of the year, personal messages were once again regularly being exchanged between Cuban and Russian leaders.[59]

In May 1993, the Russian vice premier Vladimir Shumeiko made a follow-up visit to Cuba, where he signed new agreements on economic cooperation and—in what struck many observers as a reversal of the commitment to strictly commercial relations—agreed to a credit of $350 million, primarily intended for modernization of Cuba's sugar industry. (In practice, most of this money was held up by resistance from the Ministry of Finance, which argued that since Cuba already owed Russia an estimated $20 billion it should not be given any more.)[60] Shumeiko also emphasized publicly that Russia was committed to maintaining its surveillance station at Lourdes, a clear signal to the new Clinton administration that Russia was still prepared to flex its remaining muscles if necessary. At the end of 1993, after a high-level Cuban military delegation had been received at the Russian Ministry of Defense by the minister, Pavel Grachev, and after a Cuban political delegation had spent nearly a week in Moscow in early December, some commentators started to claim that the old relationship was being restored.[61] Such rumors were further fuelled early in 1994 by the inauguration of a joint organization, Ros-Cuba, apparently intended to enable Russian oil companies to use Cuba as a bridgehead for exports to other Latin American countries.[62]

There were, however, considerable tensions between the two former allies, largely deriving from the Russian government's misplaced assumption that the Cubans were so desperate for oil that they would agree to any terms. The Cubans had demanded rent for the use of Lourdes, arguing that there was no longer any ideological reason for them to grant Russia free access. While the Russians were prepared to accept this principle, they were digging their heels in over the price and proposing to pay in spare parts for weapons, rather than the hard currency sought by Havana. Nor could the two sides agree on a ratio of exchange of oil for sugar. The agreement signed in January 1993 had resulted in a barter of 1.5 million tonnes of sugar for 1.8 million tonnes of oil, but the Russians were seeking to reduce the price paid for Cuban sugar, partly because they had accumulated large stocks of refined sugar after May 1993 when a subsidy on raw sugar imports had been removed. After tense negotiations and evading the issue of concrete volumes, a general protocol was signed, although Minister of Foreign Economic Relations Oleg Davydov announced that the two parties would start on the basis of 1 million tonnes of sugar for 2.5 million tonnes of oil during 1994 and hope to negotiate an increase to 4 million tonnes of oil for 2.5 million tonnes of sugar. Even the lower figures were widely thought to be difficult to implement, given falling Russian oil production and a Cuban harvest anticipated to be far lower than the 6.33 million tonnes achieved in 1991–92.[63]

Despite a variety of bureaucratic delays and logistical difficulties, in 1994 the target of 2.5 million tonnes of oil in return for 1 million tonnes of sugar were almost met, and a further agreement was signed for 1995 in the hope that it would eliminate both shortages and speculation.[64] The Russian government might have preferred to purchase sugar on a strictly commercial basis, but it needed to secure Cuban supplies to keep prices in the shops at reasonable levels.[65] In early 1995, Castro—asked to characterize Cuba's relations with Russia—described them as "normal," noting that trade was at a relatively low level "not because of the authorities' lack of political resolve but because of the lack of organization."[66]

Rapprochement: Reassessing Russian Interests (1995–2001)

By 1995, Cuba's supporters within the Russian bureaucracy were winning the arguments. Those who had always maintained that Russia would not get a better deal on sugar supplies felt vindicated and empowered to advance incontestably pragmatic reasons for a revival of ties with Cuba. Their position was strengthened by the fact that the Cuban sugar industry seemed to be recovering, both in the context of an overall resumption of economic growth on the island and in response to a government decision to open it up to foreign invest-ment. In 1995, several leading international sugar traders offered prefinancing deals for the Cuban sugar harvest, which meant that these companies also then had an interest in working to place the export trade with Russia on a secure basis. This development seemed to offer a promising way forward for reconcil-ing the differences in commercial practice between Cuba and Russia, and elimi-nating the difficulties experienced by the 1994–95 oil-for-sugar deals.

The course of U.S.-Russian relations since the end of the Cold War also provided ample justification for the view that the privileging of links with the West was not necessarily in Russia's best interests. Not only had the Bush White House (1989–92) failed to fulfill its implicit promises to aid the restruc-turing of the Russian economy, but his successor Bill Clinton (1993–2000), who had far more sense of the strategic necessity of such measures, had also been unable to force significant aid packages through a resistant Congress. Economic crisis in Russia, beginning in 1994 and lasting until the crash of 1998, further strained bilateral relations. By mid-1994 the Clinton administra-tion, perturbed by the success of right-wing nationalists in the December 1993 elections to the Duma and by Yeltsin's reassertion of traditional Russian inter-ests such as support for the Serbs in Bosnia, effectively abandoned the idea of an alliance with Russia. The United States switched its attention to the building of relations with other post-Soviet republics, with the expansion of NATO in mind. In late 1994, Yeltsin made public Russia's opposition to any such expan-sion, and sent Russian forces into Chechnya. Domestic factors also played their part in reviving Moscow's interest in a renewed flirtation with Cuba. Both Yeltsin (in June) and Clinton (in November) were up for reelection in 1996. Yeltsin's main rival at that time was the communist Gennadi Zyuganov, whose campaign sought to take advantage of popular nostalgia for the USSR and who was cheer-leading the criticism of Yeltsin for being too pro-Western.

In that context, First Deputy Prime Minister Oleg Soskovets was sent to Cuba in October 1995 to rebuild relations and emphasize Russia's continuing interest in Cuba. Soskovets visited both the Lourdes base and the Juragua nuclear plant, where he authorized renewal of the project that had been sus-pended in 1992. Of more immediate significance to the Cubans, he arranged for the release of the $350 million credit agreed in 1993 and signed a three-year trade protocol for 1996–98 projecting an annual exchange of oil for sugar, building up to 4.7 million tonnes of sugar for 9.5 million tonnes of oil in 1998.[67] The following February, when the Cuban air force shot down two U.S. civilian aircraft flown by Miami exiles, the Russian government issued no con-demnation. Arguably, Yeltsin was killing two birds with one stone: using Cuba, an issue of relatively minor international significance, to strengthen his position both with the United States and with domestic opponents, in a situation where he had little scope for major initiatives on either front.

Although Soskovets' visit was important in reestablishing a degree of trust, the real shift in Russia's attitude towards Cuba can be dated to the change of foreign ministers from Andrei Kozyrev to Evgeny Primakov in 1996. Primakov sought to reshape foreign policy to carve out an appropriate international role for the Russian Federation.[68] He was not unsympathetic to critics of Yeltsin's approach who argued that while much that was good about Soviet foreign policy had been rejected, much that was bad had been retained. He argued that relations with Latin America, which he described as a dynamic region committed to diversification, were a priority for the new Russian emphasis on multilateralism.[69] During his first year as foreign minister, Primakov toured the region on a number of occasions, visiting Cuba, Mexico, Venezuela, Argentina, Brazil, Colombia, and Costa Rica.

Thus, rapprochement with Cuba was seen in Moscow as only one aspect of a broader initiative towards Latin America, a region with which Russian officials increasingly identified much in common. First, they saw it as an independent bloc in a multipolar world, with an interest in promoting diplomatic solutions through institutions such as the United Nations rather than supporting or acquiescing in U.S. hegemony. The role of Latin American countries in international affairs was increasing markedly, the Russians maintained, as their foreign policies started to transcend the previous emphasis on regional matters.[70] Primakov's successor as minister of Foreign Relations, Igor Ivanov, identified the Balkans crisis as the context in which Russians and Latin Americans became aware of their shared global perspectives.[71] Analogously, Latin American countries and Russia also agreed that globalization should not be abandoned to the transnational corporations, but that states could and should intervene to ensure that the process did not set in stone existing inequalities between more and less developed nations.[72] Second, Latin American economies were performing well after economic reforms and offered an attractive and dynamic market for Russian goods, especially in the aerospace, nuclear, and energy industries.[73] Third, the region offered practical demonstrations of successful economic integration projects such as the Mercosur trading bloc.

Finally, there were parallels in the recent history of Latin American countries and Russia, notably their experiences with redemocratization and economic reform. In the late 1990s and early 2000s, the journal of the Russian Academy of Sciences' Institute of Latin America regularly included articles analyzing the comparative politics of transition and the impact of globalization on Latin America. Russian experts focused special attention on the region's privatization policies, banking and financial reforms, social security reforms, and introduction of stocks and shares. There were also parallel foreign debt experiences: in February 2000, Russia successfully concluded negotiations with the London Club and later that year began talks with the Paris Club, having drawn on Latin America's experience of such negotiations.[74] There was also a sense that Russia could learn from Latin American models of conflict resolution—in Central America, between Chile and Argentina, Peru and Ecuador, Peru and Colombia—and from their policies against drug trafficking, organized crime and terrorism.[75]

Vladimir Putin, who became president on January 1, 1999, moved Russia's pro–Latin American policy up a gear: his own new approach to foreign relations included reference to the strengthening of political dialogue and cooperation with the region.[76] He took several steps to realize that new-found commitment during 2000, notably establishing personal contacts with Mexico's president, Ernesto Zedillo, Venezuela's Hugo Chávez, and Chile's Ricardo Lagos. Specifically in relation to Cuba, Putin's government took advantage of the occasion of the fortieth anniversary of the reestablishment of diplomatic relations between the two countries in May to emphasize Russia's rediscovered interest in developing relations "proceeding from long-term interests of our peoples, on the basis of respect and mutual benefit . . . especially in the trade and economic field."[77] In December 2000, Putin himself lent substance to these words by spending four days in Cuba on an official visit, the first to Latin America by a leader of the Russian Federation.

Both parties put some effort into the occasion. Putin stated shortly before setting off for Havana that Russia had mishandled relations with Cuba in the aftermath of the collapse of the Soviet Union.[78] He described Cuba as "an old friend and faithful partner" and stated that a revival of relations would be in Russia's economic interest, publicly acknowledging that Cuba had not been the only one to lose out from the abrupt cessation of economic ties in 1991–92: "Unfortunately for us, in the years when our economic contacts collapsed, many important aspects of our mutual activity were squandered, and the position of Russian enterprises was taken by foreign competitors."[79] He emphasized that he sought practical business deals to reestablish Russia's role in the Cuban market, which looked increasingly promising as the economy resumed growth after five very difficult years in the early 1990s. The Cuban government had adopted some economic reforms, abolishing the state monopoly over foreign trade, permitting the establishment of joint ventures with foreign capital, and opening up areas to free trade. Spanish and Canadian firms, in particular, had moved into the vacuum left by the U.S. embargo, and the Russians clearly hoped that they would be able to carve out a niche for their own companies, particularly given their history of economic and technical collaboration with Cuba. Unfinished projects from the Soviet era that the Russians hoped to revive were a nickel plant at Las Camariocas, oil refineries at Cienfuegos and Santiago, and the Juragua nuclear plant. Moscow was also interested in Cuba's increasingly successful biotechnology industry, having already signed a letter of intent in July 2000 to buy hepatitis B vaccine.[80]

Putin was met at the airport by Fidel, Defense Minister Raúl Castro, and Foreign Minister Felipe Pérez Roque. Billboards proclaimed "Welcome to Cuba, esteemed President of Russia." Afterwards, both leaders made moderately enthusiastic comments about their talks, Castro declaring that "a special boost" had been given to Russian-Cuban relations by Putin's visit.[81] Radio Havana included it as number eight on its list of the ten most important Cuban news items of the year.[82] In reality, however, little progress was made on the unresolved issues that preparatory talks had failed to settle. For the Cubans, the only concrete economic outcome of Putin's visit was the release of an outstanding $50 million credit for the development of the sugar industry, originally granted as part of the $350 million from 1993. The 1993–96 Agreement on Economic and Technical Cooperation was renewed for 2001. Other agreements were signed with respect to cooperation on legal matters such as extradition (replacing a 1984 agreement) and healthcare, the avoidance of double taxation, trade targets for 2001–05, and a project involving document collection to mark the centenary of Russia's recognition of the new Cuban Republic in 1902. The Cubans got what they were probably most interested in, namely a military cooperation agreement, signed on December 15, 2000, by Raúl Castro and the Russian defense minister Igor Dmitriyevich Sergeyev. No details are available, but the Cubans' main concern would have been to secure spare parts for their Soviet weaponry, particularly tanks and aircraft.[83]

There were no agreements on the uncompleted Soviet-era projects. The key case was Juragua, not least because of concerns about the safety of the plant, especially in the United States (any accident at Juragua could have a significant impact on Florida). Critics argued that the basic flaws in the design had been exacerbated by shoddy construction work and by the deterioration caused by inadequate mothballing after cessation of work on the plant in 1992. From 1995 onwards, both Russia and Cuba had been trying to form an international consortium to finance the remaining work on Juragua. But their efforts were stymied, largely because of pressure from the U.S. government. In June 1995, the annual foreign aid bill was amended by Cuban-American House member Ileana Ros-Lehtinen (R-Fla.) to cut $15 million of aid to Russia, as a shot across the bows to Moscow for its continuing involvement in Cuba's nuclear industry. The 1996 Helms-Burton Act specifically stated that the United States would regard making any nuclear power plant in Cuba operational as "an act of aggression which will be met with an appropriate response" and stipulated that aid should be reduced to any country that helped Cuba to build such a plant.[84] Opponents of Cuba's nuclear program were not confined to the Cuban exiles or conservative members of Congress: the Clinton administration was also against completion of the reactors, and urged other countries not to give the Cubans any technological help except in relation to safety.[85] At that stage, Cuba was not a signatory to the 1968 Nuclear Non-Proliferation Treaty; nor had it ratified the 1967 Treaty for the Prohibition of Nuclear Weapons in Latin America and the Caribbean (Treaty of Tlatelolco), which established Latin America as a zone free of nuclear weapons. Cuba signed up to Tlatelolco in 1995, but continued to maintain that the United States' occupation of Guantánamo Bay precluded it from ratifying the treaty.

Castro announced the "indefinite postponement" of work on Juragua in mid-January 1997. But Russia, which was seeking to establish itself in the small but highly competitive nuclear market, had an interest in not abandoning the project. In April, the Russians stated that they were continuing to look for an international consortium to finance the estimated $750 million needed to complete the plant, but early in 1998 the Cubans were saying publicly that such plans had been abandoned "fundamentally due to the policy of harassment by the U.S. government."[86] Both governments must have been hoping that Putin's visit would resolve the issue, but it did so, apparently, only by default. Shortly after Putin had gone home, *Granma* noted wearily that it made no sense to continue with Juragua, given the high costs, the low returns in energy, and that the Cubans were better off with their new gas-powered generator recently opened in Matanzas. The same applied to the nickel plant at Las Camariocas, begun in 1984 with the involvement of other former Comecon partners as well as the Soviet Union: the Cubans had come to the conclusion that it would be "more rational to extend the capacities of the plants we already have."[87]

The main reason that no agreements were reached was that the Russians sought to link reactivation of these projects with repayment of Cuba's Soviet debt. Putin apparently suggested to Castro that the debt could be swapped for Russian participation in joint ventures, but the Cuban government was unwilling to countenance the proposal. The Cubans, who after all have no spare resources available, have been stalling on the debt issue since November 1992, when it was first agreed that a joint working group would seek to resolve the problem. Their position is that most of the debt should be written off, on the basis that it was contracted to a state that no longer exists, under arrangements of international solidarity that are derided by the successor governments. They have also repeatedly pointed out that the damage caused to their economy by the collapse of the USSR can also be estimated in billions of dollars.[88]

It is, in any case, very difficult to calculate the value of the debt. Most of it was contracted in the transferable rubles used amongst members of Comecon, which are not easily measured against convertible currency. This problem is compounded by the fact that the difference between grant, loan, and subsidy was not always made clear in Soviet-Cuban agreements, the fudging of such issues often being the most convenient way to resolve tensions. Estimates of the amount owed by the Cubans vary from the $11 billion that the Cuban government has sometimes seemed prepared to accept to the $27 billion calculated by anti-Castro Russian parliamentarians. The Russian government claim is for twenty billion transferable rubles, which would be $690 million at today's exchange rate, but $11.8 billion in December 1991. In the press conference after the talks, Putin hinted at the problem of the debt: "The Soviet Union invested a lot in Cuba's economy. . . . This is worth billions of dollars. We have to understand what to do about this."[89] But the Cubans and the Russians simply do "not see eye to eye" on this matter.[90] Whatever the exact sum, the unresolved debt was the most significant impediment to the expansion of mutually beneficial trading ties.

Putin's visit to Cuba is best seen in the context of a series of initiatives to reestablish ties with former Soviet allies—earlier in the year he had established rapprochements with Libya, Iraq, and North Korea as part of a broader strategy of rebuilding a global role for Russia. Putin's approach to international relations consisted of "a complex synthesis of elements of the Soviet legacy, the now-revived diplomatic traditions of old Russia, and the new attitudes emerging from radical democratic changes both in the country and on the international scene."[91] He sought cooperation with the West, but not on any terms, pursuing a nimble strategy of advance and retreat to establish that Russia could not be taken for granted. Actions that could be perceived by Western allies as provocative were balanced by reassuring words and measures: Russian officials consistently sought to convince the United States that their continuing ties with Cuba were not intended as any challenge to Washington. In the late 2000 context of a disputed U.S. presidential election result, Putin pressed home his advantage. The joint declaration after his talks with Castro condemned the U.S. embargo and called for a multipolar world, but he also sent a message of congratulations to president-elect, George W. Bush, and later said that he hoped for positive relations with the new U.S. administration regardless of who was declared the winner of the disputed election. Just as he arrived in Cuba, he announced the release of a convicted American spy. All the signs seemed to be that one element of the Soviet legacy that the Russians were vigorously reviving was the old habit of using their connection with Cuba as a means of exerting leverage over Washington.

It thus came as a shock to the Cubans when Putin announced on October 17, 2001 that Russia was to cancel its lease on Lourdes, especially given his visit to the intelligence facility the previous December when he had talked about modernizing, not closing, the base. The decision, announced the same day as a new U.S. ambassador presented his credentials in Moscow and prior to Putin's meeting with Bush in Shanghai, was officially justified as a pragmatic reallocation of Russian military funds. Putin's desires to cut the military budget and to force the military to reform itself (so that, for example, it might be in a better position to defeat the Chechen insurgency) certainly cannot be doubted. His close political ally, Sergei Ivanov, was appointed defense minister in 2001 with a specific brief to persuade the armed forces to learn to live within their means.

The decision not to renew the lease on Cam Ranh Bay, announced at the same time as the withdrawal from Lourdes, was a clear signal to the Russian navy that it could no longer expect funding for its ambitions to play a strategic global role. (The Vietnamese government had not been charging any rent, but had announced its intention to do so when the lease came up for renewal in 2004.) Putin's meeting with military leaders in the Defense Ministry prior to the announcement of the two closures was described as "stormy." Afterwards, Russian general staff chief, Anatoly Kvashnin, stated that for the money the Russians paid for Lourdes ($90 million in 1992, $160 million a year from 1993 to 1995, and $200 million a year from 1996 onwards), they could fund twenty spy satellites and acquire up to 100 radar stations for the army.[92] Such figures were largely notional in terms of the Russian defense budget, however, since Cuba was paid for the base in barter, mostly spare parts for its Soviet-era military hardware and other machinery and equipment.[93] As part of its response to the Lourdes closure, the Cuban government made it public that Russian negotiators had sought to reduce the amount of rent paid by twenty-five percent to take into account the intelligence passed on to Havana. On August 17, 2001, the Cubans had officially offered to make a reduction of 12.5 percent; the next thing they heard, apparently, was the announcement of the closure.[94] There may also have been pressure on the Cubans to waive the rental altogether in part payment for Cuban debts to Moscow. Most of the savings from Russia's withdrawal from Lourdes (an estimated $300 million) came from no longer having to pay the estimated 1,500 engineers, technicians, and other personnel who worked there.

Many commentators, however, concurred with the Cuban government's interpretation of the Lourdes shutdown as a symptom of Moscow's revised priorities after the terrorist attacks on New York and Washington. Russia's continued presence there had been an issue rumbling around in Moscow's relations with Washington throughout the 1990s, without seriously affecting anything. The Clinton administration publicly accepted the Russian position that it needed the facility to monitor arms control agreements. Not surprisingly, however, Castro's opponents in Congress tried to exploit the issue: the Helms-Burton Act made provision for withholding an equivalent amount of aid from any former Soviet republic that extended a credit for the maintenance of intelligence facilities in Cuba, specifically mentioning the sum of $200 million granted for the modernization of Lourdes in late 1994.[95] In May 2000 the House of Representatives sought to enact this clause by voting to make debt rescheduling with Moscow contingent upon the closure of Lourdes, but the White House invoked a presidential waiver so that a deal made the previous year, enabling Russia to postpone the payment of $485 million of Soviet-era debts, could go ahead.

After 9/11, however, the Bush administration was ill disposed to allow its supposed allies any latitude. Putin expressed strong support for U.S. military action against the Taliban regime in Afghanistan, to the extent of pressuring former Soviet republics in Central Asia to grant American forces use of their air bases. But his claim to be behind Bush's antiterrorist coalition was made far more credible by his abandonment of two bases that were seen as vivid reminders of the Cold War, an assessment that was confirmed when President Bush responded by describing the decision as a sign that the Cold War was finally over. In the broad context of reshaping Russian foreign policy, Putin judged that the moment was ripe for a grand gesture in favor of partnership with the West in order to pave the way for new negotiations with the United States on debt rescheduling, investment, and Russia's request for admission to the World Trade Organization (WTO). His decision arose from an assessment that Russia could best consolidate its position in international affairs by means of integration, rather than confrontation, with the West. Putin also indicated that Russia might be willing to accept NATO expansion eastwards, a clear signal that Moscow sought to draw a line under the events of 1999, when NATO intervention against the Serb presence in Kosovo had alienated Moscow. In the aftermath of 9/11, the Russian government had everything to gain and little to lose by closing facilities intended to monitor U.S. compliance with treaties—such as the Anti-Ballistic Missile Treaty—that it was, in any case, unilaterally proposing to abrogate. Once again, Cuban interests were sacrificed.

The Cuban government insisted, in a relatively muted statement, that in fact "the agreement has not been cancelled, since Havana has yet to give its approval."[96] The Cubans felt betrayed, justifiably so, and a couple of Russian plane loads of canned meat and condensed milk—sent as humanitarian aid after Hurricane Michelle—were hardly adequate compensation. Ironically enough, the Lourdes station was originally built by the Soviets in 1964 as part of a package of measures to rebuild relations with Cuba after the October 1962 Missile Crisis, which was the first, but far from the last, time when Kremlin leaders took a decision over the heads of the Cubans. By the late 1990s, the intelligence gathered there was far more significant to Cuban national security than to the Russians. It was the final element of substantive Russian support for the Cuban Revolution's struggle to defend itself against aggression from the United States. In symbolic terms, moreover, the decision was disastrous for Cuba, which is clearly highly vulnerable in the context of a U.S.-declared and U.S.-defined "war on terror."

A Sweet Deal Sours

Today, Russia's main interest in Latin America—and Cuba is now seen as just one hemispheric country among others—is economic, but the development of commercial ties beyond the basic exchange of oil for sugar is in practice a relatively low priority, for both sides. Russian foreign minister Igor Ivanov warned national companies that they should expect no special favors in Cuba: they would have to compete for the Cuban market like everybody else.[97] This was only the logical consequence (and it is not hard to imagine Castro calmly pointing it out) of the "de-ideologization" of relations.

As was the case during the Cold War, constraints on expansion of trade derive primarily from logistical difficulties on both sides. Technically, of course, the possibilities for communication have improved beyond all recognition since the days—as late as 1980—when a telephone call to Moscow had to be booked twenty-four hours in advance, but numerous obstacles remain. Both economies are notorious for interruptions in production: for example, Russian oil production was in decline in the mid-1990s; Cuba's sugar crop, often for reasons beyond its control, is unpredictable. Joint enterprises are promoted in official statements as a promising line of development, as they have been regularly since the early 1980s, but the financing of such initiatives remains a major problem. In the late 1990s, there was only one Russian bank with a branch in Latin America (in Buenos Aires); only two out of more than 100 foreign banks in Moscow were Latin American.[98] This state of affairs makes the collection of payment and the arrangement of credit difficult. Russian Central Bank stipulations about ninety days on payment for foreign trade transactions also impede the development of relations (Western firms customarily allow at least 125 days, sometimes 365). There has been talk of a Russian-Latin American bank, but so far it has been only talk. Furthermore, the lack of facilities makes it harder for Russian companies to offer guarantees, carry out repairs on equipment sold, or supply spare parts.

Russian companies are notoriously weak at adapting their products, presale, to meet local requirements.[99] There is a lack of exchange of commercial information and far less coverage of Cuban affairs in general than before 1991—and what there is tends to be critical. The reduced number of specialists at the Institute of Latin America in Moscow analyze comparative processes of market reform and transition to democracy in the major Latin American republics, not Cuban affairs.[100] Overall, the infrastructure for the development of significant, lasting trading relationships is absent. In any case, the Cubans, who have lived for decades with the consequences of shoddy Soviet equipment, are not particularly interested in doing business with Russian companies. Recent articles on trade fairs in Havana give prominence to European and Canadian partners; China and Australia are also celebrated, with only passing mention made of Russia, the Czech Republic, and Poland.[101]

Meanwhile, the unresolved debt issue drags on, hindering not only Russian-Cuban relations but Cuba's international creditworthiness. In early 2001, Cuba had almost reached a deal with its Western creditors over restructuring of $3.5 billion of its medium- and long-term $11 billion hard currency debt (dating back to the 1980s default), when Russia, which became a member of the Paris Club in 1997, tried to insist on being included. Cuba had embarked on the negotiations on the explicit understanding that the Russian debt would be excluded, and Moscow agreed at that time to discuss the matter bilaterally, but changed tack when they found that they could still not shift the Cubans. In late 2001, the intergovernmental commission was reported to be working on a draft agreement by which Cuba would pay in goods and "service provision,"[102] but by 2003 Russian officials were acknowledging publicly that they had no idea when or even if the Cubans would agree to commence repayments.[103] It is telling about the extent to which Cuba became a symbol of all that was bad about Soviet foreign policy that in 1997 Moscow scaled down Vietnam's debt from about $17 billion to $3.7 billion, but has not been prepared to make similar concessions to Cuba. Cuba also owed an estimated $2.2 million to the former Czechoslovakia and East Germany, which the Czech Republic and Germany have largely absorbed.

In these circumstances, regular statements will probably still be made about the desire of both parties to diversify their trade, but little of substance is likely to be agreed on, let alone implemented. Neither economy is really strong enough to permit it. As President Putin has publicly acknowledged, during the 1990s Russia concentrated its efforts on political rather than economic reform (in contrast to China), with the result that attempts to introduce flexibility often led instead to instability and corruption.[104] In Cuba, as the government itself has stated, economic growth in the late 1990s "has still not compensated for the abrupt downturn occasioned by the collapse of the former Eastern European socialist bloc."[105] The Cubans know that they must secure supplies from other sources whenever the opportunity presents itself, and they have worked assiduously to reduce their dependence on Russian oil—highlighted by an October 2000 agreement with Venezuela under which the island economy was guaranteed 53,000 barrels per day in return for services, medical technologies, and cash.

What does remain of the pre-1991 Russian-Cuban trading relationship is the exchange of oil for sugar, for which there is still an economic rationale. Despite all the missed deadlines and mutual recriminations, the bottom line is that Cuban sugar is cheap; a chain of refining and distribution is in place that complements domestic sugar beet production; and Russia, with its extensive refining capacity, will continue to seek imports of raw sugar rather than pay the premium for the refined product.[106]

In the longer term, however, even this degree of reciprocity is in jeopardy. Cuban infrastructure and institutions remain ill equipped to deal with the complexities of the Russian sugar market as it emerged during the 1990s. Instead of a single state agency, as in the USSR, at least twelve sugar-trading companies now operate in Russia, both Russian- and European-based. Sugar remains such a politically sensitive commodity, however, that the state regularly intervenes in a variety of ways: allocating tenders for quotas of sugar imports, offering or withdrawing financial guarantees, and erratically imposing higher duties to protect the Russian sugar beet growers. Each year, depending on the prospects for the domestic sugar beet harvest, there is a race to sell imports at high prices before supplies of sugar beet bring the price down. The Cuban government had hoped that its state-to-state oil-for-sugar barter deals might insulate it from such pressures, but this did not prove to be the case.[107] Trade targets were established in the 2000 agreements, but the two parties are set for an annual round of fraught negotiations over relative prices for oil and sugar. Cuban sugar is likely to be sold to Russia for the foreseeable future (about two million tonnes was sent per year in 1999, 2000, and 2001) but not on any basis that would enable the Cubans to reinvest in their industry.

In 2002, given the absence of prospects for a viable long-term market in Russia, the Cuban government finally decided that conditions in the world sugar market were so adverse that it was no longer worth their while to try to compete in it. On both the supply and demand sides the picture looked bleak. The main factor was the rise of new producers, notably Brazil, which is now dominant in the export market and has the potential to swamp it completely.[108] This means that low prices are likely to persist for the foreseeable future. In such conditions, countries like Cuba, suffering acutely from long-term underinvestment, are most at risk. Here the effects of the Helms-Burton Act are starkly visible: several major international sugar traders offered prefinancing deals to fund the Cuban sugar harvest in 1995, but most withdrew or restricted their operations in Cuba after 1996.

In terms of markets, overall prospects are also highly discouraging. In addition to all Cuba's specific problems with Russia, by 2002 sugar trade analysts were arguing that "In the longer run, the trend towards gradual toughening up of the Russian sugar regime is well readable and further reductions in sugar imports can be projected."[109] East European countries have largely recovered from the dislocation of the early 1990s and expanded their own production to minimize imports. Bulgaria and Romania are now matching beet production to consumption. Poland has converted itself into the third largest European producer after France and Germany. Former Soviet republics such as Kazakhstan and Kyrgyzstan intermittently purchased Cuban sugar during the 1990s, but only in small quantities, and all such governments are seeking to replace those imports one way or another. In September 2000, Cuba signed a ten-year Friendship and Cooperation Treaty with Byelorussia, along with a trade agreement based on the exchange of fertilizers, tractors, and spare parts for sugar.[110] Early in 2003, the two countries agreed to optimize production at a joint sugar refinery; again, though, the quantities involved are relatively small. Far more significantly, Cuba entertained some hopes that China might replace Russia as a secure market for most of its crop,[111] but it, too, seems to have recovered well from a shortfall in production of 2000–01, thwarting the perennial speculation amongst sugar traders that China is about to become a major net importer.[112] The European Union (EU) is itself an exporter, and even if an eventual reform of agricultural policy reduces subsidies, East European suppliers, themselves potential EU members, would be most likely to fill any gap. In the face of all these obstacles, the Cuban government announced a restructuring of the sugar industry to concentrate on sugar by-products and domestic consumption. In 2003, Cuba's sugar harvest—at 2.2 million tonnes—was its lowest for seventy years, raising severe doubts about its capacity to meet Russia's requirements.

Conclusion

In political terms, Cuban-Russian relations appear to have settled down at a relatively low level. On human rights, the Russian Federation's support at the UNHRC has been reliable since 1996—even in 1999, when Cuba's new Law for the Protection of the Cuban National Independence and the Economy, stipulating lengthy jail terms for anyone deemed to be a dissident, meant that Cuba lost the vote again, having won it the previous year.[113] In early 2000, Russia came down on the right side, from Havana's point of view, in the highly sensitive case of Elián González when it called for his return to Cuba. In April 2003, the Russian government declined to join the EU and long-standing Cuban sympathizer Mexico in condemning the Castro regime for arresting and imprisoning seventy-five dissidents and for executing three leaders of a group that hijacked a ferry in a bid to get to the U.S. mainland.

East European states, however, have been highly critical of Cuba. In April 2000, the Czech Republic and Poland jointly sponsored a motion censuring Cuba, which was passed, as in the previous year. When the United States lost its seat on the UNHRC in 2001, the Czech Republic assumed the mantle of introducing an annual resolution condemning Cuba's human rights record. The Cuban government, unsurprisingly, is suspicious of its former allies: in May 2000, *Granma* denounced a Polish delegation to Havana—supposedly there to discuss scientific-technical collaboration—for meeting "counterrevolutionaries."[114] The following January, two Czechs were arrested in Cuba for "encouraging internal subversion" on behalf of the U.S. organization Freedom

House.[115] In a move widely interpreted as retaliation for Czech actions in the UNHRC the previous year, the Cuban government announced that the two Czechs would be put on trial for subversion, rather than merely deported as would be the usual outcome of such incidents. The matter was resolved after the two men read out a signed statement at Cuba's Foreign Ministry, admitting that they had—unwittingly—broken Cuban law by meeting dissidents.[116] Partly as a result of all these tensions, Cuba's trade with the East European countries has virtually ceased (see Appendix, Table 1), although Havana buys spare parts as and when it can.

One consistent element in Moscow's policy towards Cuba is its continued support for the lifting of the U.S. economic embargo and the normalization of U.S.-Cuban relations. Russian foreign policy experts interpret Washington's determination to maintain the sanctions in place, which they repeatedly assert is "contrary to the interests of the United States itself and of U.S. business," as primarily the result of internal politics.[117] Russian officials insisted throughout the 1990s that Cuba no longer represented any security threat to the United States; after the Russian withdrawal from Lourdes, the claim became even more credible.[118] Moscow has probably been seeking to reassure the Bush administration that Cuba—sometimes included in the "axis of evil," sometimes not—does not pose a threat either in terms of terrorism or weapons of mass destruction. After former U.S. president Jimmy Carter had been taken on a tour of Cuba's biological research laboratories in 2002, the Russian foreign minister issued a statement to the effect that "the goodwill of the Cuban government [in giving Carter] free access to biological facilities, should eliminate all U.S. concerns about any possible biological weapons programs pursued by Cuba."[119] The Russians took the opportunity to endorse Carter's view that it was time to normalize U.S.-Cuban relations and to lift the embargo.

The two nations can find common cause in resisting Pax Americana, although since Cuba's term on the United Nations Security Council (UNSC) ended, its views carry far less weight. In any case, the united position is tactical rather than strategic, for the Cubans have little to lose by digging their heels in, while the Russians have a number of pressing reasons to make an accommodation with U.S. wishes when it comes to the crunch. If the two countries took a radically opposed stance on the U.S. war against the Taliban regime in Afghanistan, Putin's reluctance to support the Bush administration's commitment to regime change in Iraq brought Moscow and Havana closer together again. Autumn 2002 saw a series of joint statements opposing the use of force against Iraq and calling for the strengthening of the United Nations as a force for peace. Russia and Cuba declared themselves to be particularly "alarmed by strategies and doctrines that appeared recently trying to justify unilateral military actions in circumvention of the UN Security Council."[120] In a distant echo of Cold War collaboration, an account of a recent vote at the International

Atomic Energy Agency to refer North Korea to the UNSC for being in breach of the international body's nuclear safeguards noted that "Russia and Cuba abstained."[121] Russian-Cuban discussions of such matters tend to take place at the level of first deputy foreign minister or below; in other words, both countries grant moderate, but not great, significance to their exchanges.

For the foreseeable future, the Russian government is committed to integration with the West—even Moscow's adamant opposition to the U.S.-led imposition of "regime change" in Iraq in March-April 2003 was followed by a concerted effort (on both sides) to pave over the damage done to bilateral relations. The Russians may occasionally "play the Cuba card," just to remind Washington that their support cannot be taken for granted, but all concerned know that this is largely an empty gesture given that Russia no longer has any strategic interest in the island. Moscow would prefer the United States to normalize relations with Cuba; Washington would like Moscow to exert its remaining leverage to pressure Castro to implement political reforms—but the two governments are likely to agree to differ on this issue, accepting that even if either of them were willing to budge, then Castro certainly is not. For their part, the Cubans have no reason to trust the Russians. Their predicament of increasing economic and political isolation means that they have little choice but to take allies as they find them, but their expectations are unlikely to extend much beyond preserving an exchange of moderate quantities of oil for sugar. Mojitos may have become fashionable in Moscow recently, and the city has recently acquired its very own Club Che, but the vast Russian Soviet-era embassy on Havana Bay is likely to remain underoccupied indefinitely.[122]

Notes

1. From different perspectives, the following authors all tell much the same story: Jan S. Adams, *A Foreign Policy in Transition: Moscow's Retreat from Central America and the Caribbean, 1985–1992* (Durham: Duke University Press, 1992), chapter 4; H. Michael Erisman, *Cuba's Foreign Relations in a Post-Soviet World* (Gainesville: University Press of Florida, 2000), chapter 5; Carmelo Mesa-Lago, ed., *Cuba After the Cold War* (Pittsburgh: Pittsburgh University Press, 1993), chapters 2 and 3; Wayne S. Smith, ed., *The Russians Aren't Coming: New Soviet Policy in Latin America* (Boulder: Lynne Rienner, 1992); Yuri Pavlov, *Soviet-Cuban Alliance: 1959–1991* (New Brunswick: Transaction, 1994). Pavlov, who was head of the Soviet Foreign Ministry's Latin American Directorate from 1987 to 1990, gives the most detailed and revealing account.

2. It was thirty months from November 1959, when Castro first issued an invitation to leading politburo member Anastas Mikoyan to visit the island, to May 1962, when Cuba was included in the Soviet May Day slogans as a member of the socialist community; it was thirty months from President Gorbachev's visit to Havana in April 1989 to his surprising announcement of the withdrawal of Soviet troops in September 1991.

3. The publication of such a low figure was largely intended to silence public con-

cern. In practice, scope remained for high subsidies to Cuba and other allies in the 26.4 billion rubles allocated in the budget for "financing of foreign trade" (see Ye Arefyeva, "Mysterious Line in the Budget-Specialist's Thoughts on One Area of Our Foreign Ties," *Izvestiya*, January 9, 1990, 7, in *Current Digest of the Soviet Press*, February 14, 1990).

4. For a good summary of the effects of the disintegration of the USSR on the Cuban economy, see Andrew Zimbalist, "Teetering on the Brink: Cuba's Current Economic and Political Crisis," *Journal of Latin American Studies* 24, no.2 (May 1992): 407–18. Also see Susan Eva Eckstein, *Back From the Future: Cuba Under Castro* (Princeton: Princeton University Press, 1994), especially chapter 4; Archibald R. Ritter and John M. Kirk, eds., *Cuba in the International System* (U.K.: Macmillan, Basingstoke, 1995); Max Azicri, *Cuba Today and Tomorrow: Reinventing Socialism* (Gainesville: University Press of Florida, 2000), especially chapter 2.

5. Section 205(a)(7) of the 1996 Cuban Liberty and Democratic Solidarity (Helms-Burton) Act specifies that the United States will not accept any Cuban government with either Fidel Castro or his brother Raúl in it, even a transitional government.

6. Mijaíl Braguin, "¿Qué factores entorpecen la cooperación económica ruso-latinoamericana?," *Iberoamérica* (Moscow), nos. 1–2 (2001): 174.

7. Nicolai N. Petro and Alvin Z. Rubinstein, *Russian Foreign Policy: From Empire to Nation-State* (New York: Longman, 1997), 230.

8. Mikhail Gorbachev and Zdenek Mlynar, *Conversations with Gorbachev* (New York: Columbia University Press, 2002), 88–89. Yuri Pavlov confirms the view that Gorbachev was committed both to preserving Soviet friendship with Cuba and to avoiding intimidation of a weaker ally (*Soviet-Cuban Alliance*, 131). Castro did his inimitable best to strengthen Gorbachev's resolve by keeping up a constant stream of assertions to the effect that "Comrade Gorbachev . . . came to our country not in order to tell anybody . . . what to do or what not to do. That . . . is the remarkable thing about Comrade Gorbachev" (Castro/Gorbachev news conference, Moscow TV, April 5, 1989, in *Foreign Broadcast Information Service: SOV-89-064* [hereafter FBIS], April 5, 1989, 26–27).

9. Fidel Castro interviewed by Tomás Borge, *El Nuevo Diario* (Managua), in *FBIS: LAT-92-109*, June 5, 1992, 19–21.

10. See Vladislav Chirkov, "How Are Things, Compañeros?," *New Times*, January 1987, 18–19; "An Uphill Task," *New Times*, August 1987; and Carlos Rafael Rodríguez, "A Difficult But Steady Ascent," *New Times*, October 19, 1987, 16–17 (a reply published at Cuba's insistence). Castro's speeches during 1988 were particularly outspoken. See, for example, his Moncada anniversary speech, July 26, 1988, in *Granma Weekly Edition*, August 7, 1988, 4, when he condemned "mechanisms . . . smacking of capitalism."

11. Fidel Castro, interviewed in *El Sol de México*, February 3, 1995, 1, 20.

12. "Our fear [is] that imperialism, as it has done so many times . . . will understand peace to mean peace between the great powers, reserving for itself the right to oppress, exploit, threaten and attack the countries of the Third World. It might be Nicaragua one day, Cuba the next, another day some other third world country" (Fidel Castro, "En el

acto central por el XXX aniversario del triunfo de la Revolución Cubana," January 4, 1989, in *Cuba Socialista* (Havana) 37 (January–February 1989): 58 (my translation).

13. "A Unique Document—To Whom Have We 'Loaned' 85.8 Billion Rubles," *Izvestiya*, March 1, 1990, 3, in *Current Digest of the Soviet Press*, April 4, 1990. Cuba was listed as owing 15.5 billion rubles; second-placed Vietnam owed 9.1 billion rubles.

14. Valery Nikolayenko, "An Official Statement of the New Soviet Policy in Latin America," in Smith, ed., *The Russians Aren't Coming*, 61.

15. A famous exchange along these lines took place in *Moscow News*, which became an important forum for debate about Soviet foreign policy (see Andrei Kortunov, "Soviet Foreign Aid: Is it Always Put to the Wisest Use?," *Moscow News*, no. 49, December 3, 1989, 6; Sergei Tarasenko, "About Sugar with a Bitter Taste," *Moscow News*, no. 52, December 31, 1989, 6; Sergo Mikoyan, "Whom Do We Help Now?," *Moscow News*, no. 7, February 18, 1990, 13).

16. Sergo Mikoyan, "The Future of the Soviet-Cuban Relationship," in Smith, ed., *The Russians Aren't Coming*, 19.

17. Ibid., 124.

18. Fidel Castro, speech to the Fifth Congress of the National Agricultural, Livestock and Forestry Workers Union, Havana, November 22, 1991, in *FBIS: LAT-91-230*, November 29, 1991, 7–21, paragraph 38.

19. On oil, see Azicri, *Cuba Today and Tomorrow*, 34. On sugar, see Nicola Miller, *Soviet Relations with Latin America, 1959–1987* (Cambridge: Cambridge University Press, 1989), 101–2.

20. Leonid Abalkin, "We Value Our Friendship with Cuba," interview, *Pravda*, April 20, 1990, 6, in *Current Digest of the Soviet Press*, May 23, 1990.

21. *New York Times*, September 13, 1990.

22. Pavlov, *Soviet-Cuban Alliance*, 123.

23. For an account of the negotiations, see Geoffrey Berridge, "Diplomacy and the Angola/Namibia Accords," *International Affairs* 65, no.3 (Summer 1989), 463–80. Also see Tad Szulc, "The Cuban Catch in Angola Peace Terms," *Los Angeles Times*, July 24, 1988, 1, 3.

24. James A. Baker III, *The Politics of Diplomacy* (New York: G. P. Putnam's Sons, 1995), 47–48.

25. Ibid., 48.

26. Ibid., 53.

27. Ibid., 59. See also Bush and Gorbachev's joint press conference after the Malta Summit, "Question-and-Answer Session with Reporters in Malta," December 3 1989, in *Public Papers of the Presidents of the United States: George Bush, 1989*, book II (Washington, D.C.: GPO, 1990), 1636.

28. Pavlov, *Soviet-Cuban Alliance*, 147.

29. Ibid., 147–48.

30. Ibid., 149.

31. Ibid., 152.

32. Mikhail Gorbachev, *Memoirs* (London: Transworld Publishers, 1995, trans. 1997), 662, 699. George Bush also recalls that at the Malta Summit Gorbachev "made

a strong pitch for me to talk to Castro" (quoted in *All the Best, George Bush: My Life in Letters and Other Writings* (New York: Touchstone, 2000), 447.

33. Mikoyan, "Soviet-Cuban Relationship," 132.

34. Baker, *Politics of Diplomacy*, 529.

35. Ibid., 322.

36. Yuri Pavlov notes: "If a Soviet diplomat or technician on a mission to Cuba needed major surgery, he would use all his 'connections' to have it done in a Cuban hospital with modern medical equipment imported from the West rather than go to Moscow" (*Soviet-Cuban Alliance*, 125).

37. See, for example, Castro's speech on the 30th anniversary of the Committees for the Defense of the Revolution, Havana, September 29, 1990: "Even amid its problems and difficulties, [the Soviet government] has made great efforts to meet its commitments to our country" (*FBIS: LAT-90-190*, October 1, 1990, 1–16, paragraph 37).

38. Pavlov, *Soviet-Cuban Alliance*, 186.

39. Ibid., 187.

40. Estervino Montesino Segui, "The Cuban Perspective on Cuban-Soviet Relations," in Smith, ed., *The Russians Aren't Coming*, 146.

41. The text of the treaty is available in *FBIS: SOV-89-064*, April 5, 1989, 49–50 and *Granma International*, April 16, 1989, 5.

42. Pavlov, *Soviet-Cuban Alliance*, 262.

43. Yuri Pavlov, "Russian Policy Toward Latin America and Cuba," in *Russian Foreign Policy Since 1990*, ed. Peter Shearman (Boulder: Westview Press, 1995), 258.

44. Ibid., 259.

45. For a vivid account of the difficulties caused by the inability to acquire spare parts, see Castro's speech at the Fifth National Spare Parts Forum, Havana, December 15, 1990, in *FBIS: LAT-90-245*, December 18, 1990, 1–12.

46. Radio Havana, May 12, 1999, <www.radiohc.org>.

47. Report by the Federation of American Scientists, "Cuba's Nuclear Reactors at Juragua" and "History of the Cuban Commercial Nuclear Program—Timeline: 1987," September 2, 1999, available <http://www.fas.org/nuke/guide/cuba/main.html>.

48. Castro, speech to the Juragua power plant workers, Cienfuegos, September 2, 1992, in *FBIS: LAT-92-177*, September 11, 1992, 3–7.

49. "Nuclear Safety: Concerns with the Nuclear Power Reactors in Cuba," study by the U.S. General Accounting Office, August 1, 1995 (quoted in Scott Parrish, *Russia, Cuba, and the Juragua Nuclear Plant*, Center for Nonproliferation Studies, Monterrey Institute of International Studies, <www.nti.org/db/nisprofs/over/juragua/htm>).

50. Pavlov, "Russian Policy" 62.

51. For a survey of the Russian sugar market, see Jonathan Kingsman, ed., *Sugar Trading Manual* (Cambridge: Woodhead Publishing, 2000), section on CIS by Jan de Walden of Tate and Lyle and Vladimir Mkrtoumian of STELS Limited. During the Soviet era, and into the early 1990s too, figures for consumption were almost certainly exaggerated, for they were based on monitoring distribution rather than sales.

52. Ibid., section 2, 15: total Soviet sugar production in 1990 was over nine million tonnes, five million of which came from the Ukraine; in 1997 the former Soviet Union

(FSU) countries produced just over four million tonnes—a contraction of fifty-five percent.

53. Licht's *International Sugar and Sweetener Report*, January 23, 1992, 76–77.

54. Miller, *Soviet Relations*, 74–75.

55. International Sugar Organization (hereafter ISO), *Statistical Bulletin*, December 1994, 10, table 11.

56. Vladimir Shumeiko, cited in Leonid Velekhov, "Full Circle: Mr. Shumeiko Finds Golden Mean in Relations with Cuba," *Sevodnya*, December 29, 1993, 3, in *Current Digest of the Post-Soviet Press*, January 26, 1994.

57. *Latinskaia Amerika*, nos. 10–11 (1992): 54–57. Yermakov was deputy head of the Russian Foreign Ministry's Department of Central and South America.

58. Yevgeny Bai, "Russian Military Considers Castro Brothers Allies," *Izvestiya*, November 30, 1993, 3, in *Current Digest of the Soviet Press*, December 29, 1993.

59. Pavlov, *Soviet-Cuban Alliance*, 264.

60. Leonid Velekhov, "Russia-Cuba Relations: The Primacy of 'Ideology,'" *Perspective VI*, no. 4, (March-April 1996): 2 (see Boston University Institute for the Study of Conflict, Ideology, and Policy, <www.bu.edu/iscip/vol6/Velekhov.html>).

61. Leonid Velekhov, "Old Friends: Russians and Cubans—It Seems They Are Brothers Forever After All," *Sevodnya*, December 22, 1993, 3, in *Current Digest of the Post-Soviet Press*, January 19, 1994.

62. Licht's *International Sugar and Sweetener Report*, January 19, 1994, 70–71.

63. Yevgeny Bai, "Moscow Avoids Quarrel with Cuba by Signing Treaty that Can't Be Implemented," *Izvestiya*, December 28, 1993, 3, in *Current Digest of the Post-Soviet Press*, January 26, 1994; Licht's *International Sugar and Sweetener Report*, January 6, 1994, 39.

64. Reuters, "Cuba to Satisfy Russia Sugar Demand in 1995–6," January 10, 1995, in ISO, *Market Report*, January 1995, 7.

65. "Sugar in Russia is the Most Expensive in the World," *Moscow News*, no. 6, February 11–17, 1994, 9.

66. Fidel Castro, interviewed in *El Sol de México*, February 3, 1995.

67. "Relations with Russia Strengthened," *Granma International*, October 25, 1995, 4.

68. For a summary, see Leonid Gankin, "Primakov's Campaign Speech," *Moscow News*, no. 25, June 27–July 3, 1996, 5. For more details, see Evgeny Primakov, *Godui v bolshoy politike* (Moscow: Sovershenno Sekretno, 1999).

69. See an interview with Primakov, "Vemos con optimismo las perspectivas de las relaciones con América Latina," *América Latina* (Moscow), no.2 (3), 1996, 5–8.

70. Igor Ivanov, "Rusia y América Latina: relaciones de cara al futuro," *Iberoamérica*, nos. 1–2 (2001): 157.

71. Igor Ivanov, "Rusia y América Latina: La distancia geográfica no separa a los pueblos," *Iberoamérica*, no. 4 (1999): 5.

72. Interview with Ivan D. Ivanov, vice-minister of Foreign Relations, in *Iberoamérica*, no. 1 (2000): 6.

73. Alexander Sizonenko, "Por qué tenemos interés por América Latina," ibid., 14.

74. Víctor Semionov, "La deuda externa de Rusia y América Latina: problemas, tendencias y perspectives," *Iberoamérica*, no. 3 (2001): 97–108. Also see Semionov and Lev Klochkovsky, "External Debt Management in Latin America and Its Relevance to Russia," in *Latin American and East European Economies in Transition: A Comparative View*, ed. Claude Auroi (London: Frank Cass, 1998), 8–28.

75. Sizonenko, "Por qué tenemos," 13.

76. Ivanov, " Rusia y América Latina: relaciones," 155.

77. Letter from Russian foreign minister Igor Ivanov to Cuban foreign minister Felipe Pérez Roque (quoted, in "Cuba is Russia's Important Partner—Ivanov," *Itar-Tass Report*, <www.freerepublic.com/forum/a391461fd0179.htm>.

78. Quoted in "Putin to Visit Russia's Former Cold War Ally Cuba," *Reuters*, December 12, 2000.

79. Quoted in "Putin Pledges Deeper Economic Ties with Cuba, Latin America," *Associated Press*, December 12, 2000.

80. Patricia Grogg, "Russia-Cuba Trade Ties," *DAWN* (Pakistan), July 19, 2000, <www.DAWN.com/2000/07/19/int16.htm>.

81. Quoted in "Russia and Cuba Relive Old Times in Shadow of Debt," *Reuters*, December 16, 2000, <www.indianexpress.com/ie/daily/20001216/iin16019.html>.

82. "Las diez noticias cubanas más importantes del 2000," Radio Havana, December 26, 2000.

83. Analisi Difesa (Italian defense analysts), "Cuba Signs Military Agreements with Russia and China," n.d., probably late December 2000, <www.analisidifesa.it/numero 10/eng/cinacubaeng.htm>. Cuba signed a military agreement with China at about the same time.

84. See Sections 101 (3), 106, and, specifically on Juragua, 111 of the Helms-Burton Act.

85. Parrish, *Juragua Nuclear Plant*.

86. Cuban trade minister Ricardo Cabrisas, quoted in *Miami Herald*, February 23, 1998.

87. Arsenio Rodríguez, "Prevaleció la voluntad política," *Granma*, December 19, 2001, <www.granma.cubaweb.cu/temas7/articulo201.html>.

88. *Reuters*, "Russia and Cuba Relive Old Times."

89. Quoted ibid.

90. Oleg D. Davydov, *Inside Out: The Radical Transformation of Russian Foreign Trade, 1992–1997* (New York: Fordham University Press, 1998), 169.

91. Quoted in Igor Ivanov, "The New Russian Identity: Innovation and Continuity in Russian Foreign Policy," *Washington Quarterly* 24, no. 3 (Summer 2001): 12.

92. Richard Balmforth, "Russia Ends Cold War Chapter by Quitting Cuban Spy Base," *Johnson's Russia List*, October 18, 2001, <www.cdi.org/russia/johnson/5496-1.cfm>.

93. Jon Boyle, "Analysis—Cuban Base Closure a Sea Change in Russian Strategy," *Johnson's Russia List*, October 18, 2001, available <http://www.cdi.org/russia/johnson/5497-1.cfm>. Pavlov also says that the rent was spare parts for weapons (see *Soviet-Cuban Alliance*, 262).

94. Editorial, "Una obligada respuesta," *Granma*, October 6, 2001.

95. Section 106 (d). A presidential right of waiver is written into the act.

96. "Declaración oficial del Gobierno de la República de Cuba," *Granma*, October 17, 2001.

97. Ivanov, "Rusia y América Latina: relaciones," 163.

98. Petro and Rubinstein, *Russian Foreign Policy*, 233.

99. Braguin, "¿Qué factores entorpecen?," 167.

100. Vladimir Davydov, "El Instituto de Latinoamérica en el contexto de la latinoamericanística nacional y mundial," *Iberoamérica*, no.1–2 (2001): 8–22, especially 13–14 on developments after 1991.

101. *Granma International*, November 5, 2000, 9; special supplement, September 2001 (n.d.); and November 10, 2002.

102. "Moscow and Havana agree on Cuban debt payment," *Pravda*, November 30, 2001, available <englishpravda.ru/world/2001/11/30/22600.html>.

103. See, for example, the speech by Deputy Prime Minister and Finance Minister Alexei Kudrin to the Duma, quoted in "About One Billion Dollars Return to Russia Annually," *Pravda*, April 25, 2003, available <englishpravda.ru/main/2003/04/25/46383.html>.

104. "Anti-Terror Support, but Putin is all Business," October 19, 2001, *CNN.com*, <www.cnn.com/2001/BUSINESS/asia/10/19/putin.apec/>.

105. Raisa Pages, "Economic Stability Over Last Five Years," *Granma International*, January 1, 2001, 11.

106. Cuban sugar cane is processed by Russian refineries after the national sugar beet harvest is over, with no interruption in production (see Russian Federation ambassador to Cuba, Andrei Dmitriev, "Concrete Steps in Cuban-Russian Relations," *Granma*, August 27, 2000, 6).

107. In April 1996, for example, ships carrying Cuban sugar were held up in the Black Sea for nearly a month while the Russian import company, Alfa-Eko, sought to drive down the price in order to compensate for the combination of high world oil prices and low prices for refined sugar flooding into Russia from the Ukraine. By early 1997, it was clear that the barter deal had gone sour as a result of the uncomfortable mixture of market economy principles and residual communist practices. An attempt to revive it in 1999, at the lower level of 1.5 million tonnes of oil for 800,000 tonnes of sugar, quickly reached an impasse, with the Russian Ministry of Fuel and Energy stating that no more oil would be sent to Cuba until proper contracts were issued in relation to both oil and sugar (see *Reuters*, "Market Forces Pressure Russian Oil—Cuba Sugar Deal," January 29, in ISO, *Market Report*, January 1997, 8; Licht's *International Sugar and Sweetener Report*, May 21, 1999, 275, and June 25, 1999, 334.

108. In 1990, Brazil produced 8 million tonnes of sugar and exported 1.6 million tonnes. In 1998 it produced 18 million and exported 8.2 million. It is by far the world's largest sugar producer.

109. ISO, *Market Report*, August 2002, ii.

110. Mireya Castañeda, "A Treaty of Solid and Sincere Friendship," *Granma International*, September 10, 2000, 5.

111. In April 2001, Cuba and China signed eight trade accords, including a commitment by the Chinese to modernize Cuba's telephone system and a $150-million credit

for Cuba to purchase Chinese television sets. On an official visit to Havana, Chinese president Jiang Zemin affected to be blithely unperturbed by a continuing dispute with the United States about spy planes. A Chinese foreign policy expert said in Beijing: "By improving ties with Cuba . . . Beijing wants to send Washington the message that it cannot be pushed around" (quoted in "Reports of Cuba Shipments Could Hurt Sino-U.S. Ties," *Associated Press*, June 12, 2001, <www.cnn.com/2001/WORLD/asiapcf/east/06/12/china.cuba/index. html>).

112. China's 2003 sugarcane crop was set to reach a record high of 10 million tonnes, up from 8.8 million tonnes in 2002 (ISO, *Market Report*, April 2003, I). Its imports are expected to remain at around one million tonnes per annum, about three-quarters of a million tonnes short of its WTO quota, set when China joined in November 2001.

113. See United Nations, *Commission on Human Rights Annual Reports*, New York and Geneva, appropriate years. The Russian Federation abstained in 1996 and 1997, but voted with Cuba from 1998 to 2004. In turn, since 2000, Cuba has supported Russia against attempts to condemn human rights abuses allegedly perpetrated by Russian troops in Chechnya.

114. "The Polish Government's Counterrevolutionary Adventure in Cuba," editorial, *Granma International*, May 21, 2000, 3.

115. "The Truth About Arrest of Czech Citizens who Encouraged Subversion," *Granma International*, February 4, 2001, 5; "Czechs Detained in Cuba Admit Their Guilt," *Granma International*, February 11, 2001, 11.

116. "Czechs to Meet Havel After Cuba Ordeal," *Reuters*, February 6, 2001.

117. Ivanov, "Rusia y América Latina: relaciones," 9.

118. Ibid.

119. "Russia Urges U.S. to Lift Embargo Against Cuba," Interfax News Agency, Moscow, *BBC Monitoring*, May 15, 2002.

120. "Cuba, Russia 'Alarmed' by Prospect of Unilateral Military Action," Interfax News Agency, Moscow, *BBC Monitoring*, October 2, 2002. Also see "Russia, Cuba Oppose Use of Force Against Iraq," ITAR-TASS, *BBC Monitoring*, October 30, 2002.

121. "U.S. Wants U.N. to Scold, Not Sanction, North Korea," February 13, 2003, *CNN.com*, <www.cnn.com/2003/WORLD/asiapcf/east/02/12/nkorea.nuclear/>.

122. Martha Mercer and Dmitry Mozheitov, "Moscow's Clubs Embrace a Cuban Cocktail," *Lifestyle* (Moscow), August 2, 2002; Lucas Romriell, "Che to Revolutionize Moscow's Latin American Scene," *Lifestyle*, January 24, 2003, <www.lifestyle.ru/?obj=34213 and 30790>.

3

Inter-Alliance Conflict

Cuba, Europe, and America's Global Reach

Chris McGillion

The U.S. sees engagement as a reward; the Europeans see engagement as a prospect.

Senior Official, Bureau of Western Hemisphere Affairs, Department of State, October 2002

At the end of the 1980s, the collapse of the Soviet empire ushered in a so-called New World Order or what some Washington ideologues described, more candidly, as a "unipolar" world. During 1990s, however, the United States was forced to grapple with the consequences of its success in "winning" the Cold War, particularly the resurgence and intensification of intercapitalist economic rivalries. The world market had displaced ideology as the new battlefield, with allies and former enemies competing to carve out new spheres of influence and profit. While the U.S. still managed to get its own way on most issues, it has nonetheless been forced to deal with a geoeconomic environment of proliferating challenges as various allies have sought more aggressively to pursue their own interests and agendas.

Global hegemony has been an openly declared goal of American governments since the end of the Cold War. The first Bush White House sought to recreate a world of uncontested U.S. power, in the process subordinating the ambitions of competitor allies in Europe and Japan to American global leadership and priorities.[1] The Clinton administration's strategy of "enlargement" closely mirrored the Bush policy framework. "Only one overriding factor can determine whether the U.S. should act multilaterally or unilaterally, and that is America's interests," National Security Council(NSC) Adviser Anthony Lake told a Johns Hopkins University audience in September 1993.[2] Over the rest of the decade, senior Clinton foreign policy officials continued to assert that "the need for America's global leadership was more important than ever."[3] The 2002 George W. Bush National Security Strategy Doctrine further extended the unilateralist commitment to incorporate the notion of preemptive action:

"we will not hesitate to act alone, if necessary, to exercise our right of self-defense by acting preemptively [against terrorists and their organizations]." That includes "convincing or compelling states to accept their sovereign responsibilities."[4]

The demise of the Cold War, however, gave new impetus to one of the key historical divisions in postwar Europe, that between the "Atlanticists"—led by Britain—who typically accepted a subordinate position within a U.S.-directed world order in return for a privileged secondary role and the "nationalists"—represented by France—driven by a different vision of European-American relations, one in which the former pursued foreign policies more independently of the latter. Since the early 1990s, the nationalists have been in the ascendancy, reflected in a greater willingness than ever to contest Washington's posture on a broad array of political, defense, and economic/trade issues.[5] Encouraging this trend has been the deepening unilateralism so evident in post–Cold War U.S. foreign policy and a perception in European capitals that they are now dealing with an arrogant hegemon willing to "go it alone" and dismissive of international law as an obstacle to be gotten around, or ignored, in pursuit of White House objectives.

Politically, major rifts have emerged between the transatlantic allies over a number of issues. These include Europe's belief that engagement is the most effective way of dealing with former Cold War adversaries in the Third World; and the U.S. refusal to support new international organizations such as the International Criminal Court or participate in new multilateral initiatives ranging from the Ottawa Treaty banning anti-personnel land mines to the Kyoto Global Warming Protocol to the Comprehensive Test Ban Treaty. Since September 11, 2001, divergent approaches to prosecuting the global "war on terror" led French foreign minister Hubert Vedrine to describe the U.S. stance as "simplistic" and accuse Washington of acting "unilaterally, without consulting others, making decisions based on its own view of the world and its own interests."[6] In private, according to senior aides, George W. Bush smoldered about gutless "European elites."[7]

In early 2003, these tensions exploded in a particularly bitter disagreement over America's policy toward Iraq. Defense Secretary Donald Rumsfeld dismissed French and German concerns about a U.S.-led preemptive strike against Saddam Hussein as the voice of "old Europe" that was totally out of touch with the new global configuration of power.[8] President Bush amplified what this meant in response to a question about possible declining allied support for his open-ended "war on terror": "At some point we may be the only ones left. That's ok with me. We are America."[9]

In European capitals, the response to the Bush preemption doctrine was overwhelmingly hostile. Apart from the broader challenge it posed to the survival of the post-war system of multilateral institutions and coalitions, senior government officials interpreted this U.S. assertion of the right to act preemptively as sending the continent an unmistakable message: "This is an empire and we will not allow anybody to get close to our capabilities and we are ready to act to prevent that from happening"; one put it even more succinctly: "You [Europe] have become irrelevant."[10]

Beyond security, there has also been a proliferation of bilateral economic/trade disputes over issues ranging from steel to agriculture and aircraft to wheat gluten and wine. In November 2000, the European Union (EU) trade commissioner, Pascal Lamy, warned that the "problems seem to get worse, not better." During a speech some weeks later, U.S. ambassador to the EU, Richard Morningstar, lamented the inability of both sides "to resolve our list of disputes, which are growing in both number and severity [and] . . . beginning to overshadow the rest of the relationship."[11] Prominent among them was Washington's application of global economic sanctions in pursuit of foreign policy goals and specifically the extraterritorial "reach" of the Helms-Burton law and the Iran-Libya Sanctions Act (ILSA), both of which targeted European firms doing business with Cuba, Iran, and Libya. Not since 1982—when the Reagan administration blocked subsidiaries of American multinationals from selling technological equipment to the Soviet Union for its trans-Siberian gas pipeline project and imposed sanctions on Western Europe for defying its embargo—has this issue of U.S. extraterritorial legislation become such a bone of contention between Alliance partners.

Tightening the Cuba Embargo: Europe's Response

Europe's anger over post–Cold War America's ongoing economic war against Cuba initially erupted following passage of the 1992 Cuban Democracy Act (CDA) that targeted the subsidiaries of U.S. multinationals trading with the island nation. At risk was annual trade between EU member states (mostly American subsidiaries) and Cuba valued at around $600 million. In a formal diplomatic protest to the State Department, the EU's executive arm, the European Commission (EC), condemned the proposed legislation as a "violation of the general principles of international law and the sovereignty of independent nations [with] the potential to cause grave damage to the transatlantic relationship" and urged President Bush to exercise the veto if it reached his desk for signature.[12] British trade minister Richard Needham bluntly declared that London would not accept any attempt to "impose US laws on UK companies" and that Whitehall alone "will determine the UK's policy on trade with Cuba."[13] Prior to George Bush's decision to sign the CDA into law on October 22, 1992, several European allies had announced their intention to take countermeasures to nullify the impact of this extraterritorial legislation. In April 1993, on the eve of U.S.-European trade talks with the new Clinton administration, the EC released its annual report on trade barriers that singled out the CDA for specific attack. Europe's principal fear was that this signaled a policy shift whereby "U.S. domestic concerns [would now] take precedence over U.S. trade law."[14]

The Europeans had every right to feel concerned given that incoming president Bill Clinton had expressed unqualified support for the CDA during the 1992 election campaign and, once in office, did nothing to indicate there would be any slackening in Washington's determination to squeeze and destabilize the Cuban economy. Although the value of trade with Cuba varied considerably from one country to another, by 1994 the EU nations accounted for thirty-eight percent of Cuba's imports and twenty-nine percent of its exports, up from around six percent of the island's total global trade in 1989, albeit within the context of Cuba's overall trade contraction.[15] Renewed investment and commercial interest in Cuba were also accompanied by expressions of interest in developing ties among German, Dutch, Spanish, and other European private multinational banks.[16] Moreover, portents of a major rift with Washington over new legislation submitted to Congress in January 1995 by Senator Jesse Helms (R-N.C.) and Representative Dan Burton (R-Ind.) that would impose harsher sanctions on countries trading with, or investing in, Cuba were unmistakable. For the moment, however, they were easy to ignore.

One reason was Europe's failure to translate their complaints and threatened retaliation over the CDA into action. In practice, they did almost nothing, which led Washington to discount similar threats from these quarters about Helms-Burton if it became law. Consequently, when the EU sent a letter to House Speaker Newt Gingrich (R-Ga.) in March, describing key provisions of the bill as "objectionable" and "illegitimate" and warning that its extraterritorial thrust had the "potential to cause grave damaging effects to bilateral EU-US relations," it was easy to ascribe an element of "cry wolf" to the message.[17] In addition, Europe's disquiet, like that of the U.S. business community, was tempered by the unlikely prospect of Helms-Burton becoming law: "The Europeans weren't getting too anxious about Helms-Burton at that point," recalled a State Department official then based at the U.S. Mission in Brussels. "The Europeans were alarmed that the legislation had been proposed but they were confident that the administration was doing everything it could to oppose it."[18] State Department officials working directly with the EU took the criticisms seriously, but generally interpreted them as part of broader European attack on Washington's proclivity for applying unilateral economic sanctions as a blunt instrument in pursuit of foreign policy goals. Director of the Office of Cuban Affairs, Dennis Hays, described one response to Helms-Burton by diplomats and government officials on both sides of the Atlantic: "Oh God, another headache. First it was Iran, now we're going to do more to Cuba and then its going to be Iraq, and then what about Libya. To these guys it was just one more issue, just one more pariah country and do we really want to piss off the EU over yet another of these matters?"[19]

At this point, there was certainly no indication that the White House had decided to answer that question in a manner that would have ameliorated or soothed European concerns. Although senior Clinton foreign policy officials harbored misgivings about key provisions that appeared to impinge on the president's constitutional responsibilities and were likely to create frictions with allies, they had already gone on record in support of the basic intent of Helms-Burton, and interagency discussions during 1995 had not produced an unequivocal White House decision to oppose the legislation. In all probability, this position was not unrelated to the administration's unease and suspicions about what the Europeans were up to in their "reaching out" to Cuba. "The big issue for us with the Europeans at the time was not really our actions," said a Brussels-based U.S. diplomat. "Our concern then was that the Europeans were moving forward rather quickly to implement an economic agreement with the Cubans on development assistance."[20] In Washington, recalled the president's special representative on Cuba, Richard Nuccio, a decision was made to shift away from the "'kick 'em in the nuts' approach" favored by Deputy Secretary of State for Inter-American Affairs Michael Skol that would have meant automatically opposing the initiative in favor of applying diplomatic pressure on the EU governments to attach "some conditionality" to any cooperation accord they signed with Havana.[21] In other words, U.S. officials at home and abroad were seemingly less worried about the potential ramifications of a Helms-Burton law for administration policy or Alliance relations and more concerned about what plans the Europeans had for engaging Cuba.

In November, an EC delegation from Italy, France and Spain visited Havana for meetings with senior Cuban government officials. In a none-too-subtle rebuff to Washington's approach, their report concluded that dialogue was the best means of promoting political and economic reforms on the island. The Europeans did not retreat from this judgment over the following months despite two major provocations by the Cuban government.

The first surrounded the visit to Cuba in February 1996 by EC vice president Manuel Marin to negotiate an aid agreement that would commit the Castro government to respect human rights and permit a gradual opening up of the island's political and economic systems. In return, Marin offered EU development and economic cooperation and support for Cuba's membership in the Rio Group of Latin nations, which would bring a new degree of international respect and recognition. When Washington first became aware of the impending economic cooperation agreement in the latter half of 1995, Richard Nuccio visited six European capitals to lobby for the inclusion of a "democracy clause" that was part of similar agreements the EU had reached with

Mexico and Indonesia. "This time we weren't trying to block any agreement, we were just trying to better it," Nuccio explained. U.S. pressure on Marin to wrest concessions did not end with Nuccio's trip. On February 7, the day Marin was scheduled to leave for Havana, U.S. ambassador to the EC, Stuart Eizenstat, personally delivered a blunt message: the White House desired to attach its own conditions to any EU-Cuban development aid agreement. While most were consistent with EU demands for reform of the civil code in respect to property, the rule of law, free speech, and the like, "the final demand," said Nuccio, "was that Castro accept [Marin's] meeting with [opposition bloc] Concilio Cubano and understand that the EU would officially recognize Concilio and extend its protection, and acknowledge that these [dissidents] were legitimate figures who were now under the protection of the EU."[22] In return for meeting these conditions, Cuba could expect Washington to make a reciprocal concession—or the first of its much vaunted "calibrated responses" promised in return for substantive reforms on the island.

While an accommodating Marin agreed to transmit the offer to Fidel Castro, he dismissed any suggestion that this amounted to a new-found consensus between the White House and the EU over how to approach the "problem" of Cuba. The EC vice president still regarded the aid agreement as a fundamentally European initiative that was part and parcel of "a very commonsensical approach that was quite different from U.S. policy."[23] The Cuban president, however, failed to perceive any difference. After eleven hours of talks with Marin, he rejected every item on the latter's agenda. Marin was permitted to meet with Concilio Cubano members, but no sooner had he boarded his plane for the return flight to Europe than those he had spoken to, and other leaders of the group, were arrested. Castro's action was interpreted in some quarters as a deliberately planned attempt to kill off a joint EU-U.S. initiative that would have bolstered local support for domestic opponents of the Castro regime. This view may also have been shared by senior administration officials.[24] On the other hand, if Castro had qualms about the possible impact of the conditions on offer for better relations with the EU or the U.S., he simply could have rejected them outright. This had been the approach taken when the Caribbean Community (CARICOM) initially requested specific human rights commitments in return for closer ties. To have embarrassed the EC's vice president in this way was completely unnecessary and would have been tantamount to using a sledgehammer to crack a nut.

Whatever Castro's motives may have been, the development aid agreement was put on hold. But neither this experience nor the far more provocative shoot down by Cuban jet fighters of two unarmed civilian planes piloted by members of the Miami exile group, "Brothers to the Rescue," less than three weeks later could dent the Europeans' unshakeable confidence that engagement was the best way to encourage reforms in Cuba. While condemning the shoot down as a criminal act, the White House decision to embrace Helms-Burton quickly refocused their anger. Said a French diplomat: "We don't think one country has the right to tell another who they can trade with."[25] The EU issued an equally pithy statement: "This extraterritorial extension of US jurisdiction has no basis in international law."[26]

Initially, at least, the severity of individual countries' protests varied according to their economic exposure in Cuba and the importance of the Washington relationship. On one point, however, there was a firm consensus: this latest effort by the Clinton White House to subordinate allies' interests to its foreign policy goals was unacceptable. "We heard from all of the EU countries very loudly who were saying they didn't like this bill," said a high-ranking official in State Department's Office of Cuban Affairs. "Whenever senior level officials from the White House, State, or any other agency traveled overseas they were hit with this."[27] Another State Department official said the barrage of criticism was presented in "the most undiplomatic language I've ever seen."[28]

The Europeans were particularly upset by Washington's attempt to legitimate and impose "secondary boycotts" on nations trading with countries on the U.S. embargo list, and they threatened to retaliate. "There will be a price to be paid," vowed a senior official in Britain's Department of Trade and Industry.[29] Foreign Minister Malcolm Rifkind accused the Clinton administration of weakening Alliance unity and posing a threat to global free trade as a result of its "short-sighted, unilateral actions." Nor could he resist pointing out the fundamental contradiction in U.S. policy of opposing Arab attempts to boycott companies dealing with Israel only to turn around and support equivalent measures to prevent countries from trading with Cuba. "The cases are precisely comparable," he insisted.[30] No provision of Helms-Burton, a senior State Department Inter-American Affairs official recalled, triggered more hostility than Title IV (barring senior executives of foreign companies "trafficking" in "confiscated" Cuban property from entry into the United States): "It was hugely controversial in our relations with the Europeans who were saying 'that sounds like extortion to us.'"[31] This was no empty rhetoric. To underscore just how objectionable it considered Helms-Burton, the EU initiated procedures to bring the United States before the World Trade Organization (WTO) disputes settlement panel.

That even the conservative government of Britain's John Major, who traded as much as any of his predecessors on the "special relationship" with Washington, took a leading role in protesting Helms-Burton and initiated legislative countermechanisms, revealed the scope and the depth of Europe's anger over Clinton's decision. The German Federal Republic's response was no less significant, given its historically cautious approach toward the revolutionary regime in Havana: no diplomatic ties between 1963 and 1974; a largely formal relationship over the next two decades; and German business' limited attraction to the Cuban economy even after a reunited Germany inherited the former East's economic investment in the island. Only weeks after Clinton signed Helms-Burton into law, Bonn signed a bilateral investment promotion and protection accord with Cuba. Foreign Minister Klaus Kinkel vigorously attacked Washington's newfound enthusiasm for "secondary boycotts" and during talks with U.S. secretary of state Warren Christopher told him that the EU "will not let the matter drop."[32] The French were no less appalled by Clinton's action. Unease over what was viewed in some quarters as Paris' excessive deference to the Castro regime was set to one side as the leaders of all political parties unanimously condemned Helms-Burton.[33] During a White House meeting in mid-June, EU president, Jacques Santer, and Italian prime minister, Romano Prodi, told Clinton "in no uncertain terms" that Europe vehemently opposed U.S. economic sanctions against Cuba.[34] On Capitol Hill, Democratic senators Claiborne Pell (R.I.) and Christopher Dodd (Conn.) worried that Helms-Burton was "unit[ing] our friends against our Cuban policy" and "beginning to undermine U.S. leadership in . . . international fora."[35]

The Crisis Deepens

The conflict over Helms-Burton was never about the need for major political and economic reforms in Cuba but was a direct outcome of Europe's belief that dialogue and engagement were more effective tactics than economic warfare in bringing such changes about. In early May the EU temporarily broke off formal talks with Havana over future economic cooperation, citing the Castro government's inflexible posture over the pace and scope of internal changes. While this decision could be interpreted as a partial concession to Washington, it also reflected the consensus over longer-term objectives that motivated Cuba policy on both sides of the Atlantic.

Even so, as the then Group of Seven (G-7) leading industrialized countries prepared to meet in late June 1996, a British official made it clear that President Clinton and the American delegation "will hear from their six closest allies and trading partners how wrong-headed and ill conceived Helms-Burton is, and how by shooting at their foes they are injuring their friends."[36] During the summit, French president Jacques Chirac warned Clinton that Helms-Burton and analogous legislation being debated on Capitol Hill targeting Iran and Libya could only fracture Alliance unity without achieving U.S. policy goals. "Taking an entire population hostage," Chirac said with Gallic flourish, "is not elegant."[37] Under pressure, Clinton signed a joint economic communiqué committing all governments to avoid trade and investment measures that contravened WTO rules and Organisation of Economic Co-operation and Development (OECD) codes. According to EU president Santer, this was "an unambiguous signal that go-it-alone tactics are not the way to settle one's trade problems." His vice president and trade commissioner, Sir Leon Brittan, said that the communiqué delivered the U.S. a "muffled but very sharp rap over the knuckles."[38]

Europe's anger was met with a combination of arrogance, dismissiveness, and threats. "Countries that are teeing off on us now," State Department spokesman Nicholas Burns retorted, "ought to just sit back and cool it and understand that we're going to implement this law."[39] When Clinton announced in July that he would defer implementation of Title III (granting former U.S. owners of nationalized properties in Cuba the right to sue foreigners who invested or trafficked in these enterprises in American courts) for six months, Deputy NSC Adviser Sandy Berger observed that "the meter will be ticking" on Cuba's trading partners nonetheless.[40] "This is bullying," commented Canada's foreign minister, Lloyd Axworthy. "But in America you call it global leadership."[41] To a senior White House official, it was the return to the world of a single superpower that best explained Clinton's decision to act unilaterally and ignore worldwide opposition to Washington's Cuba policy. In the post–Cold War era, he said, America is *the* dominant global hegemon and those of its allies leading the charge against Helms-Burton would ultimately come to terms with that reality: "It breaks the rules, but it works, and the President says, 'We're doing it.' In the end, they'll get over it. We're America, and they'll get over it."[42]

The conflict flared anew in mid-July, following the State Department's diktat to the Canadian mining multinational Sherritt that it divest itself of its nickel-cobalt holdings in Cuba within forty-five days or face the prospect of its nine senior executives, two of whom were British citizens, being prevented from entering the United States. In London, Ian Lang, secretary of state for Trade and Industry, told the American Chamber of Commerce that such an action could only damage bilateral ties. In Washington, the British Embassy delivered a trenchant protest to the State Department over this "disgraceful and preposterous" blacklisting. Such methods, Lang caustically observed, were no way to promote democracy in Cuba.[43] The Foreign Office described the letters as "a wrong-headed restriction" on the ability of Sherritt executives to travel freely and "to do business." To emphasize the British concern, Prime Minister Major sent a private letter to the White House registering his displeasure with the Helms-Burton legislation.[44]

In mid-July, EU foreign ministers met to draw up a list of possible retaliatory measures in response to Helms-Burton, which France's Herve de Charett had no need to remind his colleagues "is directly contrary to the rules which govern international trade."[45] EC trade spokesman Peter Guilford was equally pointed in declaring that "the application of the Helms-Burton act to Cuba sets a dangerous precedent that needs to be nipped in the bud."[46] The meeting concluded with an announcement that actions ranging from blacklisting American companies, to requiring U.S. business executives to obtain visas for travel to EU countries, to taking the dispute to the WTO, would be implemented if President Clinton failed to renew the waivers on key provisions of Helms-Burton that were due to expire the next day. "The best way to get change in Cuba," said an exasperated Sir Leon Brittan "is not to clobber your allies."[47] This sentiment coincided with a desire to prevent the conflict from escalating further, if at all possible. To this end, British foreign secretary Malcolm Rifkind sought to dampen down the rhetoric by suggesting that what was occurring was "a rift, not a crisis."[48]

Irrespective of Rifkind's choice of words, the U.S. business community knew enough to fear the worst. At a minimum, individual companies would be subject to European laws designed to counter Helms-Burton; in the worst-case scenario, they could be dragged into a major confrontation between America and its trade allies. "The business community cared about Helms-Burton because it complicated relations with other countries," an involved Department of Commerce official recalled. "We tended to make that point in the administration rather more actively than anybody else."[49] Clinton's decision to postpone the Title III "trafficking" provision for at least another six months averted any immediate escalation of the dispute. The EU "welcome[d] the decision as far as it goes," while continuing to remonstrate with Washington over the fact that the extraterritorial nature of the law had not been addressed and that it still hovered over European companies and individuals like a "sword of Damocles." EU trade commissioner Brittan was visibly underwhelmed by the White House action, terming it "a very limited response" to European concerns. Not only was Title IV (visa restrictions) still in effect, but Clinton could reinstate Title III (lawsuits) at any time if he so desired. Europe restated its support for the "American objective" of political democratization in Cuba while disassociating itself from the means the U.S. seemed bent on employing to reach the goal. It cannot be achieved, British trade secretary Ian Lang remarked, by "attack[ing] trading partners in other parts of the world who are carrying out legitimate business in Cuba."[50]

This half-hearted European support for Clinton's latest "concession" paralleled continuing moves to establish a list of agreed-upon measures that would allow for a rapid counterresponse to Helms-Burton if the occasion should arise. Some EU officials favored immediate reprisals. The French trade minister Yves Gaillard showed his impatience by declaring that his government "would not leave the answer solely to the European Union. If French firms were hit," he warned, "there would also be a French response taking the form of legislative and legal sanctions."[51]

After testifying before a July 1996 House subcommittee hearing, the State Department's coordinator of the Office of Cuban Affairs, Michael Ranneberger, was questioned about administration efforts to convince the Europeans to "play ball" on Cuba and Helms-Burton. He responded with a sober, and somewhat pessimistic, appraisal. The Europeans remained "profoundly disturbed by the legislation, despite all the efforts we have made, and I think they are serious about retaliatory legislation." Ranneberger assured legislators that the White House had made no concessions to its allies on the continent: "we have given no ground on this and we have been very, very strong in defense of it."[52] This statement to some extent contradicted administration rhetoric about a cooperative effort between the U.S. and Europe to promote change in Cuba.

In mid-August, the White House launched a global diplomatic offensive to mobilize support for its Cuba policy and limit the negative impact of Helms-Burton. The president's newly appointed special envoy, Under Secretary of Commerce Stuart Eizenstat, assisted by United Nations ambassador, Madeleine Albright, and former Democratic chairman of the House Foreign Affairs Committee, Dante Fascell, were given the task of "build[ing] international support" for Washington's anti-Castro policy. On the eve of his visit to European capitals, Eizenstat said the message he would be carrying is that the quid pro quo for future presidential waivers of Helms-Burton provisions would be allies' willingness to take "concrete steps" to intensify the pressure on the Cuban government.[53] Other U.S. officials described the objective as one of trying to "elicit a sufficient response from other countries to minimally at least meet the terms of the [Helms-Burton] Act and avoid imposing sanctions if at all possible which could have then resulted in counter sanctions."[54] All the indications were that it was going to be an uphill battle.

To Eizenstat's dismay, he met a veritable avalanche of criticism wherever he went during his fourteen-day trip to the continent. In Brussels, Sir Leon Brittan bluntly told him that Helms-Burton was "not the right way to achieve [desired reforms in Cuba]," that it was a "repugnant" law that "offends and attacks America's trusted allies." German economic minister Guenther Rexrodt voiced his government's strong opposition and reiterated Brittan's comment that it was "the wrong way" to pursue political and economic changes on the Caribbean island.[55] Even the newly elected conservative Aznar government in Spain, despite its public calls for an opening up of the Cuban political system, provided an unsympathetic audience for Eizenstat's pleas. British foreign secretary Rifkind summed up the European consensus on Helms-Burton: "We are entirely of the one view in the European Union that any attempt at extra-territoriality is unacceptable. . . . The issue is clear and unanimous."[56]

Determined to keep the pressure on Washington, the EU took its case to the WTO in early October 1996. The global body agreed to convene its disputes panel to adjudicate on whether the U.S. law violated international trade rules. The Americans responded predictably: the WTO's future could be at "serious risk" if it delivered a verdict in favor of the complainants.[57] Meanwhile, the EU also began compiling a "watch list" of U.S. corporations that might pursue litigation against European investors in Cuba. In another round of meetings later that month in Paris, Amsterdam, Rome, The Hague, Copenhagen, and Brussels, Clinton's special envoy once again ran into the proverbial brick wall of European intransigence over any compromise with Helms-Burton. Adding to Eizenstat's discomfort, the EU foreign ministers agreed on a set of regulations to counter both Helms-Burton and the more recent U.S. legislation restricting trade with Libya and Iran. European companies were instructed to ignore any threat of legal prosecution in American courts under Helms-Burton. If the U.S. claimant was successful, the target company could countersue in European courts for the amount of damages incurred.[58] Following his return to Washington, a much chastened White House special envoy told a Chamber of Commerce meeting that "it would be hard to overstate to you the level of anger and resentment in Europe and Latin America about this issue based on what they see as the principle of extraterritoriality from their perspective and more so than any practical damage to their actual interests."[59]

Taking Helms-Burton to the WTO: "United States vs. Everybody Else"

When President Clinton signed Helms-Burton into law, the EU trade spokesman angrily reminded the White House that one of the WTO's key principles "is that you don't export your laws and your principles to other countries."[60] In June 1996 when the EU first asked the global body to institute consultations on Helms-Burton, the U.S. government began to qualify its enthusiasm for the WTO's procedures. "After hundreds if not thousands of discussions with the Latin countries, the European countries, Canada and Mexico, we understand their concerns," proclaimed State Department spokesman Nicholas Burns in totally rejecting the EU course of action. "They ought to understand a few things. [Helms-Burton is] the law of the land. We implement U.S. law. We're going forward with it."[61] At the G-7 meeting in Lyon, France, later that same month, EU officials told Clinton that such "go-it-alone" tactics were contrary to the spirit of inter-Alliance relations.

Officially, Washington continued to deny that Helms-Burton violated the letter of the WTO rules, although some U.S. officials privately questioned this interpretation. Inside the State Department "there were some differences of opinion at the policy level," said one participant in agency discussions. "Those in the Department who strongly supported the WTO thought a dispute about Cuba policy was not what the WTO was there to handle. The minority view in State was that we would win. The third option was to apply the 'national security exemption.' The issue was not purely trade and not purely Cuba policy."[62]

Given the complexity surrounding this issue it was clearly going to be difficult to find a resolution satisfactory to all sides and consistent with the intentions of Helms-Burton. Advising the Europeans to simply accommodate themselves to a fait accompli was hardly likely to mollify those governments whose multinational corporations were under threat from this latest piece of U.S. extraterritorial law. The dilemma for the White House was of a different kind: if it allowed the EU to proceed with its WTO challenge, with only a "minority" of knowledgeable State Department officials confident enough to predict a verdict in Washington's favor, it might have dealt the U.S. law a powerful setback, triggering a virulent congressional backlash over an issue that Clinton had little stomach to contest. "Politically, you couldn't let the EU proceed with the WTO challenge," said one State Department official. "The WTO was already under fire and being questioned by members of Congress. And our attempt to get others to join the WTO, and our efforts to build the WTO up as a credible organization would have been completely undermined."[63]

For these reasons, a compromise solution had to be found. Temporary waivers on the implementation of Titles III and IV might satisfy Congress since they left the legislation on the statute books and it could be enforced retroactively. But for precisely that reason the Europeans were likely to remain vehemently opposed to the legislation. Still, the White House wanted to ensure that it remained "in a strong position to defend the waiver."[64] What this suggested was that, irrespective of the intention of Helms-Burton, any decision on waivers was always going to be based on pragmatic, rather than principled, considerations.

In mid-October, responding to Washington's lack of substantive flexibility, the EU requested the WTO to organize a disputes panel to examine whether Helms-Burton contravened WTO rules. This was not the message the White House was waiting to hear from the EU; it immediately vetoed the request, contending that the issue in dispute was one of diplomacy, not trade. U.S. officials began applying intense pressure to permanently terminate this EU challenge. The effort was couched in terms of "further discussions," but the U.S. representative to the WTO, Ambassador Booth Gardner, left America's allies in no doubt what this meant: "What we hope happens between now and November 20 [when the EU would have a second opportunity to request a disputes panel, which would then be automatically set up under WTO rules] is that we will work with the EU and that *they will reconsider* whether or not this is the appropriate forum of discussion" (my emphasis).[65] In other words, the aim of "further discussions" was to convince the allies to give ground and accept the American position. One frustrated European official complained that the Americans "[are] trying to frighten us away from pressing a panel, and just letting sleeping dogs lie."[66]

The EU's refusal to capitulate to Washington's threats led the State Department to adopt an even more threatening posture. Ambassador Gardner warned that "proceeding further with this matter would pose serious risks" to the WTO, which was still "a very fragile institution." Stuart Eizenstat cautioned the Europeans that if they insisted on dragging the U.S. before the WTO over Helms-Burton it would likely "invite an incitement of [domestic] protectionist pressure."[67] The EU's trade commissioner, Sir Leon Brittan, dryly commented that "my American friends seem to have a hard time understanding that if they had not enacted this law, we wouldn't be discussing it."[68]

An exasperated Clinton administration now shifted tack to its third option, arguing that Helms-Burton was permissible under the WTO's "national security exemption" that allows a member state to take "any action it considers necessary for the protection of its essential security interests" in circumstances involving fissionable materials or arms trafficking, or in respect to action "taken in time of war or other emergency in international relations."[69] Eizenstat, in full hyperbolic mode, told a Washington conference on Helms-Burton that Cuba still posed a national security threat to the United States as well as Latin America: "[The U.S.] has had a bipartisan policy since the early 1960s under President Kennedy based on the notion that we have a hostile and unfriendly regime 90 miles from our border, and that anything done to strengthen that regime will only encourage the regime to not only continue its hostility but, through much of its tenure, to try to destabilize large parts of Latin America."[70] In making such a claim, he seemed oblivious to a 1995 Pentagon report on "U.S. Security Strategy for the Americas," which described the island nation as posing no military threat to the United States, as well as dismissive of the extent of Cuba's reintegration, politically and economically, within Latin America over the previous decade.

Constructing a "national security" defense of Helms-Burton also sat oddly with a rationale constantly invoked by Washington to justify tightening the Cuba embargo: the absence of political democracy on the island. Explaining why he supported the Helms-Burton provisions against Cuba but opposed secondary boycotts of Israel, President Clinton argued that the latter targeted a country "simply because [it] exists" and was therefore unacceptable, whereas the former "is directed against the only country in our hemisphere which is not a democracy."[71] Thus it was incumbent on the Europeans and other allies to drop their opposition to Helms-Burton and participate in what White House spokesman Mike McCurry described as "the effort to confine Cuban Communism to the trashbin of history."[72]

Not only was this the first time since the establishment of the global free trade body that a government had invoked a "national security" argument to defend its position; this precedent-setting American stance also raised the possibility of other countries acting in a similar fashion to quarantine their restrictive trade practices from scrutiny by the WTO. One European trade diplomat feared that any such refusal to play by the WTO rules "would be like pressing a nuclear button" targeting the multilateral trade system.[73]

As the crisis in transatlantic relations deepened and the November deadline produced no resolution of the problem, the WTO Disputes Settlement Body agreed to a second EU request for a panel to investigate whether Helms-Burton violated WTO rules. But in their search for a compromise solution, the Europeans also adopted a "Common Position on Cuba," which identified the promotion of democratic reform and respect for human rights in Cuba as core policy goals. This declaration produced another six-month presidential waiver of Title III but failed to extract a more permanent American response.

On February 12, 1997, in a last ditch effort to avoid litigation, the EU requested a one-week postponement to the formal start of the disputes panel hearing—in the hope that this might produce some reciprocity on the part of the White House. At the same time, Washington's national security defense continued to evoke scorn and ridicule from those governments it was intended to impress. EU trade commissioner Brittan termed the U.S. position "not credible" and a threat to the viability of the organization. "For the WTO to be effective," he said, "it must not be possible for one country to evade its operation simply by proclaiming that national security is involved, however farfetched such a claim may be."[74] The State Department would not budge, insisting that Helms-Burton was "a foreign policy issue" and, as such, the WTO could not adjudicate on it.[75]

The conciliatory EU stance produced no substantive concessions from the White House. On February 20, after further meetings failed to produce any proposals that would meet European concerns, the WTO named three international experts to judge the legality of Helms-Burton within global trade rules and set an April 14 deadline for the EU to present its brief.

In Washington, enraged Clinton officials announced that the U.S. would boycott the proceedings on the grounds that the WTO lacked the authority to pass judgment on an issue of American national security. "We will not show up [when the panel convenes]," an irritated senior administration policymaker declared. "We do not believe anything the WTO says or does can force the U.S. to change its laws." Stuart Eizenstat was equally dismissive: the WTO has "no competence" to rule on matters of foreign policy.[76] "We were deadly serious about that," recalled State's Michael Ranneberger, who attended the high level interagency meetings that framed this response. "We would have walked away from it."[77] A steadfast Sir Leon Brittan dismissed the U.S. argument as fanciful: "It is not credible to suggest that protection of U.S. national security requires interference in the legitimate trade of European companies with Cuba."[78] As far as the Europeans were concerned, the United States had placed itself above the very international trade law it had been the driving force in promoting.

Still, a U.S. boycott of WTO proceedings could well have proven fatal for the fledgling trade organization. At the very least, Washington's refusal to recognize the authority of any umpire in this dispute would have set transatlantic relations on a runaway collision course. The stakes were high and the pressure for some sort of circuit breaker enormous. "It was a real cliffhanger," said one Clinton official. "In the end the Europeans realized we were prepared to walk and risk the whole WTO in the process."[79] On April 11, three days before what U.S. officials described as a "drop-dead date" for ending the challenge, Eizenstat and Brittan announced they had successfully negotiated a deal. The reckless threat posed to the global trade body and the Alliance by Washington's stubbornness had been temporarily removed.

Under the terms of the agreement, the EU deferred its challenge to Helms-Burton until October 15; in return, the White House agreed to continue waiving Title III as well as to "open a dialogue" with Congress to seek the amendment or elimination of other contentious aspects of the law.[80] In the meantime, both sides would collaborate on devising investment rules to govern property confiscated by the Cuban government after 1959. But for all practical purposes the arrangement asked more of the Europeans than it did of the Americans. Eizenstat made it quite clear where the onus for a successful outcome lay: "As this process unfolds, the administration will open a dialogue with the Congress with a view toward obtaining an amendment providing the President with waiver authority for Title IV of the Libertad [Helms-Burton] Act *once these bilateral consultations are completed and the EU has adhered to these agreed disciplines*" (my emphasis).[81] In effect, the EU was being saddled with the responsibility for making prior concessions to the White House on a promise—not a guarantee—that the Congress would respond by giving Clinton the legislative changes he sought.

The April 11 agreement postponed the crisis but remained far from solving it. Indeed, the proposed "understanding" had triggered a vigorous debate among the EU countries themselves, during which Belgium, France, Italy, and Spain "expressed reservations, some of them quite vehemently."[82] The Dutch European Affairs minister Michiel Patijn described this U.S.-EU deal as a "precarious armistice."[83] German foreign minister Guenther Rexrodt called it "a step in the right direction" but emphasized that "it is still unacceptable that a country aims to carry out its foreign policy goals by imposing sanctions against companies in third-party countries."[84] Washington remained on notice that the Helms-Burton extraterritorial provisions were unacceptable and that any new American measures against European companies would trigger an immediate reopening of the WTO disputes panel.

While the conflict had been temporarily defused, two potential obstacles seemed certain to complicate any successful longer-term resolution: the proposed new investment "disciplines" the Europeans were being asked to adopt were clearly intended to deter further EU (and other Western) investment in Cuba; and White House policy was more than ever hostage to the demands of Congress. Even Stuart Eizenstat conceded, "there [was] no guarantee" that the legislators would give their "seal of approval" to any negotiated settlement.[85]

If U.S. negotiators imagined that the April 11 agreement would freeze European investment in Cuba, they were wrong. On April 25, less than a week after the EU formerly suspended its WTO challenge, France signed a major new trade deal with Cuba and warned the Clinton administration not to interfere with its companies doing business in the island nation. Washington's predictable criticism of the French initiative was dismissed by the other EU countries who insisted that it did not breach the April 11 agreement or complicate efforts to resolve the larger dispute between the U.S. and its allies over economic relations with Castro's Cuba. Nevertheless, the timing of the agreement between Havana and Paris was important. It very clearly signaled that the EU objection to the global application of U.S. trade laws was as strong as ever and that the temporary suspension of the WTO option did not mean that the Europeans had any intention of lamely falling into line behind Clinton's Cuba policy. When the State Department's Nicholas Burns told reporters, apropos of the French decision, that "we do not favor any other countries normalizing their economic relations with Cuba," France's industry minister, Franck Borotra, sharply retorted that his country was "an independent republic" and "master of its own decisions."[86]

No sooner had U.S. and EU negotiators begun the arduous task of trying to strike a permanent agreement on Helms-Burton than congressional hardliners started to toughen their position ahead of any "dialogue" with the White House on watering down the Cuba trade sanctions legislation. According to Capitol Hill insiders, "discussion drafts" of two bills proposed eliminating any future waiver of Title III or conditioning such waivers on Europe's willingness to accommodate a set of demands, including the withdrawal of its challenges to Helms-Burton in the WTO and North American Free Trade Agreement (NAFTA).[87] Irrespective of the fate of these drafts, their mere existence indicated that the administration would have an uphill battle to extract any concessions from the legislature to meet EU objections to Helms-Burton.

Over the next six months, ongoing discussions between EU and U.S. officials remained inconclusive. Disagreements persisted over a number of key issues: whether disciplines on expropriated property to "inhibit and deter" such investment should apply only to new investments or imply a blanket prohibition on all investment in "confiscated" enterprises; whether European companies with investments in expropriated properties who decide to resell those properties should be subject to the disciplines or not; whether the disciplines should apply to improvements in existing investments or not; and whether to include guidelines relating to the extraterritorial application of national law or confine the disciplines to situations in which companies are receiving contradictory directives from two trading partners.

Any possibility that the EU's October 15 deadline for an accord would be reached seemed remote. For good measure, the White House was now fighting the "war" on two fronts. Not only had it failed to persuade Congress to reconsider the impact of Helms-Burton on America's trade allies; on the contrary, the mood among Capitol Hill lawmakers for even harsher action against Cuba seemed to intensify. In the House, Florida Republican Bill McCollum introduced legislation to strip the president of his authority to keep postponing Title III, while Senator Jesse Helms (R-N.C.) wrote to Secretary of State Madeleine Albright demanding that Clinton implement Title IV.[88] Some powerful legislators interpreted the EU decision to suspend its WTO challenge as a sign that the hardline, uncompromising stance "works"; and that Clinton's attempt to avoid a nasty imbroglio with America's leading allies by diluting the more contentious parts of Helms-Burton was an unnecessary concession to blustering governments.

During a three-day visit to Washington in late September 1997, EU trade commissioner Brittan was subdued about the possibility of "convert[ing] the armistice into a lasting peace." Following meetings with U.S. trade representative Charlene Barshefsky and members of Congress he told a press conference that "we're working hard [but] it takes two to tango."[89] The core sticking point was reaching an accord on the confiscated property issue, whether it should be applied retroactively or only to future investments. As the October deadline fast approached, Washington also kept pressing the Europeans to support tough disciplines on investment in Cuba, including a ban on government commercial assistance to any business deal involving expropriated property formerly owned by American citizens.[90]

To make matters worse, a new potential obstacle to resolving the Helms-Burton conflict arose when the French oil multinational, Total, signed a $2 billion natural gas development contract with Iran in late 1997 in contravention of the Iran-Libya Sanctions Act (ILSA), another piece of extraterritorial legislation passed by Congress and signed into law by Clinton during 1996. It authorized the president to impose sanctions on any company investing more than $40 million in Libya or $20 million in Iran annually on the grounds that both were sponsors of international terrorism. Secretary of State Albright denounced the Total contract as "beyond her understanding" and accused France of refusing to support American efforts to isolate Iran.[91] White House threats to impose sanctions under ILSA unless Total rescinded the agreement provoked widespread scorn in Europe. Newly elected French prime minister Lionel Jospin bluntly rejected this latest Washington effort to "impose [its] laws onto the rest of the world," while EU officials warned that any U.S. retaliation against Total would be "illegal and unacceptable" and lead to automatic renewal of the WTO panel on Helms-Burton.[92] The British government offered a more subtle but equally pointed warning: the White House should "reflect long and hard about the wisdom of taking any action against Total."[93]

Rhetoric aside, the Europeans were still reluctant to get involved in a new trade war with the world's only superpower. Although frustrated by Washington's perceived lack of flexibility and failure to "to show genuine commitment" to negotiate a solution to the problem, the EU decided to indefinitely extend the October 15 deadline and not resume its complaint to the WTO over Helms-Burton.[94]

On Capitol Hill, Representatives Lee Hamilton (D-Ind.) and Phil Crane (R-Ill.), authors of new legislation to limit the use of trade sanctions, not only reflected their support of the anti-Cuba embargo business lobby but also a concern that Helms-Burton posed a dangerous threat to the future of the WTO. "If ongoing U.S.-EU talks on an 'out of court settlement' failed," observed Hamilton, "just about every scenario points to a weakening of the rules-based international trade system."[95] But they were in a clear minority. For the powerful anti-Castro lobby in the House and the Senate, any move to weaken or terminate key provisions of Helms-Burton was an unacceptable dilution of the administration's commitment to bring about the collapse of the Castro government.

A significant breakthrough remained elusive. Washington's insistence that the onus was on the other side to move the discussions "off dead center" virtually guaranteed that any final agreement would be a drawn out affair. The EU's signal that it would do all within its power to avoid a return to the WTO likely emboldened American officials in the belief that an uncompromising approach would eventually produce a result acceptable to the White House. "What we have been trying to achieve in the negotiations . . . is effective disciplines, one that would fully achieve the objective of inhibiting and deterring investments in illegally expropriated property," Assistant Secretary of State for Economic and Business Affairs, Alan Larson, told a congressional hearing on the WTO disputes panel. "We have made clear that while we are talking about a global set of disciplines [they must] cover American property in Cuba that was expropriated illegally without consultation."[96]

In January 1998, President Clinton extended the Title III waiver and agreed to review the overall sanctions policy. EU officials cautiously welcomed the latter, while reserving final judgment until "we . . . see what it means in reality."[97] But later that month, in a decidedly provocative move, which served to highlight the sharply differing approaches to Cuba, the EU published details of a plan to establish a committee responsible for putting together a business opportunities guide and for organizing seminars in Havana "to discuss ways of attracting investment in Cuba."[98] The EU ambassador to the United States called this initiative "in line with" Europe's belief that engaging Cuba was "the most likely catalyst for bringing about economic change to the island."[99]

Despite a continuing stalemate in negotiations over the expropriated properties issue, the Europeans were not about to attempt to reactivate the WTO panel. On April 20, the EU issued a statement that the panel would be allowed to lapse, with the caveat that a new panel would be launched if the U.S. imposed sanctions against European companies under either Helms-Burton or the ILSA. "We still have the panel in our back pocket," said EU spokesman Nigel Gardner. "If action is taken against European companies we will use it immediately." He insisted that the decision was merely "a technical development" that did not indicate any weakening of political pressure on the White House to annul the legislation.[100] Addressing the European Parliament's Foreign Affairs Committee, Sir Leon Brittan described "extraterritorial legislation" as still the most serious problem between America and its alliance partners, and said that Europe would not be satisfied with "just a ceasefire."[101] It wanted the issue resolved once and for all. While denoting his pleasure with the EU decision, the now–under secretary of state, Eizenstat, remarked that there was still "a long way" to go."[102]

On May 18, the EU and the U.S. reached an agreement on a package of measures to settle these two festering trade disputes, although the prospect of permanent solutions would depend on Clinton's success in getting Congress to come on board. In signing an "Understanding on Disciplines," the White House gave assurances that European companies would receive permanent waivers from both Helms-Burton and the ILSA and made a commitment to seek congressional authority to grant a Title IV "visa restrictions" waiver without delay; the Europeans agreed to deny government loans, subsidies, or political risk insurance to companies that invest in nations with an "established record" of illegal expropriations and to participate in establishing a global registry of confiscated properties that would be subject to these "binding principles," enabling the former owners to pursue redress in Europe and possibly around the world. State Department officials left no doubt that Cuba with its 5,911 registered U.S. claimants was the main target. Under Secretary Eizenstat termed the agreement "the biggest blow ever struck for the protection of property rights of U.S. citizens and against the efforts of Castro to expropriate property." In subsequent congressional testimony, he optimistically declared that as a result of this "historic breakthrough . . . we have chilled investment [in Cuba] in ways that have not happened in 37 years."[103] The EU, however, made it clear that it would not move to fulfill its side of the bargain until the permanent Title IV waiver had been exercised. It also extracted a White House promise to keep renewing the Title III "trafficking" waiver until the end of the Clinton presidency and to lobby Congress to make it permanent given the EU's efforts to promote democracy and human rights in Cuba.

In sum, the "Understanding on Disciplines" was a highly conditional arrangement with plenty of trip wires that could reignite the dispute. The U.S. concessions had a "trust us" aura about them. If the White House had the legal authority to waive ILSA provisions of its choosing, it could not make the same claim about Helms-Burton. Any tampering with that act required congressional assent. In contrast to Eizenstat's attempt to put the best possible spin on the agreement, the EU chairman and British prime minister, Tony Blair, spoke in more measured tones about the breakthrough having "avoided a showdown over sanctions."[104] Notwithstanding Brussels' quid pro quo for the "disciplines" to become operative, senior Clinton officials were still unable to conceal their delight over what they interpreted as a commitment by EU member states "not to upgrade their political or economic relations with Cuba until or unless Cuba improved their human rights and democratic record."[105] The State Department's Cuba Office was more candid in appraising the administration view of the May 18 deal: "We were trying to come up with a political arrangement. We were not trying to change the law—we've moved beyond that."[106]

On Capitol Hill, meanwhile, the signals were not promising, casting real doubts over Clinton's ability to deliver on his end of the bargain even if he was genuinely committed to doing so. "Congress certainly didn't buy off on the May 18 agreement," one knowledgeable legislative insider put it.[107] "The key word in the agreement is 'try,'" explained Andrew Semmel, who was monitoring the debate out of Republican senator Richard Lugar's office. "I don't think there's many people, if anybody, up here who thinks that there is any chance whatever for fundamental legislative redrafting of Helms-Burton. But everybody thinks the jawboning with the Europeans is worthwhile. Everybody wants the Europeans to be more compliant with whatever the intentions of Helms-Burton were."[108] But if the congressional debate revealed a widespread skepticism about Clinton's agreement with the EU, some legislators were more dismissive than others as they pursued their own anti-Castro agendas. Chairman of the Senate Foreign Relations Committee, Jesse Helms, was positively scathing about the disciplines: "It will be a cold day in you-know-where before the EU convinces me to trade the binding restrictions in the Helms-Burton law for an agreement that legitimizes their theft of American property in Cuba."[109]

On June 18, Helms and House International Relations Committee Chairman, Ben Gilman (R-N.Y.), wrote to Secretary of State Albright demanding a number of changes to tighten up the agreement with the Europeans before they would consent to any tampering with Helms-Burton provisions. They attacked the disciplines as "weak sanctions" that would be "almost impossible" to enforce. "We are far from convinced," the letter concluded, "that [the disciplines] will inhibit or deter the unscrupulous companies that are willing to do business with the likes of Fidel Castro."[110] To assuage their concerns, Albright gave an ironclad "commitment" to reinstate Title IV if the Europeans failed to comply with the understanding.[111] Not surprisingly, Clinton proceeded to drag his feet on the permanent waiver "promise." Meanwhile, Brussels signaled there would be no further unilateral compromises over Helms-Burton.

The Policy Differences Widen

Europe's uncompromising position on Helms-Burton was tempered by a concern to ensure it did not risk any fundamental rupture in transatlantic ties. The most obvious expression of this outlook was a growing convergence over the importance of accelerating reforms in Cuba's political economy. Early intimations of this shift had surfaced in May 1996, following the defeat of Felipe González's socialist government in Spain. The new conservative prime minister, José María Aznar, declared his intention to align more closely with the Clinton White House and the Miami exile community leadership, and was soon pressuring the EU to link increased cooperation with Havana to an accelerated opening of the political system and greater respect for civil liberties.[112] On December 4, the EU reluctantly adopted what was essentially the Spanish argument as a binding policy on its members.[113] A formal document, titled the "Common Position on Cuba," and signed by all EU finance and economics ministers, declared that henceforth future economic aid to Cuba would be tied to the nature and pace of political changes on the island. "The Europeans didn't particularly like being shoe-horned into this 'Common Position,'" observed a State Department official, but they were realistic about the price that had to be paid to secure another Title III waiver.[114] Stuart Eizenstat termed the EU document "a major advance."[115]

Paradoxically, the Europeans appended their signatures to a document that highlighted the different approaches favored on either side of the Atlantic in dealing with Cuba. It encouraged a peaceful transition to democracy based on Castro government initiatives, not external coercion, and linked future aid to periodic EC reports confirming visible progress toward democracy, including respect for human rights. At the same time, the EU remained committed to its dialogue with Havana, acknowledged the economic reforms that had been implemented, and pledged to continue humanitarian aid disbursements through appropriate nongovernmental organizations. A Dutch Foreign Ministry official emphatically denied U.S. assertions of a direct relationship between the "Common Position" and Helms-Burton: "This is absolutely not the case."[116] Engagement, not coercion, he explained, was the driving force behind European actions.

While genuflecting to U.S. sensitivities, the accord did not fundamentally impair Cuban-European relations. The EU still adhered to its basic engagement posture, and the "Common Position" did nothing to quell continental opposition to Helms-Burton. European governments, traders, and investors continued to frustrate Washington's best efforts to force them out of the Cuban economy or discourage efforts to seek out new business opportunities. Between 1994 and 1997, EU-Cuban two-way trade grew at a modest but steady rate: the value of EU exports to Cuba increased from 579 to 978 million euros, while imports from Cuba rose from 322 to 454 million. During approximately the same period (1993 to 1997), boosted by the 1995 Foreign Investment Act, the combined number of joint ventures between French, Italian, Spanish, and United Kingdom companies and the Castro regime increased from 31 to 127.[117] By December 1998, all joint ventures—largely concentrated in the petroleum, mining, and tourist sectors—topped 340 and, according to Foreign Investment Minister Ibrahim Ferradaz, forty percent had been signed post-Helms-Burton.[118]

Senior Clinton policymakers were reluctant to acknowledge these deepening bonds between Europe and Cuba. For them, the Castro regime was still, as secretary of state–designate Madeleine Albright informed the Senate Foreign Relations Committee in January 1997, "an embarrassment to the international community."[119] For the Europeans, the embarrassment was not Cuba, but rather a U.S. government still clinging to a Cold War outlook that belonged to another era.

Nevertheless, American policy certainly impeded Cuba's economic recovery. While the total number of joint ventures with foreign capital jumped from 212 in mid-1995 to 260 in 1996, the fact that this number fell about thirteen percent below Castro government expectations was attributable largely to the impact of Helms-Burton.[120] It was the sense of uncertainty created by the legislation—whether investors were specifically targeted or believed they might be vulnerable to its provisions—that led to pullouts, cutbacks, or restructuring of activities to circumvent confrontations with Washington. In particular, British, French, and Spanish companies engaged in sugar financing operations were forced to restructure their lending activities to avoid any confrontation with the Title III trafficking provision.

At a January 1997 off-the-record press briefing, Stuart Eizenstat noted "12 instances at least where activities on confiscated property were stopped or activities refrained from" in order to avoid charges of trafficking.[121] Testifying before a House subcommittee in May 1998, the State Department's coordinator for Cuban Affairs, Michael Ranneberger, increased the number to nineteen and informed legislators that another twelve foreign-based companies were currently being investigated "about their activities in Cuba." He claimed, with some justification and considerable satisfaction, that these "implementation efforts have had a significant negative impact on the Cuban economy," rendering the investment climate more "risky and unstable."[122]

Cuba's vice president, Carlos Lage, agreed that key provisions of Helms-Burton "had complicated" his government's relationship with a number of foreign companies, and even Fidel Castro pointed to "serious negative consequences," especially for the sugar industry.[123] According to Lage, some $200 million in promised financing for the 1997 harvest was a casualty of U.S. pressures: "More than through action on particular firms, [Helms-Burton] harms us through intimidation."[124] Such investment setbacks were compounded by the difficulties in obtaining alternative sources of overseas financial assistance, particularly medium or long-term loans, which would likely remain off limits prior to a restructuring of Cuba's $11 billion plus hard currency foreign debt. This lack of access to external finance, he said, largely explained a projected 2.5 percent economic growth rate in 1997 compared with 7.8 percent in 1996.[125] In February 1998, Foreign Investment Minister Ferradaz conceded that sixty-three projects had been "dissolved" over the past few years "for various reasons," among them, presumably, the Helms-Burton legislation.[126]

Not all foreign investors were intimidated by the threat of U.S. prosecution. While two Madrid-based hotel chains, Occidental Hoteles and Paradores Nacionales de Tourismo, abruptly postponed plans in July 1996 to build new hotels in Cuba, the *New York Times* reported that most of the fifty Spanish companies already operating in Cuba "have not wavered."[127] They included one of the island's biggest foreign investors, the Sol Melía hotel group, which reaffirmed its intention to push ahead with a $275 million flotation to boost its operations and, if necessary, sacrifice the one U.S.-based property it owned, a hotel in Miami.[128] Moreover, the Occidental and Paradores decisions were not dictated exclusively by concerns over Helms-Burton; the general cooling of relations between the Aznar government and Havana and the EU adoption of the "Common Position" on cooperation with Cuba also played a part.

In March 1998, Cuba's future access to foreign financial capital received a potential boost when Japan, the island's biggest creditor, signed a restructuring deal that covered $769 million of debt owed to 182 Japanese companies. A successful rescheduling of Cuba's short-term bilateral debt with Italy followed soon after.[129] While these agreements didn't open the floodgates, France later announced it was increasing its export credit provision to Cuba to $185 million in 1998 and $200 million in 1999 and would support Havana's request to the Paris Club for a renegotiation of its commercial debt.[130] Over the same two-year period, Britain's public and private sectors also increased the amounts of credit guarantees they were prepared to advance to Cuba. The Government Development Corporation (CDC) established a new $30 million medium term lending facility to finance Cuban purchases or leasing of capital equipment and announced that Cuban-owned enterprises, as well as joint ventures with foreign capital, if they satisfied the CDC's "due diligence" requirement, would be eligible for loans; the Banco Nacional de Cuba signed an agreement with the London-based insurance broker Lambert Fenchurch that would give it access to international insurance cover guarantees, thus increasing its ability to finance new trade and investment operations; and in September 1999, the two governments signed a rescheduling agreement for $27 million of short term debt owed by Havana, thus enabling Whitehall to resume medium term export credit cover for Cuba.[131]

The short-term debt rescheduling negotiations between the Paris Club group of creditor nations and Fidel Castro's government through 1999 only served to emphasize Europe's determination to engage Cuba while remaining sensitive to U.S. concerns. The negotiations proceeded cautiously—not only for reasons having to do with Cuba's limited capacity to repay, but because of Washington's publicly expressed opposition to any "special treatment" for that part of the island's debt owed to the Paris Club.[132] Signals from the Clinton administration that it would not move to block the negotiations may have been influenced by the fact that none of Cuba's Paris Club debt was owed to U.S. institutions and that the French-chaired "technical committee" established to deal with the Cuban debt had no American member. Days after they began in late September, one source privy to the talks described them as "the most positive" yet between the two sides.[133]

In June 1998, the EU had again demonstrated its commitment to constructive engagement when, over strong U.S. objections, it admitted Cuba to observer status in the African, Caribbean, and Pacific (ACP) group of countries. Ironically, Spain's rightist Aznar government took credit for the decision. This invitation was a diplomatic coup for Havana, notwithstanding European anger over Castro's crackdown on dissidents after passage of a harsh new internal security law in March and the EU's clear expectation that, in return, the Castro government must show significant progress in "human rights, good governance, and political freedom."[134]

Almost six months later, in January 1999, the official in charge of Inter-American Affairs at the NSC, James Dobbins, hit back at Europe's "doubters" in Congress and elsewhere: "The European Union has given us a pledge, and we believe is adhering to it, not to improve relations with Cuba unless Cuba makes significant steps in the areas of democracy and human rights. That doesn't mean they're going to put an embargo in place, and we didn't expect it; but neither are they going to give them preferential trade arrangements or concessional credits, and they haven't done either of those things."[135] Nor, however, did it mean that the Europeans had any intention of abandoning their engagement approach in the absence of "significant steps." While the latter was a precondition for the EU's "full cooperation," its most recent biannual report reaffirmed the desire of all member states "to become a *partner* with Cuba with a view to progressively and irreversibly opening up the Cuban economy" (my emphasis).[136]

Reflecting one year later on the May 1998 "Understanding" that mothballed the EU's WTO challenge to Helms-Burton, a senior Department of Commerce official expressed a rather jaundiced view of what exactly had been agreed to. It seemed, to him, mostly "smoke and mirrors," such as Europe's promise to take arms export controls into account in dealing with Cuba. "We haven't seen much of that," he said, "and I live in dread and fear of being called up to the Hill [Congress] and asked about that."[137] Assistant Secretary of State Alan Larson was more concerned that the administration might backtrack on its commitments at the risk of "losing its window of opportunity for burying its bitter differences with Europe over investment in Cuba." Speaking to a meeting of the U.S.-Cuba Business Council in Miami, he warned that "we'll lose the Europeans if we don't get it done this year."[138] If Larsen's sentiments were shared by others in the executive branch, as is likely, a key hurdle loomed as high as ever; Congress was still in no mood to cooperate, no matter the impact on transatlantic relations. A State Department Cuba official privately conceded it was "obvious that a waiver of Title IV is dead. There is no hope for it. The EU knows that and it may blow up very soon. There is a lot of pressure on the Hill for a Title IV determination. The Europeans are clear that if it involves a European company all bets are off."[139]

On July 1, 1999, the State Department lit a fuse when it asked the Spanish hotel group Sol Melía to reply "expeditiously" to a charge that one of its hotels in eastern Cuba was built on land seized from U.S. citizens in 1961.[140] Pressured by Jesse Helms, the department formally notified the hotel chain in August that not one, but three, of its hotels in Cuba were on land claimed by a South Florida family.[141] Any application of Helms-Burton against Sol Melía obviously posed a threat to the "disciplines" accord and was likely to put the EU and Washington back on a collision course in the WTO.

Sol Melía executives, nonetheless, remained sanguine about their problem, describing State's "please explain" letter as a "routine procedure" about which they were "absolutely not worried."[142] Irrespective of the outcome, the company announced it would maintain its operations in Cuba. "Not only are we going to stay there," said one defiant Sol Melía director, "but we are going to grow."[143] The Spanish government took a less relaxed approach. Punitive action against Sol Melía, warned Foreign Minister Abel Matutes, "would unleash a reaction from the European Union and its governments," not to speak of an immediate appeal by Madrid to the WTO.[144] EU headquarters in Brussels advised that it was watching the situation "very closely."[145] As the issue dragged on into December with no end in sight, External Affairs Commissioner Chris Patten left American lawmakers in no doubt that the Europeans had drawn their line in the sand. "I don't think it's for us at the moment necessarily to do any more," he observed.[146] To this point, the EU had not formally enacted its investment disciplines; nor had the Clinton White House lived up to its end of the May 1998 agreement.

Meanwhile, Washington had become embroiled in yet another potentially damaging trade dispute involving Cuba and the Europeans that had its origins in a 1996 decision by the Bermuda-based Bacardi Company to begin selling Havana Club rum in the United States even though its registration of the trademark had lapsed more than two decades earlier. The Cuban government was granted the rights to the abandoned trademark by the U.S. Trademark and Patent Office in 1976 and subsequently transferred them to Havana Club Holdings, a Cuban-French joint venture. Pernod Ricard, the French company that now held the U.S. rights, brought suit in U.S. courts on the grounds that Bacardi had violated its legal rights. Bacardi responded by approaching a key member of the anti-Castro Cuba lobby on Capitol Hill, Florida senator Connie Mack (R), who quietly inserted Section 211—stating that trademarks associated with companies expropriated by the Cuban government could not be recognized, renewed, or issued in the United States without the consent of the original owner—into the 1999 Omnibus Appropriations Bill. With its passage into law, there was no possibility that Pernod Ricard could obtain a legal judgment upholding its suit.[147]

The EU demanded repeal of Section 211—to no avail. The pressure applied by Bacardi's congressional allies, notably Jesse Helms and Dan Burton, ensured that Secretary of State Albright would make little headway in efforts to solve the dispute. Incensed by Washington's foot-dragging, the EU decided to take its case to the WTO, charging that Section 211 contravened America's obligations under the Intellectual Property Rights (TRIPs) agreement to which it was a signatory. John Howard, the U.S. Chamber of Commerce's director of international policy, wondered why the administration was willing to risk "an unnecessary fight at the WTO *of our own making*, when we have so much else at stake in the global trading system" (my emphasis).[148] By year's end, the dispute was still unresolved with no satisfactory solution in sight.

Collectively, the Europeans maintained a united front on their earlier commitments to promote political liberalization and respect for human rights on the island. The 1998 EU decision to extend observer status to Cuba at meetings of the ACP nations, for instance, was made on the understanding that full membership in an aid and trade pact (Cotonou Agreement), under negotiation between the EU and the ACP states to replace the Lomé Convention, would be withheld until Havana made substantial progress on human rights and democratic reform. Cuba dug in its heels over what it considered "discriminatory and interfering" conditions as the final details of the new accord were being negotiated in early 2000.[149] Even though twelve of the fifteen member European governments were reportedly still willing to allow the Cubans to join, the EU members of the United Nations Human Rights Commission (UNHRC) supported the commission's April resolution condemning the Castro government over its human rights record.[150] Furious, Havana withdrew its bid to join the EU-ACP pact and canceled a forthcoming EU delegation visit.

If these actions signaled the most serious rift in relations between Havana and Brussels since the ill-fated visit by Manuel Marin in February 1996, Washington could only take limited satisfaction from the outcome. New economic initiatives confirmed Europe's determination to quarantine the issue and not let it become a roadblock to expanding links with the island. Following on the official bilateral debt accords previously signed by France, Italy, and Spain, the Cuban-German debt agreement was another measure of Europe's willingness to accommodate particular conflicts within a broader-based policy of engagement with Cuba. In May, Bonn and Havana signed a bilateral debt renegotiation accord covering $99 million of short, medium, and long-term debts owed by Cuba. That same month, Cooperation and Development Minister Heidemarie Wieczorek-Zeul became the first member of a German government to visit Cuba in more than forty years. While there, she announced the resumption of official development aid and the restoration of Germany's export credit cover. Six months later, the German machine company, Sket, negotiated an estimated $40 million contract, financed by three of the country's major banks, to build a steel rolling mill in Cuba.[151]

The message from the Elysée Palace was an equally firm desire on the part of the Jospin government to expand trade ties with Cuba. Less than four months after Paris had renewed its annual food-for-sugar barter deal with Havana, valued at $180 million, a French trade mission to the island in June identified $75 million of potential business for national power generating, transport, railway, and engineering companies.

Spain's response largely mirrored that of France. In April 1998, a delegation representing more than 100 Spanish companies visited the island, signaling the possible beginnings of a thaw in a sixteen-month-long chilly relationship between Madrid and Havana. Addressing a University of Havana conference later that year, Foreign Minister Abel Matutes restated his government's strong support for reforms in the island's political economy, but told his audience they should be implemented by Cubans "without impositions, embargoes or pressures from abroad."[152] In January 2000, the Franco-Spanish tobacco giant Altadis announced a massive $500 million purchase of one half of Cuba's state tobacco selling company, Habanos. Another prominent Spanish company, Ibersuizas, began negotiations with the Cuban government over a $150 million investment in the island's cement industry that were still ongoing in July when the Iberia Group announced an agreement to set up two joint ventures in Cuba's aviation sector—the first of their kind involving Spanish firms.[153] Also hoping to encourage greater participation by national companies in the island economy, the Italian government established a Foreign Trade Institute office in Havana following a visit to Cuba by Foreign Undersecretary Mauro Fabris in late October.

Havana's partially successful strategy of seeking to reschedule debts owed to foreign governments on an individual basis was a way of getting around the obstacles in the way of dealing with the Paris Club group of official creditors—in particular, U.S. opposition to Cuban membership in the International Monetary Fund and the World Bank and Cuba's 1986 declaration of a unilateral moratorium on debt service payments on official bilateral loans. But even here some progress was discernable in late 1999 when a Paris Club delegation visited Havana for discussions about rescheduling the $3.5 billion in hard currency owed to member countries. Ongoing talks culminated in a September 2000 Paris Club decision to try and begin a multilateral rescheduling deal with the Castro government.[154]

The EU remained as determined as ever to protect the interests of its member nations' companies from the "long reach" of U.S. laws. Repeated EU appeals had failed to induce the Clinton administration to overturn the contentious Section 211 of the 1999 Omnibus Appropriations Act in order to resolve the "Havana Club" dispute. Lobbying efforts on Capitol Hill had proved equally fruitless. When a U.S. appeals court ruled in February 2000 that Pernod Ricard could not register the Havana Club trademark in view of Section 211, the EU took the matter to the WTO dispute settlement process. That July, frustrated by Washington's refusal "to enter substantive discussions on the issue," the EU formally requested that a panel be established to review the law on trademark rights.[155] Another two months passed with no resolution in sight, at which point the WTO agreed to a second EU request to establish the panel.

As a result, two years after the Eizenstat-Brittan "Understanding" had temporarily diffused a major inter-Alliance trade conflict, there was now a distinct possibility that it might flare up again. The reasons could be found in the same dynamics that had driven the EU-U.S. dispute over Cuba since George Bush signed the CDA into law in October 1992: Washington's insistence that it knew best on Cuba and that the rest of the world should fall into line behind its policy; the Europeans' refusal to subordinate their own national interests to U.S. demands and assume the role of submissive partners; the failure of both sides to achieve a lasting settlement because of the determination by congressional hardliners to see every letter of their sanctions' laws enforced; and a refusal by the White House to resist this pressure in the wider national interest.

As the second Clinton administration wound down, U.S. officials were left to ponder what the past four years meant—beginning with Helms-Burton and ending with Section 211—for Cuba policy and transatlantic relations. "We succeeded in doing what it is almost impossible to do," lamented an almost disbelieving State Department official working on Cuba. "The one thing that unites the European Union member states is Helms-Burton. Every single one of them, even the ones who completely agreed with us on human rights, rejected Helms-Burton."[156] The difficulty of coping with Alliance partners far less willing to accommodate U.S. foreign policy interests than they were during the Cold War era was not lost on America's diplomats: "For a long time we could persuade people to go along with us but that is not necessarily the case anymore. Helms-Burton was something that we thought we would be able to get people to accept but it wasn't as easy as we thought."[157] This was a lesson Clinton's successor, promising an even harsher approach to Cuba, was about to learn.

Competition and Confrontation: The New Conflict over Cuba

In one of his last executive actions, Clinton suspended implementation of Title III of Helms-Burton for a further six months in January 2001. That relieved the immediate pressure on the incoming president, George W. Bush, to demonstrate his anti-Castro credentials and removed the immediate EU concern about an early showdown with the new administration. A senior State Department official recalled "a lot of fear" that the legislation "was going to become an even bigger problem under Bush."[158]

The Europeans, however, could not afford to leave anything to chance—much less to the vagaries of U.S. domestic politics. Both privately and publicly they let it be known that they would fiercely challenge any new attempt to implement the extraterritorial provisions of Helms-Burton. According to State Department officials, Paris and Madrid were particularly active in raising the issue "at extremely high levels" within the Bush White House. The French, said one, were doing it simply because they "enjoy bringing it up as much as possible," while Spain's motivation was much more specific: a concern over the possible retargeting of Sol Melía, which managed twenty-two hotels on the island.[159]

The EU reaffirmed its stance in mid-March after Secretary of State Colin Powell made a noncommittal statement to a House International Relations Committee hearing about whether the president would continue to exercise the waiver, saying that this option would be considered "when we believe there are serious, great, overriding national interests for which waiver authority is provided."[160] At a Brussels meeting, EU trade commissioner Pascal Lamy assured Sol Melía's managing director that the EC would oppose any U.S. attempt to impose sanctions on the hotel group's Cuban investments.[161] In the lead-up to the April UNHRC vote on a resolution condemning the Castro government's human rights record, several EU countries highlighted their opposition to U.S. sanctions by inserting into the resolution a statement criticizing the Cuba embargo. The attempt failed but only after heavy lobbying by American officials of other UNHRC members to delete the offending words. Bush personally confronted the depth of European anger at the June EU-U.S. summit in Gothenberg, Sweden, where delegates told him that WTO proceedings would be reactivated if any of their companies were targeted under the Helms-Burton legislation.[162]

On July 13, Bush announced a number of initiatives to tighten the embargo. These included a commitment of more funds to enforce restrictions on remittances to Cuba, a crackdown on unlicensed travel to the island, and increased support to anti-Castro dissidents. He also repeated remarks made in his Cuban Independence Day address on May 18 that U.S. sanctions amounted to "not just a policy, but a moral statement"[163] and committed his administration to oppose any attempt to weaken them. Three days later, the president announced that Title III of Helms-Burton would be waived for another six months. By maintaining the Clinton approach, Bush effectively rendered the provision dead in the water and, thus, any thought of reviving the EU's WTO challenge moot. But just as the administration continued to insist that "there won't be any discussion" on the May 1998 "Understanding" with the EU to seek a permanent waiver of Title III from the Congress,[164] the Europeans were equally forthright in maintaining that they "would never waive our rights to challenge Helms-Burton in the WTO."[165]

For all practical purposes, the threat of a direct conflict over lawsuits involving European investments in Cuba had passed. "It's assumed on both sides, or at least on the European side, that the U.S. will continue to renew the Title III waiver," observed a State Department European Affairs official in late 2002. "Now if, for whatever reason, the U.S. was not to renew the waiver again then, of course, the WTO case would come back. But for the moment I don't think anyone in the administration would be advocating that we stop renewing it."[166] EU officials concurred with this assessment: "Our assumption is that a regular waiver is part of the understanding. So we're assuming that things are ok and the U.S. is aware that if things, for whatever reason, turn out not to be ok then there's the WTO and other things [that we would do] and that would just sour everything."[167]

Much the same fate befell Title IV of Helms-Burton. Bush continued to stall implementation on national security grounds, but removing it from the statute books—an objective Washington agreed to pursue in May 1998—had fallen into what one senior State Department Western Hemisphere official described as "a state of diplomatic purgatory."[168] While the EU remained in no doubt that "if there were to be a Title IV action then it wouldn't take too long for everything to spiral out of control again," the likelihood of such a scenario occurring seemed more and more remote. "Obviously the Europeans are interested in a more permanent arrangement but I think they recognize that under this present administration that's all they are going to get," a Department Europeanist confided, "and given the fact that the United States has not upset the cart by vigorously pursuing any action against European companies, then people are happy just to let things stay as they are."[169]

Titles III and IV, according to this official, remained little more than "sticking points" in transatlantic relations with the European attitude now basically reduced to that of "going through the motions": "every time the president is due to make a waiver they bring it up as a basic agenda item, but as just kind of a check mark, 'we're looking forward to the president's waiver' to check it off the list."[170] A Western Hemisphere Affairs colleague related a similar experience. During a meeting with European Commission officials in the latter half of 2002 to discuss a range of issues, "they went through their recitation about Helms-Burton, but what was interesting about the conversation was that while they had to say this issue was a talking point, they made it clear in the way they presented it that they were just going through the motions."[171]

The other piece of Cuba-related legislation left in dispute from the Clinton era—Section 211 of the 1999 Omnibus Appropriations Act—was headed for a similar impasse. In August 2001, the WTO panel ruled that Section 211 did partly contravene WTO rules on intellectual property rights. The Bush administration successfully appealed the decision but the judges coupled this second ruling with a demand that the law be changed because it discriminated against Cuban nationals' rights to claim a trademark in the United States.[172] The EU then set three deadlines (December 2002, June and December 2003) requiring the U.S. to bring its Omnibus legislation into line with this ruling. The Bush administration made no effort to push for the repeal or amendment of Section 211 as each deadline came and passed. In January 2004, the EU extended the deadline for a further twelve months, hoping that a bipartisan bill submitted for Senate consideration (actively supported by the U.S. business community) would finally force the White House to initiate talks with Cuba to ensure both countries adhere to trademark protection agreements.[173]

European enthusiasm for economic engagement with Cuba was not dampened. Indeed, the value of two-way trade between Cuba and Western Europe increased at a faster rate between 1997 and 2000 compared with the 1994–97 period.[174] Beginning in 2001, a combination of factors severely limited Cuba's ability to pay for imports in hard currency and to service its debt repayments: the global economic slowdown producing a slump in commodity prices, oil price hikes, the closure of the Russian intelligence gathering facility at Lourdes (for which Moscow had been paying an estimated $200 million a year in rent), and a sharp fall in tourist revenues following the September 11 terrorist attacks on New York and Washington. As well, growing frustration with the rules and regulations governing commercial dealings in Cuba led to a marked slump in new European investment.[175] Nonetheless, some European countries had developed an economic stake in Cuba that had subtly changed the dynamics of their relationship with the island in ways that threatened to trigger new disagreements with American policymakers.

The Aznar government was a case in point. A vocal critic of the Cuba's domestic political structures and human rights record, Spain was also Cuba's major European trading partner; in 2000, total bilateral trade was close to $900 million that both sides had a vested interest in isolating from the more fractious aspects of the relationship. "Spanish interests and ties in Cuba have become so important that it is essential to maintain and expand them," explained Spain's economic and trade consul in Havana, Luis López Moreno. "It is no longer possible for either party to back away."[176] The often times testy nature of the political relationship notwithstanding, Madrid constantly opposed the U.S. embargo as "inappropriate, unjust and counterproductive."[177] Individual investors and traders were also starting to take a much longer view of their Cuban operations, preparing for the time when the U.S. embargo and travel ban is lifted. In October, the director of Sol Melía's Cuba operations, Gabriel Canaves, revealed the Spanish hotel chain's plan to "make strategic investments in places where tomorrow there will be an adequate return, and in hotels where an American tourist would really want to stay when he comes to Cuba."[178] The same month the economic attaché at the French Embassy in Havana, Pierre Sella, commented on how his country's investors were positioning themselves for the day relations between the U.S. and Cuba improved: "We're preparing for this change with a new distribution of our exports in favor of capital goods for industry, infrastructure and transportation. It's normal that Cuba would want to diversify its suppliers, and we're preparing for that."[179]

Such expressions of a longer-term commitment challenged a widespread assumption among American business interests that European economic activity in Cuba was more or less opportunistic and would not survive post-embargo competition from the North. Kirby Jones, a prominent consultant to U.S. corporations interested in pursuing trade and investment opportunities in Cuba, put it this way in early 1999: "The Europeans and Canadians, and others, are trying like hell to get stuff started so that when the Americans come in there'll just be an auction."[180] Whether or not this perception was initially valid, Europeans had now adopted a more nuanced approach based on the belief that they could indeed compete with the Americans once the embargo was lifted.

Even Bush State Department Western Hemisphere officials were starting to have doubts about a post-sanctions "American takeover" and contemplating the possibility that foreign investment in Cuba might well become a "bigger [EU-US] issue down the line," given the EU community will "want to protect their investments and see the investments of their nationals be profitable if possible." But what clearly raised Washington's hackles was the belief that EU investor strategies were directly linked to the end of the U.S. travel ban prohibiting most American citizens from legally visiting Cuba: "Unfortunately it's the American tourists that they are betting their profit on. I think it's up to the U.S.

government to be honest about that. We're not prepared to support their businesses that profit because ultimately they profit a regime that we have major problems with."[181]

The Europeans were also acutely aware of the potential for a new kind of dispute with the U.S. over Cuba. "American companies are well prepared to take advantage of the situation [in Cuba]," said one EU trade official. "And that's the problem and we recognize that. But what we say is don't fall prey to the politics of it and we won't either."[182] This seemed a rather forlorn hope; the politics of Washington's confrontational approach versus Europe's constructive engagement was unlikely to disappear in the near or medium term. An EU-Cuba specialist gave vent to both the frustration and the dilemma that Europe had confronted ever since the end of the Cold War when it came to relations with Fidel Castro's government: "Throughout the two Bush administrations, and Clinton's, there has been a constant pressure from the U.S. to take a hard line with Castro regardless of what the EU was doing. The messages that were delivered at every opportunity have been the same. We are constantly asked to do more at the local level in Havana, to meet with the opposition, to promote human rights and to promote democracy." Washington's relentless pressure on the Europeans "to be more firm and punitive with Castro" has had a negative impact in two respects: it has "contaminated" EU policy toward the U.S. and complicated EU relations with Cuba.[183]

The EU was still locked into its 1996 "Common Position" that identified the promotion of democratic reform and respect for human rights in Cuba as core policy goals and tied economic aid to the nature and pace of political changes on the island. In July 2001, a visiting EU parliamentary delegation offered some hope that talks might resume when it commented favorably on Castro government's economic initiatives, notably in the tourist and foreign investment sectors, while remaining critical of the lack of political reforms. It was not until August that the frostiness in the relationship began to thaw, coinciding with the arrival in Havana of Belgium's deputy prime minister and EU president Louis Michel, who told waiting reporters that it was important to resume the political dialogue "as fast as possible [and] without one side imposing conditions on the other."[184] After returning, he met with EU foreign ministers, where it was agreed to restart the dialogue on one condition: the Castro government "must send us some signals."[185] The concessions sought, though, were rather modest, including Havana's support for United Nations conventions on civil, political, social, and economic rights and a moratorium on the death penalty.

By December 2001, the political dialogue was back on track. The EU interpreted the expansion of religious freedom in Cuba, no executions in the past two years, the release of political prisoners, and Havana's ratification of some United Nations human rights instruments as positive developments that "could create an appropriate framework" for further dialogue and cooperation.[186] Even Spain, the harshest critic of Cuba's human rights performance, supported renewal of the political dialogue on the grounds, said Foreign Minister Josep Pique, that it would offer "greater room for manoeuvre to exert pressure" for more improvements.[187]

Paradoxically, however, this collective effort was being simultaneously undermined by the actions of EU members acting individually and placing little or no conditionality on their bilateral dealings with Havana—as continuing aid, trade, and debt accords attested. Moreover, while European officials still exhorted their Cuban counterparts to "do a lot more" to improve the island's human rights record, these urgings had a "matter of course" quality to them, just as lobbying on behalf of specific political prisoners and meeting with dissidents were generally as far as the Europeans were prepared to go in offering practical assistance.[188] In mid-2002, the EU foreign ministers could not hide their disappointment at the continued absence of "major changes on the part of the Cuban government towards the aims of the 'Common Position'" and that the measures taken to date were still "only the first steps."[189] But the EU indicated no desire to exclude Cuba from the ongoing process of deepening ties with the Latin American region, emphasizing that "tangible results" could only occur if the process of political dialogue with Havana was maintained.[190] Aside from the ongoing tussle over Cuba's suitability for admission to the Cotonou Agreement—and thus eligibility for EU aid and preferential market access—the EU commitment to democracy promotion in Cuba amounted to essentially ritualistic initiatives, ranging from the annual condemnation of the Castro government at the UNHRC to highly general statements by senior EU officials that "if Cuba wants to improve its relationship with the European Union, then it should set about improving its human rights record."[191]

On the other hand, the Europeans seemed to take demands for economic reform on the island, where immediate and tangible interests were at stake, much more seriously. While the sharp fall in new direct foreign investment from $448 million in 2000 to just under $39 million in 2001 was part of a subregional trend, as these figures indicate it was particularly dramatic in the case of Cuba. In June 2002, the EU summarized its myriad concerns about the operating business environment in a document presented to Vice President Carlos Lage. The study prefaced its criticisms by pointing out that European companies had become the island's "principal economic partner" and were committed to Cuba's "long term" development. But excessive laws and regulations (often lacking clarity and inconsistently applied), bureaucratic red tape, excessive utility costs, and the altering of joint venture agreements were inhibiting investment expansion. The document called for a "greater juridical security and a reliable and transparent legal framework" in relation to foreign investments; an end to discriminatory laws; increased flexibility for the non-

Cuban partner in joint venture operations; changes to labor regulations; and a rationalization of the tax system. These and other issues should be the subject of a "frank, constructive and respectful dialog[ue]." The pressure for change, though, would not come by beating the Cubans with a stick; a more promising strategy was to offer the carrot of Europeans' "good intentions" together with "technical aid in anticipation of the more ambitious programs which would be available as progress is made in these processes."[192]

In early December, EU and Cuban officials concluded talks in Havana with a joint communiqué hailing a "new stage" in relations between the two sides.[193] On returning to Brussels, the delegation of Europarliamentarians labeled the "Common Position" both "useless" and "anachronistic." One member of the delegation asserted that no Cuba-based ambassador from any EU country now supported it.[194] Although the "Common Position" received another vote of approval before year's end, it had become little more than an in-principal commitment. Buoyed by this show of support, Castro declared that Cuba would renew its request to join the Cotonou Agreement, noting that some of the conditions the EU had placed on Cuba's membership had been "tempered in some form."[195] Against this background it was no great surprise when the EU Council of Ministers decided to extend the "Common Position" deadline for the next assessment of Cuba's human rights progress from six to twelve months and the EC announced it would open an office in Havana in 2003.[196]

Just as President George W. Bush, eighteen months earlier, had balanced his soft-pedaling on Title III of Helms-Burton with a package of tougher measures toward Cuba, the European Union adopted a similar strategy by honoring the Cuban dissident Oswaldo Payá Sardiñas with its prestigious Sakharov Award for the promotion of human rights in December 2002. The founder of Cuba's Christian Liberation Movement, Payá was the driving force behind the Varela Project, which had gathered 11,000 signatures in May on a petition to the Cuban National Assembly calling for a constitutional change on a number of issues including basic political rights, an amnesty for political prisoners, a new electoral law, and free and fair elections. The White House was not overly impressed by what it regarded as a purely symbolic gesture; it did little to change the prevailing sentiment in Washington that the Europeans were not applying sufficient pressure on Castro to implement political and economic reforms or that "their diplomatic missions in Havana should be more vigorous in their outreach to [Cuban] civil society."[197] Two months earlier, for instance, a senior State Department official had nominated the Varela Project as precisely the kind of initiative deserving of the EU's material support because it gave the latter "a great opportunity to basically put their money where their mouth is." In language that recalled Washington's 1996 attempt to have the EU extend its protection to the Cuban dissident group Concilio Cubano, he added that if the Europeans "really care about these conditions on the island, Varela is the perfect thing to support. The question back to Europe is 'Ok, if you want to talk about democratic transition, if you want to talk about engagement with the island, here you now have an opportunity to do that.'"[198]

According to this same U.S. official, the Europeans had long since dumped any "romantic notions" they might once have harbored about dealing with the Castro regime. For all their pretense about pursing an independent approach toward Cuba, the Europeans privately still looked to Washington as an insurance policy if things went wrong. "When something happens on the island, they're going to expect us to deal with the issue. They want us to be respectful of their investments on the island and then, in effect, they want us to be the guarantor if there is a tumultuous transition. That puts us in a position where it's not unreasonable of us to ask for some deference in terms of how we want to deal with any change on the island. So that's been always one of the dynamics of this. The Europeans always get very high and mighty on their soapbox. To put it very bluntly, undiplomatically, when the shit hits the fan they're expecting us to take care of it." The message to the European investors in Cuba should the "shit hit the fan" was just as unequivocal: "They need to get the hell out of the way."[199]

EU officials view the situation quite differently. America's Cuba policy, said one, "does not really fit into the normal foreign policy power of the United States; it is much more a domestic policy issue."[200] If Washington's approach has been overly influenced by the right-wing Cuban-American community and its congressional allies, observed another, "for the rest of the world Cuba is almost entering the mainstream."[201] What America's trade allies have increasingly demonstrated is that they are not only prepared to deal with the Castro government but to live with the institutional structures of the Cuban Revolution while advocating more transparency and political democratization.

Europe's response to the regime's unusually harsh crackdown on the dissident community in March 2003 meshed with this approach. The EU immediately condemned the summary trials and long prison sentences meted out to many of those arrested as "unacceptable"; warned Havana that it could negatively effect aid and trade ties; and indicated that it put a question mark once again over Cuba's application to join the Cotonou Agreement.[202] On May 19, Cuba withdrew its application to join the agreement, citing Europe's preoccupation with the island's human rights performance that it termed a pretext for imposing "unacceptable conditions" for treaty membership.[203] Nonetheless, Brussels pushed ahead with plans to establish an office in Havana, insisting that the "difficulties in political and human rights that we find will not diminish the importance of our presence there."[204] In keeping with this approach, the

EU drew back from an Italian government minister's proposal that "a kind of European embargo" against Cuba should be imposed if the crackdown persisted.[205]

On June 5, the EU presidency sent a message to Cuban authorities that it was "deeply concerned" about the human rights situation and called for the swift release of all political prisoners. The message also informed Havana that the EU had decided to impose some mild political sanctions on the island such as limits on high-level bilateral government visits and reductions in the profile of member states' participation in Cuban cultural events. Additionally, the EU would invite more Cuban dissidents abroad to participate, for example, in ceremonies hosted by European embassies marking significant national holidays and would immediately reevaluate its "Common Position" on Cuba.[206] Significantly, however, trade, aid, and investment ties were not affected.

An angry Castro responded by dismissing EU leaders as "a small gang, a mafia" who had "joined with the Yankee imperialists."[207] Over the next few days he led big demonstrations outside the Spanish and Italian Embassies and in a televised address to the nation again accused the EU of being "tugged along by the United States."[208] Cuban officials were particularly incensed over the decision to invite dissidents to European diplomatic functions. Foreign Minister Felipe Pérez Roque warned that it would turn European ambassadors into the "hired hands" of U.S. Interests Sections, targeting Spain's Cultural Center in Havana as an example par excellence.[209] But EU officials were sanguine about this backlash. EC commissioner Chris Patten explained the thinking behind their approach when responding to a journalist's question about whether EU policy on Cuba was moving closer to the U.S. position. "There's no difference between our approaches," Patten said. "We both deplore the human rights record of the Castro regime, but it's not been obvious to us that trying to cut off all contact with Cuba has been as successful as all of us would have liked in changing the regime and changing the way it behaves."[210] Constructive engagement, in other words, remained EU policy toward Cuba. Patten had mentioned the words "regime change" in passing, but stressed that the EU could maintain a normal relationship with Castro's Cuba as long as the regime modified its approach to human rights. In contrast to the Bush White House, the EU appeared to be taking issue with a particular Cuban policy decision rather than an entire political system and gave no indication that the March crackdown had produced a fundamental rupture in relations.

This remained the case even as tensions increased between Havana and Brussels. In July, the EU released its latest assessment of the "Common Position." The report concluded that the human rights situation in Cuba had "severely deteriorated" and that a "lack of economic reforms and the absence of economic freedom" were daily making the lives of ordinary Cubans more difficult. It also singled out the Cuban state media for conducting an "unacceptable campaign of personal vilification against certain Member States' Heads of Government." In light of these criticisms, the EU put Havana on notice that it "expects a new attitude from the Cuban authorities and major reform efforts in all these fields" and indicated that future aid would be provided "only if the [Cuban] people directly benefit or if a contribution to economic opening and reforms in Cuba is guaranteed."[211] Castro's response invoked questions of sovereignty and independence. National dignity, he told a political rally, required Cuba to turn its back on EU aid.[212]

Despite this new chill in relations, the EU executive was determined to keep its new Havana office open and to leave the offer of aid on the table.[213] Even the forced closure of the Spanish Cultural Center in September did not suggest to EU officials that a permanent break in relations between Havana and Madrid was likely, nor did it shake their commitment to a policy of constructive engagement.[214] Proof of the latter came in February 2004, when a discrete message was relayed to Cuban officials that the EU would respond "immediately" to some concrete sign that the human rights situation on the island was improving.[215] Still unhappy over recent EU decisions, the Castro government rejected the overture. For the most part, however, relations with individual European countries remained strong—particularly in the areas of trade and investment. The exceptions were Spain and Italy, but the March election of a socialist government in Spain—and the clear intention of new president, José Luis Rodriguez Zapetero, to pursue a foreign policy more independent of U.S. global interests than that of his predecessor—held the promise of a circuit-breaker in Spanish-Cuban relations that might even lead to a more sympathetic EU approach toward Cuba.[216]

Certainly, the Europeans took a far less incendiary approach than the U.S. to Cuba during the April 2004 UNHRC debate over the island's human rights record. Whereas the Bush representative denounced the Castro regime for "oppress[ing] the Cuban people," the EU delegate acknowledged "the efforts of Cuba to give effect to the social rights of its population despite the negative consequences of economic isolation." At the same time, the EU supported the resolution to further its objective of "encourag[ing] a process of transition to a pluralistic democracy and respect for human rights."[217]

The Europeans' willingness to stay the course on improved relations with Cuba contrasts markedly with what has been the overriding purpose of U.S. policy, put into sharp focus by a senior official of the Clinton administration at the end of the 1990s: "To me the point of the various strategies of the embargo was not to change Castro's mind or to change Cuba while Castro was still in power; to gain Castro's acquiescence in democracy in Cuba, or to force him to change. The point of the embargo was to impoverish the government so it could not be adventurous and to make sure that when Castro's end comes there would be insufficient movement to make possible a continuation of that regime."[218] It is precisely this issue on which future conflict between the EU and the U.S. over Cuba policy cannot be ruled out.

Conclusion

The collapse of the Soviet Union removed any potential security threat to Western Europe and in the process downgraded the importance of America's Cold War military "umbrella," thereby making it more difficult for the White House to impose its global priorities on senior Alliance partners. The post–Cold War era also witnessed the rise of the European Union as a powerful economic bloc in its own right and a greater assertiveness on the part of its member nations—individually and collectively—in pursuing their own world-wide interests. The combined result has been to increase tensions across the Atlantic over a range of foreign policy and trade/investment issues. One of the most consistent and, before the war in Iraq, one of the most bitter, disagreements has been over relations with Fidel Castro's government in Cuba.

While both the U.S. and its European allies share the ultimate goal of promoting political and economic reform in Cuba, they differ fundamentally over how best to bring this about. The U.S. remains wedded to an unreconstructed Cold War approach based on the politics of hostility and isolation—leading to a regime change—as a precondition for fully normalized relations. The Europeans, on the other hand, have developed a more nuanced approach that values dialogue and engagement with Havana while reserving the right to criticize specific government policies.

These contrasting approaches, of themselves, would not have triggered a series of major disputes were it not for Washington's continuing attempt to bludgeon allies into accepting its solution to the "problem of Cuba"—most strikingly via the extraterritorial provisions in the 1992 Cuban Democracy Act and the even more punitive 1996 Helms-Burton law. The European response has combined selective accommodations with a refusal to capitulate entirely to these U.S. policy initiatives. That Cuba—a relatively minor issue in post–Cold War transatlantic ties—has become a source of friction also reflects European concerns about Washington's propensity to jettison free trade principles and agreements when they clash with what it defines as "overriding foreign policy interests."

The dispute over Cuba, then, speaks to a larger issue. The U.S. is still the dominant hegemon—based largely on its continuing military and ideological superiority—but its economic and, to a lesser extent, political power is no longer uncontested. The Cold War coalition to confront communism has been transformed into a world of proliferating rivalries and challenges as Washington's European allies in particular seek more aggressively to defend and pursue their own interests. Clearly signaling this new global rivalry, Swedish prime minister Goeran Persson told the June 2001 U.S.-EU summit in Gothenburg that Europe's mission was to serve "as a balance to U.S. domination."[219] In the new world of global economic competition, U.S. diktats on the conditions of international trade and capital flows are more likely to be resisted than in the past. While the U.S. appears able to get its way on most occasions, Europe's resistance to its Cuba policy indicates that the White House does so with increasing difficulty; and that it is, nonetheless, willing to pursue a unilateralist foreign policy even if it means placing at risk the transatlantic relationship.

Notes

1. See Patrick E. Tyler, "U.S. Strategy Plan Calls for Insuring No Rivals Develop," *New York Times*, March 8, 1992, 14.

2. "From Containment to Enlargement," in U.S. Department of State, *Dispatch*, September 1993, 658–64.

3. Nancy E. Soderberg, "The Continuing Need for America's Global Leadership," in U.S. Department of State, *Dispatch*, October 28, 1996, 541.

4. "Full Text: Bush's National Security Strategy," *New York Times*, September 20, 2002.

5. See James Petras and Morris Morley, "Contesting Hegemons: U.S.-French Relations in the 'New World Order,'" *Review of Inernational Studies* 26, (2000): 49–67; Ivo H. Daalder, "Are the United States and Europe Heading for Divorce?," *International Affairs* 77, no.3 (July 2001): 553–67.

6. Quoted in Suzanne Daley, "French Minister Calls U.S. Policy 'Simplistic,'" *New York Times*, February 7, 2002.

7. Quoted in David E. Sanger, "Allies Hear Sour Notes in 'Axis of Evil' Chorus," *New York Times*, February 17, 2002.

8. France, Germany, and Belgium rejected an American request in NATO to plan for Turkey's defense in the event of war with Iraq. See Karen De Young, "Bush Decries Attempt to Block War Plans," *Washington Post*, February 11, 2003.

9. Quoted in Bob Woodward, *Bush at War* (New York: Simon & Schuster, 2002), 81.

10. Quoted in Glenn Frankel, "New U.S. Doctrine Worries Europeans," *Washington Post*, September 30, 2002.

11. Quoted in Raymond J. Ahearn, *U.S.-European Trade Relations: Issues and Policy Challenges*, Congressional Research Service, December 16, 2002, June 6, 2002, 2–3.

12. Quoted in *CubaINFO*, October 27, 1992, 2.

13. Quoted in "UK Rejects Trade Ban on Cuba by US," *Financial Times* (U.K.), October 21, 1992, 5.

14. EC commissioner quoted in *CubaINFO*, April 30, 1993, 1.

15. See Joaquín Roy, *Cuba, the United States, and the Helms-Burton Doctrine* (Gainesville: University Press of Florida, 2000), 108; Gabriel A. Ondetti, "Western Eu-

ropean and Canadian Relations with Cuba After the Cold War," Trinity College Programs in International Studies, Washington D.C., Caribbean Project: Cuba Briefing Paper Series, no. 9 (November 1995): 4.

16. Economist Intelligence Unit, *Quarterly Economic Review of Cuba*, 3rd quarter 1995, 16; Pascal Fletcher, "Western Banks Test the Water in Cuba," *Financial Times*, August 15, 1995, 4.

17. Quoted in *CubaINFO*, April 6, 1995, 2–3.

18. Confidential interview 1, by author, Washington, D.C., May 18, 1999. Department of State official involved with Cuba policy, 1995–2000.

19. Dennis Hays, interview by author, Washington, D.C., May 14, 1999. Director, Office of Cuban Affairs, Department of State, 1993–95.

20. Confidential interview 1.

21. Richard Nuccio, interview by author, Falls Church, Virginia, May 20, 1999. Department of State, Cuba official and White House special representative on Cuba, 1993–96.

22. Ibid.

23. Confidential interview 1.

24. See Richard A. Nuccio, "Cuba: A U.S. Perspective" in *Transatlantic Tensions*, ed. Richard N. Haass (Washington, D.C.: Brookings Institution Press, 1999), 16.

25. Quoted in Anne Swardson, "Allies Irked by Bill to Deter Their Trade With U.S. Foes," *Washington Post*, March 7, 1996, A20.

26. Quoted in *CubaINFO*, March 21, 1996, 7.

27. Confidential interview 2, by author, Washington, D.C., May 14, 1999. Senior official, Office of Cuban Affairs, 1995–98.

28. Quoted in Steven Lee Myers, "Clinton Troubleshooter Discovers Big Trouble From Allies on Cuba," *New York Times*, October 23, 1996, 1.

29. Quoted in Paul Blustein and Thomas W. Lippman, "Allies Angered by U.S. Boycott Policy," *Washington Post*, May 10, 1996, A31.

30. Quoted in Bruce Clark et al., "Rifkind Hits at Cuba Trade Curb," *Financial Times*, May 30, 1996, 4.

31. Confidential interview 3, by author, Washington, D.C., May 18, 1999. Department of State, senior Inter-American Affairs official with Cuba responsibilities, 1996–2000.

32. Quoted in *CubaINFO*, May 23, 1996, 2.

33. See Joaquin Roy, "Europe: Cuba, the U.S. Embargo, and the Helms-Burton Law," in Haass, ed., *Transatlantic Tensions*, 32.

34. Quoted in Thomas W. Lippman, "Europeans Assail U.S. Trade Curbs," *Washington Post*, June 13, 1996, A20.

35. Senate Committee on Foreign Relations, Subcommittee on Western Hemisphere and Peace Corps Affairs, *The Libertad Act: Implementation and International Law*, 104th Cong., 2nd sess., July 30, 1996, 8, 10.

36. Quoted in *CubaINFO*, July 11, 1996, 9.

37. Quoted ibid.

38. Santer and Brittan quoted in Guy de Jonquieres and David Buchan, "Clinton Yields to Pressure Over U.S. Trade Initiatives," *Financial Times*, July 29/30, 1996, 1.

39. Quoted in *CubaINFO*, June 13, 1996, 3.

40. Quoted in John F. Harris, "Clinton Delays Law Allowing Cuba Suits," *Washington Post*, July 17, 1996, A22.

41. Quoted in David E. Sanger, "Talk Multilaterally, Hit Allies With Stick," *New York Times*, July 21, 1996, E3.

42. Quoted in Steven Erlanger and David E. Sanger, "On Global Stage, Clinton's Pragmatic Turn," *New York Times*, July 29, 1996, 17.

43. Quoted in Rupert Cornwell and Andrew Marshall, "Britain Attacks U.S. Bar on Cuba Links," *The Independent*, (U.K.), July 12, 1996, 1.

44. See "Allies Slate U.S. on Law to Punish Cuba Traders," *The Australian*, July 13–14, 1996, 15. Also see British foreign office quoted in "Allies Slate U.S."

45. Quoted in Sarah Helm, "EU Threatens Trade War Over Anti-Cuba Laws," *The Independent*, July 16, 1996, 10.

46. Quoted in "EU Set to Retaliate Against U.S.," *Financial Post* (Canada), July 13, 1996, 9.

47. Quoted in "Europeans Agree On Steps to Retaliate For U.S. Cuba Curbs," *New York Times*, July 16, 1996, 9.

48. Quoted in Lionel Barber, "Europe Vows to Act on U.S. Anti-Cuba Law," *Financial Times*, July 16, 1996, 1.

49. R. Roger Majak, interview by author, Washington, D.C., May 11, 1999. Assistant secretary of Commerce for Export Administration, 1995–2000.

50. All quotations taken from the following sources: "Clinton Delays Law"; Craig R. Whitney, "Europe Gives Clinton Stand on Cuba Law Cold Shoulder," *New York Times*, July 18, 1996, 15; Ian Black and John Palmer, "Europe Reacts Coolly to Clinton Delaying Tactics," *The Guardian* (U.K.), July 18, 1996, 13; Guy de Jonquieres et al., "EU Unites Over U.S. Measures Against Cuba," *Financial Times*, July 18, 1996, 6.

51. Quoted in "France to Hit Back if Hurt by Helms-Burton," *Reuters News Service* (hereafter *RNS*), July 25, 1996.

52. House, *Implementation of the Cuban Liberty and Democratic Solidarity (Libertad) Act of 1996*, 104th Cong., 2nd sess., July 11, 1996, 21.

53. Quoted in Thomas W. Lippman, "U.S. Allies to Seek Reform in Cuba," *Washington Post*, August 19, 1996, A19.

54. Majak interview.

55. Brittan and Rexrodt quoted *CubaINFO*, September 19, 1996, 2.

56. Quoted ibid.

57. Quoted in Frances Williams and Nancy Dunne, "EU Forces Dispute Panel on Cuba Trade," *Financial Times*, November 21, 1996, 1.

58. Stephen Bates and John Palmer, "EU Unites in Defiance of U.S. Cuba Law," *Guardian Weekly* (U.K.), November 3, 1996, 1.

59. "Eizenstat Addresses Status of Further Presidential Suspension of Right of Action Under Title III of Helms-Burton," reprinted in *U.S.-Cuba Policy Report*, November 27, 1996, 2.

60. Peter Guilford, quoted in Paul Lewis, "Cuba Trade Law: Export of U.S. Ire and Politics," *New York Times*, March 15, 1996, D3.

61. Quoted in Lippman, "Trade Curbs."

62. Confidential interview 4, by author, Washington, D.C., May 17, 1999. Department of State official involved with Cuba policy since 1995; Office of Cuban Affairs, 1997–2000.

63. Confidential interview 1.

64. Confidential interview 3.

65. Quoted in Wendy Lubetkin, "EU Brings Helms-Burton Law Before World Trade Organization," *U.S. Information Agency Wireless File*, October 16, 1996 (hereafter *USIAWF*).

66. Quoted in Gail Russell Chaddock, "U.S. Puts World Trade at Risk in Cuba Fight," *Christian Science Monitor*, October 22, 1996, 14.

67. Gardner quoted in Wendy Lubetkin, "WTO Accepts EU Request for Panel on Helms-Burton Act," *USIAWF*, November 20, 1996; Eizenstat quoted in Warner Rose, "Taking Helms-Burton to WTO Seen Inciting Protectionism in U.S.," *USIAWF*, November 21, 1996.

68. Quoted in David E. Sanger, "Europe Postpones Challenge to U.S. on Havana Trade," *New York Times*, February 13, 1997, 9.

69. Quoted in Francis Williams and Nancy Dunne, "EU Forces Dispute Panel on Cuba Trade," *Financial Times*, November 21, 1996, 1.

70. Quoted in *CubaINFO*, February 27, 1997, 5–6.

71. Quoted in Lippman, "Trade Curbs."

72. Quoted in John Palmer and Jonathan Freedland, "Europe Poised for Trade War with U.S. Over Cuba," *The Guardian*, July 16, 1996, 3.

73. Quoted in Guy de Jonquieres, "Showdown on Cuba Trade," *Financial Times*, February 3, 1997, 1.

74. Quoted in David Fox, "EU Warns WTO Facing Immeasurable Damage From U.S.," *RNS*, February 12, 1997.

75. Nicholas Burns, quoted in "U.S. Disappointed by EU Move Over Cuba Law," *RNS*, February 13, 1997.

76. Quoted in David E. Sanger, "U.S. Rejects Role for World Court in Trade Dispute," *New York Times*, February 21, 1997, 1; Paul Blustein and Anne Swardson, "U.S. Vows to Boycott WTO Panel," *Washington Post*, February 21, 1997, A12.

77. Michael Ranneberger, interview by author, Washington, D.C., May 19, 1999. Coordinator, Office of Cuban Affairs, Department of State, 1995–2000.

78. Quoted in Sanger, "U.S. Rejects Role," 7.

79. Ranneberger interview.

80. Quoted in Paul Blustein and Thomas W. Lippman, "Trade Clash On Cuba Is Averted," *New York Times*, April 12, 1997, 1.

81. "Eizenstat Statement on U.S.-EU Helms/Burton Agreement," *USIAWF*, April 11, 1997.

82. "Europe Backs Down on Helms-Burton," *Latin American Weekly Report*, April 15, 1997, 170.

83. Quoted in "Europeans Disavow Tough U.S. Stance on Cuba," *RNS*, April 19, 1997.

84. Quoted in "Germany Welcomes Pact With U.S. on Cuba Trade," *RNS*, April 18, 1997.

85. Quoted in Blustein and Lippman, "Trade Clash," 20.

86. Burns quoted in "U.S. Criticizes Franco-Cuban Investment Pact," *RNS*, April 18, 1997; Borotra quoted in Marcel Michelson, "France Signs Cuba Deal, Warns U.S.," *RNS*, April 25, 1997.

87. See "Text: Draft Bills on Title III" and "Congress Considers Revoking Title III Waiver of Helms-Burton Act," *Inside US Trade*, May 16, 1997.

88. *CubaINFO*, October 23, 1997, 2.

89. Quoted in "EU's Brittan–Working Hard To End Spat With US Re Cuba/Libya," *RNS*, September 24, 1997.

90. See, for example, Assistant Secretary of State Alan Larson, "Transcript of Press Conference," Brussels, *USIAWF*, October 14, 1997.

91. Quoted in "Franco-American Ties Tense Once More," *RNS*, October 4, 1997.

92. Jospin and EU officials quoted in "Jospin Defends Total, Rebuffs US Sanctions," *RNS*, September 29, 1997; Roger Cohen, "France Scoffs At U.S. Protest Over Iran Deal," *New York Times*, September 30, 1997, 12.

93. Quoted in "EU, U.S. on Collision Course over Total Contract," *RNS*, September 30, 1997.

94. Quoted in Douglas Hamilton, "EU Rejects U.S. Bid To Talk Round Anti-Cuba Law," *RNS*, October 17, 1997.

95. Quoted in *CubaINFO*, November 13, 1997, 5.

96. House Committee on International Relations, Subcommittee on International Economic Policy and Trade, *WTO-Dispute Settlement Body*, 105th Cong., 2nd sess., March 30, 1998, 12.

97. Quoted in "EU Welcomes U.S. Review of Sanctions Policy," *RNS*, January 9, 1998.

98. "EU Plans to Increase Investment in Cuba," *CUBANEWS*, March 1998, 6.

99. Quoted in *CubaINFO*, February 26, 1998, 7.

100. Quoted in Neil Buckley, "EU Holds its Fire in Cuba Law Dispute—Helms-Burton WTO Case Lapses," *RNS*, April 22, 1998; Adrian Croft, "EU Allows Helms-Burton Challenge to Lapse," *RNS*, April 20, 1998.

101. Quoted in Adrian Croft, "EU's Brittan Hopes for Helms-Burton Agreement," *RNS*, April 21, 1998.

102. Quoted in David E. Sanger, "Europeans Drop Law Suit Contesting Cuba Trade Act," *New York Times*, April 21, 1998, 8.

103. Quoted in Christopher Marquis and Jodi A. Enda, "Miami Lawmakers Cool to New Rules," *Miami Herald*, May 19, 1998; House Committee on International Relations, *Economic Sanctions and U.S. Policy Interests*, 105th Cong., 2nd sess., June 3, 1998, 11, 17.

104. Quoted in Dan Balz, "U.S. Eases Stand on Cuba, Iran Sanctions," *Washington Post*, May 19, 1998, A15.

105. Quoted in Jeffrey Ulbrich, "U.S. Agrees to Ease Trade Sanctions," *Washington Post*, May 18, 1998.

106. Confidential interview 4.

107. Confidential interview 5, by author, Washington, D.C., May 11, 1999. Congressional Cuba specialist, who monitored the legislative debate over Cuba policy, 1993–2000.

108. Andrew Semmel, interview by author, Washington, D.C., May 14, 1999. Foreign affairs adviser to Senator Richard Lugar since 1987.

109. Quoted in Balz, "U.S. Eases Stand."

110. Quoted in "U.S. Lawmakers See Loopholes in US-EU Cuba Pact," *RNS*, June 18, 1998; "White House, Congress Spar Over Deal with E.U.," *CUBANEWS*, July 1998, 8.

111. Quoted in *CubaINFO*, August 4, 1998, 4.

112. See Wolf Grabendorff, "The Relationship between the European Union and Cuba," in *Cuba and the Caribbean*, ed. Joseph S. Tulchin et al. (Wilmington: Scholarly Resources,1997), 224–25.

113. It is in the nature of EU statements and policy documents that the search for a consensus often results in the stance of the most hardline member being adopted even if this is not necessarily the view of all member states.

114. Confidential interview 4.

115. Quoted in *CubaINFO*, December 12, 1996, 6–7.

116. See Wayne Smith, "Helms-Burton: A Loose Canon?," Washington, D.C., Center for International Policy, available <http://ciponline.org/loosecan.htm>. Smith summarizes a conference on the pros and cons of the Helms-Burton Act held February 10–11, 1997.

117. See Jorge F. Pérez-Lopez, "Foreign Investment in Cuba in the Second Half of the 1990s," *CubaSource*, April 30, 2000, <www.cubasource.org/pdf/perez_DFICuba.pdf>; Economic Commission for Latin America and the Caribbean, *Preliminary Overview of the Economies of Latin America and the Caribbean 1998* (Santiago: United Nations, 1998), 72; Dalia Acosta, "Cuba: First 100 Percent Foreign Investment in Energy," *RNS*, February 10, 1999; *Latin American Monitor: Caribbean*, August 1999, 4. On major features of the 1995 Foreign Investment Act, see Max Azicri, *Cuba Today and Tomorrow* (Gainesville: University Press of Florida, 2000), 153.

118. European Commission, *External and Intra-European Union Trade-Statistical Yearbook (Data 1958–2000)*, Luxembourg, 2001, 34, 38. Also see H. Michael Erisman, *Cuba's Foreign Relations in a Post-Soviet World* (Gainesville: University Press of Florida, 2000), 150, 152.

119. Senate Committee on Foreign Relations, *Nomination of Secretary of State*, 105th Cong., 1st sess., January 8, 1997, 67.

120. Economic Commission for Latin America and the Caribbean, *Economic Survey of Latin America and the Caribbean 1996–1997* (Santiago: United Nations, 1997), 197; "Big Cuban Slowdown is Now Certain," *Latin American Regional Reports: Caribbean*, August 19, 1997, 4.

121. Transcript, Department of State, Office of the Spokesman, "Off-the-Record Briefing," January 3, 1997.

122. Transcript, "Statement before the Subcommittee on Trade, House Ways and Means Committee," May 7, 1998.

123. Quoted in Maria C. Werlau, "Update on Foreign Investment In Cuba: 1996–97," *Cuba in Transition: Volume 7* (Miami: Association for the Study of the Cuban Economy, 1997).

124. Quoted in "Cuba's Economy Slows Down Drastically," *Latin American Regional Reports: Caribbean*, December 2, 1997, 4.

125. "Call for Efficiency as Growth Falters," *Latin American Regional Reports: Caribbean*, October 28, 1997, 2; also see "Cuba's Economy Slows."

126. Quoted in *Latin American Monitor: Caribbean*, March 1998, 4.

127. "Spanish Companies in Crossfire of U.S.-Cuba Battle," *New York Times*, July 20, 1996, 40.

128. Tom Burns, "Sol Melía Presses Ahead with IPO," *Financial Times*, May 29, 1996, 30.

129. "Cuba Scores Breakthrough in Deal With Japanese Private Creditors," *CUBANEWS*, April 1998, 6; "New Setbacks for Cuba in 1998," *Latin American Regional Reports: Caribbean*, January 19, 1999, 5.

130. Economist Intelligence Unit, *Country Report: Cuba*, 3rd quarter 1998, 24; "Cuba to Join First Europe-Latin Summit," *Miami Herald*, September 24, 1998; *CUBANEWS*, November 1998, 2.

131. Ibid., 25; also see Pascal Fletcher, "Havana Signs Insurance Deal with UK Broker," *Financial Times*, November 7, 1998 and "Debt Deal Opens Way to UK Credit Cover for Cuba," *Financial Times*, September 23, 1999, 7.

132. Quoted in Pascal Fletcher, "Debt Talks With Paris Club," *Financial Times*, September 29, 1999.

133. Quoted in Pascal Fletcher, "Paris Club Finds Cuba Receptive to Future Debt Deal," *RNS*, September 30, 1999.

134. Quoted in Roy, "Europe: Cuba," 40.

135. Transcript, Department of State, Office of the Spokesman, "Senior U.S. Officials Speak on Cuba Policy," January 5, 1999.

136. Quoted in *CubaINFO*, January 11, 1999, 6.

137. Majak interview.

138. Quoted in Jane Bussey, "Official Defends Deal on Cuba," *Miami Herald*, March 10, 1999, C3.

139. Confidential interview 1.

140. Quoted in Juan O. Tamayo, "U.S. Poised to Bar Execs of Firm Operating in Cuba," *Miami Herald*, July 3, 1999.

141. Christopher Marquis, "U.S. Eyes Spanish Firm's Cuba Holdings," *Miami Herald*, August 12, 1999.

142. Quoted in "Spanish Hotel Group Says Not Concerned With U.S. Sanctions Threat," *BBC Monitoring Service: Latin America*, August 31, 1999.

143. Quoted in Isabel Garcia-Zarza, "Spain's Sol Melía Undeterred in Cuba by U.S. Threat," *RNS*, November 4, 1999.

144. Quoted in *CubaINFO*, October 5, 1999, 5.

145. Quoted in *CubaINFO*, August 24, 1999, 3.

146. Quoted in Adrian Croft, "EU Appeals For U.S. 'Understanding' on *Cuba* Law," *RNS*, December 16, 1999.

147. See Anya K. Landau and Wayne S. Smith, "American Trademarks Threatened: Conferees Call for Repeal of Section 211 Aimed at Cuba," *International Policy Report*, Washington, D.C., Center for International Policy, September 2001, 1–3.

148. Quoted in *CubaINFO*, July 5, 1999, 3.

149. Quotations in Pascal Fletcher, "Cuba Protests UN Censure," *Financial Times*, April 18, 2000 and "Cuba Drops Bid to Join EU Trade and Aid Pact," *Financial Times*, April 30, 2000.

150. See Pascal Fletcher, "Cuba Snubs Brussels, Cancels Visit from EU Delegation," *Financial Times*, April 20, 2000.

151. Pascal Fletcher, "Germans Plan Cuba Steel Mill," *Financial Times*, November 1, 2000.

152. Quoted in Andrew Cawthorne, "Spain Urges Change in Cuba but Opposes Pressure," *RNS*, November 11, 1998.

153. Pascal Fletcher, "Cuba Seeks to Reassure Investors," *Financial Times*, July 17, 2000; "Iberia to Form Two Joint Venture Companies in Cuba," *RNS*, July 7, 2000.

154. See Economist Intelligence Unit, *Country Report: Cuba*, 4th quarter 1999, 25–26; *Country Report: Cuba*, 1st quarter 2000, 26; *Country Report: Cuba*, June 2000, 30; Pascal Fletcher, "Creditors in Attempt to Reschedule Cuba's Debt," *Financial Times*, October 4, 2000.

155. Quoted in *CubaINFO*, July 5, 2000, 8.

156. Confidential interview 1.

157. Confidential interview 2.

158. Confidential Interview 6, by author, Washington, D.C., September 14, 2001. Office of Cuban Affairs, Department of State.

159. Ibid.; confidential Interview 7, by author, Washington, D.C., November 1, 2002. Office of European Union and Regional Affairs, Department of State.

160. FDCH Washington Transcript Service, *Hearings on U.S. Foreign Policy*, Part 2 of 3, March 7, 2001.

161. *Foreign Broadcast Information Service Daily Report: WEU-2001-0321* (hereafter *FBIS*), March 17, 2001.

162. Economist Intelligence Unit, *Country Report: Cuba*, May 2002, 19.

163. Quoted in James Gerstenzang, "U.S. Gets Tough on Its Cuba Restrictions," *Miami Herald*, July 12, 2001.

164. Confidential interview 7.

165. Matthew King, interview by author, Washington, D.C., November 7, 2002. First secretary, Trade, European Union, Delegation of the European Commission.

166. Ibid.; confidential interview 7.

167. King interview.

168. Confidential interview 8, by author, Washington, D.C., October 31, 2002. Bureau of Western Hemisphere Affairs, Department of State.

169. King interview; confidential interview 7.

170. Confidential interview 7.

171. Confidential interview 8.

172. "WTO Sides With U.S. on Trademarks," *Associated Press*, January 2, 2002. In contrast to its determined opposition to a WTO determination on Helms-Burton, Washington has been willing to allow the Bacardi complaint to proceed, most likely because it is confined to a single company and could not plausibly be interpreted as having any national security implications. It would also have been extremely awkward to oppose

the WTO disputes panel hearing when the senior State Department hemisphere official, Assistant Secretary Otto Reich, was a former Bacardi lobbyist.

173. See "New Reprieve for Washington in Havana Club Affair," *Agence Europe*, January 24, 2004; "U.S. Patent Office Confirms Cuban-French Firm's Right to Havana Club Trademark," *Noticen*, March 4, 2004.

174. European Commission, *External and Intra-European Union Trade-Statistical Yearbook (Data 1958–2000)*, 34, 38. Joint venture investments by European firms increased at a modest rate through most of the 1990s. According to the Economic Commission for Latin America, for example, Spanish, French, Italian, and British firms together accounted for forty new ventures in 1998. Also see Ian F. Fergusson and Jennifer E. Stevens, *Cuba: An Economic Primer*, Congressional Research Service, June 20, 2002, 12.

175. See Marc Frank, "Foreign Investment in Cuba Falls, EU Wants Reform," *RNS*, July 8, 2002.

176. Quoted in Patricia Grogg, "Cuba-EU Dialogue to Continue Despite Rift on Rights," *RNS*, November 5, 2002.

177. Spanish foreign minister Josep Pique, quoted in *FBIS: WEU-2001-0322*, March 22, 2001.

178. Quoted in Larry Luxner, "Melía to Invest Millions in Two New Resorts; Chain Already Manages 22 Cuban Hotels," *CUBANEWS*, November 2002, 1.

179. Quoted in "French Investment in Cuba Extends to Rum, Hotels, Energy and Telecoms," *CUBANEWS*, October 2002, 9.

180. Kirby Jones, interview by author, Washington, D.C., May 12, 1999. President, Alamar Associates, a consultancy working with U.S. corporations interested in pursuing trade and investment opportunities in Cuba. In mid-2001, major British and German delegations of business executives and government officials visited Cuba and returned encouraged by the possibilities for boosting trade and investment with the island. Also see Domingo Amuchastegui, "Cuba and the EU: The New Honeymoon," *CUBANEWS*, June 2002, 7.

181. Confidential interview 8.

182. King interview.

183. Confidential interview 9, by author, Washington, D.C., October 31, 2002. Senior official, European Union, Delegation of the European Commission.

184. Quoted in "European Officials Start Visit in Cuba," *Miami Herald*, August 23, 2001. Also see *FBIS: WEU-2001-0826*, August 25, 2001.

185. Quoted in *FBIS: LAT-2001-0909*, September 9, 2001.

186. Quoted in Grogg, "Cuba-EU Dialogue."

187. Quoted in *FBIS: WEU-2001-0507*, May 7, 2001.

188. French foreign minister Hubert Vedrine quoted during talks with Cuban foreign minister Felipe Pérez Roque, in *FBIS: WEU-2002-0225*, February 25, 2002.

189. Quoted in *FBIS: WEU-2002-0617*, June 17, 2002.

190. Quoted in Ibid. Also see Richard Youngs, "The European Union and Democracy in Latin America," *Latin American Politics and Society* 44, no.3 (Fall 2002): 121–22.

191. EU External Affairs commissioner, Chris Patten, quoted in Adrian Croft, "EU Aims at Cuba's Rights Record on Summit Eve," *RNS*, May 16, 2002.

192. European Union, *The Legal and Administration Framework for Foreign Trade and Investment by European Companies in Cuba*. This note was sent to the Castro Government in late June 2002. The Cubans responded with their first concession in July when the deputy minister for foreign investment announced plans to establish a one-stop office to process applications from potential foreign investors. Also see Frank, "Foreign Investment in Cuba Falls"; Patricia Grogg, "Cuba-Govs Cut Red Tape to Lure Investors," *Reuters Business Briefing*, July 18, 2002.

193. Patricia Grogg, "Cuba-European Union: Political Thaw," *Inter Press Service News Agency*, December 3, 2002.

194. Quoted in Stephen Temple, "Europarliamentarians Speak Out Against 'Common Position' on Cuba as Key Dissident Visits Europe," *World Markers Research Centre, WMRC Daily Analysis*, December 16, 2002.

195. Quoted in "Cuba Will Renew Request to Join European Aid Pact," *Dow Jones International News*, December 9, 2002.

196. Joaquín Roy, "EU-Cuba Relations Are Warming Up," *Miami Herald*, January 10, 2003. Also see "EU/Cuba," *Agence Europe*, December 11, 2002.

197. Confidential interview 8.

198. Ibid.

199. Ibid.

200. Confidential interview 9.

201. King interview. In February 2003, France and Cuba signed a new bilateral cooperation agreement, while the head of a visiting Belgium delegation announced a program to help develop the island's tourist and transport sectors. See "Cuba, France Sign 7m-Euro Cooperation Agreement," *BBC Monitoring Americas*, February 10, 2003; "Belgium to Help Cuba Develop Tourism and Transport Sectors," *BBC Monitoring Americas*, February 6, 2003.

202. Quoted in "EU Blasts Cuban Repression," *EFE News Service*, March 26, 2003. Also see George Parker and Patrick Rucker, "EU Warns Castro Over Crackdown," *Financial Times*, April 19, 2003.

203. Quoted in Nancy San Martin, "Cuba Withdraws from European Pact," *Miami Herald*, May 20, 2003.

204. Quoted in "EU 'Disappointed' with Cuba but Will Continue Economic Stimulus," *Agence France-Presse*, June 12, 2003.

205. Quoted in "Italy Ready to Propose EU Sanctions Against Cuba," *Agence France-Presse*, April 29, 2003.

206. "Declaration by the Presidency, on behalf of the European Union, on Cuba," 9961/03 (Presse 157), June 5, 2003, *Europa Rapid Press Releases*, <http://europa.eu.int/rapid/>.

207. Quoted in "Castro Slams EU as 'Allies of Fascist Imperialism,'" *WMRC Daily Analysis*, June 9, 2003.

208. Quoted in Anita Snow, "Cuba Continues European Union Bashing; Dissidents Worry About Consequences," *Associated Press*, June 14, 2003.

209. "EU Kowtowing To US With New Aggressive Policies," *Dow Jones International News*, June 12, 2003.

210. *European Commission Videconference on EU-US Relations*, Washington Delegation, June 17, 2003, transcript by Federal News Service, Washington, D.C.

211. See "Council Gives Harsh Picture of Situation in Cuba but Leaves Door Open for Political Dialogue," *Agence Europe*, July 24, 2003.

212. "Cuban Government Confirms it is Turning its Back on EU Aid to Preserve 'Dignity,'" *Agence Europe*, August 5, 2003.

213. See "EU Says Seen no Cuba Move on Human Rights," *RNS*, September 3, 2003; "EU Demands Cuba's Castro End Crackdown on Dissent," *Dow Jones International News*, September 4, 2003.

214. See Mar Marin, "EU Does Not Foresee Break in Relations with Cuba, Official Says," *EFE News Service*, October 26, 2003.

215. "EU Overture to Havana Rejected," *EFE News Service*, February 24, 2004.

216. See, for example, "Cuba Sees Prospects for Improving Madrid-Havana Ties," *EFE News Service*, March 30, 2004.

217. See United Nations Commission on Human Rights, "Commission Adopts Measures on Situations in Cuba, Belarus, Turkmenistan, Democratic People's Republic of Korea," press release HR/CN/1087, April 15, 2004, <www.un.org/News/Press/docs/2004/hrcn1087.doc.htm>.

218. Michael Skol, interview by author, Washington, D.C., May 6, 1999. Principal deputy secretary of state for Inter-American Affairs, 1993–95.

219. Quoted in Ambrose Evans-Pritchard, "Europe Mounts Challenge to Global Cop," *Sydney Morning Herald*, June 16, 2001, 19.

4

"Sleeping with an Elephant"

The Impact of the United States on Canada-Cuba Relations

Peter McKenna and John M. Kirk

> Americans should never underestimate the constant pressure on Canada
> which the mere presence of the United States has produced. . . . Living
> next to you is in some ways like sleeping with an elephant. No matter
> how friendly and even-tempered is the beast, if I can call it that, one is
> affected by every twitch and grunt.
> **Pierre Elliott Trudeau, 1969**

In mid-April 2003, in an apparent fit of pique, U.S. president George W. Bush cancelled his first official state visit to Canada, slated for May 5. Just one day later, he announced that, roughly around that time, Australian prime minister John Howard would be visiting him at his Texas ranch. The April 17 edition of the *Toronto Globe and Mail*, Canada's national newspaper, carried a cartoon showing Canada's prime minister, Jean Chrétien, consulting a calendar in search of an alternative date ("Let's see . . . how about Thursday? Is Thursday good for you?" read the caption), while an Uncle Sam caricature, complete with welder's gear and torch, burns the Canadian invitation to Bush. Less than a month earlier, U.S. ambassador to Canada, Paul Cellucci, launched a blistering attack on Ottawa's decision not to participate in the invasion of Iraq and singled out the personal attacks on President Bush by some members of the Liberal government. (By contrast, Australia sent two thousand troops—hence the invitation to Crawford, Texas, to which Chrétien has never been invited.)[1]

The U.S. media, which mostly backed the war effort fervently, also poked fun at Canada—describing it as "France-lite" (a reference to France's opposition to the war), "Soviet Canuckistan," and even "Cuba North." Public opinion surveys of U.S. consumers showed that almost half were considering dumping Canadian products in favor of those from member countries of the U.S.-led "coalition of the willing." Ottawa, to a large extent, remained aloof from these pressures, maintaining its position of support for a multilateral solution to the Iraq question. Put simply, it understood the U.S. position, but politely rejected the invitation to participate in the U.S. campaign. In some respects, this is a recent illustration of what has been the Canadian position on Cuba for some forty-five years.

This chapter is headed up by a provocative quotation on Canada-U.S. relations by former Canadian prime minister, Pierre Trudeau. And Trudeau was absolutely correct. Canadians are indeed affected by even the slightest of policy decisions taken in Washington. The two economies are intimately connected and intertwined (with more than eighty-five percent of Canadian exports going to the United States). The two countries share similar (but not identical) cultural values and global interests as well as a 6,400-kilometer border. And they have been allies in several major international conflicts, including World War II, the Korean War, and the 1999 crisis in Kosovo. At the same time, Ottawa does have different foreign policy priorities and prescriptions. One striking example is its policy toward the Cuban Revolution; for over forty years now Canada has pursued a different strategy and tack to those of its "elephant" neighbor to the south.

That said, prime ministers and cabinet ministers, along with their officials in Ottawa, do recognize that Canada's most important foreign policy relationship is with the United States—and most certainly not with Cuba.[2] (In terms of trade, total annual bilateral trade between Canada and Cuba amounts to approximately twelve hours of one day of trade between Canada and the United States.) In practice, this means that Canada has had to craft or formulate its Cuba policy by factoring into the equation the expected U.S. response and reaction to it. Stated differently, one cannot understand Canadian-Cuban relations without first viewing that relationship through the Canada-U.S. prism.

This does not mean, however, that Canada's position toward revolutionary Cuba is expressly made in Washington, or indeed that Ottawa crafts its policy fearful of official U.S. reaction. Rather, the policy approach is generally calibrated and implemented within the wider context of Canada-U.S. relations. Indeed, the policy differences between Canada and the United States toward Cuba are partly in reaction to Canada's increasing "integration" or "interdependence" with the United States, a topic that is omnipresent in any analysis of Canada-U.S. relations.[3]

Historically, the existence of the Canada-Cuba-U.S. triangle has always been present—as John Diefenbaker's private criticism of Washington's unilateral decision making at the time of the 1962 Cuban Missile Crisis, Pierre Trudeau's high-profile visit to Cuba in 1976 (the first by a NATO leader), and Ottawa's cool response to Havana during the government of Brian Mulroney in the 1980s all amply demonstrate. At no time, though, has the "U.S. factor" precipitated a complete break in Canada's relations with Cuba—even if that was (and still remains) the preferred U.S. course. Nor has Canada been close to taking such a decision. In fact, it is often in spite of U.S. pressure that Canadian governments have charted an independent course vis-à-vis Havana, and one that is strikingly different from Washington's on several fronts. In general, Canada, as a medium-sized power, strongly prefers multilateralist impulses to any unilateralist thrust—hence its concern about the U.S. tactics in the 2003 Iraqi conflict.

Over the years, these differences have had both positive and negative repercussions for Canada.[4] On the positive side, Canadian governments have been able to play the "Cuba card" to their political and electoral advantage, symbolically demonstrating to both domestic and international public opinion that Canada's foreign policy is made exclusively in Ottawa. This element of nationalist discourse, which inevitably revolves around a declaration of political sovereignty, is extremely important as a counterbalance to the frequent claim that Canadian policy is excessively influenced by Washington. On the negative side, it has occasionally placed Ottawa and Washington at loggerheads—engendering prime ministerial–presidential ill will, expressions of diplomatic displeasure, blatant attempts at pressure, and periodic howls of protest from U.S. policymakers.

Ottawa does not make a point, however, of frequently highlighting the differences with Washington over Cuba or doing anything rash that would needlessly raise the ire of the latter—such as supplying military hardware to the Cuban government. In essence, therefore, the real challenge of Canada's relations with Cuba is to conduct that bilateral relationship in a way that is not intended to flaunt or poke Americans in the eye. As a result, it is a very delicate policy high-wire act for officials in Ottawa to walk: ever committed to a "constructive engagement" approach with Havana, while reassuring Washington that it obviously remains Canada's most important overall bilateral partner.[5]

Accordingly, the purpose of this essay is threefold in nature: first, to outline briefly the nature and extent of Canadian-Cuban relations since 1989 (especially in light of U.S.-Cuban relations since the end of the Cold War); second, to examine Washington's response to Canada's Cuba policy and how that reaction has manifested itself instrumentally; and, third, to detail Canada's response to what it sees as a heavy-handed U.S. policy and to discuss whether or not that pressure was actually successful in altering Canada's Cuba policy. The chapter closes on a brief discussion of U.S. pressure and its effectiveness, along with a number of general observations and conclusions about the Canada-Cuba-U.S. triangle.

It needs to be said from the very outset that it is extremely difficult to determine with any precision the exact impact of the United States on Canada's Cuba policy. We accept that it does indeed have an impact—but quantifying precisely what that impact is makes for an incredibly challenging undertaking, since we are not privy to confidential conversations between U.S. and Canadian political leaders. Indeed, we can never be sure that Canada responded in a certain way on the Cuba file on its own or because of U.S. pressure tactics (or some combination of the two). Having said that, there is clearly enough material available in the public domain, and through personal contacts in the Canadian government, to provide a general framework for discussion.

Canadian-Cuban Relations Since the Cold War

Since the end of the Cold War in the early 1990s and the onset of a unipolar world, the Canadian-Cuban relationship has experienced its fair share of diplomatic highs and lows. The lows mostly coincided with the years of Brian Mulroney's second term as Canada's prime minister (1988–93). His Conservative government placed Canada-Cuba relations on the proverbial back burner—if not in the political deep freeze. Out of deference to the United States and his personal friendship with President George H. W. Bush, Mulroney was simply not prepared to jeopardize relations with Washington by cozying up to Castro's Cuba. As a result, he did nothing to improve ties with Havana, leaving it to atrophy. Significantly, however, he also did not do anything to deliberately break the long-standing bilateral relationship.

The bilateral relationship that Trudeau (1968–79) had sought to cultivate, particularly in the early part of his government, was effectively allowed to die on the vine from lack of governmental attention and nourishment. Under Mulroney, there would be no ministerial visits, no development assistance initiatives, no cultural exchanges, and no plan to have an actively engaged Canadian ambassador in Havana. In fact, there would be very little diplomatic and political dialogue between the two countries—while trade and commercial relations would continue below the radar screen.

When Mulroney announced his political retirement in early 1993, there were no signature events to mark the Canadian-Cuban relationship. Notwithstanding Cuban efforts to engage the Canadians across a wide range of policy areas, they were essentially rebuffed at every opportunity.[6] By way of illustration, during the so-called "storm of the century" in March 1993, which left an enormous amount of infrastructural damage across Cuba in its wake, the best that the Mulroney government would grudgingly muster as regards assistance to the island was a miserly amount of powdered milk and surplus seed potatoes (which were slated to be plowed under anyway). The fact of the matter is that the exceptionally U.S.-friendly government of Brian Mulroney could not have cared less about Canada-Cuba relations. And when he did think of the relationship at all, it was only to make sure that it did not unduly complicate relations with the Bush White House.[7]

In sharp contrast, the incoming Liberal government of Jean Chrétien (1993–2003) embraced a policy of constructively engaging the Cubans. Minister for Foreign Affairs Andre Ouellet challenged the Clinton White House to turn the page on Cuba as it had done on Vietnam: It is "a country that . . . is no longer a threat in any way, shape or form [to the United States]."[8] Addressing the June 1994 annual General Assembly of the Organization of American States (OAS) in Belem, Brazil, Secretary of State for Latin America and Africa, Christine Stewart, reiterated Canada's desire to see Cuba reintegrated into the hemispheric community of states. In her prepared remarks to the delegates, Stewart stated pointedly that Cuba's continued "exclusion" from the OAS— which had been undertaken largely at the behest of the United States in 1962— was an unhealthy situation for all of the countries of the Americas.[9] In an obvious reference to U.S. policy toward Cuba, Stewart went on to explain: "It is in all our interests, individually and as an organization, as well as in the interests of the people of Cuba, that we support a process of change in Cuba that is positive and orderly."[10]

That same month the sixteen-year suspension on Cuba's eligibility for Canadian development assistance, instituted by the Trudeau government over Cuba's Angola involvement, was revoked. Ottawa also decided to extend Canadian International Development Agency credits to local enterprises to help fund feasibility studies regarding possible joint ventures with Cuban companies and state entities. At the December "Summit of the Americas" meeting in Miami, Prime Minister Jean Chrétien called for an end to Cuba's regional isolation and the renewal of its OAS membership. He was one of the only participating heads of state to publicly challenge the U.S. embargo policy, observing that Washington had no qualms about trading with other nondemocratic regimes in the Third World.[11]

Dialogue at the ministerial level, begun almost immediately with the new government, continued with the marking of the 50th anniversary of diplomatic ties between Canada and Cuba in March of 1995. On a working visit to Ottawa, Cuban foreign minister Roberto Robaina met with a group of cabinet ministers and senior Canadian officials.[12] While the visit drew sharp criticism from some members of the U.S. Congress, the bilateral meetings went ahead in a cordial and professional manner. The discussions, for the most part, focused on trade and investment considerations, international political developments, and questions about economic and fisheries cooperation. As is customary, Canadian officials raised the thorny issue of democratic development and respect for human rights with their Cuban counterparts.

In the last ten years there has been an "on-again, off-again" quality to Canadian-Cuban relations. People-to-people contacts have been noticeably strengthened (largely through tourism: in 2002, some 400,000 Canadians took their vacations on the island). Bilateral trade has declined somewhat—principally as a result of Cuba's economic difficulties. And in terms of diplomatic exchange, the record has been decidedly uneven. The issue of human rights has dominated the Canadian agenda, while the Cubans have indicated their inability to improve this situation because of increasing U.S. hostility. For this reason, the bilateral relationship has waxed and waned during this period—as the following discussion illustrates.

One of the most interesting elements of Canada's constructive engagement approach toward Cuba took place in late January 1997, when Foreign Minister Lloyd Axworthy undertook a two-day visit to Havana. Over the course of high-level discussions and negotiations, both sides agreed to a much-heralded fourteen-point Canada-Cuba Joint Declaration for bilateral cooperation in a variety of areas, including human rights, good governance, and economic development. At a joint conference with Cuban foreign minister Robaina prior to leaving the island, Axworthy denounced the latest addition to Washington's embargo—the 1996 extraterritorial Helms-Burton Act—for "undermining the fundamental principles of international law" and reaffirmed Ottawa's belief that only "active engagement and dialogue" could bring about desired changes in Cuba's political economy.[13] This rather extraordinary trip, which was vigorously opposed by officialdom in Washington, marked the first time in almost forty years that a Canadian foreign minister had actually set foot on Cuban soil.

Two months later, and while attending the first OAS Washington Conference on the Americas, Minister Axworthy once again reiterated his support for Canada's policy of dialogue and exchange with the Cuban government. In his closing keynote address, he noted the following: "It is time to start building bridges with Cuba and engaging it on issues of concern, in order to encourage positive change."[14] He pointed to the recent visit to Ottawa of Vice President Carlos Lage and Canada's agreement to accept a number of Cuban political prisoners as evidence that dialogue and engagement can produce positive results. Axworthy also reminded his audience of Canada's continued support for Cuba's full reintegration into the inter-American fold and the role that the hemispheric forum could play in engaging the Cubans. According to Axworthy, "surely the time has come for all OAS members to consider when the suspended 35th member of the organization, Cuba, could once again be seated at the table."[15]

Arguably, the most significant component of Canada's policy of constructive engagement was the April 1998 visit to Cuba of Prime Minister Chrétien. Although the two-day visit did not lead to any ground-breaking agreements between the two countries, it did solidify an already close and cordial bilateral relationship.[16] In private, Canadian officials said the main purpose of the trip was to pose "a highly visible symbolic challenge" to Washington's continued attempts to maintain Cuba's regional political isolation.[17] In contrast to the last visit to Cuba by a Canadian prime minister, Pierre Trudeau in 1976, which produced little beyond photo opportunities and evident personal rapport between the two leaders, this time around the meeting had a more substantive outcome. Apart from three agreements to cooperate on health, sports, and audio-video production, Chrétien was able to announce significant progress toward concluding a bilateral investment protection treaty, under which Havana agreed to immediately pay $8.4 million in compensation to a Canadian life insurance company whose assets were nationalized after 1959. One Canadian government official could not resist drawing the obvious contrast, terming the deal "a lesson to the Americans about what they ought to be doing instead of passing the Helms-Burton law and placing an embargo on Cuba."[18] The investment and compensation agreements also sharply challenged those U.S. officials who insisted that Ottawa had nothing to show for its policy of engagement. There was, however, no major progress on the human rights front, despite a vague promise from President Castro to "consider" signing onto the United Nations International Covenant on Economic, Social, and Cultural Rights. Still, Chrétien lectured the Cuban leader, in what were reportedly some testy exchanges, on the kinds of political and economic reforms that Cuba would need to make in order to be welcomed back into the wider hemispheric family. Lastly, the prime minister asked for the release of four prominent political prisoners (the so-called "Group of Four"), had some of his officials meet with a select group of Cuban dissidents, and met personally with Cuba's Catholic cardinal, Jaime Ortega.[19]

The Canadian approach was put to the test in February 1999 when the Castro government passed a draconian new internal security law and immediately sentenced the leaders of the Group of Four to substantial jail terms for "collaborating with the U.S. embargo." The Chrétien government, annoyed that its request had been rebuffed, responded quickly. Canada expressed its displeasure with Cuba in a tersely worded statement from the Prime Minister's Office that read: "Cuba sends an unfortunate signal to her friends in the international community when people are jailed for peaceful protest."[20] Accordingly, the prime minister ordered a full review of bilateral relations, effectively halting Canadian efforts to reintegrate Cuba in the hemisphere, suspending any planned ministerial visits, and canceling a joint Canada-Cuba health care program in Haiti—but stopping well short of imposing economic sanctions or aborting initiatives designed to facilitate political liberalization.[21] One Canadian official characterized Ottawa's response in the following manner: "Continued engagement, curtailed activity."[22]

At the same time, both Chrétien and Foreign Minister Axworthy vigorously defended the policy of engagement as precisely the right approach in dealing with circumstances of this kind. "We have a strategy of constructive participation and when something like that happens, we have some flexibility," Chrétien explained. "We can react. If we didn't have relations with [Cuba] we couldn't react."[23] It means, said Axworthy, that "[we can] broach problems very openly, very frankly and very directly," such as his reminder to Castro that

Ottawa's support for readmission to the OAS was contingent on Cuba's "willingness to accept some form of dissent or difference of opinion."[24]

While the Cuba policy review reaffirmed support for constructive engagement and ongoing bilateral economic relations, Prime Minister Chrétien announced that Canada was going "to put some northern ice on the middle [of the policy]" to register its displeasure over the human rights situation on the island.[25] This translated into a freeze on new aid programs subject to a case-by-case review, a temporary halt to lobbying for Cuba's reentry into the OAS, and a suspension of high-level ministerial visits.

Frictions in the Canada-Cuba relationship in 1999 recalled a similar deterioration in ties that occurred in 1976, triggered by Cuba's military involvement in Angola. On that occasion, the Trudeau government also retaliated by cutting aid programs. But whereas sensitivity to U.S. policy concerns was a major factor in Trudeau's decision, it was less important in the deliberations of Chrétien policymakers. In September, newly appointed international trade minister, Pierre Pettigrew, dismissed any likelihood that Canada would shift away from its long-held Cuba policy line: "The best way to help countries [like Cuba] to [implement reforms] is not to isolate them or marginalize them, but is the opposite—to engage them and integrate them into world markets."[26]

This was not a message primarily intended to reassure Havana. Rather, it was meant to sharply demarcate Ottawa's approach to Cuba from the one pursued by Washington. Obviously U.S.-Canadian relations were not about to founder over what was a relatively low priority issue for both countries. But Canada was putting its southern neighbor on notice to expect stiff resistance to all attempts to dictate what it should and shouldn't be doing when it came to ties with Cuba. Thus, while Ottawa was quite prepared to express its irritation with Havana's continuing crackdown on dissidents by lobbying in support of the resolution before the April 2000 United Nations Human Rights Commission (UNHRC) meeting condemning Cuba's human rights record, the Chrétien government saw no inconsistency in its senior diplomat in Havana, Ambassador Keith Christie, appearing on Cuban state television and declaring the U.S. embargo "antiquated and unworkable."[27] Ottawa's interpretation of constructive engagement allowed for differences of opinion with Havana—even reprimands—within an overall approach that remained cordial and cooperative.

A Dynamic All their Own

It was no surprise, then, that even with the release of three members of the Group of Four in May 2000, the "northern ice" on the relationship that Chrétien had spoken about earlier barely melted. Nor was there any sign of improvement with the appointment, just prior to the November 2000 federal election, of John Manley as Canada's new minister of Foreign Affairs. From the beginning, it was clear that this former industry minister would not replicate Axworthy's interest in Cuba or his personal commitment to enhancing Canadian-Cuban relations.[28]

Indeed, in mid-March 2001, Minister Manley confirmed what most people had already suspected—namely, that Cuba would not be invited by the host country Canada to attend the Third Summit of the Americas in Québec City.[29] Speaking before Canada's Foreign Affairs and International Trade parliamentary committee, Manley was unequivocal: "Canada agrees that Cuba is not ready to participate in the summit because it lacks a commitment to democratic principles."[30] He then went on to say: "There hasn't been any demonstration of an acceptance of democratic standards."[31] Clearly, the Chrétien government was still annoyed at the Cuban approach to the human rights question and wanted to send a very definite message of disappointment to Havana.

At the conclusion of the summit, the frostiness of the Canadian-Cuban relationship was evident in Chrétien's closing comments about Cuba's absence from the table. Basically, he intimated that the Cubans had no one to blame but themselves, and he stressed that future acceptance of Cuba into the inter-American community would require changes in the areas of democratization and human rights. He also said that he had tried to assist the Cuban government during his April 1998 visit to Havana, pleading with President Castro to improve his country's human rights record in exchange for easing Cuba back into the inter-American fold. According to Chrétien, he told Castro plainly: "'Let us help you to help yourself, and Castro said no to that.'"[32]

Six days later, Castro showed his irritation with the Canadian government and Chrétien's closing remarks—voicing his displeasure publicly at a nationally televised roundtable discussion. An obviously animated Castro used words like "fanatic" and "a tool of U.S. foreign policy" to describe Chrétien and his statements about Cuba.[33] Castro went on to say that the former prime minister, Pierre Trudeau, would never have said publicly that he had spent four hours lecturing the Cubans on human rights when they had not requested that advice in the first place. The May Day parade shortly afterwards satirized Chrétien as a U.S. puppet and clearly indicated that the relationship was in trouble.

In early November 2002, however, there was a slight improvement in bilateral ties when a junior cabinet minister from the Chrétien government visited Cuba. As the Secretary of State for Latin America and Africa, Denis Paradis led a trade mission (along with a handful of parliamentarians and representatives from seventy Canadian companies) to participate in the 20th Havana International Trade Fair. He also met with senior Cuban officials, inaugurated a cultural exhibit commemorating Pierre Trudeau's life, and spoke with students at the University of Havana.[34]

But just as relations were beginning to thaw, the Cuban government lowered the temperature once again. In April 2003, the revolutionary leadership took actions that would set back Canadian-Cuban relations when it moved swiftly and forcefully to silence outspoken opponents of the regime. (Not surprisingly, the international outcry was loud and critical, manifesting itself in toughly worded resolutions at the annual UNHRC session in Geneva.)[35] Ottawa was unlikely to look positively on the largest crackdown on dissidents in Cuba in several decades—with some seventy-five critics being sentenced to jail terms ranging from six to twenty-eight years.

Initially, Canada's response was low key and cautious—perhaps reflecting the bureaucratic battles being waged within the Department of Foreign Affairs between the "hawks" and "doves" on the Cuba file. Shortly thereafter, though, Cuba's ambassador to Canada was called in and told that Ottawa had "extreme concern" over the dramatic clampdown and was "deeply disturbed" by the tough prison sentences meted out.[36] In addition, a protest letter was handed over to the Cuban emissary to present to Foreign Minister Felipe Pérez Roque. Two weeks later, Canada supported an OAS resolution condemning human rights abuses in Cuba and calling on Havana "to immediately free all unjustly arrested Cubans."[37]

If Canadian-Cuban relations have taken a step backward, this is merely emblematic of their overall bilateral relationship since 1959. Canada and Cuba clearly have strong differences of opinion on many matters, perhaps symbolized by Canada's consistent vote against Cuba at the UNHRC, while it frequently supports Havana's condemnation of the U.S. embargo at the United Nations General Assembly every November. It is a normal relationship, and one in which both sides politely agree to disagree on certain policy questions. But it *is* normal (in contrast to the *abnormal* and dysfunctional U.S.-Cuba ties) and is based upon the ability to discuss these differences. Indeed, when asked about the April crackdown at a press conference, Prime Minister Chrétien remarked: "I believe it's better to be engaged and talking than to ignore the problem . . . I know that if you don't do anything it could be much worse."[38] And the on-again, off-again nature of those relations is unlikely to change in the short term.

From a policy standpoint, it is important to recognize that the respective objectives of both Canada and the United States toward Cuba are essentially the same—namely, fostering meaningful political and economic reforms in Cuba. Where there are fundamental differences in the Canadian and U.S. approaches to Cuba, however, is mainly in the prescribed means to attain these aims. Indeed, the differences, it should be emphasized, are largely over style, strategy, and chosen policy instruments. Here the differences are noticeable. Washington claims that the policy of constructive engagement followed by the Chrétien government has been largely unsuccessful. For its part, Ottawa points to the lack of success in U.S. policy over ten presidential administrations, claiming that an unwavering policy of hostility has not worked.

More specifically, where Washington resorts to a belligerent and aggressive tone toward Cuba, Canada opts instead for a more respectful and open, pragmatic style. And where the U.S. government typically subscribes to a confrontational and isolating strategy, Canada believes in the virtues of dialogue and engagement. Finally, where the United States prefers a policy prescription based on sanctions, provocative measures, and coercing allies, Ottawa advocates a policy menu that is grounded in positive inducement, constructive interaction, and multilateral cooperation.[39]

In the final analysis, Ottawa believes that Washington's hard-headed approach toward Castro's Cuba is ultimately flawed and ill conceived. Moreover, it has not worked in forty-five years. Alternatively, Canada's political leadership is utterly convinced that its approach will eventually bring about positive change—and in a less traumatic fashion over time. It sees significant merit in ministerial visits, economic and trade relations, cultural exchanges, and government-to-government development assistance programs. Of course, neither Canada nor the United States is likely to change its Cuba policy, since each is deeply committed to its own approach, and for its own domestic political reasons.[40]

Not surprisingly, the Cubans have been particularly interested in solidifying and enhancing friendly relations with Canada at every turn. Their motivations for doing so are obvious and numerous—and it is ultimately a win-win situation for Havana since there are few costs or conditions attached. Clearly, the Cuban government is interested in enhancing trade relations with a western, industrialized country like Canada—which can supply Cuba with high-tech equipment, consumer durables, and a key source of badly needed foreign investment. (And if that country is the neighbor, and largest trading partner, with the United States, then so much the better.) Only recently has the Cuban economy exhibited signs of economic improvement, after several painful years of incredible hardship, power blackouts, high unemployment, and food shortages. While the country has not completely turned the corner economically, two-way trade with Canada was especially important during the "Special Period" of the early 1990s.

Of course, Cuba's relations with Canada also provide the Cuban government with important political and symbolic benefits. It is valuable for Havana to showcase its friendly relationship with a charter member of the exclusive Group of Eight (G-8) industrialized countries, particularly a country that is willing to work cooperatively with Cuba. Moreover, the high-profile manner in which Prime Minister Chrétien and senior members of his cabinet have been received in Havana, with widespread media coverage and much fanfare, reflects the symbolic importance that the Cuban government attaches to the bilateral relationship and to the message it sends to the rest of the world. In a global architecture in which the United States reigns as the sole and indispensable "hyperpower," and makes no effort to hide its disdain for the Castro government, Canada in many ways stands out as a positive example for the rest of the world. Cuba's working relations with Canada, then, confers a certain degree of international respectability and credibility on the Castro government that can be repackaged by Havana for domestic as well as external consumption.

Simply put, close relations with Canada offer a significant number of benefits to Cuba without onerous preconditions. Most significantly, having full-blown relations with Canada, a close neighbor and ally of the United States, highlights the misguided and outmoded nature of Washington's failed approach to revolutionary Cuba. Cuban authorities also know that the Canadian government does not do Washington's bidding and that it does not intend to do anything to destabilize the Castro regime or to punish the Cuban people; instead, it aims to work constructively by dialoguing with the Cubans. Down the road, a strong and vibrant relationship with Ottawa could prove useful to Havana, should it wish to normalize relations with Washington, to seek reinclusion in the OAS, or to secure some form of associate status with any future Free Trade Area of the Americas (FTAA) initiative. Such decisions would obviously be taken by Havana alone, but if it did want someone to speak for it, Canada would be a useful choice.

Resisting U.S. Diktats

To understand Washington's reaction or response to Canada's Cuba policy, one has to first grapple with U.S. policy toward Cuba in general. Of course, one of the problems with U.S. policy is that it is constantly changing—that is, moving the goal posts whenever the Cubans make any strategic or calculated moves forward. For the most part, though, Washington wants—first and foremost—to see a "regime change," with Fidel Castro removed from power and an abrupt end brought to the Cuban Revolution.[41] This objective has remained constant even before the United States applied the Trading with the Enemy Act to dealings with Cuba and broke diplomatic relations with Havana in January 1961.

Second, the U.S. government would like to see a transition (preferably peaceful) to an open Cuban society—replete with meaningful democratic, political, and economic reforms—according to the dictates and specifications of Washington. (Business advantages for U.S. investors—as has been seen in the "rebuilding" of Iraq—are of course to be expected.) This seemingly new Cuba would eventually hold multiparty elections, respect individual rights and freedoms, and embrace a full-blown market-capitalist economy. It would also be expected to accept U.S. hegemony. Finally, Washington has been steadfast in its aim of securing financial compensation for U.S.-owned properties that had been confiscated after the 1959 revolution.

In order to attain these policy objectives, ten U.S. administrations, including that of George W. Bush, have sought to implement—in some form or another—a strategy of confrontation of, hostility to, and isolation of Cuba. Various policy instruments, including attempted assassinations of Fidel Castro, economic embargoes, a U.S.-supported invasion, and initiatives to isolate Cuba diplomatically within multilateral forums, have been used over the years. More recently, efforts to tighten the U.S. blockade, to incite political turmoil in Cuba, and to make threatening noises about Cuba being next on the list after "Operation Iraqi Freedom" have been employed.[42]

One of Washington's most frequently used policy tools, and arguably the least effective, is to pressure Western allies to halt—or at least scale back—their relations with Cuba. Most assuredly, Canada has in no way been exempted from U.S. efforts to alter its policy approach toward Cuba. In fact, it is an open secret that successive U.S. administrations—from Eisenhower onward—have been frustrated and displeased with Canada's generally cordial diplomatic relations with Castro's Cuba. Obviously, they would prefer that Ottawa sever all of its political-diplomatic, economic-investment, and cultural-tourism linkages with the tiny Caribbean island. The thrust of their criticism ultimately boils down to their view that Ottawa's relations with Havana only serve to undermine U.S. policy toward Cuba.

While Washington has not overtly exploited trade differences with Ottawa as a lever to pressure for changes in the latter's Cuba policy, it was not uncommon for American officials to express disapproval of Canada's approach. Since the early 1960s, every U.S. president has indicated, at some point, his strong dissatisfaction with the state of Canadian-Cuban relations—with remarks either directly to Canada's prime minister or through proper diplomatic channels.[43] One can be reasonably sure that President John F. Kennedy explained the finer points of U.S. policy toward Cuba to Prime Minister John Diefenbaker; that President Nixon spoke to Prime Minister Pierre Trudeau about Cuba; that President Ronald Reagan informed Prime Minister Brian Mulroney about Cuba's pariah status; and that President Bill Clinton cautioned Prime Minister Jean Chrétien about coddling the Castro dictatorship.

It is probably also fair to assume that U.S. authorities—especially during the Reagan and the elder Bush years—did not have to speak loudly to the Mulroney government about Cuba. Prime Minister Mulroney, who was firmly committed to "good relations, super relations" with the United States, was certainly not going to rock the Canada-U.S. apple cart (as Trudeau had) for the sake of Cuba.[44] Therefore, he did not need any coaxing or persuading to downgrade Canadian-Cuban relations. That said, Canadian governments—regardless of political stripe—have all responded firmly when they have seen Washington undertake extraterritorial measures to support its aggressive policy toward Cuba. This has happened on several occasions.

While verbal pressures from the top levels may have been unnecessary, members of the U.S. Congress still felt it prudent to subject Canada to some form of economic arm-twisting. It began with the 1990 passage of the "Mack amendment" (named after the Republican senator from Florida, Connie Mack), which essentially sought to extend the U.S. economic embargo internationally by making it illegal for U.S. subsidiaries abroad to do business with Cuba. It also called for imposing sanctions against (or halting aid to) any country that buys sugar or other products from Cuba. Notwithstanding Mulroney's obsession with strengthening Canada-U.S. relations, his government actually responded swiftly and substantively to the Mack amendment. Secretary of State for External Affairs Joe Clark called it "an intrusion into Canadian sovereignty" and, in a strongly worded letter to American secretary of state, James Baker, suggested the administration "weigh fully the impact the Mack Amendment will have on U.S.-owned enterprises in Canada as well as on our bilateral relationship."[45] More concretely, Ottawa invoked the 1985 Foreign Extraterritorial Measures Act (FEMA), which required Canadian-based companies—including those of U.S. multinationals—to ignore the provisions of the amendment. Additionally, it instructed those same companies to inform the Canadian government of any instructions from head offices in the U.S. to contravene the Canadian law. In the end, George H. W. Bush, sensitive to Canadian and international criticism of the amendment, vetoed the legislation.

Following on the heels of the Mack amendment was the so-called "Cuban Democracy Act" (CDA), sponsored by Democratic congressman from New Jersey, Robert Torricelli, and passed in November 1992. In general, the law was intended to tighten the U.S. economic embargo against Cuba and thus precipitate the downfall of Fidel Castro. To do so, the act incorporated the Mack amendment provision blocking American subsidiaries trading with Cuba and even prevented any vessel from entering a U.S. port for a period of 180 days if that cargo ship handled any freight to or from revolutionary Cuba. It also stipulated that U.S. aid would be cut to those countries trading with Cuba and that tax benefits for U.S. companies would be ended if they allowed their subsidiaries to conduct normal business activities with Havana.[46] Once again, the Mulroney government responded by condemning the new law and by invoking "blocking" measures under FEMA. Minister of Justice Kim Campbell described the move as necessary "to protect the primacy of Canadian trade law and policy."[47] Expressing deep reservations about the extraterritoriality of the act, Ottawa threatened to fine Canadian-based subsidiaries several thousand dollars or a maximum jail sentence of five years for not respecting Canada's law. It is instructive to note, however, that Ottawa neglected to charge or prosecute any of the U.S. subsidiaries in Canada (including Pepsi Cola, Heinz, and Eli Lilly) for actually violating FEMA.

One of the first disputes involving the CDA surfaced in June 1993 when Canadian travel operators suddenly found they could no longer make bookings on flights linking cities in other countries to Havana. Fearful of violating the CDA, the Colorado-based company that provided computerized flight information to Canadian clients simply terminated the service. Kim Campbell immediately attacked the United States for attempting "to regulat[e] what we do in Canada. . . . If we want to send our people there, that's our business."[48]

Ottawa's fierce resistance to U.S. efforts to squeeze the Cubans economically at the expense of Canada continued under the Liberal government of Jean Chrétien, which came to power in a landslide majority in October 1993. It first surfaced in a major way in June 1995 when four Cuban subsidiaries (joint venture agreements with Cuban government enterprises) of the Alberta-based Sherritt International Corporation were added to a U.S. Treasury Department list of "specially designated nationals of Cuba" barred from selling products in the United States or doing business with U.S. subsidiaries in other countries. As the largest single foreign investor in Cuba, funding a range of nickel, oil, gas, agricultural, and tourist projects, it was not surprising that this Canadian multinational should have been singled out for special attention. But what particularly angered U.S. officials was Sherritt's large-scale investment in the running of the formerly American-owned Moa Bay mining company. With the introduction of new technology, management skills, and incentives schemes, Sherritt, in association with a Cuban state company, had almost doubled the plant's annual output of nickel and cobalt to twenty thousand tons. Moreover, the joint partners intended to invest $165 million in new capital over the four-year period 1996 to 1999 with the objective of increasing yearly production to twenty-four thousand tons. For its part, Sherritt was willing to sacrifice U.S. market share and build up successful alternative markets in Asia, Europe, and Canada rather than withdraw from Cuba.[49] For Ottawa, however, Washington's action against the four subsidiaries had implications far beyond the balance sheet of any particular Canadian corporation. The U.S. Treasury decision, Foreign Affairs Department official Charles Larabie observed, "sends a bad signal to everybody—not just Sherritt."[50]

Within weeks, the Canadian Senate Foreign Affairs Committee released a report sharply critical of U.S. policy toward Cuba and its impact on Canadian enterprise on the island. Referring to the Clinton plan to create a blacklist of foreign companies doing business with Cuba, the report stated that "no country ought to try to impose its own boycott against Cuba, or any other country, in an extraterritorial fashion."⁵¹ Months later, Foreign Minister Andre Ouellet reiterated that "Canada will not tolerate any interference in the sovereignty of Canadian laws" and, to drive the message home, said his government would implement new regulations to block Washington's efforts to restrict trade between Cuba and U.S.-owned subsidiaries in Canada.⁵²

But Ottawa's hostility toward the U.S. economic war against Cuba was most clearly demonstrated in the case of the extraterritorial Cuban Liberty and Democratic Solidarity (Helms-Burton) Act that was signed into law in March 1996. Helms-Burton, which was the heir of the CDA, also internationalized the blockade against Cuba by imposing stiff penalties on foreign companies renting or owning properties in Cuba that were previously expropriated from U.S. citizens by the revolutionary government.⁵³ According to Title III of the act, these same foreign businesses (now operating on property that had been nationalized over forty years earlier) could be subject to lawsuits in U.S. courts by the original owners—and their U.S. assets could be legally seized as financial compensation or damages for "trafficking" in stolen property. In addition, Canadian executives and shareholders, along with their spouses and minor children, who benefited from these "confiscated" properties would be effectively banned from entering the United States under Title IV of the act.

The reaction from Jean Chrétien's government was both immediate and robust. Canada promptly made its concerns known to the highest levels of the U.S. government—including the White House—and sought an exemption from the anti-Cuba law. Ottawa then began an intensive lobbying campaign in Washington as well as working collaboratively with its European Union (EU) partners, members of the Commonwealth, and allies within the World Trade Organization (WTO) to have the law repealed.

Incensed by the extraterritorial provisions of Helms-Burton, Canada's international trade minister, Art Eggleton, exploded: "If the United States want to get at Cuba, that's one thing. But what they are doing here is contrary to the relationship we have had with them and it is a violation of NAFTA [North American Free Trade Agreement]." After conferring with U.S. Trade Representative Mickey Kantor, he described the bill as setting a "dangerous precedent."⁵⁴ What Canada primarily objected to, said Prime Minister Jean Chrétien, was "the notion of extraterritorial application of American law."⁵⁵ During a March speech at Johns Hopkins University in Baltimore, the newly appointed foreign minister, Lloyd Axworthy, bluntly reminded the U.S. government that it had consistently opposed "secondary boycotts" in the case of Israel but now chose to support such action in the case of Cuba, as well as other countries (notably Iran and Libya) with which it had major foreign policy conflicts. "One cannot have it both ways," Axworthy told his audience. "One cannot unilaterally pick and choose which international rules to accept and which to ignore."⁵⁶

In May 1996, Eggleton—in a highly publicized speech in Washington—attacked the U.S. government for its protectionist-minded behavior.[57] More important, perhaps, was the minister's veiled threat about possible retaliatory action by Canada against the United States. The Canadian government also contemplated drafting a series of countermeasures—including so-called "antidote" legislation that would mirror the Helms-Burton Act (and thus presumably allow Canadian citizens to sue for damages against U.S. corporate assets in Canada if they are found in violation of Helms-Burton), as well as introducing a visa requirement for U.S. citizens entering Canada.[58]

One month later, the Canadian government's continuing offensive against Helms-Burton was still gathering momentum—working closely with its NAFTA partner, Mexico, and utilizing whatever multilateral leverage it could muster. At the June OAS General Assembly in Panama, the Canadian delegation, along with the Mexicans, drafted a resolution challenging the legal integrity of the Helms-Burton law. In a vote of 33 to 1, the assembly backed the Canadian-inspired resolution, which instructed the Inter-American Juridical Committee (IAJC) "to examine and decide upon the validity under international law of the Helms-Burton Act at its next regular session, as a matter of priority, and to present its findings to the Permanent Council."[59] Needless to say, a very angry and despondent U.S. delegation stormed out of the hemispheric meeting in disgust. Once again, Canadian policy had revealed a degree of independence that was quite surprising.

Shortly thereafter, Ottawa made known its plans to counter Helms-Burton by introducing legislation to amend the Foreign Extraterritorial Measures Act. Besides issuing "blocking orders" (declaring that judgments handed down by U.S. courts would not be enforced in Canada), the proposed legislation would also permit "Canadians to recover in Canadian courts any amounts awarded under those foreign rulings, along with their court costs in Canada and the foreign country."[60]

In the first punitive measures implemented under the aegis of Helms-Burton, the State Department mailed letters to the senior executives of Sherritt International on July 10, 1996, informing them that the recipients, company shareholders, and their families would be barred from entry into the United States unless the multinational divested itself of its Cuban nickel-cobalt operations within forty-five days. Defending the extension of the ban to children of the principals, the department's Nicholas Burns opined that this would "strengthen the deterrent effect."[61] A Canadian International Trade Department official characterized the move against Sherritt, whose Cuban assets by now totaled around $250 million, as "a very retrogressive step" that could immeasurably damage the global trading system.[62]

As the July deadline approached for the implementation of Title III, Canada's foreign minister, Lloyd Axworthy, attacked not only Washington's embargo policy but also its refusal to concede that the Castro government had introduced major domestic economic reforms during the 1990s. He referred to its liberalizing laws governing foreign investment and profit remittances, introducing taxation policy, and privatizing sectors of the economy. President Clinton decided to activate Title III but to postpone the possibility of Americans taking legal action against foreign corporations for six months, until February 1997. While calling the suspension "a step in the right direction" and, in light of domestic political factors (Clinton's determination to win Florida in the November presidential election), "about as good as we could get," senior Canadian officials believed that it did not go far enough. "There is no question that we are going to have to continue to keep the pressure on," Foreign Minister Axworthy declared, mindful of the fact that Title IV, for instance, remained operative. "This does not mean in any way that we should lessen our efforts to make the bill much more acceptable, or to get rid of it entirely."[63] International Cooperation Minister Pierre Pettigrew responded to the Clinton compromise in a like-minded fashion, indicating that his government would proceed with new legislation giving affected Canadian corporations the power to sue to recover damages awarded any U.S. companies in American courts and including "blocking orders" that would make it impossible for legal judgments resulting from Helms-Burton and similar laws to be enforced. As far as International Trade Minister Eggleton was concerned, Washington "still [has] a gun to our heads."[64]

Once again, Canadian officials highlighted the contradictions in U.S. policy. Noting Washington's preference for engagement over confrontation in its dealings with China but not Cuba, Lloyd Axworthy offered a diplomatic but nonetheless telling comment: "I wouldn't call it hypocrisy, but I would say there is a certain inconsistency that should be examined. They want to engage in a constructive dialogue with the Chinese. . . .I think it should apply equally 90 miles offshore."[65] State Department officials dismissed such criticism as betraying a lack of realism and scolded the Canadian approach for its alleged lack of results.

In a further effort to mobilize allied support for Helms-Burton, special White House representative on Cuba, Stuart Eizenstat, traveled to Canada, Mexico, and a number of European capitals between August 30 and September 13. In Canada, he made no headway whatsoever in discussions with senior foreign policy and trade officials. "We reiterated our position of strong opposition to Helms-Burton," said Art Eggleton, "and we're not backing off that one iota."[66] Eizenstat was similarly rebuffed at a meeting with the influential Business Council on National Issues where he proposed that Canadian companies adopt more stringent trade and investment standards. The business leaders' refusal to make any concessions to Clinton's envoy was writ large in the decision by Sherritt International, the primary global corporate target of

Helms-Burton, to hold its Board of Directors meeting in Havana on September 13.

Eizenstat had barely set foot back in Washington when the Canadian government took additional measures to underscore its refusal to buckle to White House pressures. First, it agreed to finance construction of a third terminal at Havana's international airport using an export credit facility (totaling $225.5 million) "reserved for politically sensitive projects with dubious commercial prospects."[67] Second, it introduced legislation into parliament that would not recognize U.S. court decisions based on Helms-Burton and would ignore collective judgments made against Canadian firms, allow local companies to file countersuits against U.S. subsidiaries whose parent company resorted to Helms-Burton to pursue damages, and give the Canadian government power to financially punish local firms that capitulated to provisions of the American legislation. On October 9, 1996, the House of Commons approved the bill. That same week, Canada also decided to join an EU request to the WTO challenging the legality of Helms-Burton as "an interested third party."

But in December, it was Canada's European allies who now applied subtle pressure on Ottawa to support a tactical policy shift in order to limit friction with Washington, thereby encouraging the Clinton White House to waive Title III of Helms-Burton, due to be activated in February 1997, for a further unspecified period. The EU adopted a binding policy linking expanded trade ties with Cuba to improvements in human rights and movement toward political democracy on the island. Foreign Minister Axworthy summarily rejected the European decision "as just not the approach that we're using." At a news conference in early January 1997, International Trade Minister Eggleton's language was even more dismissive: "If the European Union wants to cosy up to them [the Americans] on the Helms-Burton law, fine, but not us. . . . We think it's far more effective to engage Cuba."[68]

On January 3, President Clinton suspended Title III for a further six months. The announcement provoked little enthusiasm among Canadian officials. Eggleton termed it "disappointing," not least because other unacceptable Helms-Burton provisions still remained in place, and then launched a no-holds-barred attack on the basic thrust of U.S. policy: "It continues to be unacceptable behavior by the United States in foisting its foreign policy onto Canada and other countries, threatening Canadian business, threatening anyone who wants to do legal business in Cuba."[69] During a meeting at Canada's Washington Embassy, Axworthy made it clear to Stuart Eizenstat that his government would not accommodate the U.S. policy position—in the least.[70]

Before long, Ottawa demonstrated that this was not a commitment to mere abstract principle or rhetorical gesture. Invoking the FEMA, it ordered Wal-Mart Canada, the subsidiary of the giant U.S. retail corporation, to rescind a decision to withdraw its inventory of eighty thousand Cuban-made pajamas.

Wal-Mart Canada had acted to preempt threatened sanctions against its parent corporation under the 1992 CDA banning U.S. subsidiary trade with Cuba. Annoyed Treasury Department officials indicated they would not let the issue rest. "Our interest," said one, "is in enforcing the embargo."[71]

Amid the escalating Wal-Mart conflict, the State Department announced that four more Sherritt International executives would be barred from entering the United States. Mixing disgust with anger, Trade Minister Eggleton called Washington's action an "all-time low."[72] These frictions notwithstanding, however, both sides were concerned to avoid any serious rupture in bilateral ties stemming from policy differences over Cuba. Clinton and Chrétien, for instance, agreed to disagree over Cuba when they conferred at the White House in early April. The Canadian prime minister would not retreat from his government's belief that constructive engagement was the "best way to resolve the problem," while the American president obstinately refused to consider that option.[73]

On April 11, agreement was reached between the United States and the EU to temporarily suspend the latter's challenge to Helms-Burton in the WTO in return for a White House promise to seek congressional assent to renegotiate those provisions of the legislation dealing with foreign companies investing in "confiscated" properties in Cuba. The Canadian response was lukewarm. While describing the postponement as encouraging, Art Eggleton stressed that it hardly met Ottawa's basic objection: "I want to get rid of [Helms-Burton]. I want to either amend it or end it."[74] He also bluntly stated that Canada reserved the right to contest Helms-Burton under the NAFTA dispute procedures if the U.S.-EU negotiations failed to produce a satisfactory result.

Paradoxically, the Canadians soon came under attack for what seemed to have been a policy decision to hold their fire until the outcome of the EU challenge in the WTO was clarified.[75] The EU itself, which only months earlier had been pressuring Ottawa to downplay its differences with the United States over Cuba, publicly took Canada to task for this perceived reluctance to take the fight up to Washington. Leading the attack was Trade Commissioner Sir Leon Brittan. "The EU was told that it wasn't a question of whether [Canada would challenge Helms-Burton under NAFTA] but when," he declared, "so I find it a little curious that we have gone ahead and challenged the United States [in the WTO] and taken a high profile action and got some progress . . . and Canada has held back on NAFTA." He accused the Chrétien government of being "scared."[76]

There was clearly a kernel of truth in the implication that attached to Brittan's comment; Ottawa was vulnerable to the charge that a number of its initiatives opposing Helms-Burton seemed little more than empty gestures. The Justice Department, for instance, despite amendments to FEMA giving it the authority, had launched no prosecutions related to either the CDA or Helms-

Burton. Ottawa's reluctance, however, to translate into practice its threat to challenge Helms-Burton on the grounds that it violated NAFTA is perhaps more explicable. Ambassador to the United States Raymond Chrétien was under no illusion that any resort to a NAFTA disputes panel would be treated by Washington in the same dismissive manner as the latter had dealt with European initiatives in the WTO. U.S. officials simply said they wouldn't show up before a disputes panel. "If the Americans tell you in advance, 'if you do this, we'll not even talk to you, we'll not even appoint our judges, we'll not even play the game,' what can you do?," asked Chrétien.[77] But, while acknowledging the need to walk a fine line over Cuba so as not to cause major damage to its relations with the United States, Canada continued to pursue an independent policy based on engagement, not confrontation.

Following its reelection in June 1997, the Chrétien government gave no indication that Canada's vigorous opposition to Washington's economic warfare against Cuba would abate in the near future. Newly appointed trade minister, Sergio Marchi, was quick to reaffirm his predecessor's hope that the Clinton administration would abandon the U.S. trade embargo on the Caribbean island: "It doesn't help Cuba, it doesn't scare Cuba, and it certainly doesn't help the United States."[78] Stepping up the war of words in September, Marchi threatened to withdraw Canada's participation in the Organisation of Economic Co-operation and Development (OECD) negotiations over a Multilateral Agreement on Investments (MAI) if Washington continued to punish foreign companies investing in Cuba.[79]

An Uneasy Appeasement

The Canadian government's continued vigorous support of trade and investment links with Cuba went beyond profits and a commitment to free trade. Equally important was the opportunity it provided to move out from under the U.S. foreign policy shadow, to reaffirm the country's own distinctive approach in international affairs. "For Canada there is a definite symbolic aspect to our ties with Cuba," the vice-chairman of the House of Commons Foreign Affairs Committee, John English, explained. "It is important to us to have a sense that we can act independently in the world—that we can have a foreign policy that is our own."[80]

But such considerations did not find favor in Washington. To Ambassador Chrétien's plaintive question of what could Canada do to accommodate American concerns, senior U.S. policymakers had a simple and straightforward answer: "Fall into line behind us." Speaking at a foreign policy conference in early 1998, special White House envoy Stuart Eizenstat singled out, and upbraided, Canada for its failure to aggressively promote democracy and condemn human rights abuses in Cuba. Although forced to admit that the sanctions policy was hurting American firms and that unilateral actions of this kind often don't work, he believed it imperative that the nations of the world speak with one voice on Cuba. His audience was left in no doubt as to whose voice that should be.[81]

Canadian political and business leaders thought otherwise. Neither Eizenstat's proposal nor a fourth presidential waiver of Title III satisfied Foreign Minister Lloyd Axworthy, who called "the whole embargo and the Helms-Burton bill . . . totally counterproductive" that continued to subject Cuba to "a form of economic victimization."[82] This stance was guaranteed to harden with news that the State Department was again putting Canadian firms under the Helms-Burton spotlight. Genoil Inc. of Calgary, a subsidiary of the Montreal-based St. Genevieve Resources, which had several off-shore oil and gas concessions in Cuban waters, was cautioned that it could face sanctions for "trafficking" in formerly owned U.S. assets. Undeterred by these threats, Genoil began negotiations with the Cuban state oil company, Cubapetroleo, on drilling a $2.5 million exploration onshore well in the southeastern part of the island. Agreement to proceed was announced in January 1999.[83] Canada's biggest corporate investor offered its own, no less emphatic, response to Eizenstat's request: Sherritt International announced it would build a $150 million power generating plant on the island and purchase a 37.5-percent stake in Cuba's monopoly cellular telephone company.[84] In mid-March, standing alongside a poker-faced U.S. secretary of state, Madeleine Albright, in Ottawa, Axworthy told reporters that the American economic embargo of Cuba was not working and that the Chrétien government would continue to oppose it.[85]

While the Helms-Burton Act still remains on the congressional books, its full impact has been blunted by presidential decree. International condemnation, and pressure from Canada and the EU, has succeeded in halting the full implementation of the anti-Cuba law.[86] In fact, every sitting president since 1996 has agreed to waive, on a six-month basis, the Title III provisions on allowing lawsuits to proceed.

Helms-Burton was not the only issue involving Cuba that was causing some friction in the Canada-U.S. relationship. Indeed, when news broke in early January 1997 that Canada's Foreign Affairs minister would be visiting Cuba, it was strongly opposed by Washington—which made its displeasure perfectly clear to the Canadian government. Not surprisingly, nothing short of canceling the trip would be satisfactory to the U.S. side. As State Department spokesperson Nicholas Burns made clear in response to a question from a Canadian journalist: "It doesn't make sense to reward a dictator in our hemisphere who is completely behind the times. You reward him by sending your foreign minister down to visit, by having visits as usual, by trading. And we think that's wrong."[87] In an effort to reduce the diplomatic rhetoric, President Bill Clinton noted: "I'm skeptical, frankly, that . . . the recent discussions between the

Canadians and the Cubans will lead to advances. I believe that our policy is the proper one, but I'm glad that the Canadians are trying to make something good happen in Cuba."[88]

U.S. dissatisfaction with official Canadian visits to Cuba took on greater significance when word was leaked at the Summit of the Americas in Chile that Jean Chrétien himself would be traveling to Havana in late April of 1998. Since no Canadian prime minister had visited Cuba for some twenty years, Washington was obviously concerned about the international legitimacy and respectability that such a visit would confer on the Castro government. Senior American officials sought to scuttle the visit by openly questioning the value of sitting down for late night dinners with Fidel Castro to talk about democracy and political prisoners. National Security Council Adviser Sandy Berger summed up the U.S. view firmly: "We have not seen much evidence that constructive engagement with Cuba has produced any material results with respect to human rights or democracy."[89] In the end, though, the Chrétien visit proceeded in the face of stiff U.S. opposition.

At times, however, Ottawa has made concessions to the U.S. position, and occasionally, Canada refrains from doing something on the Cuban file out of deference to Washington. This seems to have been the case with respect to the April 2001 Summit of the Americas in Québec City, when an expected invitation to Cuba to attend was not forthcoming. All hemisphere countries—with the exception of Cuba—were invited. Canadian officials wrapped their noninvitation in the cloak of human rights and the lack of democracy in Cuba (even though several of the less savory governments represented in Québec were no paragons of democracy), but the real reason was more obvious and less judgmental.

Clearly, the Chrétien government knew that it would be considered a major slap in the face to the United States to have President Castro sitting around the table with the other regional heads of state and government, including President George W. Bush. The writing was on the wall: if Castro attended, then President Bush would not have made an appearance. Needless to say, it was clear to everyone in official Ottawa: Canada would not jeopardize Canada-U.S. relations and the prospect of a hemisphere-wide free trade agreement (a major Canadian foreign economic policy aim) for the sake of the Cubans. While there was no apparent direct pressure on Ottawa to capitulate in terms of the list of invited dignitaries, the anticipated negative U.S. reaction was very much on the minds of officials in Canada's Department of Foreign Affairs and International Trade.

Similarly, at times, Washington's pressure is direct, unsubtle, and even blunt. The most recent example of Washington's pressure tactics came in the form of a charge under the 1917 U.S. Trading with the Enemy Act and the Cuban Assets Control Regulations (the nuts and bolts of the economic embargo). James Sabzali, a Canadian citizen living in Philadelphia and working for a U.S. chemical company named Purolite, ran afoul of the blockade policy by orchestrating the sale of "ion exchange resins" to Cuba—where they were subsequently used for water-purification systems in hospitals and factories.[90] That made Sabzali the first Canadian to be charged and tried for knowingly and willingly conspiring to violate U.S. laws against Cuba. (The fact that this occurred in the midst of an orgy of food purchases by Cuba from American companies—in all some $255 million—reveals the absurd nature of this legislation.) Clearly, the prosecution of Sabzali was intended, in part, to send a commercial chill through Canada and deter Canadian businesspeople from looking at Cuba for possible investment opportunities in the future.[91] As a result, Canadian businesses exporting goods to Cuba have to be extremely careful that they do not run foul of a particularly mean-spirited U.S. government, and one that is determined to tighten the screws on Havana.

When Paul Martin was sworn in as Canada's twenty-first prime minister in mid-December 2003, very little had changed in Canada-Cuba relations for quite some time. A noticeable chill continued to characterize the overall relationship, and no ministerial exchanges between the two countries had taken place since the major crackdown on dissidents in April of that same year.[92]

The fundamental "pull" and "push" factors underscoring Canadian-Cuban relations remain the same, but the new government's obsession with improving the tone of Canada-U.S. relations makes it highly improbable that Martin will seek to strengthen or enhance relations with Cuba.[93] It was clear from their meeting in Monterrey, Mexico, during the Summit of Americas in mid-January 2004, that both Martin and George W. Bush are intent on establishing a warm working relationship. This, despite the fact that Canada is out of step with Washington—and closer to the Latin Americans in insisting that issues of equity and social development cannot be ignored for the sake of neoliberal free market orthodoxies.[94] Still, in a press conference following the summit, Martin said he detected some "very, very good vibes" between himself and the U.S. president.[95] He is clearly not about to jeopardize them, much less Canada's improved ties with Washington, by new efforts to engage with Havana—especially knowing that the payoff to Canada of any such approach would likely be small.

At the same time, any perception that Martin was compromising Canadian sovereignty by embracing the Bush White House would undoubtedly cause him major problems. He knows full well that Jean Chrétien was elected in 1993, to a large extent, because of the seemingly obsequious behavior towards the Reagan and Bush administrations by his predecessor, Brian Mulroney. In the long run, this fear of showing deference to Washington might well prove to be the strongest argument in favor of the status quo in bilateral relations with Cuba. Martin's precious few words about Cuba at Monterrey confirmed his preference for a "stay-the-course" type of Cuba policy. His statement about the lack of democracy in Cuba and a desire to promote positive reforms in that country are certainly consistent with Canada's policy over the last five years or so. There is, then, little chance that Ottawa will soon move to melt the bilateral ice in Canada-Cuba relations. The most likely probability in the short term is a Cuba policy more along the lines of maintaining the current status quo of continued engagement at a reduced level of activity.[96]

Conclusion

It seems reasonably obvious from the previous discussion that U.S. attempts to disrupt Canada's Cuba policy have been largely unsuccessful. While the efforts to put obstacles in the way of Canada-Cuba relations have given officials in Ottawa reason to pause, to deliberate on the nature of those pressures, to show occasional deference, and to calculate an appropriate policy response, it has not resulted in any significant readjustment of Canada's Cuba policy. Indeed, whenever Canada has altered the tenor of its relations with Havana, it has done so not because of U.S. intimidation or pressure, but rather according to its own foreign policy interests and on the basis of its reading of the situation in Cuba.[97]

Still, U.S. efforts to influence Canada's Cuba policy have persisted and varied over the years, as the strange case of James Sabzali manifestly confirms. But the nature and extent of the pressure has often been sporadic and episodic—as opposed to relentless and sustained. More important, the Cuba file takes up a relatively minor portion of the overall Canada-U.S. relationship and never to the point of severely damaging their bilateral relations. Both governments understand the rules of the Cuba game: pressures will be applied and rebuffed accordingly; public statements on the Castro government will be critical in tone; Canadian nationalist discourse will be respected; and each country will simply agree to disagree on the thorny question of Cuba.

It is important to recall that Canada's policy toward Cuba is never a function of one single explanatory variable and, in fact, is the result of a complex series of factors. To be sure, it would be a huge mistake to assume that Canada's Cuba policy can be fully explained by the (unsubtle) exigencies of the Canada-U.S. relationship. In fact, the making of that policy involves the pushing and pulling of a combination or constellation of factors: to wit, bureaucratic politics, individual political ministers, commercial interests, nongovernmental organizations, and external (including U.S.) pressures.

Nonetheless, Canada's Cuba policy cannot be fully understood unless it is viewed in terms of the Canada-Cuba-U.S. triangle. In other words, Canada's policy toward Havana is a function not just of relations with Cuba, but also of its implications for the Canada-U.S. relationship. At times, this has placed

Canada in the unique position of being touted as a possible mediator or inter-locutor between Havana and Washington. More often than not, though, it has created headaches for its relations with both Cuba and the United States.

In practice, Ottawa tries to walk a fine line by maintaining cordial relations with Havana and, simultaneously, sustaining remarkably close relations with Washington. Accordingly, Canada does not go out of its way to flaunt its differences with Washington over the Cuba file. That does not mean that it refrains from acknowledging its relations with Cuba; rather it tries not to do anything that would unnecessarily antagonize the United States—such as invit-ing Fidel Castro to make an official visit to Canada (as distinct from his "un-official" visit to Vancouver en route back from Japan to Havana in 2003).

As for the United States, it still espouses an approach that subtly (and not so subtly at times) pressures Canada to tone down or minimize its relations with Cuba. Yet, as the case of Canada's opposition to war against Iraq in 2003 clearly demonstrated, Washington can and does makes its displeasure known; but it is not in a position to punish Ottawa for taking a strikingly different policy response.[98] The fact remains that the White House cannot retaliate eco-nomically against Canada (and a two-way trade flow of $2 billion-plus a day) any more on the issue of Iraq than on Cuba without, at the same time, shooting itself in the foot.[99] As one Canadian journalist has noted: "Canada supplies 94 percent of U.S. natural gas imports, nearly 100 percent of its electricity im-ports, 53 percent of the uranium for its nuclear power generation, and 17 percent of its crude oil imports."[100]

Officialdom in Washington also recognizes, reluctantly, that friends can sometimes disagree on policy matters and still remain friends and allies. Addi-tionally, the United States knows full well that pushing the Canadians too hard on Cuba would be largely counterproductive, since Ottawa could indeed re-taliate, particularly with its energy resources. More to the point, Washington refrains from pressuring Ottawa too much on its Cuba policy because it does not want to impair seriously the overall bilateral relationship. This is especially true since the United States is inevitably going to need Canada's help in other areas—whether in the reconstruction of Iraq or in supplying a seemingly insa-tiable U.S. thirst for energy resources and possibly even water.

So while it is true that U.S. pressure makes itself felt in no uncertain terms, in the final analysis it does not dictate Canada's policy toward Cuba. If it did, Canadian prime ministers and senior ministers would never have visited Ha-vana, Canada would have honored the U.S. economic embargo, and Ottawa never would have established a particularly successful development assistance program for Cuba. It may well be true, however, that the Canada-U.S. dynamic plays a larger role in the more mundane, day-to-day political operation of the Canadian-Cuban relationship: for instance, supporting critical resolutions at sessions of the UNHRC or at the OAS, issuing strong condemnations of any political crackdowns in Cuba, and raising the issue of human rights with the Cubans at every opportunity. But on the major thrust of the policy, U.S. pressure has had only a minimal impact. It is still unclear how U.S. foreign policy (complete with its new, and dangerous, doctrine of preventative or preemptive strikes) will play out in the post-Iraq era. The "twitch" and "grunt" of the "elephant" is likely to continue to influence Canadian foreign policy toward Cuba. But if the past forty-five years are anything to go by, they will be largely resisted.

Notes

1. A *Toronto Globe and Mail* cartoon of March 27, 2003, parodying Saddam Hussein's tactic of having several "body doubles" as a security precaution, shows the Canadian prime minister having breakfast with his astonished wife. Three others, identical to Mr. Chrétien, are also sitting at the table. The headline in the paper the prime minister is reading states, "Chrétien reacts to growing U.S. anger," and his explanation to his surprised wife for the unexplained guests is simple: "Doubles" (A18).

2. Whenever one contemplates Canada's Cuba policy, it is necessary to remember that Canada is largely dependent upon the U.S. marketplace for its economic survival. As the closing of the Canada-U.S. border in the wake of the tragic 9/11 terror attacks amply demonstrated, Canadians can ill afford to have any border slowdowns or to be impeded from accessing the market of its largest trading partner. That some forty percent of Canada's economy depends upon commercial interaction with the United States creates a certain sense of vulnerability and susceptibility to policies and pressures emanating from Washington.

3. For a discussion of the rationale underpinning Canada's Cuba policy, see Peter McKenna and John M. Kirk, "Canadian-Cuban Relations: A Model for the New Millennium?," *Global Development Studies* 1, nos. 3–4 (Winter 1998–Spring 1999): 396–401. It goes without saying that there are domestic political pressures on Canadian governments to stand up to Washington on Cuba, to defend Canadian sovereignty, and to promote Canadian economic interests.

4. See John M. Kirk and Peter McKenna, *Canada-Cuba Relations: The Other Good Neighbor Policy* (Gainesville: University Press of Florida, 1997).

5. For an examination of the Canada-U.S. dynamic within the Organization of American States (OAS), see Peter McKenna, "Canada, the United States, and the Organization of American States," *The American Review of Canadian Studies* (Autumn 1999): 473–93.

6. See Kirk and McKenna, *Canada-Cuba Relations*," 122–45.

7. Ibid., 125–28.

8. Quoted ibid., 154–55.

9. See Government of Canada, "An Address by the Honorable Christine Stewart, Secretary of State (Latin America and Africa), to the 24th General Assembly of the Organization of American States," *Statements and Speeches*, June 7, 1994, 4.

10. Ibid.

11. *CubaINFO*, December 15, 1994, 3–4.

12. Department of Foreign Affairs and International Trade, "Robaina Visit to Mark 50 Years of Diplomatic Ties Between Canada and Cuba," *News Release*, no. 56, March 17,1995, 1.

13. Quoted in Douglas Farah, "Cuba Signs Broad Pact with Canada," *Washington Post*, January 23, 1997, A22.

14. Department of Foreign Affairs and International Trade, "Notes for an Address by The Honorable Lloyd Axworthy, Minister of Foreign Affairs, to the Organization of American States Conference of the Americas," *Statement*, March 6, 1998, 5.

15. Quoted in Kathleen Kenna, "Canada Blasts U.S. on Cuba," *Toronto Star*, March 7, 1998, A2.

16. For a critical assessment of the visit, see Marcus Gee, "Chrétien's Cuban Folly," *Toronto Globe and Mail*, April 29, 1998, A27.

17. Colin Nickerson, "Canadian Premier Sets Havana Visit," *Boston Globe*, April 20, 1998.

18. Quoted in "Havana to Compensate Canadian Firm for Nationalization," *Miami Herald*, April 27, 1998.

19. See Paul Knox, "Castro to Consider Rights Cases," *Toronto Globe and Mail*, April 28, 1998, A1.

20. See Government of Canada, Office of the Prime Minister, "Statement by the Prime Minister," March 15, 1999.

21. See Joel-Denis Bellavance, "PM Orders Review of Cuban Relations After Critics Jailed," *National Post*, March 16,1999; Allan Thompson, "Canada's Diplomatic Aid for Cuba Put on Hold," *Toronto Star*, March 17, 1999.

22. Confidential interview with Canadian Foreign Affairs official, by author, Ottawa, June 8, 2000.

23. Quoted in "Canada, Spain Condemn Cuba's Sentencing of our Dissidents," *Miami Herald*, March 17, 1999.

24. Quoted ibid.; "Cuban Trial Step Backward, Axworthy Says," *Toronto Globe and Mail*, March 3, 1999.

25. Quoted in Jeff Sallot, "New Cuban Ambassador Gets Cool Official Reception in Ottawa," *Toronto Globe and Mail*, June 30, 1999.

26. Quoted in Andrea Hopkins, "Canada Trade Minister to Stand Firm in Disputes," *Reuters News Service* (hereafter *RNS*), September 9,1999.

27. Quoted in *Latin American Monitor: Caribbean*, April 2000, 4.

28. See Peter McKenna and John M. Kirk, "Canadian-Cuban Relations: Is the Honeymoon Over?," *Canadian Foreign Policy* 9, no.3 (Spring 2002): 49–63.

29. The Cubans were not pleased with the decision, describing the noninvitation as "arbitrary" and "second-level" treatment (*Correspondence from Camilo García*, Second Secretary of Cuba's Embassy in Ottawa, March 19, 2001).

30. Quoted in Peter McKenna, "Manley Courting Bush with his Cold Shoulder to Cuba," *Hamilton Spectator*, March 29, 2001.

31. Quoted in Ian Jack, "Ottawa Shifts Policy on Cuba, Supports Bush," *National Post*, March 16, 2001.

32. "Closing Press Conference of the Summit of the Americas," *CBC Television*, April 22, 2001.

33. See Paul Adams, "Castro Rails Against Canada, Chrétien," *Toronto Globe and Mail*, April 27, 2001, A12.

34. See Jeff Sallot, "Canada's Trade Mission to Cuba Signals Thaw," *Toronto Globe and Mail*, November 2, 2002, A6; Peter McKenna and John Kirk, "It's Time to Make up With Cuba," *Toronto Globe and Mail*, November 6, 2002, A12.

35. Kevin Sullivan, "Cuban Dissidents Reel Under 'Wave of Repression,'" *Washington Post*, April 6, 2003, A15; "Cuba Bars UN Human Rights Envoy," *Washington Post*, April 19, 2003, A14.

36. Quoted in Paul Knox, "Graham Protests Against Cuban Trials," *Toronto Globe and Mail*, April 8, 2003, A8.

37. Quoted in "OAS to Debate Resolution Condemning Cuba on Rights," *Washington Post*, April 22, 2003; Pablo Bachelet, "U.S. Fails to Pass Anti-Cuba Resolution at OAS," *Washington Post*, April 23, 2003.

38. Quoted in "Fidel Castro's Friends in Ottawa," *National Post*, April 25, 2003.

39. See Peter McKenna and John M. Kirk, "Canada, Cuba and 'Constructive Engagement' in the 1990s," in *Canada, the U.S. and Cuba: Helms-Burton and Its Aftermath*, ed. Heather N. Nicol (Kingston, Ontario: Center for International Relations, 1999), 57–76.

40. Ibid.

41. See, for example, Stephen J. Randall, "Cuba–United States Relations in the Post–Cold War Transition," in *Canada, the United States, and Cuba: An Evolving Relationship*, ed. Sahadeo Basdeo and Heather N. Nicol (Miami: North-South Center Press, 2002), 75–93; Wayne S. Smith, "Shackled to the Past: The United States and Cuba," *Current History*, February 1996, 49–54.

42. See John King, "Bush to Stand Firm on Cuba Embargo," CNN.com, May 20, 2002; Scott Lindlaw, "Bush Hardens Stance on Cuba Embargo," *Washington Post*, May 20, 2002. In early April 2003, as the war in Iraq was winding down, U.S. ambassador to the Dominican Republic, Hans Hertell, was quoted as saying: "I think what is happening in Iraq is going to send a very positive signal, and it is a very good example for Cuba" (see "U.S. Ambassador In Dominican Republic Says Iraq an Example for Cuba," *Latin America Working Group*, April 10, 2003).

43. See, for example, Morris Morley, "The United States and the Global Economic Blockade of Cuba: A Study in Political Pressures on America's Allies," *Canadian Journal of Political Science* 17, no.1 (March 1984): 25–48.

44. Those were precisely the words that Mulroney used in an interview with the *Wall Street Journal* just after being elected prime minister in September 1984 (quoted in Lawrence Martin, *Pledge of Allegiance* (Toronto: McClelland & Stewart, 1993), 57.

45. Quoted in "Canada Protests U.S. Effort to Block Firms From Trading With Cuba," *Miami Herald*, November 2, 1990, 1A, 13A. Also see William Claiborne, "Canada Blocks U.S. Effort to Expand Embargo," *Washington Post*, November 1, 1990, F1, F4.

46. See Sahadeo Basdeo, "Helms-Burton Controversy: An Issue in Canada-U.S. Foreign Relations," in Basdeo and Nicol, eds., *Canada, the United States, and Cuba*, 6–26.

47. Quoted in Gillian McGillivray, "Trading With the 'Enemy': Canadian-Cuban Relations in the 1990s," Trinity College Programs in International Studies, Washington D.C., Caribbean Project: Cuba Briefing Paper Series, no. 15 (December 1997): 10.

48. Quoted ibid.

49. "Meet Fidel's Favorite Capitalist," *Business Week*, June 26, 1995, 58; Pascal Fletcher, "Canadians Revitalize Cuban Nickel Plant," *Financial Times* (U.K.), February 15, 1996, 35.

50. Quoted in *CubaINFO*, June 29, 1995, 3.

51. Quoted in *CubaINFO*, August 28, 1995, 2.

52. Quoted in "Canada Toughens Action Against U.S. Cuba Measures," *RNS*, January 19, 1996.

53. See Basdeo, "Helms-Burton Controversy," 6–26.

54. Quoted in Anne Swardson, "Anti-Cuba Legislation in U.S. Angers Island-Friendly Canada," *Washington Post*, March 1, 1996, A10; Michael Wines, "Senate, 74 to 22, Approves Bill Tightening the Curbs on Cuba," *New York Times*, March 6, 1996,4.

55. Quoted in Ann Swardson, "Allies Irked by Bill to Deter Their Trade With U.S. Foes," *Washington Post*, March 7, 1996, A20.

56. Quoted in Jeff Sallot, "Ottawa Condemns Bill on Libya, Iran," *Toronto Globe and Mail*, July 25, 1996, A6.

57. See Drew Fagan, "Eggleton Warns U.S. About Trade Chill," *Toronto Globe and Mail*, May 7, 1996, A1.

58. See Robert Russo, "Canada May Hit Back at U.S. Over Cuba," *Halifax Mail-Star*, May 7, 1996, C6.

59. Organization of American States, "Resolutions Adopted By the General Assembly At Its Twenty-Sixth Regular Session," Panama, June 3, 1996, 11.

60. Government of Canada, Department of Foreign Affairs and International Trade, "Government Announces Measures To Oppose U.S. Helms-Burton Act," *News Release*, no. 115, June 17, 1996, 2.

61. Quoted in Michael Den Tandt et al., "U.S. Bans Sherritt Officers as Penalty for Cuba Deals," *Toronto Globe and Mail*, July 11, 1996, A6.

62. Quoted in Michael Dobbs, "U.S. Announces Measures Against Canadian Firm," *Washington Post*, July 11, 1996, A14.

63. All quotes in Juliet O'Neill, "Clinton Relaxes Anti-Cuba Strategy," *Vancouver Sun*, July 17, 1996, A1; Craig R. Whitney, "Europe Gives Clinton Stand on Cuba Law Cold Shoulder," *New York Times*, July 18, 1996, 15; Drew Fagan, "Reaction Cool to Clinton's Cuba Plan," *Toronto Globe and Mail*, July 18, 1996, A12.

64. Pettigrew and Eggleton quoted in *CubaINFO*, August 1, 1996, 3.

65. Quoted in Fagan, "Reaction Cool," A12.

66. Quoted in *CubaINFO*, September 19, 1996, 1.

67. Bernard Simon and Pascal Fletcher, "Canada to Fund Cuban Airport Growth," *Financial Times*, September 21/22, 1996, 3.

68. Axworthy and Eggleton quoted in Robert Russo, "Canada Rebuffs U.S. Over Cuba," *Vancouver Sun*, December 17, 1996, A10; Laura Eggertson, "Eggleton Ready for Fight Over Cuba," *Toronto Globe and Mail*, January 4, 1997, A2.

69. Quoted in Thomas W. Lippman, "Clinton Suspends Provision of Law That Targets Cuba," *Washington Post*, January 4, 1997, A18.

70. See "Eggleton Ready for Fight," A2.

71. Quoted in *CubaINFO*, March 20, 1997, 1.

72. Quoted in Laura Eggertson. "U.S. Assailed For Barring Executives," *Toronto Globe and Mail*, March 15, 1997.

73. Quoted in *CubaINFO*, April 10, 1997, 4.

74. Quoted in "Canada Says Cuba Compromise Only a First Step," *RNS*, April 11, 1997.

75. See Laura Eggertson, "Eggleton Delays Challenge of Helms-Burton," *Toronto Globe and Mail*, February 7, 1997, B1.

76. Quoted in *CubaINFO*, May 22, 1997, 7; McGillivray, "Trading with the 'Enemy,'" 13.

77. Quoted in Randall Palmer, "Canada Wary of Taking Cuba Dispute to NAFTA," *RNS*, October 30, 1997.

78. Quoted in "Canada Trade-New Trade Minister," *Economist Intelligence Unit*, July 11, 1997, reprinted in *RNS*.

79. See Heather Scoffield, "New Canadian Trade Minister Walks Tightrope," *RNS*, September 25, 1997.

80. Quoted in Mark Clayton, "U.S. to Canada: Play With Cuba, You'll Pay," *Christian Science Monitor*, March 25, 1996, 7.

81. See Barry McKenna, "U.S. Revising Sanctions Policy," *Toronto Globe and Mail*, January 8, 1998.

82. Quoted in Paul Koring, "Axworthy, Helms Aide Slug it Out on Cuba," *Toronto Globe and Mail*, March 7, 1998.

83. *Cuba INFO*, February 1, 1999, 7.

84. See Brent Jang, "Sherritt Expanding in Cuba," *Toronto Globe and Mail*, February 6, 1998; John Partridge, "Sherritt Enters Cuban Cellular Market," *Toronto Globe and Mail*, February 28, 1998.

85. See "US, Canadian Officials Face Off On Cuba," *Journal of Commerce*, March 12, 1998.

86. See Peter McKenna, "Canada and Helms-Burton: Up Close and Personal," *Canadian Foreign Policy* 4, no.3 (Winter 1997): 7–20.

87. Quoted in Laura Eggertson and Paul Knox, "Cuba Law Swaying Canada, U.S. Says," *Toronto Globe and Mail*, January 24, 1997, A8.

88. Quoted in "Cuba Visit Likened to Appeasing Hitler," *Toronto Globe and Mail*, January 24, 1997, A8.

89. Quoted in Janice Tibbets, "Chrétien to Visit Cuba," *Halifax Sunday Herald*, April 19, 1998, A19.

90. See Joseph A. Slobodzian, "3 Men Guilty of Violating Embargo," *Philadelphia Inquirer*, April 4, 2002; Anne Marie Owens, "Conviction Over Cuban Trade a Warning: Canadian Experts," *National Post*, April 5, 2002.

91. See Peter McKenna, "Not Exactly Trading With the Enemy," *Toronto Globe and Mail*, April 5, 2002, A13.

92. However, Ottawa has not adopted an overly critical public posture toward the

Cubans over the 2003 crackdown—as the Europeans have. For the most part, Canada continues to engage the Cubans through joint efforts in health care, community participation, and cultural exhibits. Ottawa has also sought to "brand" Canada in Cuba by contributing to a public affairs program (supporting academic talks in Cuba), efforts at economic modernization and civilian society assistance.

93. There was some concern that Canada bowed to U.S. pressure over the removal of Jean Bertrand Aristide of Haiti in late February 2004. It was even criticized by the fifteen-nation Commonwealth Caribbean (CARICOM) for helping to establish such a negative precedent for democratization in the Americas (see Peter McKenna, "Martin Should Have Tried to Save Aristide," *Toronto Star*, March 2, 2004).

94. See, for example, "Address by Prime Minister of Canada, Paul Martin on the occasion of the inauguration ceremony of the Special Summit of the Americas," Monterrey, Mexico, January 12, 2004, *Organization of American States website*, <www.oas.org/speeches/speech.asp?sCodigo=04-0023>.

95. Quoted in Drew Fagan, "The Vibes Were Very, Very Good," *Toronto Globe and Mail*, January 14, 2004, A1.

96. As of early 2004, Canada's policy toward Cuba shows no signs of doing anything differently. Ottawa still subscribes to a policy of engagement, maintains its opposition to the U.S. economic embargo, and continues to register its displeasure with Title III of Helms-Burton (Confidential interview with Canadian official in the Department of Foreign Affairs and International Trade, by author, Ottawa, February 16, 2004).

97. For instance, Canada's decision to put some "northern ice" on the Canada-Cuba relationship in late 1999 had nothing to do with U.S. pressure or a desire to please Washington. See Peter McKenna and John M. Kirk, "Canada-Cuba Relations: 'Northern Ice' or Nada Nuevo?," in Basdeo and Nicol, eds., *Canada, the United States, and Cuba*, 57–72.

98. See Gloria Galloway, "U.S. Envoy Scolds Canada," *Toronto Globe and Mail*, March 26, 2003, A1; "U.S. Stung by Canada's Lack of Support," *Toronto Star*, March 25, 2003. At the Monterrey Summit of the Americas meeting in January 2004, Bush effectively terminated the chill in relations over the Iraq intervention when he announced that Canadian firms would be allowed to bid for reconstruction projects.

99. See Sinclair Stewart, "Rift Over Iraq Expected to Heal," *Toronto Globe and Mail*, April 7, 2003, B1. Often lost in the U.S. bluster is the importance to the United States of Canada as its largest trading partner. Fully seventeen percent of U.S. foreign crude is produced in Canada—greater than Saudi Arabia's exports to the United States. In 2001, U.S. exports to the province of Ontario alone were nearly twice those to Japan, while for an astonishing thirty-seven U.S. states, Canada is their largest single foreign client. Canada accounts, moreover, for fully twenty-five percent of U.S. exports abroad and imports more from the United States than all fifteen EU countries—clearly demonstrating that Washington would hurt itself in any retaliation against Canada (see Michael den Tandt, "Trade as Crucial to the U.S. as to Canada," *Toronto Globe and Mail*, March 27, 2003, B2.

100. Michael den Tandt, "Presto! Canada-U.S. Trade Fears Go Up in Smoke," *Toronto Globe and Mail*, April 8, 2003, B2.

5

Reconnecting with Cuba

How Washington Lost a Cold War in Latin America

Morris Morley

More than the economic or political blockade what is damaging the treatment of Cuba as a topic is a mental blockade.
Ernesto Samper, president of Colombia and secretary general of the Organization of American States, December 1994

From John F. Kennedy to George W. Bush, successive U.S. administrations have sought, with varying degrees of success, to isolate Cuba politically and economically from the rest of Latin America. By late 1964, only Mexico still retained diplomatic ties with the Caribbean island—partly attesting to the initial success of these efforts. The resurgence of hemispheric nationalism in the late 1960s witnessed the first tentative cracks in this regional "iron curtain" Washington had sought to construct. Over the next two decades, the impetus toward accepting Cuba back into the inter-American system steadily gathered momentum. By the 1990s, the imperial state's regional strategy was in disarray. Indeed, George H. W. Bush and Bill Clinton presided over a quickening of the process of Cuba's reintegration in concert with the almost total hemispheric opposition to White House attempts to further tighten America's economic blockade of the island nation.

U.S. policy toward Cuba during the Bush-Clinton era must be placed in the wider context of political developments in the rest of Latin America, particularly the electoral transitions that swept the hemisphere in the preceding decade. During the 1980s, Washington shifted from supporting authoritarian military rulers against "totalitarian" threats to "brokering" redemocratization processes. In most cases, the reason for this policy shift was a fear that these regimes would collapse under the pressure of economic crises, the loss of elite support, and a growing popular-social mobilization within which a resurgent left often played a leading role. Such an outcome, it was thought, might ultimately result in the election of civilians who opposed the free market economic model championed by the dictatorships or who were simply reluctant to do the automatic bidding of foreign bankers and governments. The experience of the "early" transitions in Peru (1980) and Argentina (1983) confirmed a perception that it was not only possible, but also politically advantageous, to promote a return to civilian rule in a way that preserved the existing state institutions and socioeconomic systems. By 1989, this process of redemocratization and "free markets" had spread across most of the continent and significantly included all three of the powerful ABC countries (Argentina, Brazil, Chile).

What had originated as Washington's "adaptation" to practical demands for political and social change in Latin America was soon transformed into a new political strategy for preserving the status quo. Once the formula ("democracy and free markets") was in place and the rules for electoral transitions firmly established, U.S. policymakers proceeded to promote and support "democratization" as the most effective lever for breaking down barriers to markets, privatizing public enterprises and attacking one-party collectivist states. Any regime resisting the demands of external creditors and foreign multinationals could be accused of undermining democracy, and thus deserving of rebuke or worse. Washington's judgments were less altruistic than practical; Latin America was the only region where the United States had a favorable external account to compensate for trade deficits elsewhere.

The United States exploited the "moral authority" derived from supporting electoral transitions to legitimate its hostile posture toward Cuba. As the Cold War policy justifications receded—Cuba could no longer be described as a Soviet "outpost" in the hemisphere posing a threat to its neighbors—American officials soon found a new rationale. The island was the "exception" to the regional trend; it was ruled by a nonelected regime clinging to outmoded socialist policies. Therefore, relentless pressure was warranted to force the Castro government to adopt full-blown free-market economic policies and change the island's political system in a way that would undermine revolutionary state institutions. In its absence, Cuba should remain excluded from regional organizations and be denied the legitimacy afforded by renewed or expanded ties with Latin America's democratic regimes.

Paradoxically, however, these new civilian governments were prepared to resume bilateral relations with Havana—and usually without preconditions. While sharing the ostensible U.S. objective of seeking changes in Cuba's political economy, they rejected an approach based on isolation and external pressures to bring about this result. Instead, like U.S. allies in Europe, Canada, and elsewhere, their preference was for engaging the Castro government as the most effective means of persuading it to implement domestic reforms. The justification was not only the singular failure of a punitive "isolation" strategy to achieve its stated objective(s); Latin governments were looking to maximize their own economic interests in an increasingly competitive free-market environment that the United States had done so much to encourage. By implication, a policy of engagement with Cuba also signaled that as far as the hemisphere was concerned, there were limits to the kinds of imperial state diktats it was prepared to tolerate.

From the elder Bush to the younger Bush, the post–Cold War White House was very publicly dismissive of these sentiments. Cranking up the invective, American policymakers described the Castro regime in 1990 as the "last bastion of an outdated theology" operating in "splendid isolation" from global political and economic trends.[1] In meetings with regional governments, they variously justified the White House refusal to consider normalized ties on the grounds that Cuba was a "national security threat," a "regional dinosaur," and a promoter of "international terrorism." By 2002, the absence of political democracy had risen to the top of the list. "Our main discussions on Cuba with the Latins," a senior political appointee in the State Department's Bureau of Inter-American Affairs explained, "has been about democratization, the lack of democracy, the lack of democratic processes and human rights."[2]

While the Bush commitment to free markets and deregulated economies in Latin America has remained resolute, the administration's response to the May 2002 military coup that temporarily ousted the Chávez government in Venezuela revealed the limits of its support for democracy. In contexts where these newly elected governments pursue domestic and foreign policies viewed as running counter to fundamental U.S. interests, such support remains—as it has been historically—more contingent than principled and sustained.[3] Washington's behind-the-scenes support for Chávez' opponents contrasted sharply with its insistent demands for Cuban democratization. It also contrasted with the swift and unambiguous condemnation of the coup by all of the Latin governments. The previous September, the Organization of American States (OAS), of which the United States was a charter member, had unanimously and enthusiastically embraced an Inter-American Democratic Charter (IADC) committing its signatories to the protection of duly elected regional governments. That not a single American official referred to the charter in response to the Venezuelan *golpe* raised serious questions about the real objectives of the Bush administration's Cuba policy and its commitment to democracy in the hemisphere.

Divergent Responses: The United States, Latin America, and Cuba's New Regional Policy

The disintegration of the Soviet Union accelerated shifts already under way in Cuban foreign policy. Having linked its core economic and strategic interests to the continuity of its ties with Moscow for more than three decades, Cuba's external relations were moving toward a greater emphasis on the market before Gorbachev's reforms began to come unstuck. In late 1986, Castro acknowledged the need to become more globally competitive when he launched a "rectification" program. Its key objectives included export growth and the greater accumulation of hard currency that could only be achieved by a more concerted opening than hitherto to the capitalist marketplace. The pursuit of this objective demanded, among other things, increased political and economic integration with Latin America.

The key to Cuba's new regional strategy was the consolidation of state-to-state relations. While these included political and ideological ties with the leftist Sandinista government in Nicaragua, of greater importance were the new diplomatic and economic links established with Argentina and Brazil. The policy emphasis was on maximizing short-term economic gains and foreign exchange earnings at the expense of class struggle politics. "We're in a position to work toward integration in Latin America," observed Trade Minister Ricardo Cabrisas in May 1991, "without the difference in social systems becoming an obstacle."[4] While Latin America could never hope to substitute for the loss of Soviet aid and trade or compensate for opportunities denied by the embargo, to an island cut adrift it was one lifeline that couldn't be ignored. In some of his public pronouncements, Castro even offered advice to area regimes on how to avoid "social explosions" that might be triggered by gross inequalities in wealth—a far cry from the days when the Cuba leader sought to exploit such opportunities in pursuit of revolutionary solidarity.[5]

In addition to bilateral relations, Cuba's regional strategy of subordinating revolutionary ties to market concerns also involved active efforts to participate in, and promote, hemispheric organizations, particularly those that had economic functions; and to develop links to a broad mix of nongovernmental forces—including political parties, social movements, and church groups—around specific issues ranging from human rights to the foreign debt.

Irrespective of Havana's shift toward a complex array of relations with Latin America, the elder Bush clung to Ronald Reagan's increasingly tattered regional isolation policy, rejecting mediation offers by hemispheric leaders and refusing to contemplate any modus vivendi prior to the demise of the Castro leadership. The new assistant secretary of state for Inter-American Affairs, Bernard Aronson, spelled out two main reasons for keeping Havana's regional options limited. First, "the Cold War had not ended, the Soviet Union was still an ally of Cuba and the Central American issues had not been fully resolved." Second, the Bush administration was in the business of "promoting democracy in Latin America and trying to isolate dictatorships—Peru, Guatemala, Haiti—and the effort was to maintain a consistent policy on democracy."[6] Technically Aronson's statement about the Cold War may have been correct, but the Soviet Union was in the process of substantially retrenching its overseas commitments, including those in Cuba; and ending the Central American conflict had more to do with Reagan's willingness to support the peace process already well under way than with any decisions taken in Moscow or Havana. As well, there was little consistency in Washington's readiness to engage with, and indeed on occasion offer aid to, the military rulers in Peru, Guatemala, and Haiti and its steadfast refusal to even open a dialogue with Havana.

During Senate confirmation hearings in mid-January 1989, secretary of state–designate, James Baker, told the Foreign Relations Committee "that Castro's continuing support for subversion and instability in Central America and in Chile and Colombia and other places . . . makes it extremely difficult for us to talk about normalizing relations at this stage of the game."[7] Within days of Bush's inauguration, U.S. ambassador Otto Reich demonstrated that this was an assessment Washington thought Latin leaders should share when he unsuccessfully attempted to persuade the newly elected Venezuelan president, Carlos Andrés Pérez, not to invite Castro to his own inauguration.[8]

In a confidential policy memorandum prepared in March, Baker repeated his charge that Havana was still promoting "subversion" in the Western Hemisphere and signaled that there would be no let up in U.S. efforts to pursue a policy toward Cuba that was being increasingly spurned by regional governments. Indeed, what remained of Cuba's diplomatic isolation all but crumbled during the years of the elder Bush presidency: along with Chile, Jamaica reestablished full diplomatic relations; the Dominican Republic announced its intention to move in a similar direction; Colombia upgraded ties to consular status; and Paraguay signaled that it would establish commercial and consular relations as "a first step" to the exchange of ambassadors.[9] Even Guatemala, which continued to resist this trend, offered to actively support Cuba's efforts to improve its hemisphere ties following Castro's support for peace talks between the Serrano regime and that country's guerrilla movement. Declaring that the region was Cuba's "common future," Castro himself assumed a more active profile, attending the inauguration of Brazilian president-elect, Fernando Collor, in March 1990 and the first Ibero-American Summit of Latin American nations in 1991.[10]

The Bush administration, by contrast, moved in the opposite direction. "Diplomatic demarches" protesting new links between Cuba and its neighbors became "fairly routine" said an involved State Department official. "We didn't like Cuba strengthening its relations within the hemisphere because it was counterproductive to our major policy goals and because it might mean strengthened influence among governments in the Western Hemisphere, and this might lead to eventual Cuban membership in the OAS." At the same time, given the strength of the tide running in favor of relations with Cuba, the White House was not prepared to expend a great deal of political capital in an effort to obstruct these moves: "It was not something we were prepared to go to the mat about."[11]

Bush policymakers were particularly encouraged by the electoral defeat of Nicaragua's Sandinista government in February 1990. "Now [that] they've lost their most closely aligned partner," declared a senior official, "our primary pressure is to keep Cuba economically and politically isolated until it changes."[12] To this end, and in a marked policy departure, the president set out his conditions for any future normalization of relations with Havana: the holding of free elections, the establishment of a market economy, and a reduction in Cuba's armed forces.[13] Whereas for Carter and Reagan, changes in Cuba's foreign policy had constituted the preconditions for renewed ties, the quid pro quo was now shifted to changes in Cuba's political economy. Castro was being asked to implement steps that would effectively mean an end to the Cuban Communist Party's monopoly of power, the abolition of the socialist system, and a weakening of the island's ability to defend itself. Short of such a fundamental restructuring, Cuba would remain a pariah state in the eyes of the United States—if not its Latin allies.

These allies, however, could not completely ignore Washington's feelings about Cuba. U.S. clients like Panama's president, Guillermo Endara, publicly supported tightening the economic embargo, while other heads of state, notably Argentina's Carlos Menem and Uruguay's Luis Alberto Lacalle, were vocal in demanding political redemocratization and more rapid economic changes in return for normalizing relations or restoring Cuba's OAS membership. Even the leaders of the twenty-one nations who attended the inaugural Ibero-American Summit were unanimous in pressing Fidel Castro to implement political reforms and, what Colombia's César Gaviria diplomatically termed, economic "corrections."[14] Nonetheless, the dominant sentiment was that engaging Cuba was most likely to accelerate the process of change on the island. At the 1991 and 1992 Rio Group Summits, Argentine efforts to make redemocratization a condition for Cuba's return to the inter-American "family" and wrest from the group a condemnation of the Castro regime, failed to gain the support of more than a handful of governments. Chilean president Patricio Aylwin observed that while member states supported a transition to democracy in Cuba, they rejected a "policy of pressure" to bring it about.[15]

Modest but proliferating Cuban economic relations with Latin America were further evidence of the region's divergence from the U.S. approach. In 1991, for instance, new trade, technology, and scientific cooperation agreements were signed with Brazil, Mexico, and Guyana; the Colombian government began negotiations for the state petroleum company, Ecopetrol, to refine its crude oil in Cuba; the Caribbean Community (CARICOM) group of nations established its first contact with the island to explore the possibility of new economic ties; Venezuela provided $240 million in subsidies to its exporters engaged in Cuba trade; and Mexico signed a commercial agreement with Cuba that included a $300 million line of credit, despite being owed a similar amount by the economically beleaguered revolutionary regime.[16]

When President Bush signed the Cuban Democracy Act (CDA) in October 1992, the torrent of regional criticism this new set of punitive measures against the island economy provoked should have come as no surprise to Washington. Key CDA provisions banned U.S. subsidiaries from engaging in any transactions with Cuba or Cuban nationals; barred third-country vessels from loading or unloading freight at any U.S. port for 180 days after departing a Cuba port it had entered to engage in the trade of goods and services; codified the April 1992 administrative regulation closing U.S. ports to third-country vessels carrying goods or passengers to or from Cuba or carrying goods in which Cuba or a Cuban national had any interest; and gave the president authority to declare third countries providing "assistance" to Cuba ineligible for aid under the Foreign Assistance Act of 1961 or for relief under any program for the forgiveness or reduction of debt owed to the U.S. government. Even Latin governments sympathetic to U.S. objectives in Cuba drew the line at these restrictions, which they perceived as a direct challenge to the principles of self-determination, national sovereignty, international law, and free trade.

Although the Clinton White House appeared just as eager to obstruct the island's gradual reintegration back into the inter-American community, it did, at least, concede the changed nature of Cuba's ties with Latin America, and even Pentagon officials no longer viewed the Castro regime as a "destabilizing" presence in the hemisphere.[17] An executive branch participant in the Bush and Clinton policy debates over the issue recalled: "With the end of the Soviet Union and the Cold War, changes in Cuba behavior in the hemisphere, and democratic governments getting elected who were not right-wing so they could isolate Cuba [as matter of course], the question for us was whether we try keeping Cuba isolated or try to develop a new strategy toward Latin Americans who wanted to develop ties with Cuba."[18] But this greater sensitivity to regional developments did not amount to a rejection of the assumptions on which Bush policy had operated. "The defense of democracy had become the most important political issue in Latin America itself," Michael Skol, principal deputy assistant secretary of state for Inter-American Affairs (1993–95) explained. "So the logic of it was that we had to work against the Castro regime, not because it was a threat any longer to the United States or other Latin American countries," but because consistency demanded that Washington could not promote democracy across the region and ignore its absence in Cuba.[19]

According to Richard Nuccio, the Cuba policy specialist on Congressman Robert Torricelli's (D-N.J.) staff in the early 1990s, "democracy-promotion" also resulted as a strange mixture of ritualistic denunciation and diplomatic realism during the Bush years. He gave the example of a yearly State Department cable transmitted to American Embassies around the world, "particularly in Latin American and the Caribbean, saying 'be sure to go in and tell the Foreign Ministry how bad Cuba is and that you shouldn't renew diplomatic ties with Cuba' but the aim was to deliver it to a minor official because we didn't really want to call attention to it." Clinton diplomats, however, took these "fairly routine" cables much more seriously. "There was a kind of escalation of those kinds of demarches during '93 and '94," said Nuccio, then senior policy adviser to Clinton's assistant secretary of state for Inter-American Affairs, Alexander Watson, "due partly to the efforts of Michael Skol and State's director of the Office of Cuban Affairs, Dennis Hays. Skol was of the old 'kick 'em in the nuts to get their attention' school of U.S. diplomacy. He wanted to go around and berate governments and tell them 'don't you know who we are, don't you know who you are messing with.'"[20] Hays was just as committed to "as tough a line as possible opposing Cuba's reentry into Latin America, bilaterally and regionally" because the absence of strong U.S. disapproval would send exactly the wrong signal to hemisphere governments—in effect, that normalizing relations with Cuba was no longer an important issue for Washington that, in turn, would simply accelerate the trend.[21]

The Clinton administration's fulsome embrace of the Bush approach to Cuba presented regional governments with a dilemma. They too knew that the old days of ideological rivalry and military confrontation were over, and the security concerns that had once justified Washington's iron curtain around Cuba no longer pertained. Moreover, they had their own reasons to want to reengage with Havana. Cuba remained symbolically important in the politics of the Americas: it had long been a ploy of some Latin regimes to make measured overtures to the island whenever they felt the need to reaffirm their independence from U.S. policy; where electoral democracy was constrained by the prevailing free market economic orthodoxy and beholden to the International Monetary Fund (IMF) and foreign private banks, reaching out to Cuba offered one way of accommodating leftist domestic constituents whose demands for redistributive policies and a reckoning for the brutal days of military dictatorship were unlikely to be met. Importantly, better state-to-state relations could also increase the possibility of recovering debts owed by Havana, encourage trade, and facilitate agreements that would strengthen the protections for private investment on the island.

The region's increasingly pragmatic approach to the Cuba "problem" was given added impetus by Havana's conciliatory demeanor, including its willingness to negotiate compensation packages for U.S. properties nationalized after 1959 in the context of normalization discussions and Castro's announcement of a 170,000-man reduction in the size of Cuba's armed forces. To further calm any lingering concerns, the Cuban president issued a statement that Havana had "no plan to export" its political and economic model to the rest of the hemisphere and sought only "to be recognised and respected as a legitimate part of Latin America's political plurality."[22] Even if there was no obvious immediate advantage in taking up Havana's approaches, it seemed absurd to dismiss them out of hand and pass up what benefits conceivably could emerge. During the latter months of 1993, Colombia and Nicaragua restored full diplomatic relations with Cuba; the president-elect of Honduras, Carlos Roberto Reina, called for an end to Cuba's regional isolation; and Grenada received the first official Cuban delegation since the October 1983 U.S. military invasion.

If U.S. officials insisted that Cuba remained a problem for the hemisphere because it was mired in "the communist ideologies of an earlier day," from the perspective of most Latin capitals it was America's Cuba policy that was outdated and problematical.[23] None understated the need for political redemocratization in Cuba, but the majority rejected Washington's argument that satisfaction of this demand was a precondition for normalized ties. Instead of demonizing and isolating Castro, Latin governments urged a search for common ground. Argentina's president Carlos Menem attempted to reduce tensions with an offer to mediate between the two adversaries on the eve of his June 1994 White House visit. But, speaking to reporters after meeting with Clinton, he quickly backtracked, hinting that the suggestion had received a cool reception. Cuba's return to the OAS and the lifting of U.S. economic sanctions, Menem said, still depended on the Castro government implementing major political and economic changes.[24] Only weeks later, however, at the Third Ibero-American Summit in Brazil, Menem expressed the view that "democratization is now possible in Cuba."[25]

During 1994 Jamaica opened a consulate in Havana; Antigua and Barbados established diplomatic ties with the island; Grenada accepted the credentials of a nonresident Cuban consul the same week that Washington closed its embassy there; and Panama's newly elected president, Ernesto Balladares, restored relations with Cuba that had been severed by his predecessor. The Cubans pursued their own "full court" diplomatic offensive to accelerate this process. In April, Foreign Minister Roberto Robaina visited a number of Latin capitals, including Buenos Aires, Lima, and Montevideo; five months later, he embarked on a second trip, conferring with senior government officials in Ecuador, Chile, Bolivia, Brazil, and Panama. Fidel Castro capped off the year by attending the inauguration of Mexico's president, Ernesto Zedillo, where he rubbed shoulders with OAS secretary general Gaviria and a number of Latin heads of state including Eduardo Frei, the newly elected president of Chile.

Confronted by a hemisphere determined to pursue its own Cuba agenda, the Clinton White House began to shift away from largely fruitless efforts to block the restoration of bilateral ties. "We decided on a new strategy," said an NSC official, "which was to say restore diplomatic relations but condition those ties on Cuba making changes."[26] But even this proposal made little headway among Latin governments. While prepared to pay lip service to the idea by coupling the renewal of relations with verbal exhortations about the importance of reforms, they balked at conditioning ties on Cuban compliance. The coordinator of State's Office of Cuban Affairs, Michael Ranneberger, acknowledged the that this "new strategy" did little or nothing to arrest the trend: "We continued to approach them and say that we really don't think restoring ties is a good thing to do because it sends the wrong signal, that it reinforces the regime, that you give Castro a little more legitimacy. But normalizing bilateral relations has just become a way of life."[27] Still, not everyone in the administration was as sanguine about the trend. "We have never fallen on our sword over any country reestablishing normal relations with Cuba," explained a State Department Inter-American Affairs official, "but if we get wind of it we seek to discourage it."[28]

Coming Home: Latin America "Engages" Cuba

The growth in Cuba's bilateral relations with its neighbors was one thing; any attempt to bring Cuba back into regional organizations and forums was quite another. Collective reaching out to Fidel Castro's regime struck at the very heart of Washington's isolation strategy. If the idea took hold that Cuba was just another member of the hemispheric community that all the rest could— and should—deal with as a group, this would pose an infinitely more serious challenge to the U.S. view of Cuba as a "rogue" state. Above all, it would undercut U.S. attempts to force Havana to implement the kinds of political and economic changes being demanded as the quid pro quo for normalized ties.

Logically, readmitting Cuba to the peak regional body—the OAS—would have also undermined the whole rationale for the embargo and the broader regional policy approach it had come to symbolize. "Our stated objectives in Latin America were liberalized economies, the promotion of democracy and human rights," Robert Morley, the coordinator of the Office of Cuban Affairs in the elder Bush administration explained. "Cuba did not have a good record in any of these areas. As a result, Cuba's entry into the OAS, whose stated policy was to promote these objectives, would not be productive. In every aspect of our major interests, Cuba's involvement in the OAS would be counterproductive."[29] Assistant Secretary of State Aronson put it more emphatically: it was of "fundamental" importance to resist any reconsideration of Cuba's membership because to do so "would have undermined the OAS as a defender of democracy."[30]

On this issue, there was no room for flexibility. In October 1990, for instance, Argentina's Menem told a press conference that he was willing to abide by a broad consensus in support of Cuba's return to the regional body because such a move could facilitate the process of change: "[It] would give us the opportunity to dialogue with the Cubans and achieve some democratic reforms in that country."[31] But the White House would have none of it. Again, following a similar comment by Mexico's foreign minister Fernando Solana in mid-1991, U.S. ambassador to the OAS, Lawrence Eagleburger, responded tartly that his government "has a very clear position on Cuba and it will maintain it."[32] At the same time, efforts to achieve a regional consensus were being continually frustrated by governments such as Argentina's periodically shifting their positions on this issue.

The Clinton administration was equally committed to limiting Cuba's regional successes and, in the words of State's Michael Ranneberger, "our principle focus was keeping them out of the OAS."[33] Given the region's growing support for normalized relations with Havana, it was not surprising that this unbending U.S. stance had the paradoxical outcome of ensuring that the issue would continue to reverberate at hemispheric meetings. At the Fourth Ibero-American Summit in Cartagena, Colombia, in June 1994, retiring OAS secretary general, Joao Baena Soares, received a standing ovation when he declared the time had arrived "for member states to re-examine the measures adopted more than 30 years ago to suspend the Cuban government from the activities of the organization." Cuba was still part of the hemisphere and a great deal had changed since the January 1962 expulsion. "The nineties," he told the assembled delegates, "aren't the sixties."[34] Mexico, Brazil, Venezuela, and most Central American countries supported Cuba's readmission, but El Salvador and the ever-shifting Argentina lined up with the United States to force postponement of any formal discussion to a later date. "We all want political and economic changes in Cuba," said host President César Gaviria, "and we all want Cuba to return to the inter-American system should these changes take place."[35] Chilean president Eduardo Frei spoke for most of his colleagues in stating that decisions about political reforms "can be made by the Cuban government only."[36] Ironically, Washington again ensured that the issue would not quietly go away when it backed César Gaviria's successful campaign to succeed Soares as OAS secretary general. On taking up his position in September, Gaviria affirmed his support for Cuba's reintegration and questioned whether ending its isolation was not the best way to encourage the internal reform process.[37]

The White House also had to contend with the annual humiliation in the United Nations General Assembly (UNGA) over its embargo policy. In November 1994, 101 countries voted to approve a resolution calling for the lifting of the embargo (an increase of thirteen over 1993) with two against and forty-eight abstentions. An equally significant feature of the 1994 vote was that no Latin American government voted with the United States and only three (Argentina, Guatemala, and El Salvador) abstained. Even support for the annual

U.S.-sponsored condemnation of Cuba in the United Nations Human Rights Commission (UNHRC) was dwindling with the figures for 1994 at twenty-two in favor, eight opposed, and twenty-three abstentions compared with twenty-seven, ten, and sixteen respectively for 1993. It consequently came as no surprise when Secretary of State Warren Christopher told a House International Relations Committee hearing in January 1995 that there was "very strong pressure from others" against the main thrust of the U.S. policy approach to Cuba.[38]

The cleavage between the United States and its southern neighbors had been sharply exposed in December 1994 when the Clinton administration unilaterally vetoed Fidel Castro's attendance at a "Summit of the Americas" meeting in Miami. The refusal to extend an invitation to the Cuban leader was justified on the grounds that his government was undemocratic and failed to respect human rights. Although the same criteria was used to exclude Haiti's military rulers, the United States was not willing to veto Peru's Alberto Fujimori, whose armed forces had perpetrated widespread human rights abuses against the civilian population in its war to exterminate the Sendero Luminoso guerrillas and who orchestrated an *autogolpe* in 1992 by shutting down the country's legislature. Similarly, the United States had no qualms about the attendance of the Dominican Republic's Joaquín Balaguer, whose reelection was the subject of widespread allegations of vote fraud. Nor did Clinton officials show much concern about the degree of political power still exercised by the military institutions in a number of countries that had made the transition from dictatorship to democracy over the past decade. Despite pre-summit lobbying by U.S. officials to keep Cuba off the agenda, proposals by Mexico and Brazil urged Washington to open a dialogue with Havana as a first step to improving bilateral relations. Colombia's president Ernesto Samper adopted a less diplomatic approach when he addressed the delegates: "More than the economic or political blockade what is damaging the treatment of Cuba as a topic is a mental blockade."[39] Nobody could have been in any doubt as to whom he believed was responsible for this state of affairs.

But the pressure was not all one way. When Chile announced the exchange of ambassadors with Cuba in April 1995, Washington combined expressions of "disappointment" with the threat of economic sanctions. One State Department official warned that it "won't make things easier" for Chile's application to join the North American Free Trade Agreement (NAFTA).[40] In Colombia, U.S. ambassador Myles Frechette finally exhausted the host government's patience with his repeated criticisms of the latter's rapprochement with Cuba. Foreign Minister Rodrigo Pardo publicly cautioned the senior American diplomat to stop interfering in a domestic issue that was none of his business.[41] Yet, the Clinton administration remained determined to obstruct the pace of Cuba's return to the inter-American system, even if this meant taking actions that were petty or inconsequential. That August, for instance, it refused to allow Puerto Rico and the Virgin Islands to participate as observers at the inaugural Association of Caribbean States (ACS) Summit meeting in Port-of-Spain because of Cuba's inclusion and Fidel Castro's attendance.[42] Meanwhile, the State Department refused to delete Cuba from its list of terrorist states even though it could muster no evidence to show that Havana actually sponsored specific acts of terrorism in the hemisphere, let alone the rest of the world.

Visibly frustrated by what he believed was an inflexible U.S. posture, especially given the direction in which the region as a whole was moving, OAS secretary general César Gaviria told a June 1995 General Assembly meeting that the debate over Cuba "has lost all logic and rationality. The all or nothing policy has led us nowhere all these years."[43] The State Department response seemed merely to validate Gaviria's point. The crux of the matter was there for all to see, said Assistant Secretary for Inter-American Affairs Alexander Watson: Cuba was ruled by a "Stalinist government" and that alone disqualified it from readmission to the OAS.[44]

Castro's decision to authorize the shoot down of two civilian planes piloted by members of the Miami-based "Brothers to the Rescue" exile group in February 1996 did not shake Latin leaders' confidence in the good sense of their approach. While the incident may have hardened the White House resolve to tighten economic sanctions, it had a far less dramatic impact on the trajectory of Cuban–Latin American relations. The response of key hemispheric nations was, in fact, surprisingly restrained. Mexico expressed concern over the tension generated between the United States and Cuba by the shoot down and urged both sides to resolve the situation through dialogue and negotiation "strictly adhering to international law." The Brazilian Foreign Ministry issued a statement of "regret," observing that "episodes of this kind, besides causing loss of human lives, could create an atmosphere of confrontation and instability in the region." Chile's foreign minister, José Miguel Insulza, simply called Cuba's action "very censurable."[45] Washington was unable to muster any clear condemnation of Cuba's action except for a statement from Central American leaders, prepared during a meeting with Secretary of State Christopher who was visiting the area at the time.

Overall, the region cautioned a measured response, but domestic political calculations impelled Clinton to sign the Helms-Burton legislation—passed by Congress and slightly revised during negotiations with the White House—into law. One of its principal targets was foreign investors. Title III allowed American nationals to sue for damages in U.S. federal courts those persons who "traffick" in property nationalized by the Cuban government after 1959. Title IV denied foreign citizens (including CEOs and other senior corporate executives, principals, or shareholders) who were party to the expropriation of U.S. property or deemed to "benefit" from the trafficking in such property in Cuba entry into the United States. Helms-Burton also specified numerous conditions for determining when a genuine political "transition" was under way and when a "democratic" government had assumed power in Havana—thus qualifying Cuba for various types of U.S. assistance and, ultimately, the suspension of all trade sanctions.

Throughout 1996, the expanding political links between Latin America and Cuba were paralleled, and indeed overshadowed, by regional anger over this ratcheting up of the embargo. State's coordinator of the Office of Cuban Affairs Michael Ranneberger described the reaction to Helms-Burton as "horrible [and] vehement."[46] At an OAS General Assembly meeting in June, every Latin member supported a strongly worded resolution condemning the extraterritorial reach of Helms-Burton and calling on the Inter-American Juridical Committee to investigate its legality under international law. The United States was the lone dissenting voice; Ambassador Harriet Babbitt, fuming, denounced her colleagues for engaging in an act of "diplomatic cowardice."[47] Chile's foreign minister alluded to the contradiction inherent in Washington's vote against a resolution that was, first and foremost, "about freedom of trade, about economic freedom and about international law."[48] Secretary General Gaviria hinted at the need for a shift in U.S. policy and stressed that the sticking points were not over goals "but over how best to reintegrate Cuba into the inter-American system."[49] On Capitol Hill, anti-Castro legislators demanded his resignation. Gaviria's retort was short and sweet: the OAS "must deal with [every] legitimate government" in Latin America, including Cuba's.[50]

The sentiments behind that statement were to be given a powerful boost—and one that would further expose the thin veneer of regional respect for the alternative U.S. position—by Pope John Paul II during his historic visit to Cuba in January 1998. It was no surprise that the pope used his mobile pulpit to criticize Castro's government for restricting basic liberties and imprisoning political opponents; less anticipated was the degree of support the pope lent to Cuba's campaign to be accepted as a full member of the international community on its own terms. While subtly admonishing Cuba to "open itself to the world," John Paul simultaneously called on "the world to open itself up to Cuba."[51] As the pope was about to leave the island, he repeated the call but with an even sharper message: "In our day no nation can live in isolation, especially when the imposed isolation strikes the population indiscriminately, making it ever more difficult for the weakest to enjoy the bare essentials of decent living—things such as food, health, and education."[52]

The response from Latin countries was almost immediate. Scarcely had the pope left Cuba when Guatemala, citing the pontiff's call to end Cuba's isolation, reversed its 1997 decision not to open an Interests Section in Havana and announced that it was going to reestablish full diplomatic relations. Over the next five months, Haiti reopened its embassy after a two-year break in ties;

Ecuador signed a memorandum of understanding with Cuba designed to foster closer relations; the Dominican Republic renewed full diplomatic relations; Honduras, where Cuba already had an Interests Section, announced it was considering an upgrade in ties; and Argentina's president Carlos Menem cited the papal visit as reason for a possible trip to Cuba later that year. Buenos Aires also announced that while it would not play any active role in moves to reinstate Cuba's OAS membership, the Menem government "will abide by what the [OAS] Council decides."[53]

In a related development, only weeks after the pope's visit, the United States suffered an embarrassing defeat at the UNHRC when for the first time its resolution condemning Cuba's human rights record was defeated by a vote of 19 to 16 with eighteen abstentions. Of the eleven Latin members, only Argentina and El Salvador supported the resolution; this time around, Chile and Uruguay deserted Washington and joined the abstention bloc. A high-ranking State Department Latin Americanist attributed what he called this "surprising" setback to an insufficiently aggressive U.S. lobbying effort: "We had got a little complacent about beefing up co-sponsoring and didn't pay enough attention to the vote camp."[54]

While the United States was still absorbing this setback, the second Summit of the Americas got under way in Santiago with Cuba's exclusion set to dominate proceedings. Chile's foreign minister Insulza established the tone by proposing that "surely the moment has come to revise [U.S.] policy toward Cuba, which not only we do not share but also which has now been in place for 30 years or so without any impact." Brazil's president Fernando Henrique Cardoso denoted his unhappiness at Cuba's absence by calling for "integration without exclusions," while Peruvian head of state Alberto Fujimori also publicly took the United States to task over its veto of Cuba's presence at the gathering. Barbados expressed the hope that this would be the last summit without Cuba and, in his closing speech to the conference, Brazil's Cardoso referred to Cuba as "the great absentee."[55]

It is true that such statements were largely rhetoric. Expressions of disagreement with U.S. policy did not mean that the Latin Americans had much enthusiasm for doing anything about it where that meant direct confrontation with the imperial state. Cuba was not invited to return to the OAS precisely because relations with Washington took priority, and U.S. officials stuck to their line-in-the-sand approach. "To put Cuba into the family at this point or even discuss Cuba's reentry," the State Department's Peter Romero insisted, "would be very, very premature."[56] Other department officials explained the reasoning that underpinned this belief. "The OAS," said one, "is a group of democracies and Cuba doesn't belong there."[57] Some explanations were more desperate and illogical. A senior official actively involved in Cuba policymaking stressed not just concerns about the lack of democracy but also the likely impact of a Cuban presence on the U.S. role within the regional organization: "Because the OAS was in Washington it would have hobbled the organization to have Cuban views in the OAS. A very dramatic Cuban presence would have made it very tough going; the dramatic effect would have been very difficult for us."[58] At an April 1998 White House news conference, President Clinton warned that any move to readmit Cuba to the OAS "would be a big mistake."[59]

Despite U.S. efforts to block any formal discussion of the Cuba issue at the June 1998 OAS General Assembly meeting in Caracas, there was little likelihood that Washington's strictures would be heeded by those governments for whom Cuba was "the absent protagonist." Host president Rafael Caldera announced prior to the gathering that "if Cuba were to desire to return to the OAS, it would have Venezuela's support."[60] In his opening speech to the General Assembly, Secretary General Gaviria put the issue squarely on the "unofficial" agenda, noting that there was a growing regional sentiment in favor of Cuba's readmission based on "formulas of diplomacy, negotiations and a gradual approach." He also identified Cuba as "the hemisphere's most important outstanding political problem."[61] At the meeting's first session, Mexico's Rosario Green, in a not-so-subtle knock at the U.S. delegation, observed that "ignoring the problem won't make it go away."[62] Devising a formula for Cuba's readmission, however, proved easier said than done. Mexico's efforts bogged down and were ultimately shelved, due to a combination of U.S. opposition and differences of opinion among member states over whether to begin the formal process in the absence of substantive political changes on the island.[63]

The pope's call for an end to Cuba's isolation had also provided new ammunition for Latin American supporters of Cuba's readmission to the OAS. Gaviria declared that the papal visit had "created new circumstances for examining the Cuba issue."[64] Chilean government officials were convinced that the visit had done more than thirty-six years of OAS isolation to open Cuba to the world. The feeling was widely shared among delegates at the OAS's 50th anniversary celebrations in late April. Colombian president Ernesto Samper said the OAS was incomplete without Cuba; Mexico's foreign minister, Rosario Green, said the pope's visit had been "a detonator" that should break Cuba's isolation.[65] Ironically, this latest OAS tussle over Cuba was being played out at a time when Havana's public stance remained adamantly opposed to rejoining an organization it regarded as still thoroughly dominated by the United States.

The latter half of 1998 culminated an extraordinarily successful year for Cuba's regional diplomacy. During a Caribbean tour, Fidel Castro was feted in Jamaica, where even the conservative political leader Edward Seaga (who had closed down the Cuban Embassy after his presidential election victory in 1980) welcomed the Cuban leader and declared, "I don't think we need to fight yesterday's war today."[66] In Grenada and Barbados, Castro received similar red-carpet treatment, while the Dominican Republic's president, Leonel Fernández, urged him to "feel right at home." None of these anglophone Caribbean leaders commented publicly on Cuba's political system or aired misgivings they may have had about its human rights record.[67] Weeks later, in Oporto, Portugal, the Ibero-American Summit not only produced a final communiqué that included a vigorous condemnation of the U.S. embargo, but agreed that Havana would host the 1999 conference. The one bright spot for Washington was the mid-year visit to Havana by Brazil's foreign minister Luiz Felipe Lampreia, which temporarily strained Cuban-Brazilian relations after he insisted on meeting with prominent human rights activist, Elizardo Sánchez, and lectured his Cuban counterpart Roberto Robaina on the virtues of democracy and respect for human rights.[68]

In mid-January 1999, Colombian president Andrés Pastrana and Venezuela's president-elect Hugo Chávez visited Fidel Castro to discuss possible support roles for Cuba and Venezuela in the revived talks between the Colombian government and leftist guerrillas aimed at terminating the longest running conflict in Latin America. "For us, President Castro's involvement is very important," Pastrana told reporters. "He still has influence in insurgency groups and he's willing to play a role."[69] Before leaving, Pastrana signed agreements on cooperative measures in drug interdiction and law enforcement, publicly criticized the U.S. embargo, supported Cuba's readmission to the OAS, and invited Castro to pay a state visit to Colombia later in the year. That same month, another important visitor put Havana on his itinerary, Suriname's Jules Albert Wijdenbosch, the newly appointed head of CARICOM. He signed trade and cooperation agreements with the Cuban government and encouraged it to take a more active role in the CARICOM's future activities—a view that raised eyebrows among officials in the State Department and the White House.[70]

Cuba's biggest diplomatic achievement in 1999 was playing host to the Ninth Ibero-American Summit. Doubts about whether it would take place and, if so, how many countries would attend, proved unfounded. Representatives of all twenty-one member states arrived in Havana, including sixteen heads of state. Only the presidents of El Salvador, Costa Rica, and Nicaragua boycotted the summit over professed ideological differences with the Castro government; Chile's Eduardo Frei and Argentina's Carlos Menem stayed away to protest plans by Spain to continue efforts to extradite former Chilean dictator General Augusto Pinochet from Britain to face prosecution for "crimes against humanity."

While many of the visiting officials met with political dissidents and human rights activists, they also exhorted the Clinton administration "to take a similar position of talking with all Cubans, including the government."[71] The closing "Declaration of Havana" expressed a general commitment to "respect human rights and fundamental freedoms" and took the Cuban government to task over its authoritarian rule. But this was coupled with criticism of the U.S. embargo, including a specific denunciation of Helms-Burton.[72] Reflecting on Cuba's changed status, Castro told his guests that at the First Ibero-American Summit in 1991 "I was a strange bird there, an intruder whose admission to that hall had the taste of forgiveness." Today, he continued, "we do not need to be summoned or receive anyone's permission to meet like a family without exclusion."[73]

At the conclusion of a state visit to Venezuela in October 2000, Castro and Hugo Chávez signed an agreement that promised to substantially ameliorate the island's post-Soviet oil "crisis," which had forced the Cuban government to budget an extra $500 million for oil imports that year. Venezuela would supply one-third of Cuba's oil needs (53,000 barrels daily) over the next five years on preferential terms similar to those Venezuela had signed with other Caribbean and Central American nations: a fifteen-year repayment period, a two-year grace period, a two percent interest rate, and prices per barrel well below the current world market figure. This would represent an important breakthrough for a country reduced to preindustrial forms of transport in many parts of its agricultural sector. A supplementary accord took into account Cuba's limited hard currency reserves by providing for repayment in goods and services— vaccines, sugar technology, doctors, physical education teachers, and sports coaches—as well as cash.[74] Washington's criticism of the accord merely under- scored the extent to which U.S. policymakers had retreated into a state of denial. "The thinking in the administration is that Castro is an anachronism and Chávez, in associating himself with Castro, is also casting himself in an anachronistic light," commented one senior Clinton official.[75] To most Latin capitals, it was the U.S. policy of trying to maintain Cuba's regional isolation that looked increasingly anachronistic.

Approaching the end of the first post–Cold War decade, the limitations on Cuba's greater regional integration were more and more a function of decisions taken in Havana and the other regional capitals; Washington's efforts to prop up its increasingly discredited isolation policy were now largely concentrated on avoiding humiliating defeats in organizations such as the UNHRC and on keeping Cuba out of the OAS and other regional bodies where the United States exercised disproportionate influence. Discussing the 1999 UNHRC vote condemning Cuba's human rights record, the coordinator of State's Office of Cuban Affairs, Michael Ranneberger, conceded that "we put a lot of pressure on" Ecuador, Argentina, Chile, and Uruguay to get them to vote in favor of the resolution.[76] Support for Cuba's readmission to the OAS, by contrast, was being freely offered—so much so that at the commencement of his second term, Secretary General César Gaviria expressed the hope that Cuba would progress toward democracy and pluralism *and* full reintegration into the OAS family before it ended.[77] The contrasting approaches could not have been more striking.

Latin America and Cuba: Economics before Ideology

The disintegration of the regional political iron curtain around Cuba that successive U.S. governments had fought so long to maintain was hastened in the 1990s by a new and powerful impetus toward Latin economic integration. Annual meetings of the Rio Group, the Ibero-American Summit, the Miami Conference on the Caribbean and Latin America, and the Latin American Economic System (SELA) repeatedly called for an end to the U.S. economic embargo, singling out for harshest attack the new Bush-Clinton laws designed to tighten it. The closing declaration of the Rio Group's 1996 meeting was typical: it denounced "all [U.S.] attempts to impose unilateral sanctions through the implementation of laws with extraterritorial effects."[78] The 1998 Ibero-American Summit document went further, demanding not only the termination of economic sanctions but also rejection of the notion that one country should dictate another's political system.[79]

At the bilateral level, Latin governments were less and less willing to condition new trade and investment ties with Cuba on changes in the island's political economy, rejecting the U.S. position that the lack of the former would only discourage the growth of the latter. When Guatemala decided to upgrade to full ambassadorial status in January 1998, for example, the major reason given by President Alvaro Arzú was the desire to expand trade with Havana.[80] Ideology was subordinated to pragmatic politics. In the new pluralistic era, Washington's democratic allies were not prepared to sacrifice profitable relations with Cuba in the service of U.S. foreign policy goals or, as in the case of Argentina, the possibilities offered by this changed environment for negotiating the repayment of outstanding debts incurred by the Castro regime.

Despite occasional contradictory statements, the Menem government was the strongest and most influential hemispheric supporter of Clinton's Cuba policy. But in early 1996, Foreign Minister Guido Di Tella told the U.S. secretary of state, Warren Christopher, that his government no longer believed the economic changes taking place in Cuba could be dismissed as merely "incipient."[81] While President Menem publicly justified engagement with Cuba in terms of furthering democratic reforms on the island, this policy turnabout was influenced largely by the possibility of a future investment accord that would enable Buenos Aires to recover part of Cuba's $1.25 billion debt owed to Argentine companies. Bilateral talks laid the groundwork for an announcement that Secretary of International Economic Relations Jorge Campbell would travel to Havana in late October 1998 to negotiate a debt-for-equity agreement "allow[ing] Argentine investors to get sweeter-than-usual deals to take over Cuban companies."[82] In line with what ambassador to the United States, Diego Guelar, described as a "two-track policy," remonstrations with Cuba over its lack of democratic institutions and human rights record now cohabited with aggressive support for the island's reinsertion "into the region on economic and trade issues."[83] Hence, Argentina could cosponsor Cuba's admission to the Latin American Integration Association (ALADI) but refuse to actively support Cuba's readmission to the OAS.

While the growth in Cuba-Latin America economic relations during the 1990s was small in relative terms, the primary impediment was less U.S. pressure than Havana's limited hard currency resources ("capacity to pay") and its foreign debt problem. Interviewed in April 1993 about the possible resumption of oil supplies to Cuba, Venezuelan president Carlos Andrés Pérez bluntly responded that "Venezuela is not shipping one single drop of oil to Cuba, and is not planning to, unless Cuba pays at market prices on a cash basis."[84] When Venezuela sold five thousand barrels of crude oil to Cuba later in the year, it did so through international traders who did business with the island.

Nonetheless, Cuba's trade with its neighbors did rise appreciably in absolute terms after the collapse of the Soviet Union, and there were no signs of leveling off despite the impending threat of Helms-Burton. In 1990, Cuba conducted only 5 percent of its total trade with the region; by 1994, the figure had increased sevenfold to 35 percent, albeit from a base that had more than halved over the same period and in the context of an overall decline in Cuba's exports.[85] The value of Cuban-Brazilian trade during 1995 exceeded any of the previous five years; two-way trade with Panama increased from $150 million in 1994 to $400 million in 1996; with Venezuela from $60 million in 1991 to $456 million in 1997; and with Mexico experienced an almost 30 percent jump from $318 million in 1996 to $410 million in 1997.[86]

Small but growing amounts of Latin public and private investment also flowed into the Cuban economy despite a particularly aggressive State Department campaign against prospective investments in Cuban properties formerly owned by U.S. citizens. Two early Clinton administration targets were Jamaica and Honduras. The department warned Jamaican nationals who had started investing in the tourist sector to "take care" about resort property ventures or they could become embroiled in future legal problems.[87] In Honduras, American Embassy officials responded to an accusation that Ambassador William Price had informed the host government's Foreign Ministry about the dangers of Honduran nationals investing in Cuba by saying that similar notes had been forwarded to other regional capitals. The director of State's Cuba Desk explained that it was official policy to send out periodic reminders to Latin governments about the continuing U.S. claims against properties expropriated in Cuba after 1959.[88] But if these pressures forced investors to be more careful about joint ventures in "confiscated properties," the fear of U.S. retaliation did not always overcome the lure of profits. By the end of Clinton's first term, nationals from countries other than Mexico (which had a total investment stake of around $500 million) were beginning to take advantage of potential opportunities on the island. Some twenty Chilean companies, for example, had a combined $63 million invested in the financial, property, tourist, and citrus industries.[89]

Paralleling this effort to reach out to Cuba economically, Latin governments continued to attack the U.S. economic sanctions regime. The hemispheric clamor against Helms-Burton was even more vociferous and hostile than earlier denunciations of the CDA. No government was more scathing of this latest piece of extraterritorial legislation than Mexico, Washington's partner (together with Canada, another very public critic) in NAFTA. Clinton's decision to sign Helms-Burton outraged the Zedillo government and ended any sympathy in Mexico City for America's Cuba policy. In June 1996, the Mexican Congress began drafting "antidote" legislation to protect local companies from the global "reach" of Helms-Burton. At the same time, President Zedillo broached the possibility that Mexico would adopt a law not dissimilar to Canada's, blocking local companies from complying with the reporting provisions of Helms-Burton and forbidding them from paying any fines levied by U.S. courts.[90]

Given Mexico's economic, political, and strategic importance to the United States, it was not surprising that the White House exercised care when interpreting Helms-Burton as applied to its southern neighbor. Assistant Secretary of State for Inter-American Affairs Alexander Watson maintained that the administration "resisted pressure from certain elements in Congress and CANF (Cuban American National Foundation), and others, for us to take steps against the Mexicans," including demands to invoke the provision declaring Mexico ineligible for U.S. aid because of its debt assistance to Cuba. According to Watson, he personally lobbied Mexico's foreign minister to "help us out on this, not make it any more difficult than you have to, and find some other way to achieve your objectives."[91]

Two Mexican multinationals, however, were reportedly on the State Department's initial "hit list" of companies accused of "trafficking" in Cuban properties "confiscated" from American nationals after 1959: Cemex, one of the world's largest cement manufacturers, and the telecommunications conglomerate Grupo Domos, which had decided to contribute $750 million to a $1.5 billion joint venture with the Cuban state telephone system, ETECSA. Of these two groups, Cemex was potentially the more highly exposed to retaliation by Washington; sales from its U.S. operations amounted to $385 million in 1995, earning $12.4 million in profits. Only days before its top executives were apparently due to receive the State Department "warning," the company preemptively severed an agreement to provide technical advice and market Cuban-produced cement from a plant formerly owned by the U.S. Lone Star Industries, Inc. "It was more than a coincidence," said one U.S. policymaker privy to a series of meetings between department officials and Cemex lawyers preceding the company's decision to withdraw from its Cuban joint venture.[92]

But Grupo Domos arrived at its decision with equal speed; it would not be cowed into abandoning its joint venture investment with ETECSA under any circumstances. Awaiting the predicted formal State Department notification that it was in breach of Helms-Burton and that its executives would be denied entry into the United States unless they wound up their Cuban operations before the end of September, Grupo Domos was defiant. Not only was the company staying in Cuba, it intended to pursue new projects with the Castro government. The company's intransigence was undoubtedly bolstered by the financial rewards from its Cuban venture: an annual profit of around $150 million.[93] Ironically, while the Clinton administration was adopting a "get tough" posture in its dealings with Grupo Domos, there was no indication that International Telephone & Telegraph (IT&T)—the largest certified corporate claimant against Cuba, whose former properties the Mexican company was allegedly exploiting—had shown any interest in reclaiming these properties either prior to, or with the assistance of, the Helms-Burton legislation.

Encouraged by a broad segment of the Mexican business community, the Zedillo government directed its Washington Embassy to register a strong formal protest with the State Department over a letter sent to Grupo Domos warning of the risks and consequences of its Cuba investment. The protest note denounced the threat to punish the telecommunications multinational as "an illegal attempt to make the United States' extraterritorial jurisdiction prevail in Mexico."[94] Although Grupo Domos terminated business operations in Cuba the following year, it did so because of an inability to meet its financial obligations to the Cuban government, not for reasons connected with Helms-Burton.

In late August 1996, on the eve of White House special representative Stuart Eizenstat's arrival, Mexico publicly declared its satisfaction with Inter-American Juridical Committee ruling that key provisions of Helms-Burton were contrary to international law. Eizenstat found no support at all for Washington's approach; both the executive and the legislature demanded repeal of Helms-Burton and the lifting of the U.S. embargo. At a luncheon hosted by the U.S. ambassador, deputies of the country's three major political parties attacked the legislation. Eizenstat explained away this brick wall of hostility as nothing but Mexico's "really emotional attachment to the Revolution, to Castro himself, a sort of empathy with the feeling that big brother the United States has been too heavy-handed."[95] But if mere "emotional attachment" was driving Mexico's policy toward Cuba, it was also putting it on a collision path with its northern neighbor. No sooner had Clinton's envoy left than President Zedillo announced planned new laws to shield Mexican companies from Helms-Burton. At the beginning of October, the Mexican Chamber of Deputies approved by 317 to 1 a series of "antidote" laws proposed by the government. Local firms and citizens would now be able to countersue U.S. companies pursuing action under Helms-Burton; and those providing any information to U.S. courts in relation to a Helms-Burton prosecution, or failing to inform the Foreign Ministry that they were being targeted by the U.S. law, would be subject to punitive financial measures. Of course, the Mexican government was realistic about the probable limited impact of its "mirror" laws. Nevertheless, the issues at stake were deemed of such fundamental importance as to require a firm and public response.

During Clinton's second term, U.S. efforts to mobilize Latin support for the economic war against Cuba made no headway; on the contrary, they lost ground. Broadsides against Helms-Burton continued, accompanied by a modest but steady growth in commercial ties. In 1997, Cuba's two-way trade with the region totalled approximately $1.6 billion, of which an estimated $1.2 billion was with the ALADI group of countries. Between 1997 and 2000, the region (including Canada) accounted for around forty percent of Cuba's annual total trade.[96]

Likewise, the process of Cuba's return to the inter-American system showed no signs of slackening. During the last year of Clinton's presidency, for instance, Paraguay established full diplomatic relations, and Havana finally became a full-fledged member of the African, Caribbean, and Pacific (ACP) group of nations. Latin leaders encompassing a range of political outlooks continued to describe the U.S. policy approach as misguided and anachronistic. Mexico's president-elect, Vicente Fox, was heard to observe that "a policy of isolation, a policy of not having relations, does not contribute anything to having Cuba become a country of the market and a country of democracy."[97] At Fox's December 2000 inauguration—to which Castro was invited—Brazil's president Fernando Henrique Cardoso called for the lifting of the embargo. "We are not convinced that human rights are respected on the island," he said, "but we are not obsessed by the idea that Havana is a big abuser." The head of Peru's delegation, Foreign Minister Javier Pérez de Cuéllar, went even further, declaring that "Cuba must join the Latin American community especially the Organization of American States."[98] That even conservative heads of state were now openly expressing these sentiments showed the extent of Washington's isolation over Cuba.

The Caribbean "Reaches Out" to Cuba

One of the more striking developments in Cuba–Latin American economic relations during the 1990s was Havana's deepening ties with its Caribbean neighbors, because it demonstrated how far the most economically (and politically) vulnerable governments were prepared to engage Cuba. The beginning point was the establishment of a joint Cuba-CARICOM commission to promote intraregional trade, technical cooperation, and cultural ties. The implementation of the original 1992 accord had been delayed pending the resolution of a disagreement over key provisions in the draft document. Havana objected to the inclusion of references to democracy and respect for human rights on the grounds that they did not appear in similar agreements CARICOM had signed with Mexico and Venezuela. Eventually, CARICOM accepted the logic of Cuba's argument, deleted the troublesome political references from the document, and formally established the commission at its July 1993 summit in Nassau.

Dismayed U.S. officials, who had actively lobbied CARICOM members to demand political concessions from the Castro government as the price for these changes, accused the organization of simply giving in to Cuban demands.[99] On Capitol Hill, the leading anti-Castro legislators were incensed by the summit outcome. They made their feelings known in a letter from Congressman Robert Torricelli to CARICOM chairman, Prime Minister Vere Bird Sr. of Antigua and Barbuda, threatening to oppose any legislation to establish a free trade agreement between the United States and the regional grouping if the "Cuban dictatorship" benefited in any way from CARICOM's action.[100] The anger was genuine enough, although the immediate threat proved rather empty. "There has been some effort to punish CARICOM because of its new relations with Cuba," said a congressional specialist on Cuba policy. "You get a lot of rhetoric but what have they done or can they do to prevent it? Nothing."[101] In any event, CARICOM dismissed the legislators' warnings and stood by its decision.

Potentially more serious was the displeasure vented by Clinton officials at an August White House meeting with CARICOM leaders over the failure to insert any human rights or political reform demands in the agreement signed with Cuba. The State Department's Donna Hrinak raised the specter of some kind of U.S. retaliation by declaring that "people will need to have it explained to them why CARICOM believed that Cuba should, in effect, be given a bye on democracy." Jamaican prime minister P. J. Patterson was only too willing to oblige. "The Cold War is over," he said. "Countries in Europe are negotiating with Cuba [and it] is appropriate for us to have agreements with Cuba in the framework of a joint commission."[102]

The White House sought to straddle a fine line between mollifying angry legislators and not taking any precipitate action. While the CARICOM delegation was severely rebuked for its decision, there was no "punishment," only a warning that future relations with the United States would depend on members' efforts to promote democratization on the island.[103] This intentionally ambiguous message also testified to the changing nature of U.S. influence in the Caribbean. In the 1980s the Caribbean countries could count on Cold War rivalry to deliver relatively generous amounts of U.S. aid and attention. By late 1993, U.S. aid programs had almost collapsed. As well, the special economic relationship that originated with the Reagan-era Caribbean Basin Initiative (CBI)—sold by Washington as a way of encouraging private investment in these economically vulnerable nations with the promise of preferential access to U.S. markets—was under threat from NAFTA, which had already eliminated a number of advantages CARICOM countries formerly enjoyed under the CBI. Although State Department officials still voiced concern over the parlous state of the Caribbean economies, and even held out the possibility of NAFTA expansion to include CARICOM, for all practical purposes such offers were little more than promises of future benefits in return for concessions in the here and now. Under the circumstances, the Caribbean countries had to make do as best they could. Exploring possibilities within the region was an obvious first step.

At its April 1994 meeting in Kingston, Jamaica, CARICOM welcomed Havana as a founding member of a new twenty-five-member regional trading bloc, the Association of Caribbean States (ACS), established in large part to offset any negative effects of the U.S. decision to establish NAFTA with Mexico and Canada. Privately, CARICOM officials again reported that they had been pressured by the United States to keep Cuba out.[104] Once again, self-interest dictated that they resist the pressure.

The result was a major diplomatic coup for Havana. ACS membership not only promised Cuba direct economic benefits; of equal or greater importance, it complemented Cuba's participation in other regional bodies including the Caribbean Development and Cooperation Committee (CDCC) and the Latin American Economic System (SELA). The ACS provided a forum in which Cuba could discuss and help coordinate policy on a range of issues—from NAFTA parity to bilateral investment treaties. More than this, however, membership, without preconditions, now gave Cuba "meaningful visibility" in subregional affairs.[105] During the second half of the 1990s, this integration process showed no signs of ebbing. The ALADI group upgraded Cuba's observer status to full membership. So too did the Caribbean Forum (CARIFORUM) with an additional promise of support from a number of member countries for any future Cuba bid to join CARICOM. In the decade since 1987, two-way trade between Cuba and the Caribbean nations jumped from around $6 million to an estimated $65 million with Caribbean investors, notably Jamaican hotel chains, becoming increasingly visible players in the expanding tourist sector.[106]

These developments reflected both a rejection of the U.S. Cold War approach toward Cuba and a worsening of relations between the Caribbean nations and the United States. In 1997, for the eleventh consecutive year, the

United States registered a trade surplus with these countries in the amount of $1.2 billion, accompanied by a precipitous decline in U.S. economic aid levels, which tumbled from approximately $225 million in 1985 to around $25 to $30 million annually during the years 1995 to 1997.[107] Assistant Secretary of Commerce R. Roger Majak conceded that this feeling of abandonment was not altogether misplaced: "There's a perception [in the Clinton administration] that the Caribbean is a backwater now."[108] Apart from the economic advantages of trading with Cuba, engaging Fidel Castro's government was one way the Caribbean could express its frustration at being ignored by Washington.

Against a background of falling U.S. aid levels, Cuba moved to exploit this opportunity and substitute itself as an alternative source of support. During 1997, it provided financial donations totaling around $20 million, as well as skilled personnel including engineers, technicians, doctors, health workers, and sports trainers.[109] These activities were closely monitored by the Pentagon, especially the "massive and growing presence of Cuban so-called medical brigades" in Central America and the Caribbean in the wake of Hurricane Mitch: 110 doctors, nurses, and heath technicians sent to Honduras; 373 to Guatemala; 383 to Haiti; and 89 to Nicaragua. Although Defense Department officials subsequently conceded that these were "indeed legitimate medical brigades" engaged in much-needed aid and relief work, they nonetheless argued that the brigades "tended to have a security and intelligence component to them."[110]

That same year, two Caribbean prime ministers, Grenada's Keith Mitchell and Jamaica's P. J. Patterson, visited Cuba where they signed a number of economic and technical cooperation agreements, denounced the U.S. embargo, and emphasized the importance the subregion attached to Cuba's reintegration as a full member in good standing. Mitchell's meeting with Fidel Castro was particularly significant, ending almost fourteen years of estrangement following the 1983 U.S. military intervention that overturned the leftist government of Maurice Bishop.

Nonetheless, when CARICOM heads of state arrived in Montego Bay, Jamaica, in July for their annual summit meeting, they did so in the knowledge that they had failed to convince the White House about the benefits of a Cuba policy shift. Two months earlier, President Clinton had ventured to Barbados for a summit meeting with Caribbean leaders on trade and investment matters where several participants attempted, unsuccessfully, to persuade him that a policy of "constructive engagement" and support for Cuba's membership in key regional bodies was more likely to achieve Washington's sought-after goals than a demanding and hostile approach.[111] Any likelihood of a free trade accord with Cuba, however, was quickly dashed when CARICOM officials announced there were still too many differences to be ironed out between the group's free market economies and the island's statist/welfare development model. Jamaican industry minister, Paul Robertson, also referred to "political considerations involved in signing this treaty." One summit delegate acknowledged that the prospect of a harsh U.S. response to an agreement with Cuba may well have tempered the organization's resolve and been the political factor Robertson had in mind.[112] Dennis Antoine, Grenada's ambassador in Washington, pointedly observed that "the United States puts a certain price on our heads for associating with Cuba."[113]

While forced to tread carefully, the Caribbean's relations with Cuba continued to warm as its grievances and complaints against the United States multiplied. On the eve of a mid-April 1998 meeting of CARICOM foreign ministers in Trinidad and Tobago, the host prime minister, Basdeo Panday, held private talks with U.S. secretary of state Madeleine Albright. At their news conference, Panday spoke candidly about Cuba: "I don't think Cuba poses the kind of problem it did when there was a Cold War. CARICOM has taken the position that Cuba is a Caribbean state." An obviously uncomfortable Albright acknowledged that this was CARICOM's decision to take but "she made it clear this was not a prospect pleasing to the Clinton administration."[114] Two months later, Caribbean nations helped Cuba win observer status at negotiations on the new Lomé Convention between former European colonies in the ACP group of nations and the EU, which gives exports from the latter preferential treatment in European markets.

In August, Castro attended the annual CARICOM Summit in the Dominican Republic as an observer, in line with the group's policy of "dialogue and constructive engagement with Cuba."[115] At its conclusion, the host government's secretary of state, Max Puig, wasted few words in expressing the visiting leaders' key message: "The Caribbean is incomplete without Cuba."[116] In December, the United States received another "scolding" over Cuba and market access for Caribbean Basin products at the annual Miami Conference on the Caribbean and Latin America. Jamaica's Patterson told the concluding session that a number of products "of vital importance" to Caribbean economies, especially in the apparel industry, had been excluded from CBI benefits because of quotas and tariffs imposed as a result of NAFTA. Turning to Cuba, he called the embargo "unjust" and sarcastically observed that "while the [Latin American] political map is changing, the geographical map has remained the same, and the geographical map clearly indicates that Cuba is part of this hemisphere."[117]

Entering 1999, the Caribbean's disenchantment with Washington showed no signs of abating. "Far from being on the [diplomatic] back burner," said one disenchanted Caribbean leader, "we are not even on the stove."[118] The Clinton administration supported a bipartisan congressional initiative to extend NAFTA parity to the Caribbean but was still unable to deliver any concrete results; it struggled to win Capitol Hill approval for a $956 million emergency reconstruction package for the hurricane-devastated countries of Central America and the Caribbean and did itself no favors by maintaining pressure on the EU to change its banana import regime to the detriment of Caribbean producers. CARICOM secretary general, Edwin Carrington, described Washington's behavior as "like being killed by friendly fire."[119] In May, the Caribbean nations even threatened to suspend the 1997 anti-drug-trafficking Bridgetown Accord with the United States.

At its April summit meeting in Santo Domingo, the ACS encouraged Havana to take a more active role in CARICOM, urged Washington to end its embargo, and called for the island's participation in talks on establishing a Free Trade Area of the Americas (FTAA) by 2005.[120] The Caribbean's resolve to expand economic relations with the island was not shaken even by the White House success in gaining congressional approval for a limited extension of NAFTA parity to twenty-seven impoverished Caribbean and African nations who belong to the ACP group of countries receiving special EU aid and trade benefits under the Lomé Convention. Signed into law in mid-June, the Caribbean-African trade bill granted apparel manufacturers duty free access to the U.S. market. The following week, ACP secretary general, Jean-Robert Goulangang, confirmed that Cuba would maintain its observer status pending revision of the group's original Georgetown accord "that will enable Cuba to become a full member of the ACP group without taking part in the ACP/EU partnership agreement" and expressed the ACP's hope that Cuba would eventually become a participant in the EU relationship.[121] Soon after, Havana signed a trade liberalization agreement with CARICOM, which both sides viewed as the first step toward a free trade accord.

These were small and largely symbolic victories compared to the yet-to-be-achieved defeat of U.S. efforts to restrict Cuba's full reintegration into the hemisphere's affairs. But their importance was bound to be greater from Havana's perspective than it was from Washington's. Furthermore, they provided further evidence of the steady and irreversible shift in relations between Cuba and Latin America.

George W. Bush and Cuba: The New Polarization

By January 2001 Latin American governments had done virtually all they could to facilitate Cuba's reintegration into the hemisphere. Only Costa Rica, El Salvador, Honduras, and Grenada had yet to reestablish full diplomatic ties with Havana; the majority had signed trade and investment agreements with the Castro government, and Cuba was an active participant in regional organizations and forums where the United States could not exercise a veto power over the decisions taken. Washington was still the major obstacle to OAS membership, but tensions generated with some Latin capitals over the island's hu-

man rights problem had slowed the earlier regional momentum for championing Cuba's cause. Meanwhile, the almost total opposition to Helms-Burton,
and what Brazilian president Fernando Cardoso described as "the U.S. policy
to strangle Cuba," remained as firm as ever.[122] The challenge for the hemisphere now was twofold: how to manage relations with Cuba based on a belief
that engagement was the best way to encourage political and economic reform
on the island; and how to do this against the backdrop of a new administration
in Washington that showed every sign of being even less compromising than its
predecessors toward Fidel Castro's regime and no more amenable to charting
a new course in its dealings with a region where the impact of free-market
economics had produced a resurgence of nationalist and populist sentiment.

George W. Bush's appointment of a number of Cuban-Americans to key
foreign policy positions dealing with Latin America sent a clear signal regarding the approach it would take in dealing with the twin issues of Cuba and the
growing challenge to U.S. regional hegemony.[123] Other appointments also
boded ill for any moderation in Cuba policy or innovative thinking about Latin
America as a whole. A Reagan State Department official who played a prominent role in the covert war against Nicaragua, Elliott Abrams, was named
senior director of the National Security Council's Office of Democracy, Human Rights, and International Operations. Roger Noriega—who earned his
stripes in the anti-Castro cause as the senior foreign policy adviser to Senator
Jesse Helms (R-N.C.) during the 1990s—was nominated to serve as the U.S.
ambassador to the OAS. And a former political officer for the Nicaraguan
contras, Rogelio Pardo-Maurer, took over the position of deputy assistant secretary of defense for Western Hemisphere Affairs.[124] Later, in April 2002,
Daniel Fisk, another former aide to Helms, who had played a leading role in
drafting the Helms-Burton legislation, was appointed deputy assistant secretary of state for Central America, public diplomacy, and Cuba.

Senior Bush officials lost no time in spelling out their thoughts on how Latin
governments should regard the Castro regime. On March 6, Secretary of State
Colin Powell told House lawmakers that passage of a resolution condemning
Cuba's human rights record at the April UNHRC meeting was an administration "priority."[125] In the lead-up to the vote, according to one senior official,
the administration embarked on a "real pressure strategy from the President to
the Embassies" to influence the result.[126] Among those who participated in a
phone lobbying "offensive" were Vice President Richard Cheney, National
Security Council (NSC) Adviser Condoleezza Rice, and Deputy Secretary of
State Richard Armitage.[127] For all this effort, the resolution barely passed by 22
to 20 with ten abstentions. While hardly the decisive outcome Washington had
sought, Bush applauded the vote from Québec where he was attending another
Cuba-free Summit of the Americas.

The Latin votes on the committee split three ways. Argentina, Costa Rica, Guatemala, and Uruguay voted in favor; Brazil, Colombia, Mexico, and Peru abstained; and Cuba and Venezuela voted against the resolution. Havana's sharpest attacks were reserved for Costa Rica and Argentina. The former was derided as a "Yankee colony," prompting San Jose to recall its consul to the island and cancel the credentials of its resident Cuban consul—although by the end of the month, relations had been patched up to the point where Costa Rica accepted the appointment of an interim consul.[128]

The animosity between Havana and Buenos Aires ran deeper. In February, Castro had accused Argentina of "licking the Yankee boot" by supporting Washington's attacks on Cuba's human rights record, prompting the recall of Argentina's ambassador for "consultations."[129] Following the UNHRC vote, Castro and other Cuban officials delivered another round of verbal missives, including a charge that Buenos Aires was duplicitous for intentionally keeping secret until the last moment its decision to support the resolution. These "new insults at the highest level" were the last straw for President Fernando de la Rúa who decided to permanently withdraw his senior Cuba diplomat, leaving a chargé d'affaires to run the embassy.[130]

State Department officials interpreted this apparent readiness among Latin governments to publicly protest Cuba's human rights record—and to stand up to Castro's angry backlash against their protests—as a sign of a new maturity in their relations with the island. They were now praised for being "more willing to be vocal and active about raising the lack of democratic processes, the lack of human rights, and both speaking about it and acting on it."[131] Washington was also encouraged by related developments, notably the hemisphere's embrace of a democracy clause in the final communiqué of the Québec Summit of the Americas meeting and the far more comprehensive Inter-American Democratic Charter (IADC) agreed to at a special session of the OAS General Assembly some months later in Lima. The principle adopted at Québec was that an unconstitutional alteration or interruption to the democratic order in any participating state rendered its government ineligible to take part in summit processes until the rule of law had been reestablished. The IADC placed even greater responsibilities on the signatories, committing them to endorse, promote, and defend democratic rule in the hemisphere and conditioning OAS membership on "the effective exercise of representative democracy" that included, among other requirements, respect for human rights, periodic, free, and fair elections, and a competitive party system.[132]

The White House could take little credit for either initiative. Both grew out of the frustration Latin governments felt over their inability to address the challenge posed by President Alberto Fujimori's increasingly unconstitutional rule in Peru during the 1990s and the wider threat this posed to elected regimes

throughout the hemisphere. Although neither document was intended to specifically address the situation in Cuba, the implication was unmistakable: as far
as OAS membership was concerned, and arguably participation in future Summits of the Americas, the island government did not qualify. "The Charter's
emphasis on the importance of democratic processes and institutions is an
increasingly important step," a senior Western Hemisphere official in State
commented, "but it also highlighted the fact there is this exception, and Cuba
is the exception, and that the other states in the hemisphere see the democratic norm as the norm."[133] Twelve months after the IADC was signed, a
member of the U.S. Mission at the OAS remarked that the issue of Cuba's
readmission "has not come up" and would only do so as part of a democratic
transition process on the island. Just in case Latin governments signaled future
interest in departing from this scenario, the Bush administration left them in no
doubt that OAS membership was a "red line issue" it would not allow to be
crossed.[134]

The White House may have stymied Cuba's efforts to gain complete acceptance as a member of the inter-American system, but it could not win regional
converts to its hardline policy approach. In November 2001, Havana had little
trouble persuading the Ibero-American Summit to approve a motion urging
the United States to abandon Helms-Burton.[135] Meetings of Caribbean leaders
in Venezuela, the Tenth São Paulo Forum in Havana, and the ACP group in
Brussels also criticized the U.S. economic embargo.[136] Even Bush officials now
conceded that opposition to the CDA and Helms-Burton "has become part of
the [region's] operating environment; it is taken as a given, it is not going to go
away."[137] In late January 2002, Washington received an unexpected and unwanted surprise when the outgoing president of Honduras, Carlos Flores
Facusse, announced that his country had restored full diplomatic ties with
Cuba.[138]

These developments, however, did not halt the Bush administration's search
for Latin allies to lend support to its anti-Castro policy. While Havana and
Tegucigalpa were consigning past antagonisms to history, Argentina's foreign
minister Carlos Ruckauf emerged from a Washington meeting with Secretary
of State Colin Powell to announce that his country would work with the United
States "to free" the Cuban people.[139] This precipitated a new round of Cuban
attacks on Argentine "groveling" and a flurry of diplomatic broadsides between officials of both governments. In March, with the forthcoming UNHRC
vote on Cuba's human rights performance high on the agenda, Bush embarked
on his first official visit to Latin America. During talks with Peru's head of
state, Alejandro Toledo, the U.S. president "signaled the importance the United
States attache[d]" to this vote. The American ambassador repeated the message, suggesting that Peru was well placed to assume a "leadership role" at the
commission.[140]

Although relegated to observer status on the UNHRC since losing its seat in 2001, members of the diplomatic community reported that the U.S. government engaged in a sustained behind-the-scenes lobbying effort to get the Latin members of the commission to sponsor a new resolution condemning Cuba.[141] Montevido's *La República* informed its readers that Uruguay played a central role in drafting the resolution "which was purportedly reviewed by top Peruvian officials and [U.S. assistant secretary of state for Inter-American Affairs] Otto Reich."[142] Cuban foreign minister Felipe Pérez Roque accused the Bush administration of exerting "frenetic" pressure and of extracting promises from Uruguay, Argentina, and Costa Rica to vote for whatever resolution was submitted to the commission.[143]

Whatever the truth of these specific allegations, the State Department conceded that American officials "have been working with a number of countries to see whether there can be a Cuba resolution this year."[144] The outcome of these efforts suggested a compromise of sorts had been reached between Washington's pressure for an unqualified condemnation and the region's concern not to support a document that totally undermined their support for engaging Cuba. With the backing of several hemisphere nations, Uruguay formally presented to the commission a resolution that recognized Cuba's achievements in the social policy area despite an "adverse international environment," while urging the Castro government to make similar progress in human, civil, and political rights.[145] It also called for the appointment of a United Nations special representative to monitor progress in these fields.

In April, the UNHRC passed the resolution by a vote of 23 to 21 with nine abstentions. If Washington expressed pleasure at the outcome, it was positively euphoric over the contribution of the Latin governments. Uruguay, Chile, Argentina, Peru, Mexico, and Costa Rica all voted "yes"; Brazil and Ecuador abstained; and only Cuba and Venezuela cast "no" votes. This result, said one U.S. official, reaffirmed the "benchmark" 2001 UNHRC meeting "where Uruguay led a Latin American effort to draft, and then get approved" a similar resolution. "The Latins still see engagement as the way to go but it's no longer the whisper to the U.S. that 'you take care of the problem and by the way publicly we're going to say we don't like your approach.'"[146] Missing from this interpretation, however, were key contextual factors that influenced the breakdown of the vote and signified a growing cleavage between regimes mired in severe economic crises and dependent on U.S. assistance to stay afloat or else facing major domestic economic problems (Argentina, Peru, Costa Rica, and Mexico), and governments that had moved to the left or adopted a new assertiveness in challenging Washington's agenda for the hemisphere (Venezuela, Brazil, and Ecuador). Within the two groups, Mexico and Venezuela were among Cuba's most important bilateral partners—politically and economically. Although there is a stark contrast in the way relations have been managed with each, both demonstrate the limited regional appeal of Washington's continued hostile policy toward Cuba.

The election of Vicente Fox as president of Mexico in late 2000 ushered in a new and more complex relationship with Cuba. His predecessor Ernesto Zedillo had repeatedly attacked Havana over its human rights record and lack of political democracy, blocking Cuba's membership in the San Jose Pact in 1999 (thus denying it access to sorely needed subsidized oil imports) and months later delivering a provocative speech at the Ibero-American Summit in Havana calling for political change on the island. Signaling a shift toward a more amicable relationship, Castro attended Fox's inauguration and held a "cordial" meeting with the new Mexican head of state. Weeks later, the general manager of the Foreign Trade Bank arrived in Cuba to discuss ways of expanding trade on a "healthy" financial basis but without the island's foreign debt to Mexico "being an obstacle to exploring new trade paths."[147]

Nonetheless, it soon became apparent that this desire for renewed diplomacy and improved economic ties had its limits. Picking up from where Zedillo left off, Fox and his anti-Castroist foreign minister, Jorge Castañeda, were quick to focus on Cuba's human rights performance, describing it as "a source of concern."[148] On April 17, 2001, Mexico abstained on—rather than opposed—a UNHRC resolution inviting Cuba to respect human rights. In the course of the debate, Castañeda denounced Cuba's record and actively lobbied for a condemnation of the Castro government. President Fox refused to reprimand his foreign minister, but downplayed the significance of Mexico's vote, asserting that "relations with Cuba are as strong as ever."[149] Havana's anger over the abstention and Castañeda's behavior, however, was not so easily dismissed.

When a Reciprocal Protection Agreement was signed in late May, guaranteeing the security of investments in both countries, Cuban minister for Foreign Investment and Economic Cooperation, Martha Lomas, said it "opens up a new stage" in bilateral ties. Mexico's president was equally upbeat, describing the trade-investment relationship with Cuba as "very extensive and positive" and a measure of his government's opposition to the U.S. embargo policy.[150] Four months later, Cuba renegotiated its approximately $400 million foreign debt with Mexico.[151]

Nevertheless, on the eve of a brief official visit to Cuba in February 2002, Fox conceded that relations were still "somewhat chilly" but reaffirmed a commitment to "strengthen" economic ties, pursue a dialogue about regional issues of concern to both countries, and discuss human rights issues "without rancor or conflict."[152] But Mexico's ambassador to Cuba, Ricardo Pascoe, recalled that the trip did little to ameliorate outstanding disagreements and tensions due to Fox's meeting with dissidents and the behavior of Castañeda, who again displayed his barely concealed hostility toward the island regime by announcing that Mexico no longer supported the Cuban Revolution, only the Cuban Republic.[153]

The other main target of the foreign minister's anti-Castro scheming was Ambassador Pascoe, a vigorous advocate of maintaining constructive relations with Castro's government. Deliberately kept in the dark about the April 2001 UNHRC vote, as well as President Fox's plans to meet with Cuban dissidents, Castañeda and the Foreign Relations Secretariat were largely responsible for orchestrating Pascoe's replacement in September. In a scathing letter to Fox, the former diplomat complained that "an attempt was made to corner me into carrying out a series of subversive actions aimed at disrupting bilateral relations and causing a diplomatic break."[154]

To Bush State Department officials, on the other hand, Pascoe's demise indicated a positive shift in Mexico's policy. "Previous Mexican governments," said one attached to the U.S. Mission to the OAS, "appeared to more actively support the Castro government whereas you don't get that sense with the Fox administration. It is more reserved and seems to have greater doubts about that government." Acknowledging that "the Mexicans are still uncomfortable with our embargo policy and still prefer practical engagement," the official termed these differences less important than the Fox government's support for democratic change in Cuba. "We have a tactical disagreement not a strategic disagreement. We all agree on the end result."[155]

Mexico's ties with Cuba took a severe turn for the worse as a result of events that occurred at the March 2002 United Nations Conference on Poverty and Development in Monterrey. President Fox and his senior officials, under intense pressure from Washington, forced the Cuban leader to abruptly depart the gathering to avoid any possibility of an accidental Bush-Castro meeting. Furious over his treatment, Castro subsequently released an audio tape of a private telephone conversation with Fox during which the latter attempted to persuade Castro to cancel his attendance or leave prior to Bush's arrival, fearful that if their paths crossed it would "complicate" Mexico's relations with the United States.[156] Relations hit a new low in April when Fox authorized the Mexican delegate to vote in favor of the latest resolution before the UNHRC condemning the human rights situation in Cuba.

For his part, Fox continued to dismiss any talk of a major rupture in bilateral ties, downplaying Mexico's UNHRC vote and Castro's sudden departure from the United Nations summit as "incident[s] that had no lasting impact."[157] By early 2003, relations appeared to be on an upswing. Senior officials in Mexico City and Havana described Castañeda's resignation in April as a turning point, effectively ending the diplomatic war. "We are going to repair our relations with Cuba, slowly and bit by bit," commented a leading Mexican official. "It is not in our interests to have relations in a constant state of tension."[158] The Foreign Ministry also announced the resumption of high-level visits to the island.

If Mexico's economic dependence and geographic location dictated a relationship with Cuba that avoided unnecessarily provoking the region's dominant hegemon, oil-rich Venezuela was in a relatively stronger position to resist the entreaties of the United States, the IMF, and the World Bank—and thus more able to pursue a foreign policy less compliant with Washington's regional ambitions.

From the moment of Hugo Chávez's February 1998 inauguration speech when he voiced strong opposition to the U.S. economic embargo, Clinton policymakers were left in no doubt that Venezuela's populist president was intent on developing a close and mutually productive relationship with Castro's Cuba. Indeed, one of his Foreign Minister José Vicente Rangel's first acts was to seek "to improve relations" between the United States and Cuba by offering Venezuela's good offices as a mediator.[159] While initiatives of this kind were bound to irritate the White House, of greater concern was the practical assistance Chávez was prepared to extend to Havana, such as the 1999 proposal to export large amounts of petroleum to the island at subsidized prices. In early April, Venezuela also resisted subtle but unmistakable U.S. pressure to vote against Cuba at the UNHRC.[160]

Although Chávez's foreign policy decisions and nationalist rhetoric generated unease, and even hostility, in Washington, his neoliberal domestic reforms (orthodox fiscal measures, pro-foreign investment, financial deregulation, and scrupulous adherence to Venezuela's foreign debt obligations) led the Clinton administration to settle on a "wait and see" approach. Following his reelection with increased support in 2000, the tempo of Chávez' challenge to U.S. regional hegemony accelerated. This included a multiyear preferential arrangement to provide Cuba with critically needed petroleum imports based on cheap credits and a barter system. While the "oil for goods and services" arrangement was subsequently put on a cash basis, Cuba's access to this vital raw material remained intact. By the end of 2001, Venezuela had also become the island's main trading partner.[161]

Chávez also criticized Washington's Plan Colombia, offered lukewarm support to the FTAA, and refused to allow the U.S. "war against drugs" missions to use Venezuelan airspace.[162] Relations with the United States worsened after George W. Bush entered the White House. Venezuela's maintenance of friendly ties with OPEC partners, Iran, Iraq, and Libya, its opposition to Washington's antiterrorist campaign, and criticism of the U.S. war in Afghanistan enraged the hardline conservative ideologues who were largely responsible for the new administration's regional and global policies.

In April 2002, the depth of the White House commitment to democratic norms and processes in Latin America was put to the test when a military-civilian coup temporarily toppled Chávez from power. During the five months prior to the *golpe*, Assistant Secretary of State Reich and other senior U.S. officials had conferred on a regular basis with anti-Chávez military, business, and labor leaders—the future coup-makers.[163] According to one report, U.S. Navy vessels stationed in Caribbean waters provided more direct aid to the *golpistas*, supplying them with intelligence and jamming the communications of pro-Chávez forces.[164] The generals installed Pedro Carmona, the head of the country's largest business association, Fedecámaras, as interim president. He, in turn, dissolved the legislature and the supreme court, abolished the new constitution approved by a majority of the population in 1999, and moved to reverse key features of Chávez' foreign policy, including an end to oil exports to Cuba. The pro-coup managers in charge of the state-owned oil monopoly suspended exports ostensibly on the grounds that Havana owed $143 million in outstanding payments.[165]

The Bush administration refused point blank to condemn the coup—even denying that a coup had taken place because, as the State Department's Phillip Reeker put it, "the military did not take over the government."[166] No U.S. official referred to the IADC or the obligation on its signatories to come to "the defense of democracy" in precisely those circumstances that had transpired in Venezuela. Since the collapse of the coup, Washington has persisted with its efforts to challenge the legitimacy of the Chávez government and supported the domestic opposition—politically and financially—in pushing for early elections.[167]

Trying to extract some positives from the failed coup on Venezuela's relations with Cuba, a State Department OAS official suggested that Chávez had become "more sensitive to the negative image that Castro has among the Venezuelans and more careful and less ostentatious about his friendship with Castro."[168] Chávez' behavior, however, seemed to indicate otherwise. Four months after the *golpe*, he announced that Venezuela would resume subsidized petroleum shipments to the island. Chávez also floated the idea of Venezuela, Brazil, and Cuba forming an "axis of good" to challenge U.S. regional dominance.

In Brazil, the idea received a sympathetic hearing. During the last year of the Cardoso government (1994–2002), the country's relations with Washington had become increasingly frayed over issues ranging from Brazil's regional leadership ambitions, to disagreements concerning the FTAA, to its refusal to vote against Cuba in the UNHRC, to its failure to endorse the post 9/11 White House unilateralist worldview. The election of Workers Party presidential candidate Luiz Inácio Lula da Silva in 2002—on a platform that was critical of open markets, free trade, and privatization and demanded a "non-exclusive FTAA" that would include Cuba—had the potential to widen the rift.[169]

On a less dramatic scale, Cuba's political and economic ties with its Caribbean neighbors continued to expand—fueled by the latter's growing sense of abandonment by the United States and their rejection of Cold War–driven foreign policies. By the end of 2002, approximately one thousand Cuban doctors and health workers and hundreds of sports trainers were based in CARICOM countries, while some 2,500 students from the subregion were studying in Cuba.[170] Jamaica was leasing combine harvesters and hired workers from Cuba to help improve the island's sugar industry. And in early October, Grenada and Cuba reestablished full diplomatic relations for the first time in nearly two decades. In addition, Belize resisted heavy State Department pressure to convert a Voice of America relay station so it could beam Radio Martí signals toward Cuba.[171]

In early December 2002, Cuba hosted its first CARICOM Summit where the participants agreed to boost trade with the island and, in a final declaration, called on Washington to end its economic sanctions regime.[172] Predictably, U.S. officials were quick to respond with subtle warnings of unspecified future retribution. Otto Reich, newly appointed White House special envoy for the Western Hemisphere, conveyed the message personally and bluntly to Caribbean nations during an April 2003 news conference in Bridgetown, Barbados: "I would caution against hitching your wagon to a failed state."[173]

As George W. Bush passed the mid-point of his first term, the regional challenges to U.S. hegemony and White House efforts to entrench the neoliberal economic model began to multiply: a new wave of nationalist and populist leaders had been elected to political office in Venezuela, Brazil, Ecuador, and Peru; guerrilla movements continued to pose a threat to the Colombian state and regime; one of the most devastating economic crises in Argentina's history triggered a resurgence of popular anti-imperialist sentiment; large-scale demonstrations in Mexico against the impact of NAFTA policies were becoming commonplace; and Caribbean resistance to Washington's demands were growing bolder.

If these developments, at least temporarily, relegated bilateral relations with Cuba to the back burner, U.S. policymakers were nonetheless worried that Fidel Castro's government might benefit directly from this changing regional political environment—and even contribute to it in ways that would have been inconceivable only a decade earlier. While conceding that it was impossible to prevent Venezuela's Hugo Chávez or Brazil's "Lula" from "having a relationship with Cuba," any new generous economic concessions were a different matter altogether and would likely produce a more vigorous imperial state response: "If they want to do business with Cuba, then don't give them preferences. Oil is one, but trade in general."[174] Such sentiments fell on deaf ears in Venezuela: in late April 2003, the Chávez government began the export of fifty-three thousand barrels daily of oil and petroleum by-products to Cuba and signaled it was about to sign an agreement rescheduling the island's $140 million-plus oil debt. The White House also confronted the possible emergence of a new regional political and/or economic bloc, including Cuba, opposed to its agenda for the hemisphere.

The April 2003 UNHRC debate on Cuba's human rights performance further exposed the gap between the United States and Latin America when it came to dealing with the Castro regime. The resolution, sponsored by Costa Rica, Peru, Nicaragua, and Uruguay, excluded any specific condemnation of the Cuban government's record and merely requested that the personal representative of the United Nations Commissioner for Human Rights be allowed to visit the country. Even then, it was only approved by a vote of 24 to 20, with nine abstentions (including Brazil and Argentina) and Venezuela joining with Cuba in opposing the resolution. In line with their traditional "balancing" posture, Mexican officials were also quick to emphasize that their "yes" vote was not an endorsement of U.S. policy, portraying it as nothing more than a "procedural" measure aimed at encouraging Cuba's cooperation on human rights. Deputy Minister for Human Rights and Democracy Mariclaire Acosta said the vote was "consistent with [Mexico's] principles not to condemn or to criticize Cuba."[175]

This UNHRC result was all the more surprising coming as it did in the wake of the harshest government crackdown on the Cuban dissident movement in recent years. During March and April, authorities detained seventy-five human rights activists, independent trade unionists, and journalists, many of whom were tried and sentenced to long prison terms *prior* to the UNHRC vote.[176] A Costa Rican amendment to the original resolution specifically condemning the detentions, trials, and severe punishments was defeated in the commission with Mexico and Guatemala, among others, voting against it. Ultimately, despite the international outcry, Cuba received little more than a slap on the wrists.

Opposition to the Cuba economic sanctions partly explained the Latin Americans' refusal to go along with White House calls for a more punitive response. An equally, if not more important, reason was growing anger at the deepening unilateralist trend in U.S. foreign policy. Hemisphere governments exhibited a marked reluctance to militarily support Bush's open-ended, preemptive global "war on terror" and offered virtually no support for his determination to force a regime change in Iraq without specific United Nations authorization and the backing of the international community. Argentine president Eduardo Duhalde said his country's abstention vote on the UNHRC resolution "[took] into account the unilateral [U.S.] war [in Iraq]," while Foreign Ministry official Marcos Campos attributed Brazil's vote to the "political motivations [behind] proposals censuring Cuba on human rights issues [that] often go beyond human rights."[177]

The White House/State Department response to the mild condemnation of the Castro regime by the Latin representatives on the UNHRC was a mixture of disappointment and anger. The Cuban government response was more nuanced. On the one hand, it pilloried the sponsors of the resolution as "disgusting lackeys" of Washington and called Mexico and Chile "servile vassals of the great power"; on the other, it was sensitive to the constraints under which these governments were forced to operate. Foreign Minister Felipe Pérez Roque acknowledged that "it is very difficult" for regional nations to take an "independent" decision on this issue "in the midst of a complex and contradictory relationship [with the United States]."[178] Whatever calculations lay behind the wording of the resolution and the subsequent vote, both contradicted suggestions by U.S. officials that the stance taken by Latin governments at the two preceding UNHRC meetings on Cuba were "benchmark" developments in gaining hemispheric support for the American effort to promote political reform on the island. Within days of the vote, the Bush White House was subjected to a further harsh dose of unwanted and unreconciled reality when Cuba was reelected to another term on the commission.[179]

Two months later, Washington's UNHRC setback was replicated at the OAS. Speaking at the annual meeting of foreign ministers, Secretary of State Powell challenged Latin governments to work more closely with the United States "to find ways to hasten the inevitable democratic transition in Cuba." The response was decidedly unenthusiastic. The Caribbean and Brazilian delegates, in particular, questioned any debate about Cuba without the latter's participation. A senior OAS official pointed out that "members want to talk about Cuba in a balanced way [that includes] not only human rights, but also isolation of Cuba and the embargo."[180] Privately, several delegates criticized Powell's preoccupation with Cuba instead of addressing the region's major social and economic problems. Powell was doubly embarrassed when, for the first time, the OAS voted to exclude the United States from membership in the Inter-American Committee on Human Rights.

Irrespective of particular concerns or disagreements, the region's most influential nations remained committed to engaging Cuba even where cognizant of the need to adopt an approach that avoided any major rupture with Washington. In late September 2003, Brazilian president "Lula" arrived in Havana with a 100-member entourage to discuss regional trade, aid, and political integration. The visit resulted in a commitment of $200 million in new investments in Cuba's tourist, sugar, and biotechnology sectors and an agreement to renegotiate Havana's $40 million debt to Brazil. Five months later, Cuban drug technology transfers initiated a comprehensive program of technological cooperation in the pharmaceuticals and biotechnology fields that would facilitate Cuba's debt payments while allowing Havana to keep supplying the drugs until Brazil was able to start domestic production.[181]

But the turnabout in Argentina's ties with Cuba was perhaps the most revealing indicator of the failure of U.S. policy. Since the fallout from the April

2001 UNHRC vote, the gradual improvement in relations between Havana and Buenos Aires received a major impetus with the May 2003 election of Nestor Kirchner as Argentina's new president—whose inauguration Castro attended. In October, Argentina restored full diplomatic relations with Cuba. That year, both governments agreed to reduce tariffs on 1,600 items and, according to Cuban foreign minister Pérez Roque, Argentina gave a commitment to support negotiations for a "4 plus 1" trade pact between Cuba and the four-nation Mercosur economic bloc (Argentina, Brazil, Paraguay, Uruguay).[182]

Nonetheless, Kirchner was careful to ensure that improved ties with Cuba did not jeopardize his relationship with the Bush administration, especially given the importance of maintaining Washington's support over defaulted debt negotiations. Thus, following a White House meeting with the U.S. president in January 2004, he decided to cancel a proposed trip to Havana and substitute an official visit to Argentina by the Cuban foreign minister. In discussions with Pérez Roque, Kirchner's "balancing" act continued. He said that his government would not condemn Cuba at the April UNHRC meeting but would justify the decision publicly on the grounds that it was simply responding to the popular will.[183]

If Brazil and Argentina's engagement with Cuba irritated and annoyed Bush officials, Venezuela's behavior was an altogether more serious matter. By early 2004, the administration, still hopeful of achieving a regime change, was pursuing a two-track strategy: demanding that Chávez—twice elected president in free and fair elections—submit to opposition demands for a recall referendum to demonstrate "that he believed in democratic processes" (National Security Council Adviser Rice) and accusing his government of collaborating with Cuban efforts "to do everything it [can] to destabilize parts of the region" (Secretary of State Powell).[184] The Venezuelan leader's response to these charges and diktats was vehement. He called President Bush an "asshole," told him to stop interfering in Venezuelan affairs, and even threatened to cut off U.S. oil supplies.[185]

The mid-January 2004 Summit of the Americas meeting in Monterrey, Mexico, to debate a Bush administration proposal creating an FTAA by December 2005 underlined the differences between the imperial state and its southern neighbors regarding both regional development strategies and ties with Cuba. The major opponents of a 2005 deadline were the presidents of Brazil and Venezuela: the former demanding that the United States end its multibillion-dollar program of subsidies to American agricultural producers, while the latter proposed an alternative Latin American trade bloc. In a pre-summit briefing, NSC Adviser Rice again faulted Venezuela's ties with Cuba, and American officials indicated that there would be no bilateral meeting between Bush and Chávez.[186] Brazil's response to this U.S. effort to isolate Venezuela was emphatic and very public. Hours before Bush's speech to the meeting, which included statements critical of Venezuela (and Cuba), "Lula" and Chávez lunched together. Soon after, Brazilian foreign minister Celso Amorim reinforced the point of the meeting: "We maintain friendly ties with Venezuela and the Venezuelan government."[187]

Argentina's Nestor Kirchner also challenged Washington's effort to impose its will on the gathering. Angered by U.S. criticism of his country's rapprochement with Cuba and his domestic economic policies, Kirchner exhorted the hemisphere "to stop being a [U.S.] doormat" and to reject the idea that "just any free trade accord of the Americas will serve," especially one that does not address the issues of removing agricultural subsidies and guaranteeing intellectual property rights. Responding to Condoleezza Rice's warning that President Bush intended to pressure him to make "tough decisions" about Argentina's default on approximately $90 billion debt obligations to American and other foreign creditors, Kirchner predicted that he would "win by a knockout" at their bilateral meeting.[188]

Ultimately, the thirty-four heads of state agreed to support regional free trade but avoided any commitment to Washington's proposed 2005 deadline. Regional leaders such as Brazil and Argentina supported bilateral trade deals between Latin nations prior to negotiating an FTAA. The summit also balked at another Bush White House proposal that targeted Cuba in particular (and possibly Venezuela) to bar countries deemed corrupt or undemocratic from participating in regional organizations.[189]

Three months later Washington could take little satisfaction from the attitudes of the Latin American members on the UNHRC regarding Cuba's human rights performance. The 2004 resolution, which was drafted by Honduras, was little more than another mild rebuke of the Castro government. While it "deplore[d]" the March 2003 crackdown and urged Havana to "refrain from adopting measures which could jeopardize fundamental rights," the resolution encouraged Cuba to cooperate with the personal representative of the commission but "within the context of the full exercise of its sovereignty."[190] In the weeks preceding the vote, the State Department "lobb[ied] hard" among the Latin Americans for passage of the resolution.[191] The final UNHRC vote was 22 in favor, 21 against, with ten abstentions. While seven of the eleven Latin countries voted with the United States, of greater significance was the fact that the three most powerful countries in the region either abstained (Brazil and Argentina) or voted in favor but with qualifications (Mexico, whose president explained that "It's about a vote in favor of a cause, not against a nation which we have always respected and supported").[192]

Conclusion

If Washington stuck to an unreconstructed Cold War policy toward Cuba in the post-Soviet era, the same could not be said of Latin America. Since the late 1980s, there has been a major erosion of support for U.S. policy toward Cuba and a rejection of the White House rationale justifying its unbendingly hostile stance. At the same time, the latter has forced some nations (notably Mexico), dependent on large-scale U.S. economic assistance, to walk a fine line between improving Cuba ties and triggering a retaliatory U.S. response, whereas others (Venezuela and Brazil) have felt less constrained in taking a more defiant approach, and still others (the Caribbean nations) have expanded social and economic relations with Cuba as a response to U.S. neglect.

But equally significant, what matters to the United States has not been the decisive factor influencing periodic "blowups" between Cuba and its regional neighbors. These have largely been a function of "south of the border" government actions. Witness the latest of these episodes: the May 2004 decision by Mexico (and Peru) to withdraw its ambassador from Havana and expel Cuba's ambassador from Mexico City over Castro's denunciation of the Fox government's UNHRC vote in favor of the resolution criticizing Cuba's human rights record. Even then, Mexican foreign minister Luis Derbez emphasized that "there is no rupture. All channels are open, all the relationship is normal. The only exception is that we have downgraded the post of Ambassador."[193] Within a matter of weeks, both governments agreed that the ambassadors would return to their posts.[194]

The George H. W. Bush administration actively sought to maintain Cuba's isolation, even though it could no longer argue that the island still posed a security threat to Latin America. As more and more governments upgraded or renewed diplomatic relations with Cuba, Bush policymakers focused their efforts on keeping Cuba out of the OAS. "The bilateral isolation was eroding," recalled the coordinator of State's Office of Cuban Affairs, Vicki Huddleston, "so you tried to hold the line where you could."[195] Yet, by the time Bill Clinton entered the White House in January 1993, the island's reintegration into the inter-American system was well advanced, and the Castro government had already developed an increasingly complex array of political, economic, cultural, and scientific relations with its neighbors.

Latin America, in effect, had given its answer to the question of what to do about Cuba. Despite a broad consensus in support of political redemocratization and free-market economic reform on the island, most Latin governments rejected Washington's demand that these be made preconditions for engagement with Fidel Castro's revolutionary regime. If the hemisphere had little argument about the desirability of Cuba making such changes, it increasingly disputed the White House contention that only a hostile diplomacy and stringent sanctions would achieve them. Mirroring the approach taken by Europe and Canada, a conviction had formed throughout the region that such changes were more likely to result from increased contacts with the island than from its continuing isolation.

Although sensitivity to U.S. policy concerns still exerted some influence over the pace and scope of renewed ties with Cuba, as far as most regional governments were concerned Castro's shift to a foreign policy based on ideological pluralism and his selective opening up of the island economy to the world market dictated an approach based on pragmatism rather than ideological hostility. The changing configuration of global power in the post–Cold War international order also played a decisive role in shaping the hemisphere's stance. Few put it more succinctly than Dominican prime minister Eugenia Charles, among Washington's most consistent Latin American allies: "If [the United States] haven't realized the Cold War is over, we have."[196]

Paradoxically, Washington's support for Latin American redemocratization that brought to power new civilian regimes—more and more expected to live by their wits rather than on U.S. handouts—hastened the breakdown of Cuba's regional isolation during the 1980s and 1990s. Almost all elected governments subsequently renewed relations with Fidel Castro's government and developed trade and investment ties as best they could.

Even as the administration of George W. Bush sought to encourage a harsher approach to Cuba, Latin governments by and large stood firm. Tensions generated between Havana and some regional capitals over human rights, together with a greater focus on bilateral relations and Washington's continued hostility to the Castro regime, has worn down the momentum for championing Cuba's readmission to the OAS. But the United States has made no inroads into a Latin approach that balances criticism of discrete features of Cuban domestic policies with a fundamental commitment to engagement.

In sum, Latin America has concluded that Cuba should be dealt with like any other country. As a result, no U.S. president could ever again hope to forge the consensus in favor of Cuba's isolation from the rest of the hemisphere that Washington managed to achieve in the 1960s and, to a lesser extent, in the 1970s. In May 2003, Brazilian president Luiz Inácio Lula da Silva underscored this reality when he announced that Fidel Castro would be invited, for the first time, to attend the next meeting of the Rio Group of nations in 2004.[197] Castro's triumphant visit to Argentina that month also showed he was still a key factor in Latin American domestic politics.[198]

Given Washington's promotion of a more competitive regional economic environment and a resurgence of political nationalism and populism, the United States could not blame anyone but itself if its Cold War approach toward Cuba was one the rest of Latin America rejected. Indeed, by making an exception of Cuba and frustrating its complete return to the inter-American family of nations, the White House risks inadvertently making the Caribbean island once again a rallying symbol for the popular left in Latin America and those governments intent on pursuing foreign and domestic policies at variance with imperial state interests.

Notes

1. Quoted in Rowan Scarborough and Bill Getz, "Left Nearly Alone, Cuba Faces a Crisis," *Washington Times*, March 1, 1990, 6; Ann Devroy, "U.S. Employs 'Verbal Policy' in Attempt to Isolate Castro," *Washington Post*, April 3, 1990.

2. Confidential interview 1, by author, Washington, D.C., October 31, 2002. Senior official, Bureau of Western Hemisphere Affairs, Department of State.

3. See, for example, Morris H. Morley, *Washington, Somoza and the Sandinistas: State and Regime in U.S. Policy Toward Nicaragua, 1969–1981* (New York: Cambridge University Press, 1994), 9–30; James D. Cochrane, "U.S. Policy Toward Recognition of Governments and Promotion of Democracy in Latin America Since 1963," *Journal of Latin American Studies* 4, no.2 (1972): 275–91.

4. Quoted in "Cuba Invites Trade With Latin States," *Miami Herald*, May 18, 1991, 8A.

5. Quoted in "'No Strings' to Co-Operation," *Latin American Regional Reports: Caribbean*, September 29, 1988, 2.

6. Bernard Aronson, telephone interview by author, Washington, D.C., May 17, 1999. Assistant secretary of state for Inter-American Affairs, 1989–93.

7. Senate Committee on Foreign Relations, *Nomination of James A. Baker III*, 101st Cong., 1st sess., January 17 and 18, 1989, 85.

8. See "Moscow Chill vs. Nod From Bush," *Latin American Weekly Report*, February 19, 1989, 10.

9. Quoted in *CubaINFO*, August 2, 1991, 3.

10. Quoted in "Castro Returns to Latin Roots," *Latin American Monitor: Caribbean*, March 1989, 637.

11. Robert Morley, telephone interview by author, Washington, D.C., May 19, 1999. Coordinator, Office of Cuban Affairs, Department of State, 1988–91; Latin American director, National Security Council staff, 1991–93.

12. Quoted in Paul Bedard, "US Putting Cuba in a Vise, Quayle Tells Vets," *Washington Times*, March 6, 1990, A3.

13. See Gil Klein, "Bush Lays Down His Conditions for Normal Relations With Cuba," *Washington Post*, March 20, 1990, A14.

14. Quoted in Edward Cody, "Latins Nudge but Castro Won't Budge," *Washington Post*, July 19, 1991, A15.

15. Quoted in *CubaINFO*, December 18, 1992, 4.

16. See Luis L. Vasconcelos, "The Limits and Possibilities of Cuban-Brazilian Relations," in *Cuba's Ties to a Changing World*, ed. Donna Rich Kaplowitz (Boulder: Lynne Rienner, 1993), 189; Boris Yopo H., "Latin American Perspectives on the Cuban Transition," Trinity College Programs in International Studies, Washington D.C., Caribbean

Project: Cuba Briefing Paper Series, no. 3 (July 1993): 3. Also see *CubaINFO*, February 28, 1991, 3; August 23, 1991, 4; October 25, 1991, 4; November 15, 1991, 5.

17. Raimundo Ruga, telephone interview by author, Washington, D.C., May 12, 1999. Cuba desk officer, Department of Defense, 1993–97; chair, Secretary's Cuba Task Force, summer 1994.

18. Confidential interview 2, by author, Washington, D.C., May 12, 1999. Department of State Cuba official, Bush administration; senior Latin American official with Cuba responsibilities in the first and second Clinton administrations.

19. Michael Skol, interview by author, Washington, D.C., May 6, 1999. Deputy secretary of state for South America 1990; principal deputy secretary of state for Inter-American Affairs, 1993–95.

20. Richard Nuccio, interview by author, Falls Church, Virginia, May 20, 1996. Staff aide to Congressman Robert Torricelli (D-N.J.) with special responsibility for Cuban affairs, 1991–93; Department of State Cuba official and White House special representative on Cuba, 1993–96.

21. Dennis Hays, interview by author, Washington, D.C., May 14, 1999. Director, Office of Cuban Affairs, Department of State, 1993–95.

22. Quoted in *CubaINFO*, July 16, 1993, 6.

23. Secretary of State Warren Christopher, quoted in *Washington Report on the Hemisphere*, June 25, 1993, 2.

24. See *CubaINFO*, July 16, 1993, 5.

25. Quoted in *Foreign Broadcast Information Service Daily Report: LAT-93-134* (hereafter *FBIS*), July 15, 1993.

26. Confidential interview 2.

27. Michael Ranneberger, interview by author, Washington, D.C., May 17, 1999. Coordinator, Office of Cuban Affairs, Department of State, 1995–2000.

28. Confidential interview 3, by author, Washington, D.C., May 18, 1999. Department of State, senior Inter-American Affairs official with Cuba responsibilities, 1996–2000.

29. Morley telephone interview.

30. Aronson telephone interview.

31. Quoted in *CubaINFO*, October 5, 1990, 2.

32. Quoted in *CubaINFO*, June 19, 1991, 3.

33. Ranneberger interview.

34. Quoted in Andres Oppenheimer and Mimi Whitefield, "OAS Warms to Possibility of Cuba's Return to Group," *Miami Herald*, June 18, 1994, 13A.

35. Quoted in *FBIS: LAT-94-116*, June 16, 1994.

36. Quoted in *FBIS: LAT-94-117*, June 17, 1994.

37. "Gaviria Inaugurated as OAS Secretary-General; Discusses Cuba, Haiti, Other Issues," *BBC Monitoring Service: Latin America*, September 1, 1994.

38. House Committee on International Relations, *Evaluating U.S. Foreign Policy*, 104th Cong., 1st sess., January 12,19, and 26, 1995, 102.

39. Quoted in *CubaINFO*, December 15, 1994, 4.

40. Quoted in *CubaINFO*, April 27, 1995, 7.

41. See *CubaINFO*, May 18, 1995, 9.

42. See *CubaINFO*, August 28, 1995, 4.

43. Quoted in *FBIS: LAT-95-108*, June 6, 1995.

44. Quoted in James Brooke, "Latin America Now Ignores U.S. Lead in Isolating Cuba," *New York Times*, July 8, 1995, 5.

45. All quotations in *FBIS: LAT-96-039*, February 27, 1996.

46. Ranneberger interview.

47. Quoted in Larry Rohter, "Latin American Nations Rebuke U.S. for the Embargo on Cuba," *New York Times*, June 6, 1996, 6.

48. Quoted in "OAS Vote Should Not be Seen as Pro-Cuba-Chile," *Reuters News Service* (hereafter *RNS*), June 7, 1996.

49. Quoted in *CubaINFO*, September 19, 1996, 6.

50. Quoted in James Morrison, "Embassy Row: Gaviria for Lunch," *Washington Times*, October 15, 1996, A13.

51. Quoted in Tracey Eaton and Alfredo Corchado, "Pope Brings a Message of Hope to Cuba," *Dallas Morning News*, January 22, 1998.

52. Quoted in Tracey Eaton et al., "Pope Ends Trip to Cuba Amid Cries for Liberty," *Dallas Morning News*, January 26, 1998.

53. Argentine OAS representative, Alice Martínez Rios, quoted in "Gaviria Sees Cuba Back in the OAS, But Washington Cool," *RNS*, March 26, 1998.

54. Confidential interview 3. This explanation drew an angry response from prominent anti-Castro legislators. See House Committee on International Relations, Subcommittee on the Western Hemisphere, *Latin America and the Caribbean: An Update and Summary of the Summit of the Americas*, 105th Cong., 2nd sess., May 6, 1998, 18–19.

55. All quotations in Chris Aspin, "Uninvited Cuba Still in Spotlight at America's Summit," *RNS*, April 14, 1998; "Heads of State Unhappy at Absence of Cuba at Summit," *BBC Monitoring Service: Latin America*, April 21, 1998; "Heeding Pope's Call to End Isolation," *Latin American Weekly Report*, May 5, 1998, 198.

56. Romero quoted in Tom Brown, "U.S. Dismisses Calls for Cuba's Return to OAS," *RNS*, April 30, 1998.

57. Confidential interview 4, by author, Washington, D.C., May 14, 1999. Senior official, Office of Cuban Affairs, Department of State, 1995–98.

58. Confidential telephone interview, by author, San Francisco, California, December 21, 1999. Senior Department of State official, 1994–97.

59. "Press Conference by the President," White House, Office of the Press Secretary, April 30, 1998, transcript.

60. Quotations in "Cuba, Absent Protagonist at OAS Assembly," *RNS*, May 30, 1998. It was Venezuela's ambassador, Francisco Pararoni, who described Cuba as the "absent protagonist."

61. Quoted in "Mexico, US Face Off Over Cuba and Operation White House," *RNS*, June 4, 1998; "OAS Decides It Can Do Without Cuba," *Latin American Weekly Report*, June 9, 1998, 259.

62. Quoted in "U.S. Seeks To Bar Cuba Debate at OAS," *RNS*, June 2, 1998.

63. See "Foreign Minister Reaffirms Desire to See Cuba Return to OAS Membership," *RNS*, June 3, 1998; Maria Azpiazu, "Bid to Return Cuba to OAS is Shelved," *Miami Herald*, June 3, 1998.

64. Quoted in David Hashel, "Gaviria Seeks Cuba Back in OAS, But Washington Cool," *RNS*, March 26, 1998.

65. Quoted in Tom Brown, "U.S. Dismisses Calls."

66. Quoted in "Castro Begins Caribbean Tour," *Miami Herald*, July 30, 1998.

67. See Serge F. Kovaleski, "Fidel Castro is Cheered in Grenada," *Washington Post*, August 3, 1998; Reudon Eversley, "In Barbados Castro Calls for a United Caribbean," *Miami Herald*, August 2, 1998; "Castro Plays Elderly Statesman," *Miami Herald*, August 20, 1998 for Fernandez quote; "Castro Wows 'em in the Caribbean," *Latin American Regional Reports: Caribbean*, August 25, 1998, 2.

68. *FBIS: LAT-98-153*, June 2, 1998. Interestingly, Clinton refused to meet Elizardo Sánchez when the dissident visited the United States in late 1993, or even to acknowledge or reply to his letters.

69. Quoted in Deborah Ramírez, "Colombia Looks to Castro to Broker Peace," *South Florida Sun-Sentinel*, January 15, 1999. While Castro was reluctant to take "a leadership role" in any mediation, he offered to participate in a joint effort with other countries if the Colombian government and the guerrillas could agree on terms (quoted in Tim Johnson, "Colombia Leader Takes New Stance on Cuba Ties," *Miami Herald*, January 17, 1999).

70. Ramírez, "Colombia Looks to Castro"; Dalia Acosta, "Castro Strengthens Vital Ties With Colombia, Venezuela," *Inter-Press Service*, January 18, 1999.

71. Foreign Minister José Vicente Rangel, quoted in Andres Oppenheimer, "Venezuelan Says He'll Meet With Cuban Dissidents," *Miami Herald*, June 30, 1999.

72. See John Rice, "Summit of Gains, Losses," *Miami Herald*, November 18, 1999.

73. Quoted in "Leaders at Summit Call for Democracy in Cuba," *Miami Herald*, November 17, 1999.

74. Larry Rohter, "Venezuela Will Sell Cuba Low-Priced Oil," *New York Times*, October 31, 2000. By 2004, Cuba had sent around twelve thousand doctors, teachers, sports coaches, sugar industry experts, and other specialists to Venezuela.

75. Quoted in "U.S. Loses No Sleep Over Cuba-Venezuela Ties," *RNS*, November 1, 2000.

76. Ranneberger interview.

77. "Americas/OAS Chief Urges Cuba Solution," *BBC World Service*, September 15, 1999.

78. Quoted in *CubaINFO*, September 19, 1996, 6.

79. See *CubaINFO*, October 26, 1998, 5.

80. "Minister Restates Government's Opposition to US Embargo on Cuba," *RNS*, January 31, 1998.

81. Quoted in "Argentina Changes Its Approach," *Latin American Regional Reports: Caribbean*, February 29, 1996, 7.

82. Andres Oppenheimer, "Latin Nations Poised for Summit," *Miami Herald*, October 17, 1998.

83. Guelar quoted in Andres Oppenheimer, "Argentina Clarifies Stance on Cuba," *Miami Herald*, November 21, 1998; senior foreign ministry official quoted in Oppenheimer, "Latin Nations Poised for Summit."

84. Quoted in *CubaINFO*, April 30, 1993, 3.

85. *Latin American Monitor: Caribbean*, May 1995, 6; Brooke, "Latin America Now Ignores U.S.," 1,5.

86. See *CubaINFO*, November 30, 1995, 6; Economist Intelligence Unit, *Country Report: Cuba*, 4th quarter 1999, 24; Domingo Amuchastegui, "Cuba's Reengagement with the Caribbean: Setbacks and Successes," Trinity College Programs in International Studies, Washington D.C., Caribbean Project: Cuba Briefing Paper Series, no. 22 (November 1999): 7–9.

87. "Concern that New Caricom-Cuba Joint Commission Could Antagonize the US," *Latin American Regional Reports: Caribbean*, January 27, 1994, 1.

88. See *CubaINFO*, November 5, 1993, 5.

89. *Latin American Regional Reports: Mexico & NAFTA*, May 9, 1996, 2; "Recovery Goes on But Doubts Linger," *Latin American Regional Reports: Caribbean*, August 29, 1996, 2.

90. Anthony Palma, "Canada and Mexico Join to Oppose U.S. Law on Cuba," *New York Times*, June 13, 1996, 8.

91. Alexander Watson, interview by author, Arlington, Virginia, May 13, 1999. Assistant secretary of state for Inter-American Affairs, 1993–96.

92. See Mary Beth Sheridan, "New U.S. Law's Penalties Spur Cemex to Pull Out of Cuba," *Los Angeles Times*, May 30, 1996; U.S. policymaker quoted in "Cemex Quits Cuba to Avoid U.S. Sanctions," *RNS*, May 29, 1996.

93. Leslie Crawford, "Mexican Groups Prepare Cuba Defense," *Financial Times* (U.K.), May 28, 1996, 6; "Domos Uncowed by Helms-Burton Bar," *Latin American Weekly Report*, September 5, 1996, 404.

94. Quoted in *FBIS: LAT-96-105*, May 30, 1996.

95. Stuart Eizenstat, interview by author, Washington, D.C., September 16, 2001. Special White House representative for the promotion of democracy in Cuba, 1996–98.

96. "Heeding Pope's Call to End Isolation," 198; H. Michael Erisman, *Cuba's Foreign Relations in a Post-Soviet World* (Gainesville: University Press of Florida, 2001), 150, 195; Economist Intelligence Unit, *Country Report: Cuba*, May 2001, 28.

97. Quoted in *CubaINFO*, July 26, 2000, 6.

98. Cardoso and Cuéller quoted in "The United States Should Lift the Economic Embargo," *RNS*, December 12, 2000.

99. See H. Michael Erisman, "Cuba's Evolving CARICOM Connection," in *Cuba in the International System*, ed. Archibald R. M. Ritter and John M. Kirk (New York: St. Martin's Press, 1995), 136.

100. Quoted in *Washington Report on the Hemisphere*, September 19, 1993, 136. Also see *FBIS: LAT-93-156*, August 16, 1993.

101. Confidential interview 5, by author, Washington, D.C., May 11, 1999. Congressional Cuba specialist, who monitored the legislative debate over Cuba policy, 1993–2000.

102. Hrinak and Patterson quoted in *CubaINFO*, September 3, 1993, 1–2.

103. See Erisman, "CARICOM Connection," 139.

104. See "Caricom Leaders Disregard US Objections to Cuba's ACS Membership," *Latin American Regional Reports: Caribbean*, July 28, 1994, 1.

105. Anthony T. Bryan, "Cuba's Relations with the Caribbean: Reversal of Bad

Fortune?," in *Cuba and the Caribbean*, ed. Joseph S. Tulchin et al. (Wilmington, DE: Scholarly Resources, 1997), 174.

106. "Latin America and the Caribbean—Cuba Looks For Greater Ties With Its Caribbean Neighbors," *RNS*, July 16, 1998; "Caricom-Cuban Joint Commission," 1.

107. See Raymond J. Ahearn, *Trade and the Americas*, Congressional Research Service, March 17, 1999, 8; Glenn Garvin, "Castro, in Grenada, Revisits Cuban Role," *Miami Herald*, August 3, 1998; "Caricom-Cuban Joint Commission," 1.

108. R. Roger Majak, interview by author, Washington, D.C., May 11, 1999. Assistant secretary of commerce for Export Administration, 1995–2000.

109. Kovaleski, "Fidel Castro Cheered."

110. John Merrill, telephone interview by author, Washington, D.C., May 11, 1999. Director for Caribbean and Central American Affairs, Department of Defense, 1997–99. On the Cuban medical personnel figures, see Amuchastegui, "Cuba's Reengagement," 6.

111. See Larry Rohter, "Caribbean Nations, Ignoring U.S., Warm to Cuba," *New York Times*, December 21, 1997, 8.

112. Quoted in *CubaINFO*, July 10, 1997, 4.

113. Quoted in Larry Luxner, "With Economy in Doldrums, Grenada Courts Cuban Ties," *CUBANEWS*, December 1997, 7.

114. Panday and Albright quoted in Stanley Meisler, "Caribbean Ally of U.S. Takes Dim View of Cuba Policy," *Miami Herald*, April 6, 1998.

115. Quoted in "Castro Plays Elderly Caribbean Statesman," *Miami Herald*, August 20, 1998.

116. Quoted in "Castro Calls For Alliance Against United States," *RNS*, August 26, 1998.

117. Quoted in Don Bohning, "Jamaica, EU Fault U.S. on Cuba, Market Access," *Miami Herald*, December 12, 1998.

118. Quoted in Tony Best, "U.S.-Caribbean Relations Worsen," *CARIBNEWS*, May 18, 1999, 3.

119. Quoted in "Caribbean Nations Suspend Treaty with U.S. Due to Banana Dispute," *CNN/Associated Press*, March 7, 1999.

120. See "Caribbean Countries Seek Tariff System for New Trade Bloc," *Los Angeles Times*, April 18, 1999.

121. "Cuba Calls For Its Integration, As Fully Fledged Member, Into ACP Group, Outside Partnership Agreement with EU," *RNS*, June 23, 2000.

122. Quoted ibid.

123. See William LeoGrande's chapter for details.

124. Bush's reshuffling of his Latin America policy team in early 2003 indicated no change in the administration approach to Cuba or the region. His effort to renominate Otto Reich was derailed by incoming chair of the Senate Foreign Relations Committee, Richard Lugar (R-Ind.) who told Secretary of State Powell that it was time for the appointment of a "big leaguer" to be assistant secretary for Inter-American Affairs, "someone who . . . can reach out to a multitude of situations" (quoted in G. Robert Hillman, "Sen. Lugar Objects to Renomination of Top Envoy to Latin America," *Dallas Morning Herald*, December 14, 2002). Reich was transferred to the NSC with primary

responsibility for coordinating long-term policy initiatives dealing with Cuba, Mexico, and the Caribbean. His replacement at State, U.S. ambassador to the OAS, Roger Noriega, a hardliner on Cuba and highly regarded by the Cuban-American lobby, was reportedly opposed by Secretary Powell who had recommended Anne Patterson, a career diplomat and current U.S. ambassador to Colombia, for the position. John Maisto, the senior director for Western Hemisphere Affairs at the NSC, took over Noriega's post at the OAS.

125. Quoted in "Powell Says UN Rights Censure a Priority," *RNS*, March 7, 2001.

126. Quoted in Pablo Alfonso, "U.N. Panel Condemns Cuba for Rights Abuse," *Miami Herald*, April 19, 2001.

127. See *U.S.*Cuba Policy Report*, April 2001, 2.

128. See *FBIS: LAT-2001-0425*, April 25, 2001; *FBIS: LAT-2001-0426*, April 26, 2001.

129. Quoted in *FBIS: LAT-2001-0203*, February 3, 2001.

130. Quoted in *FBIS: LAT-2001-0504*, May 4, 2001.

131. Confidential interview 1.

132. For the text of the IADC, see Organization of American States Web site, <www.oas.org>.

133. Confidential interview 1.

134. Confidential interview 6, by author, Washington, D.C., October 28, 2002. Department of State official attached to the U.S. Mission at the Organization of American States.

135. See "Ibero-American Tackles Terror, Economic Crisis," *New York Times*, November 25, 2001. This ongoing criticism of Helms-Burton was all the more significant as it *followed* President Bush's July decision to extend the waiver on implementation of the most contentious extraterritorial provisions of the legislation.

136. See "USA: Caribbean Leaders Back Regional Free Trade Zone," *Reuters Business Briefing* (hereafter *RBB*), December 13, 2001; Economist Intelligence Unit, *Country Report: Cuba*, August 2001, 17.

137. Confidential interview 6.

138. See "Honduras Re-Establishes Ties With Cuba," *New York Times*, January 27, 2002; "Honduras: Foreign Minister Calls Normalizing Ties With Cuba 'A Sovereign Act,'" *BBC Monitoring Service: Latin America*, February 1, 2002. This left just two Latin American nations—El Salvador and Costa Rica—still to normalize relations.

139. See Marc Frank, "Cuba Says Argentina 'Boot Licking' Washington," *RNS*, January 30, 2002.

140. Quotations in "Bush Discusses Cuba Censure with Peru," *RNS*, March 25, 2002.

141. See "Latin Americans Attack Cuba at U.N. Rights Meeting," *RNS*, April 10, 2002; Nancy San Martin, "Latin American Nations Expected to Back Cuba Censure," *Miami Herald*, April 9, 2002; *FBIS: LAT-2002-0411*, April 11, 2002. The Czech Republic had decided not to sponsor a new resolution.

142. Quoted in Dalia Costa, "Human Rights Debate Tangles Latin American Relations," *RBB*, April 9, 2002.

143. See Patricia Grogg, "Cuba Assails Latin Americans' Betrayal on U.N. Commission," *RBB*, April 5, 2002.

144. Quoted in San Martin, "Cuba Censure."

145. Quoted in Nancy San Martin, "Latin Nations Find Unity in Rebuke of Cuba," *Miami Herald*, April 19, 2002. Uruguay's leading role reignited the bitter personal dispute between Castro and President Jorge Battle, whom the Cuban leader verbally savaged as a "Judas" and a "lackey" of the United States. Uruguay cut diplomatic ties over what Battle termed these "affronts," then partially backtracked three days later by deciding to maintain consular relations with the island (see Anahi Rama, "Affronted Uruguay Cuts Diplomatic Ties with Cuba," *RNS*, April 23, 2002; "Uruguay to Keep Relations With Cuba," *New York Times*, April 27, 2002).

146. Confidential interview 1.

147. Quoted in *FBIS: LAT-2001-0208*, February 7, 2001.

148. Quotations in *FBIS: LAT-2001-0401*, April 1, 2001; *FBIS: LAT-2001-0412*, April 12, 2001.

149. Quoted in *FBIS: LAT-2001-0425*, April 25, 2001. Also see "Mexico Abstains on Human Rights Motion," *Latin American Mexico & NAFTA Report*, May 1, 2001, 4.

150. Lomas and Fox quoted in *FBIS: LAT-2001-0530*, May 30, 2001 and *FBIS: WEU-2001-0602*, June 2, 2001.

151. *FBIS: LAT-2001-1002*, October 2, 2001.

152. Quoted in "Mexico's President Making Cuba Trip," *New York Times*, February 2, 2002; Ginger Thompson, "Mexican Leader Visits Castro to Repair Damaged Ties," *New York Times*, February 4, 2002.

153. See "Sobering for Castro," *Latin American Mexico & NAFTA Report*, February 12, 2002, 2.

154. Quoted in *FBIS: LAT-2002-0903*, September 30, 2002.

155. Confidential interview 1.

156. Quoted in David González, "Castro Defies Fox of Mexico as Once-Warm Ties Sour," *New York Times*, April 23, 2002. Also see Patricia Grogg, "Rows with Uruguay, Mexico Strain Cuba's Ties With Region," *RBB*, April 24, 2002; Karen DeYoung and Kevin Sullivan, "Bush Urges Nations to Use Aid as Tool Against Corruption," *Washington Post*, March 23, 2002; "Cuba Says U.S. Pressured Mexico," *New York Times*, March 22, 2002.

157. Quoted in *FBIS: WEU-2002-0505*, May 5, 2002.

158. Quoted in Ricardo Chavira, "Cuba, Mexico Resume Friendly Relationship," *Dallas Morning News*, March 19, 2003.

159. Quoted in "Cuba Denies Asking Venezuela to Mediate with USA," *BBC Monitoring Service: Latin America*, February 6, 1999.

160. See José Zambrano, "Caracas Bucks U.S. Cuba Policy," *RNS*, April 23, 1999; *FBIS: LAT-1999-0422*, April 21, 1999.

161. See *Latin American Andean Group Report*, October 2, 2001, 6.

162. Plan Colombia has been the centerpiece of U.S. policy toward Colombia since the early 1990s. For a detailed analysis, see James Petras and Morris Morley, "The

Geopolitics of Plan Colombia," in *Masters of War: Militarism and Blowback in the Era of American Empire*, ed. Carl Boggs (New York: Routledge, 2003), 83–108.

163. See Christopher Marquis, "Bush Officials Met with Venezuelans Who Ousted Leader," *New York Times*, April 16, 2002; Karen DeYoung, "U.S. Details Talks With Opposition," *Washington Post*, April 17, 2002; Hector Tobar et al., "Rapid-Fire Coup Caught Chávez Foes Off Guard," *Los Angeles Times*, April 22, 2002; Maurice Lemoine, "Venezuela: A Coup Countered," *Le Monde Diplomatique*, May 2002, 11.

164. See Duncan Campbell, "American Navy 'Helped Venezuelan Coup,'" *The Guardian* (U.K.), April 29, 2002.

165. See "Venezuela Resumes Cuba Oil Shipments," *New York Times*, September 8, 2002.

166. Quotations in Jonathan Wright, "U.S. Withholds Support for Reinstated Chávez," *RNS*, April 15, 2002. Also see Omar G. Encarnacion, "Venezuela's 'Civil Society Coup,'" *World Policy Journal* XI, no.2 (Summer 2002): 45.

167. See, for example, Marcela Sánchez, "Bush's Venezuelan Breakdown," *Washington Post*, December 21, 2002; Pablo Bachelet, "U.S. Working for Early Elections in Venezuela," *RNS*, December 21, 2002; Bart Jones, "US Funds Aid Chávez Opposition," *National Catholic Reporter*, April 2, 2004.

168. Confidential interview 1.

169. Quoted in *FBIS: LAT-2002-0620*, June 20, 2002.

170. See *FBIS: LAT-2002-0421*, April 21, 2002; Anthony Boadle, "Cuba's Castro Cements Caribbean Support," *RNS*, December 9, 2002; "Regional Leaders Ask End to Cuba Embargo," *Inter Press Service*, December 9, 2002.

171. See Tim Johnson, "Belize Refuses to Broadcast Radio Martí," *Miami Herald*, June 11, 2002.

172. Addressing the heads of state, Guyana's president and CARICOM chairman, Bharrat Jadgeo, called the U.S. trade embargo "anachronistic in this era of globalization and trade liberalization" (quoted in "Cuba Will Renew Request to Join European Aid Pact," *Dow Jones International News*, December 9, 2002).

173. Quoted in "US Envoy Cautions Caribbean Against Deeper Ties with 'Totalitarian' Cuba," *BBC Monitoring Americas*, April 4, 2003.

174. Confidential interview 1.

175. Quoted in Richard Waddington, "U.S. Commission Urges Cuba to Accept Envoy's Visit," *Washington Post*, April 18, 2003. Given President Fox's desire to improve Mexico's political ties with the United States, however, it is interesting to note the White House declaration two days before the vote that Mexico *would* be supporting the resolution. This elicited a "still undecided" response from Fox, but turned out to be an accurate call.

176. See Anita Snow, "Cuba Criticized for Jailing Dissidents," *Washington Post*, April 8, 2003.

177. Duhalde quoted in "We Won't Denounce Cuba But We Decry U.S. Actions," *Dow Jones & Reuters*, April 15, 2003; Campos quoted in "Brazil to Abstain from UN Vote on Cuba's Rights Record," *Dow Jones & Reuters*, April 17, 2003.

178. All quoted in "U.N. Keeps Pressure on Cuba Over Human Rights," *New York Times*, April 17, 2003; "Cuba 'Offended' by Latam Support for Critical U.N. Resolu-

tion," *Dow Jones & Reuters*, April 18, 2003. Days later, the United States, Costa Rica, and Nicaragua cosponsored a draft resolution at an OAS Permanent Council meeting condemning the crackdown on Cuba's dissidents. But two-thirds of the delegates voted that the council did not have the authority to debate the issue and the resolution was shelved.

179. See Marika Lynch, "Cuba is Reelected to U.N. Rights Panel; U.S. Angered," *Miami Herald*, April 30, 2003.

180. Quotations in Paul Richter, "U.S. Seeks United Action Against Cuba," *Miami Herald*, June 10, 2003.

181. Anita Snow, "Brazil and Cuba Cement Ties With Government Accords Business, Deals," *Associated Press*, September 28, 2003; Tanja Sturm, "Cuba and Brazil in Pharmaceutical Technological Transfer Deal," *WRC Daily Analysis*, February 26, 2004.

182. "Cuba and Argentina Restore Ties," *New York Times*, October 13, 2003.

183. See "Argentina: Cuba Ties Strengthened Further," *Latinnews Daily*, February 27, 2004.

184. Rice quoted in Carol J. Williams, "Cuba is Just a Friend, Venezuela Tells Suspicious U.S.," *Los Angeles Times*, February 15, 2004; Powell quoted in Tracey Eaton, "Cuba's Alliance with Venezuela Seen as Threat to U.S. Influence," *Dallas Morning Herald*, January 9, 2004. Also see "Top Administration Official Warns Castro," *Miami Herald*, January 7, 2004; "U.S. Cites Angst Over Venezuela-Cuba Ties," *Miami Herald*, January 6, 2004.

185. Quoted in "Chávez Insults Bush and Threatens to Cut Oil Off," *Latinnews Daily*, March 1, 2004.

186. See "US Scolds Venezuela's Chávez on Cuba, Recall," *Agence France Presse*, January 9, 2004; Tim Weiner and Elisabeth Bumiller, "Expectations Are Low for Progress at Americas Summit," *New York Times*, January 12, 2004.

187. Quoted in "Bush Achieves Little at Summit," *Dow Jones International News*, January 14, 2004.

188. Kirchner quotations in Richard Boudreaux, "Bush Visits Neighbors No Longer So Friendly," *Los Angeles Times*, January 12, 2004; Dudley Althaus and Patty Reinert, "Special Summit of the Americas," *Houston Chronicle*, January 14, 2004. Rice quoted in "Bush Achieves Little."

189. See "Bush Makes Concessions to Western Hemisphere Leaders at Summit," *Knight Ridder*, January 14, 2004.

190. Quoted in United Nation's Commission on Human Rights, "Commission Adopts Measures on Situations in Cuba, Belarus, Turkmenistan, Democratic People's Republic of Korea," press release HR/CN/1087, April 15, 2004, <www.un.org/News/Press/docs/2004/hrcn1087.doc.htm>.

191. Department official quoted in Nancy San Martin, "U.N. Panel to Vote on Cuba," *Miami Herald*, April 14, 2004.

192. Quoted in "Cuba and Mexico Clash Over U.N. Rights Vote," *Reuters*, April 15, 2005. The Cuban representative on the UNHRC also opposed the resolution. Just prior to the vote, Fox invited Castro to attend the May summit of European, Latin American, and Caribbean nations to be held in Guadalajara.

193. Quoted in Alistair Bell, "Mexico Says Open to Dialogue with Cuba Despite Row," *Reuters*, May 3, 2004. Also see Ginger Thompson, "Mexico and Peru Withdraw Ambassadors From Cuba," *New York Times*, May 3, 2004.

194. See "Cuba, Mexico Decide to Return Ambassadors," *Miami Herald*, May 27, 2004.

195. Vicki Huddleston, interview by author, Washington, D.C., May 17, 1999. Deputy and then-coordinator of the Office of the Coordinator of Cuban Affairs, Department of State, 1989–93.

196. Quoted in *CubaINFO*, April 12, 1993, 4. Entering its fourth year in office, the George W. Bush administration seemed no closer to acknowledging this reality as it applied to Cuba. During the March 2004 presidential elections in El Salvador, the White House actively supported the conservative ruling National Republican Alliance (ARENA) candidate, Tony Saca, who promised to continue his party's free-market and pro-U.S. policies; endorsed a Central American free trade agreement with the United States; and declared that he would not restore diplomatic ties with Cuba. At the same time, Bush officials warned about the likely consequences of the nation voting for the Farabundo Martí National Liberation Front (FMLN) nominee, Schafik Hándal, who wanted to review the ARENA government's economic model; reopen negotiations on a free trade accord; withdraw El Salvador's 380 troops from Iraq; and pursue closer relations with Cuba. Assistant Secretary of State Roger Noriega said Salvadorans should consider "what kind of relationships a new government would have with us" (quoted in Richard Boudreaux, "Businessman Wins Salvadoran Presidency," *Los Angeles Times*, March 22, 2004). Otto Reich, White House special envoy to the region, was more explicit: "We could not have the same confidence in an El Salvador led by a person who is obviously an admirer of Fidel Castro and Hugh Chávez" (quoted in John Rice, "Saca Wins El Salvador Presidential Race," *Miami Herald*, March 22, 2004). Also see Mary Beth Sheridan, "Pro-U.S. Candidate Wins in El Salvador," *Washington Post*, March 22, 2004. Washington got the result it desired.

197. See Frances Robles, "Latin Leaders Will Invite Castro to '04 Summit," *Miami Herald*, May 25, 2003.

198. See Daniel Grech and Kevin Hall, "Argentines Swoon Over Visiting Castro," *Miami Herald*, May 27, 2003.

6

In the Shadow of the Giant

Cuban Internationalism in the Third World

H. Michael Erisman

Whoever heard of Cubans conducting a global foreign policy.
Henry Kissinger, 1978

Revolutionary Cuba is unique among smaller states in the sense that it has a tradition of foreign policy activism on a much broader scale than its size, population, natural resources, and other conventional measures of power would seem to warrant. In stark contrast to the tendency of many smaller nations to (reluctantly) accept the premise that their fate is to be pawns in world affairs, Cuba aspired to play a highly visible, proactive role in international affairs beginning in the early years of the Revolution. Such activism repeatedly has brought Cuba—and often those countries that deal with it—into conflict with the United States. From Dwight D. Eisenhower to George W. Bush, the White House has taken exception not only to the Castro government's specific foreign policy initiatives but also to revolutionary Cuba as a symbol for the Third World of a country that dares to pursue its global affairs independently of, and often in competition with, U.S. interests and to pursue a development approach that rejects a free-for-all capitalist model.

For its part, Cuba's internationalism reflects a commitment to revolutionary principles as well as a far more pragmatic concern to win friends and allies in its struggle with the U.S. imperial state. (Overseas deployments, of course, have also served purely internal purposes such as the maintenance of an experienced, combat-ready armed forces and the provision of career "opportunities" for Cubans who might otherwise constitute a highly educated but disgruntled group of underemployed professionals.) Just as Havana's internationalist ambitions are constrained by factors other than sheer motivation—including the availability of outside logistical support and the state of its economy—so too Washington's hostility is contingent on the extent and nature of Cuban deployments, their strategic location, and the ebb and flow of ideological considerations as a priority issue in U.S. domestic policy. As a general rule, however, the

U.S. has tried to block Cuban involvement in the Third World at every turn and has continued to portray Cuba as a pariah state with which other countries should not have dealings. The reasons advanced have been varied: that Cuba is an ideological dinosaur, a major human rights abuser, undemocratic, a supporter of terrorism and, most recently, that the island government is actively pursuing a biological weapons capability that places it only one step removed from the rogue's gallery President George W. Bush defined as the "axis of evil."

Cuba, however, has not retreated from the world stage either in response to changed external or internal circumstances (the collapse of the Soviet Union; the subsequent economic difficulties of the 1990s) or in the face of U.S. opposition. Nor have its overtures to the Third World in particular proved any less welcome—although they have been modified significantly over the last fifteen years. The primary focus of this chapter is threefold: to investigate the evolution of Havana's ties with Asia, Africa, and the Middle East during the post–Cold War period; to identify the key factors that have influenced the dynamics of those links; and to probe the impact of Washington's response both on the Revolution's international agenda and on the relations of these Third World regions with Cuba. But no comprehensive understanding of these developments is possible without consideration of Cuba's internationalist foreign policy during the Cold War era and how this set the pattern both for Havana's attempts to maximize its global influence and for U.S. attempts to counter and limit the achievement of this goal.

Contesting the Cold War: Cuba, the United States, and the Third World

In the years immediately after Castro's 1959 triumph in toppling the Batista dictatorship, the Fidelistas launched an ambitious program to replicate their success elsewhere in the Third World. During the 1960s, the focus of Cuba's ideologically driven foreign policy in support of revolutions and national liberation movements shifted from Latin America to Africa. Setbacks due to the lack of popular support and an aggressive U.S. policy to prevent "another Cuba" in the hemisphere saw Havana dispatch revolutionaries to the Congo in 1965 and Guinea in 1966. Following a similar lack of success in Africa, the death of Che Guevara in Bolivia in 1967, and the 1973 military coup against the Marxist government of Salvador Allende in Chile, Cuba's revolutionary internationalism relocated along a different track: from encouraging guerilla campaigns to supporting broad-based anticolonial movements and established Third World Marxist or radical nationalist governments. [1]

One of the most spectacular examples was Cuba's intervention in Angola. In late 1975 Havana began, with Soviet logistical support, to dispatch combat troops to the country in an attempt to help the radical leftist Popular Movement for the Liberation of Angola (MPLA) defeat its Western-backed opponents and consolidate its control over the former Portuguese colony. This Cuban expeditionary force, which eventually reached a total of thirty-six thousand troops, was decisive in tipping the military balance in the MPLA's favor. The Cubans stopped the various enemy columns that were converging on Luanda, the nation's capital, and then launched their own counteroffensive, particularly against South African units that were spearheading the opposition assault and thus represented the greatest threat to the MPLA's position. Although the most serious fighting came to an end in March 1976—after the South African forces had been driven back into neighboring Namibia and the MPLA was able to assume control of the government—instability continued to plague the region until 1989 when a treaty was negotiated that provided, among other things, for Namibian independence as well as a total withdrawal of Cuban forces from Angola.[2]

This episode was pivotal in the maturation of Cuban globalism, demonstrating that Havana had the ability as well as the will to project its power overseas and thereby acquire the potential to play a crucial role in influencing the course of political developments in areas thousands of miles from home. Initially, some African and other Third World countries exhibited reservations about Cuba's decision to send combat troops to Angola, a move that ran counter to their long-standing preference to avoid internationalizing regional conflicts. Such misgivings took on added urgency when the scope of Havana's involvement expanded beyond the Angolan theater to include the Namibian conflict. But ultimately such considerations were almost unanimously overshadowed by the jubilation generated by the crushing victories over the South Africans in Angola (and later Namibia). Two years later, at least twelve thousand Cuban troops were airlifted to Ethiopia to assist its pro-Soviet military rulers resist an invasion of the country's Ogaden Province from neighboring Somalia—although, unlike the Soviets, the Cubans refused to fight on behalf of Addis Ababa against Marxist rebels in Eritrea, whose bid for independence Havana had long supported. In the final analysis, Cuba's military exploits in the Horn and southern Africa greatly enhanced its status throughout the Third World.[3]

Havana's foreign policy initiatives in this period, however, were not limited to military and security endeavors. Rather, in a move that was as unprecedented as its combat role in Africa, Cuba created a remarkable package of socioeconomic aid programs for Third World nations, which in some respects equaled and even surpassed the efforts of more highly developed countries. By the mid-1980s, for instance, Havana was sending one civilian aid worker abroad for every 625 of the island's inhabitants, the comparable U.S. figure being approximately one Peace Corps volunteer or Agency for International Development (AID) employee per 34,700 American citizens. Moreover, during the 1984–85 academic year, twenty-two thousand scholarship students from eighty-two less developed countries were attending high schools and universities in Cuba. By contrast, the U.S. government provided only seven thousand university scholarships for the entire Third World in 1985. A similar pattern emerged with respect to the Soviet Union and its Warsaw Pact allies: in 1979, Cubans represented 19.4 percent of all Soviet bloc economic technicians working in the Third World even though the island's population constituted only 2.5 percent of the combined Soviet/Eastern Europe/Cuban total.[4] Proportionately then, and even at times in overall numbers, Cuba's developmental aid efforts compared very favorably with those of the two superpowers. These efforts functioned to increase sympathy and support for the revolutionary regime among Third World populations but also offered an alternative to the neodependent ties that typically accompany official aid programs from the United States and other industrialized countries.

Although Cuba dispatched contingents of developmental internationalists across the Third World, Africa was its main theater of operations. During the heyday of such activity in the early 1980s, close to fifty percent of all such personnel were posted to Africa (over nine thousand). In 1984 they were concentrated in Angola (six thousand), Ethiopia (one thousand) and Mozambique (nine hundred) but were present in more than eighteen other countries in the region.[5]

The military aid missions, the key role in defeating South Africa's regional ambitions, the developmental assistance programs and other initiatives firmly established Cuba as a major player in international affairs. Through the 1970s, its stature was recognized not only among ideologically compatible governments and popular movements, but within the Third World more generally—and especially so in its most prominent institutional expression, the Non-Aligned Movement (NAM).[6] The NAM, which Cuba had joined as the Western Hemisphere's only charter member in 1961, was established as an organization ostensibly independent of the two Cold War superpower blocs with the objective of serving as the main institutional vehicle for promoting cooperation between the so-called developing states and representing their interests on the global stage. Cuba's internationalist, anti-imperialist foreign policy and demands for structural changes in the global economy put it at odds with a NAM that emphasized diplomacy and negotiation in pursuit of similar objectives during the 1960s. A decade later, however, the continuing failure of this strategy to extract substantial concessions from the developed countries, combined with a new focus in Cuban foreign policy on collective action to achieve economic goals through multilateral institutions, produced a more responsive audience for Havana among the NAM membership.[7]

Cuba's official designation as head of the movement in 1979 (with Fidel Castro serving as NAM's chairman until 1983) represented at one level its coming of age as a key influential member of the Third World. At another level, it reflected the impatience of the NAM for fundamental reform of the international political economy. Together, these two developments enabled Havana to be in the forefront of a new organized Third World challenge to Washington and the advanced capitalist world.

Soon after reaching the NAM's pinnacle, however, Cuba's support of the December 1979 military intervention in Afghanistan—which engendered widespread opposition among NAM members—and its refusal to vote for a United Nations resolution condemning Moscow's move (even though the resolution had very strong Third World backing) created a situation wherein Cuba was unable to exert the assertive, flamboyant leadership that many had anticipated. Instead it had little choice but to adopt a fairly cautious, low profile stance, functioning essentially as a routine caretaker rather than playing the more familiar role of firebrand on the international stage.

Cuba's globalist ambitions during the Cold War era were not entirely restricted to the African continent and the NAM; the Castro government's foreign policy and economic goals also extended to Asia and the Middle East. In Asia, the Cubans exhibited the strongest ideological affinity with revolutionary Vietnam, which Havana viewed as a natural ally in the sense that both countries were highly nationalistic and firmly committed to the principle of unconditional respect for a state's "effective" sovereignty. These sentiments helped to generate extremely cordial ties between Havana and Hanoi. At times, however, they served to complicate smooth relations between Cuba and Asia's communist giant—the People's Republic of China.

Beijing's initial response to Castro's victory in 1959 was quite positive, and the two countries quickly established strong ties. While Havana's strident anti-Americanism resonated well with Beijing, the main factor reinforcing China's friendliness was the growing tensions between Havana and Moscow following the latter's unilateral concession to Washington during the October 1962 Cuban Missile Crisis. In essence, the Chinese looked to Havana as a potentially very useful Third World ally in their own bitter dispute with Moscow. This honeymoon lasted until the island regime began to mend its fences with the Kremlin in the late 1960s and especially the early 1970s. What ensued were disagreements between Beijing and Havana over a variety of issues, most centered on what should be the most appropriate revolutionary strategy in the Third World, culminating in 1976 when China in effect allied itself with the United States and the South Africans by supporting efforts to destroy the MPLA government in Angola.[8] The Cubans viewed this as treachery of the worst kind and proceeded to pillory China as an unscrupulous imperialistic power that would stoop to anything in its attempts to bring vulnerable Third World countries under its influence.[9]

Surprisingly, however, these tensions in the Sino-Cuban relationship had for the most part little negative impact on bilateral economic relations. Instead, as

Table 2 (Appendix) indicates, trade between the two countries held fairly steady during the 1970s and then expanded significantly in the 1980s (the increase from 1970 to 1988 was 448 percent, for example) as both governments took steps that generally succeeded in neutralizing the rancor that had previously characterized their political dealings. Indeed the rapprochement proceeded so smoothly that by the end of 1990 Havana had emerged as Beijing's most important trading partner in Latin America.[10] Such momentum could not be maintained in the early 1990s as the Cuban economy was devastated by the collapse of the Soviet Union and the Eastern European socialist bloc. Cuban-Chinese trade experienced a 24.2 percent decline between 1990 and 1991 followed by an additional 15.4 percent fall in 1992.

Moving beyond the Asian socialist societies, Cuba, like practically all other nations who were making pilgrimages to the Orient in search of trade and aid, inevitably found itself drawn to the region's most powerful economy—Japan. The two countries had maintained vigorous trade relations going back to the early 1960s, with the volume involved often exceeding the figures generated in Havana's dealings with Canada and some of its main Western European partners. But as Table 2 shows, the Japanese were steadily losing ground to the Chinese in the late 1980s and early 1990s. Despite this, there were several factors (beyond the obvious attraction exerted by Japan's market potential and its vast investment resources) that functioned to sustain Havana's interest in a Tokyo connection. One was an accommodating stance on the issue of technology transfers—Japanese business executives recognized that Third World countries wanted an infusion of the most advanced technology available and, in contrast to their counterparts in many other industrialized societies, were often willing to make concessions to such desires as an unavoidable cost of doing business. Another was a willingness (which is not characteristic of many Western investors) to enter joint ventures as junior partners, thereby alleviating fears of neocolonialism that are often triggered by the idea of foreign majority ownership. Finally, Tokyo tended to offer foreign aid on terms that were often much more favorable than those of many other donor countries.

For the most part, however, Havana's hopes for a vigorous and broad-based economic relationship with Japan failed to materialize. For example, in the late 1980s and early 1990s, Japanese companies did not respond to Cuba's efforts to attract international investors, the primary problem being Havana's inability to pay off its existing debts to foreign creditors. At this point, the principal goal of most Japanese firms was to secure a return on their existing credits—not to start new projects—and Cuba was experiencing a foreign reserve shortage that made such returns unlikely, at least in the short term.[11] Consequently major Japanese corporations were extremely reluctant to test the Revolution's investment waters, a position that was reinforced by Tokyo's reluctance to risk complicating its relations with the United States by cooperating too closely with Havana.

A similar air of hesitancy surrounded Japan's Official Development Assistance (ODA) programs as far as Cuba was concerned (Appendix, Table 3). In fact, Latin America was a backburner region for ODA Cold War activity, generally attracting only about five percent of the total funds available in the late 1980s. Within this budget, Havana was accorded a rather low priority.

The Middle East was perhaps even less of a priority on Cuba's international agenda. This had not always been the case. In 1963, for instance, Havana sent a small contingent of combat forces to Algeria to help Ahmed Ben Bella's radical socialist government in its border dispute with Morocco. Ten years later, another Middle East deployment occurred when a Cuban brigade (estimated at five hundred to seven hundred troops) was dispatched to Syria at the time of the 1973 Yom Kippur war. On both occasions, these Cuban units, essentially temporary token forces, saw little, if any, frontline action and were withdrawn, or at least drastically reduced, once the particular crisis died down. Nevertheless these deployments could be seen as harbingers of the large-scale and controversial Fidelista involvements during the 1970s in the Horn and southern Africa.

For the most part, however, Middle Eastern affairs represented a relatively low-profile component of Havana's Cold War preoccupations. Indeed, generally speaking, there were probably only two broad concerns that attracted any serious Cuban attention: solidarity with the Palestinian cause, which included efforts to try to resolve disputes between Palestinian Liberation Organization (PLO) factions in order to strengthen the PLO's overall position and to protect it against divide-and-conquer tactics; and the need to promote Arab unity as a requisite for regional security, a position that on occasion led Cuba to try to define its role as that of a broker between quarreling Middle Eastern states such as Iran and Iraq.[12] Obviously a key factor influencing Cuban policy initiatives with respect to the Arabs/Palestinians was that they shared a common adversary—the United States. But in neither case did the pursuit of the policy translate into a major Cuban investment of time, energy, or resources. This relative detachment carried over into the economic realm where Cuba exported little apart from sugar to the Middle East and imported almost nothing in return.[13]

The Revolution's internationalist foreign policy merely confirmed Washington's judgment that Cuba was a rogue state intent on destabilizing friendly Third World governments and destroying the existing global order. President Carter's National Security Council adviser, Zbigniew Brzezinski, even claimed that, as a consequence of Cuban and Soviet involvement in the Horn of Africa in 1977, the Strategic Arms Limitation Talks (SALT)—in effect, détente—"lies buried in the sands of the Ogaden" and that a new phase in the Cold War had begun.[14] During the 1980s, the withdrawal of Cuban troops from Africa and the cessation of its support for the export of revolution became standard White House prerequisites for the normalizing of ties across the Florida Straits. Even after these conditions were met, however, U.S. officials would continue to view with deep suspicion the activities of Cuban foreign aid workers and occasionally dredge up unsubstantiated allegations of Cuba's Cold War behavior to justify ongoing punitive measures against the island.[15]

The Soviet Collapse and the Challenge of Economic Survival

Throughout most of the Cold War period, Cuba's close links with the Soviet bloc helped transform the Castro government into a prominent player on the global stage. This special relationship incorporated a number of key foreign policy aspects. The Soviet connection played a major role in alleviating Havana's concerns about military security. Although Cuba never became a formal member of the Warsaw Pact (the Kremlin's equivalent of the NATO Treaty), the island nevertheless was widely considered to be "covered" by its deterrent umbrella. In addition, Cuba received massive amounts of military aid from the Soviet Union and its allies that transformed its armed forces into a highly formidable organization that even the Pentagon was not anxious to confront.[16] Consequently, anxiety about possible U.S. attacks (covert or otherwise) increasingly diminished. Likewise, with respect to economic security, the extensive preferential trade and developmental aid benefits flowing from Cuba's Soviet bloc links, especially its membership in the Council for Mutual Economic Assistance (CMEA), greatly reduced Havana's vulnerability to the destabilization strategy that the United States was pursuing in its efforts to achieve regime change. These substantial bloc economic and military commitments meant that, in comparison with the early years of the Revolution, Havana no longer had to be obsessed with responding to Washington's hostility. Instead it could concentrate on developing its own distinctive role on the international stage, capitalizing on its access to Eastern European support to achieve key foreign policy goals, including efforts to extend Cuba's influence in the Middle East, Asia, and especially Africa.

This intricate and highly effective policy was, of course, based on a proposition that Havana took as a given—the continued viability of the Soviet Union and its military and economic networks throughout Eastern Europe. The collapse of the former and the dissolution of the latter had devastating impact on the configuration of Cuba's international agenda: ending the security umbrella, removing important logistical supports, and necessitating the substitution of economic security over revolutionary adventurism as the primary factor shaping its foreign policy.

This shift in priorities had its greatest impact on Cuba's Africa ties. The region quickly found itself positioned more toward the periphery of Havana's relationships with the developing world, its relative importance having been overshadowed by the Castro government's expanded links with the Caribbean/Latin American community as part of an effort to promote greater hemispheric integration and thus, it was hoped, Cuba's economic survival. The one notable exception was Cuba's relationship with South Africa, which with the collapse of apartheid reaped the benefit of years of revolutionary solidarity with the African National Congress. One of Nelson Mandela's first major acts as president was to restore diplomatic relations with Havana, and Fidel Castro was among the first heads of state to be invited to the new South Africa. Mandela himself (over the strong objections of Washington) visited Cuba in July 1991, and both he and his successor, Thabo Mbeki, have been vocal opponents of Washington policy toward the Caribbean island. Mandela demonstrated and explained the depth of feeling toward Havana during an October 1995 speech in Johannesburg: "Cubans came to our region as doctors, teachers, soldiers, agricultural experts, but never as colonizers. They have shared the same trenches with us in the struggle against colonialism, underdevelopment, and apartheid. Hundreds of Cubans have given their lives, literally, in a struggle that was, first and foremost, not theirs but ours. As Southern Africans we salute them. We vow never to forget this unparalleled example of selfless internationalism."[17] Economically, however, neither country was for the foreseeable future in any position to be of much benefit to the other.

The late 1980s and early 1990s were years in which Cuba was forced to reduce drastically its international profile and to turn its attention to cultivating state-to-state relations on more orthodox commercial footings. The devastating impact of the Soviet bloc's disintegration on the Cuban economy has been widely documented; an estimated forty to forty-five percent of the island's annual Gross National Product (GNP) was wiped out by the disappearance of the highly lucrative preferential trade and aid relations that Havana had developed with Eastern Europe (the CMEA was officially disbanded in June 1991). Such developments entailed not only deprivation and suffering for the Cuban people, but also potentially rendered the island economy more vulnerable to the pressures of the U.S. embargo. Indeed, both the George H. W. Bush and Clinton administrations sought to take advantage of what was perceived as a golden opportunity to achieve Washington's long-held goal of economically destabilizing the country to the point where Fidel Castro would be driven from power and the Revolution destroyed. As Cuba opened up to the world economy, the United States simultaneously tried to close off its options. The most extreme measures employed in this effort were the 1992 Cuban Democracy Act and the 1996 Helms-Burton Act, two pieces of extraterritorial legislation designed to punish overseas subsidiaries of U.S. corporations and foreign nationals seeking profitable economic ties with Cuba and, in the case of Helms-Burton, threatening possible U.S. retaliation in kind against any country willing to throw financial lifelines to the island.

Fully aware that the emerging post-Soviet world was fraught with serious danger not only to the high levels of social development and national sovereignty that the Fidelistas had worked so hard to achieve, but perhaps also to the Revolution itself, and that reestablishing economic security was the key to survival on its own terms, Havana moved quickly to implement the countermeasures necessary to deal with the changed international environment. The main challenge involved rebuilding and restructuring the island's global economic relations in order to pursue a more diversified set of trading partners and foreign investors (as opposed to the heavy Cold War–era reliance on the Soviet bloc) and so reduce the disruptive risks involved in any particular relationship. Although the European Union and the Western Hemisphere emerged as the focal points of these new Cuban initiatives, the relative commercial importance that Havana accorded Asia and, to a lesser extent, the Middle East, likewise increased. The new trade patterns that began to emerge are illustrated in Table 4 (Appendix).

Havana's "Outreach" to the Post–Cold War Third World

Cuba has been quite successful in diversifying its export markets and sources of supply. During the 1980s, for example, approximately eighty to eighty-five percent of the island's foreign trade was conducted with CMEA members; in 1999 at least fifty-nine percent of its export and eighty-one percent of its import business occurred with countries outside of the old Soviet bloc. In terms of increased "market share," Western Europe has been the primary regional beneficiary of this economic restructuring followed—by wide margins—by the Americas and Asia.

Cuba's commercial relations with Africa have not expanded significantly. The harsh reality is that Africa does not appear to represent a very significant factor in terms of its relevance to the pursuit of the top-priority item on Havana's current foreign (economic) policy agenda. There are various political and diplomatic considerations that nonetheless constitute strong incentives for Cuba to maintain and indeed strengthen, where it can, relations with sub-Saharan Africa. For example, Africa's votes are extremely important to Cuba in the United Nations where Havana and Washington annually vie to mobilize support behind their dueling resolutions (that is, the U.S. condemnation of the island's human rights record and Cuba's denunciation of the U.S. economic blockade). In 2002 the United Nations Human Rights Commission (UNHRC) resolution chastising Havana was passed by the narrow margin of 22 to 21 with 9 abstentions.[18] Nine of the African members voted in favor of the resolution but five voted against and one abstained. In 2004, no African member of the commission voted for the resolution condemning Cuba; ten voted against and three abstained. When the issue shifted to the United Nations General Assembly (UNGA) for the annual vote on its nonbinding resolution calling for the U.S. sanctions to be lifted, the African vote has been, and remains, solidly pro-Cuban; not one African nation has voted in favor of the resolution since it was first introduced in 1992.[19]

Such concerns have helped to sustain Havana's interest in its sub-Saharan aid programs in particular. But certain aspects of the current scenario are quite different from the Cold War days. The most obvious change is in the military/ security sphere where all prior linkages have essentially disappeared; the fundamental role of the Cuban armed forces in the post-Soviet period has shifted from external security affairs to internal economic management responsibilities; military personnel are now assigned almost exclusively to domestic rather than foreign assignments. Another change has been a shift away from the rhetoric of class struggle. In an October 1995 speech to the Cuban–Southern Africa Solidarity Conference in Johannesburg, Castro used instead the language of global social justice: "Our present struggle for the preservation of the identity and validity of our homeland, for the continuity of our revolution, and the defense of our socialism and its imperishable conquests, is also the struggle for the poor people of this earth."[20]

Developmental projects continue to receive support, although economic exigencies have almost always made it impossible to maintain the programs at anywhere near their Cold War levels. The following comparison is illustrative. In 1986 there were approximately 8,540 Cuban developmental aid workers assigned to sub-Saharan Africa (most of which were medical personnel). By 2000 that number had declined to 481 doctors and related health care specialists.[21] Efforts have and are being made to reverse this trend. At an April 2000 summit of less developed countries in Havana, for instance, a number of sub-Saharan governments announced that they were planning to make contributions to a fund to send an additional three thousand Cuban doctors to Africa.[22] Gestures of this kind underline the present-day reality that Havana cannot, as it did in the 1970s and 1980s, absorb all of the costs involved in such undertakings. Instead, either the host nations must be able to share some of the burden (which often may not be feasible for the more impoverished states) or else third parties must step forward to help, such as the trilateral operation being conducted in Mali by Cuba, South Africa, and Nigeria.[23] In general, however, getting firm commitments from either potential recipients or joint venture partners has been rather difficult. Thus, despite its surplus of highly qualified health professionals, Havana has not yet been able to recoup all of its lost Cold War ground in medical and associated aid.

Cuban–Middle East relations appear at first glance to have remained rather static. Indeed, it would be fair to say that there have been no patterns of *signifi-cant* change associated with either the transition to the post-Soviet era or to developments that have occurred since then. As Table 4 (Appendix) indicates, the basic trade configuration has remained quite stable. Admittedly there was a marginal percentage increase in the region's status as a market for the island's exports in the late 1980s and early 1990s, but these gains proved temporary. Perhaps most surprising is the fact that there has been no marked increase in the Middle East's share of Cuba's imports, for it would seem reasonable to expect heavy Cuban purchases of the region's oil once Havana's preferential arrangements with the Soviet Union and its Eastern European bloc partners (for example, Romania) had disappeared. However, to the extent that other suppliers have become more prominent, the beneficiaries have tended to be near neighbors—Mexico, Venezuela, and Trinidad/Tobago—rather than na-tions from the world's major oil-producing region. Middle East countries are conspicuously absent and today play no significant role in contributing to the island's petroleum needs.[24] Nonetheless, Fidel Castro's visit to Iran in May 2001, and Cuba's dogged opposition to the U.S.-led wars in Afghanistan and Iraq, may presage a more fruitful era in relations between Havana and the region.

Overall, Cuba's relations with Asia have also not experienced any major ups and downs during the post-Soviet period, although in some specific instances the bilateral dynamics have become quite robust (notably in the case of eco-nomic relations with China). Certainly the fact that Castro has made two major Asian tours since the Soviet bloc disintegrated (one in 1995 and another in 2003) represents an important symbolic indication of Cuba's interest in developing and capitalizing upon opportunities to enhance its stock in the region. The biggest disappointment has been its failure to expand ties with Japan, primarily due to the ongoing problem of servicing Havana's debt obli-gations to the regional power and the negative impact thereof on the whole spectrum of bilateral commercial relations. In 1987 Cuba had announced to all of its major creditors—including Tokyo—that it would not be able to repay its debts on schedule, and it remained in arrears during the very difficult financial years that followed. Table 5 (Appendix) shows the dampening effect of the debt issue on Cuban-Japanese trade; throughout the 1990s, the general pattern was one of stagnation and erosion, not growth.

In March 1998, Havana's signature on a $770 million rescheduling agree-ment covering debts owed to 182 Japanese private companies raised hopes of new Japanese investments and a boost to bilateral trade.[25] In February 2000, Tokyo reinstated its export credit cover after Cuba made its first payment on $120 million of rescheduled short-term debt.[26] But such optimism was rela-tively short-lived after the Revolution suffered a series of major economic set-backs. Among them was Hurricane Michelle, which devastated the island in

November 2001, generating $1.8 billion in damages. The difficulties this created were compounded by terrorist attacks on New York and Washington three months earlier, which triggered a general longer-term decline in international tourism, the Cuban economy's leading hard currency earner. In October 2002, the Cuban Central Bank was forced to announce that it could not satisfy the conditions of the 1998 Japanese agreement and that a revised repayment schedule would be necessary. Tokyo was now placed in the unenviable position of holding the largest single amount of outstanding Cuban hard currency debt—$1.7 billion or approximately twenty percent of the total—with few, if any, prospects for dramatically reducing this exposure in the foreseeable future. The financial difficulties resulting from these problems received a further blow when the highly influential Moody credit rating agency listed Havana as a very high-risk borrower (that is, "Caa1"—one of the company's worst categories).[27]

Predictably, given these circumstances, the dynamics of the bilateral economic relationship has tended to be more cautionary than expansive in recent years, although a delegation to Havana in May 2003 led by the head of the Latin American section of Japan's Foreign Ministry promised a renewed effort to build on bilateral ties.[28] Six months later, an economic conference between Cuban and Japanese officials discussed ways of increasing investment in and exports to the island, and a protocol was signed to boost economic, commercial, and scientific-technological ties.[29]

In contrast to the somewhat lethargic state of affairs with Japan, Cuba's ties with China in the post-Soviet era have boomed, especially since the November 1993 visit to Havana of China's president Jiang Zemin. Although no specific trade or economic accords were signed on that occasion (principally due to Cuba's inability to supply sugar exports to China),[30] and despite some subsequent bickering over trade payment arrangements,[31] the visit was hailed on both sides as a resounding success and a harbinger of even better things to come. Two years later, in December 1995, Fidel Castro took up Jiang's invitation to visit Beijing. Two factors have been instrumental in this burgeoning relationship: Havana's great interest in the Chinese model—a mixed command/free market economy operating within the context of a single-party political framework—as a viable socialist alternative to the system of global neoliberalism being advocated by Washington; and the existing trade and related links that the two countries managed to maintain (and in some cases expand) despite the debilitating economic blows that the transition to a post-Soviet world imposed on Cuba (Appendix, Table 6).

Such close ties have been supported as well as supplemented by China's willingness, not matched by many other countries, to provide Cuba with long-term "soft credits," accompanied by generous repayment provisions, worth millions of dollars. In fact, China is the only country offering Cuba this type of financial assistance to facilitate trade and investment, which has led to Chinese companies pushing foreign competitors out of the Cuba market.[32] A good example of this occurred in 2001 when Beijing extended a $150 million low-cost loan to help finance the purchase and distribution of Chinese television sets, approximately half of which were to be assembled on the island via a joint venture between the Chinese manufacturer, Nanjing Panda Electronic Company Ltd., and a local Cuban partner. To assure the success of the enterprise, competitively priced televisions produced by companies already well established in the Cuban market such as Samsung (Korea), Sony (Japan), and Phillips (Netherlands), were removed from state-run appliance stores throughout the country; and simultaneously Havana instituted an interest-free loan program to encourage and facilitate purchases of the Pandas (which were being sold at cost).[33]

In recent years, Beijing has demonstrated an interest in moving away from what was once purely a trade connection, occasionally complemented by various financing incentives, by upgrading its status to that of a direct foreign investor in Cuba and thereby joining the ranks of other major participants in the island's economy such as Spain, Canada, and Mexico. The March 2001 flagship project for this new stage in the Chinese/Cuban connection called for the construction and operation of a major joint venture tourist hotel at one of Havana's prime locations—the intersection of the central Prado Avenue and the seafront Malecon Boulevard. Other more low profile, but nevertheless potentially important, cooperative investment initiatives have involved rice cultivation projects in Piñar del Río and Granma Provinces.

In April 2001, Jiang returned to Havana where he signed agreements extending approximately $400 million in loans to Havana.[34] By 2002, Beijing had become the island's third most important trading partner, even though the trade balance clearly favored China,[35] and Jiang's successor, Hu Jintao, signaled his strong intention to maintain the direction of Chinese-Cuban relations by sending a senior official on a goodwill visit to Havana in July 2003.[36] The following April, the two nations signed an agreement to set up a joint venture biotechnology enterprise in northeastern China.[37]

The bottom line with respect to all of this Chinese activity has been a greater stake in Cuba's developmental prospects and an increasing contribution to the Revolution's economic security. This has not gone unnoticed in Washington, however. As early as 1991, the Senate considered a measure that would have tied the granting of Most-Favored-Nation trading status to China to a "significant" reduction in Beijing's aid to Havana.[38] Several years later, anti-Castroists in the Congress raised alarm bells about an alleged attempt by China to substitute for the Soviets in the area of military cooperation with Cuba—an issue that resurfaced anew under the rubric of the George W. Bush administration's "war on terror."[39]

Cuba has continued to make progress in its dealings with other Third World countries as well. In February 2003, Fidel Castro was warmly received in Hanoi. In June, he was extended an invitation to visit India during a meeting in New Delhi between the Cuban and Indian foreign ministers. But the most substantive developments centered on relations between Cuba and South Africa. Days before a visit by President George W. Bush in July 2003, Pretoria signed an agreement with Havana to strengthen South African investment in the island's mineral and energy sectors.[40] That December, the two countries declared their commitment to a range of cooperative projects involving telecommunications, health, finance, and agriculture,[41] and in March 2004, labor ministers on both sides signed a Memorandum of Understanding on employment, social security, and occupational health and safety issues.[42] These agreements, and the sentiments that underlie them, were evidence of the welcome role Cuba was again being invited to play in the affairs of southern Africa.

Challenging U.S. Hegemony: Cuba's Reemergence as a Global Actor

Cuba's flourishing trade, commercial, and sociopolitical links with the developing world are emblematic of the larger reconfiguration of the island's economic relations that has occurred in recent years. While the cultivation of new economic relations and the deepening of ties with existing partners have not produced a complete recovery from Cuba's post-Soviet economic slump, the island's economic health and security have nevertheless improved considerably since the dire days of the early 1990s. One luxury for a government that has finally weathered the worst of such a calamity is that it usually finds itself in a position where it can finally devote some serious attention to matters that heretofore had to be sacrificed to the exigencies of crisis management. In Havana's case, there are indications that the main deferred item on its foreign affairs agenda in recent years—efforts to maximize its influence on an international scale—has, once again, begun to take center stage, generating new tensions between Havana and Washington in the process.

The contemporary Cuban initiatives to exercise increased influence and leadership among the Third World community have fallen into two broad categories: policy proposals in specific issue areas and larger, more ambitious attempts to promote structural reform of various international organizations. The main venues available to less developed countries within which Havana has pursued these efforts have been the Non-Aligned Movement (NAM) and the Group of 77 (G-77), although lesser efforts have also been made within specific United Nations agencies, commissions, and conferences.[43]

The policy-specific approach has a long history in Cuban foreign affairs circles; indeed it is the strategy that Havana has most frequently employed over the years in its efforts to mobilize the developing nations behind its leadership. None has involved more effort and visibility than its attempts to resolve the Third World debt problem. Havana's aspirations to play a vanguard role in this issue area can be traced back to the mid-1980s, when Castro proposed a major plan to resolve the debt crisis then engulfing many Latin American nations (especially Mexico, Brazil, and Argentina) that he also perceived as applicable to indebted nations throughout the Third World. The core components of the Cuban proposal were threefold: first, the loans simply could not be repaid without doing serious and probably irreparable damage to the debtor countries' long-term developmental prospects; second, as a result, both financial realities and moral considerations made it incumbent upon the creditors (mostly private banks in the industrialized nations, especially the United States) to cancel repayment; and third, the governments of the developed countries should reimburse the losses experiences by their banks, defraying the costs of the operation by a modest reduction (for example, ten to twelve percent) in bloated military spending.[44]

In April 2000, a landmark event in Cuba's campaign to rejuvenate its Third World leadership aspirations occurred when Havana hosted the South Summit, which was the first time that the G-77 developing countries had ever convened a meeting where member nations were represented by heads of state (as opposed to the usual ministerial-level delegates). At this conference Cuba once again spotlighted the debt issue as a priority matter. In many respects, its analysis of the problem and its key proposal—the debt must be forgiven—had not changed radically from the 1980s. A new element was added, however, when Castro floated an admittedly somewhat vague proposition for a "one percent tax on all speculative operations [that] would suffice to finance the development of the Third World."[45] Presumably debt relief and reimbursement to creditors would be underwritten by this fund.

Reflecting Cuba's growing integration into the contemporary system of international economic networks, and given its aggressive opposition to the U.S./ International Monetary Fund (IMF)/World Bank neoliberal economic model, the Castro government has added trade reform as a major item on its Third World leadership agenda. In December 2002, as part of an effort to rally the G-77 behind its objectives, Havana submitted a comprehensive set of working principles concerning the linkages between trade, debt, and finance to the World Trade Organization (WTO). A key section of the communiqué summarizes Havana's wide-ranging position:

> The work program should address the linkages between trade, external debt, and finance from a global and multidimensional perspective, focusing on systemic problems. The debt problem cannot be solved without

adopting a comprehensive approach that embraces trade-policy issues (market access, falling commodity prices, supply constraints in less developed countries, and imbalances in the multilateral trade system) on the one hand, and development finance issues (official development assistance, debt relief and FDI [foreign direct investment]) on the other.[46]

Beyond its complex technical aspects, this WTO document is important because it serves as an excellent illustration of the more holistic perspective that Cuba has increasingly embraced in its approach to major developmental problems confronting the Third World. In other words, as opposed to its previous tendency to deal with Third World grievances as discrete and straightforward challenges, Havana now stresses to its G-77 and NAM colleagues the necessity for an integrated approach that recognizes the intricate complexity of these issues. This more comprehensive strategy was detailed in a sweeping working paper submitted to the August-September 2002 World Summit on Sustainable Development in Johannesburg, South Africa, by a broad coalition of Cuban organizations.[47] The topics covered in the document as part of the larger goal of achieving truly sustainable development included: environmental protection and compliance with targets set at the 1992 Earth Summit in Rio de Janeiro, Brazil; drought problems; energy supplies and consumption; health care; food security; and the global maldistribution of wealth.

Yet despite the increasingly ambitious scope of the Havana's attempts to mobilize the developing nations behind its policy initiatives, these efforts have tended to be overshadowed by Cuba's growing emphasis on the need to restructure the key international bodies that deal with such issues. Its Third World platform has increasingly revolved around the idea that policies are very unlikely to change until the institutions that make and implement them are reformed in a manner more responsive to Third World interests. In a speech to the opening session of the April 2000 G-77 Summit conference in Havana, Fidel Castro had explained the harsh reality to the assembled delegates:

> The political and economic influence of the US and other developed nations over multilateral organizations like the IMF, World Bank, and the WTO has had an adverse effect, in that they have used these institutions as vehicles for imposing neo-liberal globalization on the underdeveloped nations. . . . The hegemonic forces that now monopolize power see the neo-liberal model—which benefits only the major transnationals—as a means of creating an homogenized and hence more easily controlled world, without regard for the danger to the planet or the consequences confronted by humanity.[48]

Such ingrained inequities in power (and thus benefits) can only be remedied, insists Havana, by drastic structural reforms. Thus a central feature of its appeals for Third World unity and support have been proposals calling for the replacement of many existing international financial institutions with new organizations that would be specifically tailored to render them immune to control by the industrialized nations, particularly the United States.

The IMF has been a particular target of Cuba's rhetorical broadsides. "It is of crucial importance for the Third World," declared a 2003 Foreign Ministry document, "to work for the removal of that sinister institution, and the philosophy it sustains, to replace it with an international finances regulating body that would operate on democratic bases and where no one has a veto right."[49] When Havana has not argued for the abolition of such institutions it has proposed a greater democratization of their existing structures—in the United Nations Security Council (UNSC), for instance, where lesser developed countries tend to be underrepresented and their interests can be easily frustrated by a great power veto.

Another example is the United Nations Human Rights Commission (UNHRC). In recent years, the Cuban delegation has led a campaign to refocus the energies of the UNHRC from civil and political rights onto economic and social rights. Speaking before the commission in March 2002, Foreign Minister Felipe Pérez Roque argued that is "absolutely necessary to banish from this Commission the attempt to ignore the defense of basic human rights for us, the poor peoples of the Earth." In passionate tones Roque then went on to ask: "Why do the rich, developed countries fail to openly recognize our right to development and to receive financing to that end? Why is our right to receive compensation for centuries of grief and looting that slavery and colonialism imposed on our countries not recognized? Why is it not recognized our right to see the cancellation of the debt strangling our countries? Why is it not recognized our right to overcome poverty, our right to food, our right to life? Why is it not recognized our right to education, our right to enjoy scientific knowledge and our original cultures? Why is it not recognized our right to sovereignty, our right to live in a democratic, fair and equitable world?"[50] In April 2003, Cuba, along with a host of Third World countries, voted in support of resolutions before the commission concerning the right of all peoples to food, housing, and health care—resolutions that in each case the United States alone opposed.[51]

Demonstrating that his country could practice a degree of global social justice and not just preach it, Castro had declared, in March 2001, that Cuba would use its advanced biotechnology industry to help Third World countries acquire treatments for AIDS sufferers cheaper than those available from multinational pharmaceutical companies—even if this meant challenging U.S. patent laws: "We will fully support Brazil and South Africa (two countries that had announced their intention to copy 'generic' versions of far more expensive brand-name drugs), encouraging them to ignore U.S. patents and produce the drugs to save the millions of lives that can be saved."[52] Although such assistance posed a threat to international trade laws—most notably the protection of intellectual property and patents—it was consistent with the mood of frustration felt among many African, Latin American, and even European countries that not enough was being done to address the worldwide AIDS pandemic.

Indeed, later that year, developing countries succeeded in getting the WTO to issue the Doha Declaration that stated that public health issues should take precedence over WTO patent rules. One year after that agreement was reached, in November 2002, the respected British aid group Oxfam released a report on the success of efforts to provide cheaper drugs to the Third World. Accusing the United States of using "bullying" tactics on drug patents, the report concluded that Washington's "policy on patents and medicines is still heavily influenced by the narrow commercial interests of the giant pharmaceutical companies"; that the United States continued to use bilateral and regional trade agreements outside the WTO framework to pressure other countries to adhere strictly to existing patents; and that these pressures "delay or restrict the production of cheaper generic versions of new medicines" for poor people in the Third World.[53] Here was an issue of immediate practical urgency for many Third World countries on which Cuba and the United States took diametrically opposed positions reflecting two quite different views on whose interests the international trading system should seek to serve.

The most dramatic evidence that Cuba's new internationalism had produced a resurgence in the country's standing in the Third World came in the form of the announcement at the February 2003 NAM Summit in Malaysia that Havana had been chosen to host the next summit in 2006, at which time it would assume presidency of the movement. The NAM's Latin American/Caribbean caucus had, without any dissenting voices, nominated Havana as its candidate to head the group, and this recommendation was subsequently ratified by the 115 member nations, thus once again conferring upon Cuba the mantle of leadership that it had previously exercised during its somewhat ill-fated, 1979–82 tenure.

This development was not, as one might expect, fortuitous, for Havana had launched a campaign to revitalize the NAM as a vehicle through which Third World countries can collectively pursue their mutual interests on the global stage. The NAM had been a target of American hostility during the Cold War because it was viewed as having the potential to challenge U.S. power and influence in the Third World. Washington's success in promoting bilateral relations and North-South ties at the expense of interregional links based on NAM and like-minded organizations was central to the spread of free-market economic agendas across these regions of the world—in the process, limiting

Cuba's options and allies and increasing pressure on it to fall into line and jettison its welfare/development model.[54]

Cuba's vision of the NAM's role and goals in the new, post-Soviet international order was detailed in a major Foreign Ministry position paper prepared for the February 2003 Kuala Lumpur Summit. The document spelled out a number of key issues that the NAM needed to address. First, it emphasized that in today's world dominated by "unipolarism and unilateralism . . . and the process of neoliberal globalization [it is more imperative than ever] to strengthen the efforts of the countries of the South to promote their unity, solidarity and cohesion." Second, it highlighted the nature of the threat posed to multilateralism and international law by Washington's new global unilateralism that, it argued, was undermining the United Nations and the principles enshrined in international law. Third, it criticized the failure to structurally reform the UNSC and to promote the democratization of the system of international governance. The document concluded by exhorting the NAM to "unite its forces, reaffirm its political credibility and face with its own capacity and identity the complex trends in contemporary international relations." This call for united action was echoed in the summit's final declaration on continuing the effort to revitalize the movement.[55]

Cuba's effort to maximize its influence within the NAM is consistent with, and indeed would serve to enhance the pursuit of, other key foreign policy objectives. The issue of economic security, for instance, is directly linked to the Foreign Ministry's concern about the "process of neoliberal globalization." Stemming from a firmly held belief that the legitimate developmental aspirations of the world's poor majority will be systematically traduced by the power of the wealthy few within a U.S.-promoted system of unfettered global free enterprise, Cuba has long emphasized the need for organizations that can serve the two key economic security functions: providing a mechanism whereby less developed countries can function as a collective bargaining unit in negotiating the terms of their trade and financial ties with the world's major centers of economic power; and promoting broader and more vigorous currents of inter–Third World developmental cooperation.

Clearly, however, it is the perceived threat to the sovereignty and independence of Third World countries that Cuba feels must receive top-priority attention. Havana's Foreign Ministry document for the Kuala Lumpur Summit repeatedly highlighted unilateralism, the disregard for well-established principles of international law, and hegemonic arrogance as the foremost dangers confronting the global community. The concern appeared all the more urgent—for Cuba in particular and the Third World in general—in light of the Bush administration's response to the September 11 terrorist attacks on New York and Washington. Above all was its assertion of the right to use force, including preemptive military strikes, whenever it unilaterally decides that such tactics are vital to safeguarding America's national security—a claim it invoked to justify military intervention in Iraq.

The basic outline of this new U.S. strategic posture emerged from President George W. Bush's January 2002 State of the Union address, when he declared that three Third World states—Iraq, Iran, and North Korea—constituted an international "axis of evil," engaged in or supporting terrorist activities, or having or seeking to acquire weapons of mass destruction.[56] While Bush himself never referred directly to Havana within the context of such pronouncements, other administration officials did make such a connection. The most notorious instance was involved a May 6, 2002 speech by Under Secretary of State John Bolton that expanded the "axis of evil" to include Cuba, Libya, and Syria. Cuba, according to Bolton, qualified as a rogue government on multiple grounds: it "has long provided safe haven for terrorists, earning it a place on the State Department's list of terrorist-sponsoring states [and] is collaborating with other state sponsors of terror"; Fidel Castro "has repeatedly denounced the U.S. war on terrorism [and] continues to view terror as a legitimate tactic to further revolutionary objectives"; and Cuba's biomedical industry "has at least a limited offensive biological warfare research and development effort [and] has provided dual-use biotechnology to other rogue states [that] could support BW [biological warfare] programs in those states."[57]

To most observers, Bolton's argument was singularly unpersuasive, more an exercise in hyperbole and innuendo rather than fact. To Havana, though, what it revealed about Washington's attitude was no less important than the question of its accuracy. For the Third World, such declarations had a "divide-and-conquer" air to them. For Cuba, they were reminiscent of the hegemonic mentality expressed in the 1902 Platt amendment through the 1961 Bay of Pigs invasion and beyond—a potential threat to the Revolution's sovereignty and conceivably to its very existence. Given Havana's obvious lack of confidence in the ability of existing institutions like the United Nations (at least as presently structured) to provide sufficient protection against such perils, it appears to have opted for a renewed campaign of global activism as the most viable alternative option.

In June 2002, Bush elaborated further on his preemptive strike doctrine in an address to graduating cadets at West Point. "Given the goals of rogue states and terrorists, the United States can no longer solely rely on a reactive posture," he said. "To forestall or prevent such hostile actions by our adversaries, the United States will, if necessary, act preemptively." Moreover, U.S. security henceforth "will require transforming the military you will lead, a military that must be ready to strike at a moment's notice in any dark corner of the world."[58]

Castro made much of this depiction of Third World countries as "dark corner[s]" in his address to the NAM in Malaysia. It was, he said, the perception that former colonial powers now had of these regions of the world and it revealed the contempt for them that underlay their position in the international pecking order: "There is nothing like full independence, fair treatment on an equal footing or national security for any of us; none is a permanent member of the UN Security Council with a veto right; none has any possibility of being involved in the decisions of the international financial institutions; none can keep its best talents; none can protect itself from capital flight or the destruction of nature and the environment caused by the squandering, selfish and insatiable consumerism of the economically developed countries." Castro went on to say that waiting for a change of attitude on the part of the developed world was pointless: time and again promises had been made that peace and democracy and development would flow from some power projection by developed nations (George Bush's talk of a "New World Order" arising from the first Gulf War; George W. Bush's promise to promote democracy in post–Saddam Hussein Iraq) and time and again such promises amounted to nothing more than a "huge lie." The Third World had to fight for itself, Castro concluded, "by sowing ideas, building awareness and mobilizing global and North American public opinion."[59] This was not just a cry for solidarity, but a clever positioning of Cuba—and the pariah status accorded it by the United States—at the forefront of the kind of struggle the Third World faced to achieve independence and economic security.

Before returning to Havana, Castro visited Japan where he again demonstrated that Cuba fully intended to make its presence felt at the very center of the global stage: he offered Prime Minister Junichiro Koizumi his help in resolving the crisis over North Korea's nuclear weapons program.[60] Weeks later, in another sign of how Third World countries were responding to the return of a more activist Cuban foreign policy, Cuba was reelected to the UNHRC despite strong White House opposition and criticism from the European Union over the island's human rights record.[61]

Conclusion

The Cold War period witnessed an ambitious effort by Cuba to maximize its influence among other less developed countries in the context of an ideological, political, economic, and military division of the world into two competing camps. In the initial—and some might say naïve—phase of those efforts, Havana did this by attempting to export revolution via its material and ideological support of leftist guerilla movements in Africa and Latin America. When these efforts failed to produce results, however, the policy focus shifted to supporting leftist regimes (Ethiopia, Angola, Nicaragua, Jamaica, Grenada) as the need and available resources determined.

The 1970s and 1980s witnessed a parallel adjustment in Cuba's approach whereby its internationalist foreign policy was also expressed through multilateral institutions, promoting a collectivist Third World approach to solving shared social and economic problems. Oftentimes, its initiatives were directly hostile to U.S. interests, producing a consistent Washington demand that Cuba change its international behavior as a precondition for the normalization of ties across the Florida Straits.

In the early post-Soviet period, the preoccupation with economic survival forced the Castro government, largely out of necessity, to retrench these kinds of selective global investments. This in turn meant dropping much of its revolutionary rhetoric in an attempt to convince potential trade and investment partners that Cuba was a good international citizen prepared to play by the rules. None of these changes in Cuba's behavior, however, produced a positive response from Washington. Instead, they tended to intensify U.S. hostility even to the extent of suggesting that Cuba represented a danger to the rest of the world comparable to that of other rogue states that, the White House alleged, supported international terrorism and were the intent of developing weapons of mass destruction. With the disintegration of the Soviet Empire, Cuba was now much more vulnerable to a U.S. policy whose major objective was still regime change on the island.

As the Cuban economy began to revive in the later part of the 1990s, Havana again embraced an activist global foreign policy. But this return to the international stage occurred in a new context and had a new focus. Now the United States was the world's uncontested superpower, and Cuba was forced to look for friends and allies where it could in Africa, Asia, Africa, and the Middle East (as well as Latin America), and to mobilize the Third World to speak with one voice on issues that affected them all: debt, development, environment, social problems, and military intervention. This policy approach emphasizes multilateral solutions to global problems and offers a sharp contrast to America's commitment to a unilateralist foreign policy and its desire to entrench its hegemony over these regions of the world. To the extent that Cuba is successful in persuading less developed countries that its fate is emblematic of theirs and that only a common front on the part of the Third World promises any counterbalance to U.S. global dominance, Washington's unrelenting goal to destabilize the Cuban Revolution has the potential to open a new cleavage between the United States and the Third World.

Notes

1. This section draws on material in H. Michael Erisman, *Cuba's Foreign Relations in a Post-Soviet World* (Gainesville: University Press of Florida, 2000), chapters 4 and 5.

2. The two anticommunist movements contending for political power in postcolo-

nial Angola—the National Front for the Liberation of Angola (FNLA) and the National Union for the Total Independence of Angola (UNITA)—were both supported by the Ford administration, and the latter was a major recipient of covert military aid during the Reagan presidency in its efforts to topple the MPLA government.

3. For a definitive account of Cuba's African policy, see Piero Gleijeses, *Conflicting Missions: Havana, Washington, and Africa, 1959–1976* (Chapel Hill: University of North Carolina Press, 2002).

4. Julie M. Feinsilver, "Cuba As a World Medical Power: The Politics of Symbolism," *Latin American Research Review* XXIV, no. 2 (1989): 12, 15.

5. For data that covers the entire global deployment of Cuban development aid personnel, see H. Michael Erisman, "Cuba Development Aid: South-South Diversification and Counterdependence Politics," in *Cuban Foreign Policy Confronts a New International Order*, ed. H. Michael Erisman and John M. Kirk (Boulder: Lynne Rienner, 1991), 153–54, Table 9.1. Also see H. Michael Erisman, *Cuba's International Relations: The Anatomy of a Nationalistic Foreign Policy* (Boulder: Westview Press, 1985), 78–79 and three U.S. Department of State publications: *Soviet and East European Aid to the Third World, 1981*, Washington, D.C., 1983, 20–21; *Warsaw Pact Economic Aid to Non-Communist LDCs, 1984*, Washington, D.C., 1986, 16; *Warsaw Pact Economic Aid Programs in Non-Communist LDCs: Holding Their Own in 1986*, Washington, D.C., 1988, 12.

6. In 1979 the Non-Aligned Movement had 91 members, increasing to 115 by 2003.

7. For a good discussion of Cuba's relations with the NAM, see William M. LeoGrande, "Cuba's Policy in Africa, 1959–1980," Policy Papers in International Affairs, no. 13, University of California, Berkeley, 1980, *passim*.

8. For an analysis of this dispute that emphasizes its Third World dimensions, see H. Michael Erisman, "Conflicto Sino-Cubano: La Lucha Por Influencia En El Tercer Mundo," *Arieto* V, nos. 19–20 (Special Edition, 1979): 12–19.

9. For an excellent overview of the shifts and changes in Cuba-China relations since the 1959 Revolution, see Damian Fernández, "Cuba's Relations with China: Economic Pragmatism and Political Fluctuation," in *Cuba's Ties to a Changing World*, ed. Donna Rich Kaplowitz (Boulder: Lynne Rienner, 1993), 17–31.

10. Reported in *Update On Cuba*, October 10, 1990, 6.

11. Kanako Yamaoka, "Cuban-Japanese Relations in Japanese Perspective: Economic Pragmatism and Political Distance," in Kaplowitz, ed., *Cuba's Ties*, 41.

12. For a detailed discussion of these and related matters, see Damian J. Fernández, *Cuba's Foreign Policy in the Middle East* (Boulder: Westview Press, 1988).

13. John Attfield, "Cuba And The Middle East: The Gulf War and After," in Kaplowitz, ed., *Cuba's Ties*, 72.

14. Zbigniew Brzezinski, *Power and Principle* (New York: Farrar Straus Giroux, 1983), 189.

15. See, for example, House Committee on International Relations, *The Cuban Program: Torture of American Prisoners by Cuban Agents*, 106th Cong., 1st sess., November 4, 1999.

16. Cuba enjoyed special status with regard to Soviet security aid when compared to Moscow's Warsaw Pact allies. Normally the Eastern European states were expected to

reimburse the Kremlin (at least in part) for the equipment and other types of military assistance that they received. Cuba, on the other hand, paid nothing, although the Soviets did calculate some military spare parts against the rent it paid for the Lourdes Intelligence facility.

17. Quoted in Argiris Malapanis and Roman Kane, "Mandela: Cuba Shared the Trenches with Us; S. African President praises 'Unparalleled Internationalism,'" *Militant*, October 23, 1995.

18. See United Nations Human Rights Commission, "Resolutions on Situations in Iraq, Sudan, and Cuba Adopted by the Commission on Human Rights," press release, April 19, 2002.

19. Ibid. Also see Remy Herrera, "Why Lift the Embargo?," *Monthly Review* 55, no. 8 (January 2004): 51, Table 1.

20. Quoted in Malapanis and Kane, "Cuba Shared the Trenches."

21. For 1986 figures, see Table 1; 2000 data in "Despite Defections, More Cuban Medics Go to Africa," *Reuters News Service* (hereafter *RNS*), August 10, 2000.

22. See David Gonzalas, "Cuban-African Relations: Nationalist Roots of an Internationalist Policy," *Review Of African Political Economy* 27, no. 84 (June 2000): 322. As of mid-2003 it was still unclear as to whether these plans were or ever would be transformed into significant reality.

23. For details, see "Cuba and South Africa, Looking at Expanded Health Programmes in Africa," *Sapa-AFP News Service*, April 23, 2002.

24. See table "Commodity Imports By Country Of Origin, 1994–1999," in U.S. Central Intelligence Agency, *Cuba: Handbook Of Trade Statistics, 2000* (Springfield, Va.: National Technical Information Service, 2001).

25. See "Cuba Scores Debt Breakthrough in Deal With Japanese Private Creditors," *CUBANEWS*, April 1998, 6; Max Azicri, *Cuba Today and Tomorrow* (Gainesville: University Press of Florida, 2000), 172.

26. See "Japan Restores Credit Cover," *Latin American Monitor: Caribbean*, March 2000, 4.

27. See Mark Frank, "Cuba Said To Miss Japan, Mexico Debt Payments," *RNS*, October 25, 2002.

28. "Cuba, Japan Call for Closer Ties," *Xinhua News Agency*, May 23, 2003.

29. *Vietnam News Agency Bulletin*, December 26, 2003.

30. "Sugar Shortage—Trade With China," *Lloyd's List International*, November 25, 1993.

31. See Domingo Amuchastegui, "Cuba and China Step Up Cooperation but Progress has Limits," *CUBANEWS*, September 2000, 10.

32. Quoted in Mark Frank, "China's Cuba Business Takes Big Leap Forward," *RNS*, April 11, 2001. This article is an excellent summary of evolving Cuban/Chinese commercial relations.

33. For details, see Marc Frank, "In Cuba, the Pandas Are Coming, Like It or Not," *RNS*, August 22, 2001. Between 1999 and 2001, the value of Cuban imports from China jumped from $232 million to $547 million. See U.S. Central Intelligence Agency, *Cuba: Handbook of Trade Statistics 2002* (Springfield, VA: National Technical Infor-

mation Service); "Fidel Castro Arrives in China for Four-Day Visit," *Agence France-Presse*, February 26, 2003.

34. "China and Taiwan Compete in Latin American Cheque-Book Diplomacy," *Financial Times* (U.K.), May 1, 2001.

35. See Jim Randle, "Castro Arrives in Beijing for 4-Day Visit," *Euro-Cuba News*, February 28, 2003.

36. "Cuba's Fidel Castro Meets Senior Chinese Official Li Changchun in Havana," *BBC Monitoring Asia Pacific*, July 8, 2003.

37. See "China, Cuba Sign Biotechnology Joint Venture," *BBC Monitoring Asia Pacific*, April 5, 2004.

38. Quoted in *CubaINFO*, August 2, 1991, 1.

39. See, for example, "China's Ties with 'Rogue States' Under Spotlight," *RNS*, September 14, 2001.

40. "S. Africa in Cuba Investment Deal Before Bush Visit," *RNS*, July 5, 2003.

41. "SA, Cuba Cement Ties," *All Africa*, December 4, 2003.

42. "SA, Cuba Sign Memo of Understanding," *All Africa*, March 3, 2004.

43. The G-77 was formed in 1963 to provide a forum for developing countries to establish common positions on matters concerning international economic relations and to represent their interests in negotiations with the industrialized nations. Its organizational structure is quite decentralized in that it lacks a coherent core secretariat, preferring instead to rely upon permanent and ad hoc working groups as the primary vehicles for its activities. Originally composed of 77 countries, its membership in 2003 had almost doubled to 133.

44. For more information on this topic, see H. Michael Erisman, "Cuban Foreign Policy and the Latin American Debt Crisis," *Cuban Studies 18*, ed. Carmelo Mesa-Lago (Pittsburgh: University of Pittsburgh Press, 1988), 3–18.

45. A more detailed exposition of Cuba's positions on key summit agenda items can be found in Castro's opening and closing speeches to the conference. See *Granma Internacional Digital*, <www.granma.cu/documento/ingles00/009-i.html> and *Yahoo Groups: Cuba News*, <http://groups.yahoo.com/group/CubaNews/message/1281>.

46. World Trade Organization, "Working Group on Trade, Debt and Finance—Communication from Cuba," WT/WGTDF/W/18, December 19, 2002, 4. See *WTO Documents Online*, <http://docsonline.wto.org/gen_home.asp?language=1&_=1>.

47. A copy of this document can be found at <http://groups.yahoo.com/group/CubaNews/files>.

48. See WTO, "Communication from Cuba," 2.

49. See Castro's speech at the opening session of the April 2000 G-77 summit conference in Havana, *Granma Internacional Digital*, <www.granma.cu/documento/ingles00/009-i.html>.

50. "Hypocrisy and Human Rights," statement by Cuban minister of Foreign Affairs, Felipe Pérez Roque, at the 58th Session of the United Nations Human Rights Commission, Geneva, March 26, 2002, reprinted in *Monthly Review*, April 2002.

51. See "Commission on Human Rights adopts 10 resolutions and decisions on economic, social and cultural rights," *M2 Presswire*, April 23, 2003.

52. Quoted in "Cuba Issues Double Trade Challenge," *BBC News*, March 19, 2001.

53. See "US Bullying on Drug Patents: One Year after Doha," *Oxfam International Briefing Paper*, November 2002, 2.

54. See James Petras and Morris Morley, "Clinton's Cuba Policy: Two Steps Backward, One Step Forward," *Third World Quarterly* 17, no.2 (1996): 281–82.

55. Quoted from Cuban Foreign Ministry, *A Cuban Vision Of The Movement Of Non-Aligned Nations*, Havana 2003. For the summit's final declaration, see XIII Summit, Kuala Lumpur, NAM Web site, <http://www.namkl.org.my/>.

56. "The President's State of the Union Address," White House, Office of the Press Secretary, January 29, 2002.

57. Quoted in John R. Bolton, "Beyond the Axis of Evil: Additional Threats from Weapons of Mass Destruction," remarks to the Heritage Foundation, Washington, D.C., May 6, 2002.

58. "Full Text: Bush's National Security Strategy," *New York Times*, September 20, 2002.

59. "Voices in the Dark Corners," edited extract of Fidel Castro's speech to the Non-Aligned Movement Summit in Kuala Lumpur, Malaysia, *The Guardian*, March 6, 2003.

60. See "Castro Offers to Help Solve N. Korea Nuke Standoff," *Japan Policy & Politics*, March 3, 2003.

61. See Marika Lynch, "Cuba is Reelected to U.N. Rights Panel; U.S. Angered," *Miami Herald*, April 30, 2003.

Appendix

Table 1. Cuban Trade with Former Eastern Bloc Countries (millions of pesos)[a]

Total Trade	1986	1987	1988	1989	1990	1991
Bulgaria	338	353	336	354	181	38
Czechoslovakia	301	344	403	352	279	91
Hungary	124	139	105	136	36	15
Poland	114	125	102	112	50	4
GDR[b]	567	620	652	645	396	66
Romania	170	291	277	278	203	10
USSR	9273	9314	9047	8753	8709	4521

Cuban Trade with Former USSR(millions of pesos)

	1992	1993	1994	1995	1996	1997	1998	1999	2000
Byelorussia									
Imports	4	5	2	—	4	2	3	1	0.5
Exports	4	5	9	—	—	3	7	—	—
Total	8	10	11	—	4	5	10	1	0.5
Kazakhstan									
Imports	—	—	—	—	—	(—)	3	1	5
Exports	28	0.25	4	8	—	—	(—)	(—)	(—)
Total	28	0.25	4	8	—	(—)	3	1	5
Kyrgyzstan									
Imports	—	—	(—)	—	—	(—)	(—)	(—)	(—)
Exports	0.6	16	3	(—)	(—)	4	(—)	—	(—)
Total	0.6	16	3	(—)	(—)	4	(—)	(—)	(—)
Latvia									
Imports	2	(—)	(—)	—	8	(—)	(—)	—	—
Exports	2	3	6	13	7	22	—	—	—
Total	4	3	6	13	15	22	—	—	
Russian Federation									
Imports	534	86	41	57	159	112	135	125	111
Exports	607	401	279	94	457	303	355	303	325
Total	1141	487	320	151	616	415	490	428	436
Ukraine									
Imports	1	5	2	4	3	13	39	33	23
Exports	59	65	(—)	0.5	42	0.6	22	1	0.5
Total	60	70	2	5	45	14	61	34	24

(continued)

Table 1—*Continued*

Cuba Trade with Eastern Europe (millions of pesos)

	1992	1993	1994	1995	1996	1997	1998	1999	2000
Bulgaria									
Imports	2	3	2	13	9	11	21	11	2
Exports	23	11	19	36	24	17	(—)	8	(—)
Total	25	14	21	49	33	28	21	19	2
Czech Republic[c]									
Imports	5	4	5	6	17	13	30	25	11
Exports	6	(—)	0.5	1	0.25	(—)	0.25	0.5	(—)
Total	11	4	6	7	17	13	30	26	11
Hungary									
Imports	11	3	2	(—)	(—)	1	2	2	2
Exports	—	(—)	(—)	(—)	—	(—)	(—)	—	—
Total	11	3	2	(—)	(—)	1	2	2	2
Poland									
Imports	5	4	1	0.5	13	16	10	7	2
Exports	1	(—)	(—)	(—)	(—)	(—)	(—)	(—)	(—)
Total	6	4	1	0.5	13	16	10	7	2
Romania									
Imports	—	(—)	5	29	32	21	8	8	7
Exports	5	6	19	27	60	16	10	2	12
Total	5	6	24	56	92	37	18	10	19
Slovakia[d]									
Imports	—	4	2	2	10	5	9	9	6
Exports	—	0.5	1	—	(—)	0.5	—	—	(—)
Total	—	5	3	2	10	6	9	9	6

Source: Oficina Nacional de Estadísticas, República de Cuba, *Anuario Estadístico de Cuba*, Havana, 1996, 1997, and 2001.

Note: I have opted for Cuban statistics because, unlike most sources, they provide a complete series. It is probable, however, that these figures significantly underestimate the level of Russian Federation exports to Cuba during the mid-1990s, which, according to the United Nations, were worth $103 million in 1993, $87 million in 1994, $211 million in 1995, and $465 million in 1996 (*International Trade Statistics Yearbook,* Volume 1, Trade by Country, 2000). The discrepancy may be due to the fact that Russia apparently sometimes sold oil on the world market and sent the remittances to Cuba, rather than supplying the oil itself.

a. To the nearest million or 0.25 million for amounts below 1 million. (—) indicates an amount <250,000 pesos.

b. Cuba's trade with the former West Germany totalled 113 million pesos in 1990. It continued at around that level with reunified Germany for most of the 1990s, suggesting that Cuba entirely lost its economic links with the former GDR.

c. Still Czechoslovakia in 1992.

d. See Czech Republic for 1992.

Table 2. Cuban Trade with Japan and China (Total exports and imports, U.S.$ millions)

Year	China	Japan
1970	81.8	149.9
1975	99.0	778.9
1980	115.7	426.1
1985	224.3	396.2
1988	448.5	254.7
1990	561.9	168.3
1991	425.7	177.7
1992	383.0	133.0

Sources: Compiled from U.S. Central Intelligence Agency, *Cuba: Handbook of Trade Statistics—1992 and 1997* (Springfield, Va.: National Technical Information Service, 1992 and 1997); United Nations, *United Nations International Trade Statistics Handbook, 1970/1975/1980/1985* (New York, various volumes).

Table 3. Japan's Overseas Development Assistance, 1985–1990

Year	Latin America (U.S.$ millions)	Cuba (U.S.$ thousands)
1985	224.93	90
1986	316.54	230
1987	417.99	210
1988	399.29	480
1989	563.33	350
1990	561.20	550

Source: Kanako Yamaoka, "Cuban-Japanese Relations in Japanese Perspective: Economic Pragmatism and Political Distance," in Donna Rich Kaplowitz, *Cuba's Ties to a Changing World* (Boulder: Lynne Rienner, 1993), 42.

Table 4. Cuban Export Profile, 1987–1999 (U.S.$ millions)

Year	1987	1989	1991	1993	1996	1999
Western Europe	343.2	361.5	353.1	338	541	515
Latin America	81.6	157.9	235.3	65	396	259
Asia	207.4	379	349.4	130	216	125
Sub-Saharan Africa	2.3	0.5	0	0	0	2
Middle East	72.8	129.6	105	61	64	11

Cuban Import Profile, 1987–1999 (U.S.$ millions)

	1987	1989	1991	1993	1996	1999
Western Europe	508.4	723.3	851	589	1,010	1,262
Latin America	294.3	634.4	506.2	551	933	1,118
Asia	239.3	308.9	280.1	223	214	315
Sub-Saharan Africa	5.1	0	0	11	17	23
Middle East	8.4	7.2	14	10	17	13

Source: Compiled from various editions of U.S. Central Intelligence Agency, *Cuba: Handbook of Trade Statistics*.
Note: 1991 was an extremely chaotic year for Cuban trade. Good comprehensive data is lacking, and the figures must be taken somewhat skeptically.

Table 5. Cuban Trade with Japan (U.S.$ millions)

	1989	1990	1991	1992	1993	1994	1995	1996	1997	1998	1999
Exports to	144	95	142	115	51	63	89	67	109	39	56
Imports from	54	73	36	18	18	24	10	24	21	23	39

Source: Compiled from various editions of U.S. Central Intelligence Agency, *Cuba: Handbook of Trade Statistics.*

Table 6. Cuban Trade with China (U.S.$ millions)

	1989	1990	1991	1992	1993	1994	1995	1996	1997	1998	1999
Exports to	229	310	202	183	74	121	214	138	100	94	57
Imports from	212	252	224	200	177	147	146	101	156	127	232

Source: Compiled from various editions of U.S. Central Intelligence Agency, *Cuba: Handbook of Trade Statistics.*

Contributors

H. Michael Erisman is professor of political science at Indiana State University. He is the author of *Cuba's Foreign Relations in a Post-Soviet World* and coauthor of *Cuban Foreign Policy Confronts a New International Order*.

John M. Kirk is professor of Latin American studies at Dalhousie University (Canada). He is coauthor of *Canada and Cuba: The Other Good Neighbor Policy* and coeditor of *Cuba in the International System: Normalization and Integration*.

William M. LeoGrande is professor of government at American University, Washington, D.C. He is the author of *Our Own Backyard: The United States in Central America, 1977–1992* and has written extensively on U.S.-Cuban relations, most recently in *Cuba: The Contours of Change* and the *Journal of Latin American Studies*.

Chris McGillion is senior lecturer in journalism at Charles Sturt University (Australia) and a senior research fellow at the Council on Hemispheric Affairs, Washington, D.C. He is the coauthor of *Unfinished Business: America and Cuba After the Cold War, 1989–2001*.

Peter McKenna is assistant professor of political studies at University of Prince Edward Island (Canada). He is the author of *Cuba and the OAS: From Dilettante to Full Partner* and the coauthor of *Canada and Cuba: The Other Good Neighbor Policy*.

Nicola Miller is reader in Latin American history at University College, London. She is the author of *Soviet Relations with Latin America 1959–1987* and *In the Shadow of the State: Intellectuals and the Quest for National Identity in Twentieth-Century Spanish America*.

Morris Morley is associate professor of politics and international relations at Macquarie University (Australia) and a senior research fellow at the Council on Hemispheric Affairs, Washington, D.C. He is the author of *Imperial State and Revolution: The United States and Cuba, 1952–1986* and the coauthor of *Unfinished Business: America and Cuba After the Cold War, 1989–2001*.

Index